I0643864

The Phantom Heroine

THE PHANTOM HEROINE

Ghosts and Gender in Seventeenth-Century Chinese Literature

JUDITH T. ZEITLIN

UNIVERSITY OF HAWAIʻI PRESS
HONOLULU

Paperback edition 2017

Printed in the United States of America

22 21 20 19 18 17 6 5 4 3 2 1

Library of Congress Cataloging-in-Publication Data

Zeitlin, Judith T.

The phantom heroine : ghosts and gender in seventeenth-century Chinese literature / Judith T. Zeitlin.

p. cm.

Includes bibliographical references and index.

ISBN 978-0-8248-3091-5 (cloth : alk. paper)

1. Chinese literature—Ming dynasty, 1368–1644—History and criticism. 2. Chinese literature—Qing dynasty, 1644–1912—History and criticism. 3. Ghosts in literature. 4. Gender identity in literature. I. Title. II. Title: Ghosts and gender in seventeenth-century Chinese literature.

PL2296.Z42 2007

895.1'09375—dc22

2006100946

ISBN 978-0-8248-6771-3 (pbk.)

University of Hawai'i Press books are printed on acid-free paper and meet the guidelines for permanence and durability of the Council on Library Resources.

Designed by Leslie Fitch

This book is for Wu Hung and Lida with love

Contents

ACKNOWLEDGMENTS IX

NOTE ON CITATIONS AND ABBREVIATIONS XI

SELECTED DYNASTIES AND PERIODS XIII

EPIGRAPHS XIV

Introduction 1

1 The Ghost's Body 13

2 The Ghost's Voice 53

3 Ghosts and Historical Time 87

4 Ghosts and Theatricality 131

Coda: *Palace of Lasting Life* 181

APPENDIX: SELECTED LIST OF MAJOR TRANSLATED BOOK AND FILM TITLES 199

NOTES 203

GLOSSARY 251

WORKS CITED 259

INDEX 283

Acknowledgments

It is a great relief after many years to bring this book into the light of day and exorcise its specter for good. As always with a research project of this magnitude and duration, there are almost too many institutions and people to thank. I want to express my deep gratitude to the National Endowment for the Humanities and to the American Council of Learned Societies in conjunction with the Committee on Scholarly Communication with China for fellowship support, and to Philip Gossett and Janel Mueller, former deans of the Humanities at the University of Chicago, for their generous grants of research leave. Phil, in particular, believed in this project from the start; his faith in me and my work in the earliest stages was crucial.

This book would not have been possible without the assistance of Yuan Zhou, the fantastic head of the East Asian Collection at the University of Chicago's Regenstein Library, and of his learned predecessor, Tai-loi Ma, now head of the East Asian Gest Library, Princeton University. I am also particularly grateful to Martin Heijdra of the Gest Library, Chun Shum of Harvard-Yenching Library's Rare Book Room, Dai Longji, director of the Peking University Library and the staff of its Rare Book Collection, and to Liu Yanjun and the staff of the Theater Research Materials Collection of the Chinese Academy of Arts, Beijing. I am also deeply indebted to the Chinese department of Peking University, particularly Chen Pingyuan, for welcoming me as a visiting scholar in 1999–2000, and to Andrea Goldman, Guo Yingde, and Liao Ben for the benefit of their scholarly acumen and aid in navigating the Chinese libraries and theaters that year.

I owe a special debt to Stephen Owen and Marjorie Garber in planting some important seeds of this project when I was still at Harvard as a graduate student and then as a faculty member. In the mid eighties I had the privilege to hear a set of unforgettable weekly lectures by Steve that he later published as *Remembrances*. Part of this book, particularly Chapters 2 and 3, are a response, long in germination, to ideas about the relationship to the past in Chinese literature that he first brought to my consciousness then. Marge's *Shakespeare's Ghost Writers* and subsequent conversations with her first suggested to me a way to study revenants in literature outside the predictable realms of folklore and the fantastic by underscoring the intimate connection between writing and ghosts, an approach that became a cornerstone of my study.

I have been fortunate to be able to try out many of the ideas in this book with superb graduate students at the University of Chicago and Harvard. Many of them also served as invaluable research or course assistants and deserve my heartfelt thanks: Margaret Baptist Wan, Sonya Lee, Jason McGrath, Ling Hon Lam, Paize Keulemans, Fumiko Joo, Suyoung Son, Yuhang Li, Catherine Stuer, and Rivi Handler-Spitz.

For additional assistance with the illustrations for the book, I would like to thank Michael Raine, Freda Murck, Jeehee Hong, Christine Tan, Ma Meng-ching, Jim Cahill, Mei Mei, Emma Teng, Julia Orell, Nancy Berliner, Roberto Marques, and Ellen Widmer.

Over the years I have rehearsed arguments related to this book at numerous talks, conferences, and workshops. I am grateful to the many organizers of and interlocutors at these events, and to the many colleagues and friends who read sections of the manuscript, discussed issues in it with me, or offered crucial support at thorny junctures, particularly Allan Barr, Ellen Widmer, John Ziemer, Charlotte Furth, Kate Swatek, Isabel Wong, Buzzy Teiser, Yi-li Wu, Norma Field, Kyeong-hee Choi, Don Harper, David Roy, Patrick Hanan, Kang-i Sun Chang, Shang Wei, David Wang, Hua Wei, Rania Huntington, Sophie Volpp, Grace Fong, Bao Weihong, Martha Feldman, Peg Olin, Immy Humes, Elaine Hacker, and Kim Rorschach.

Dorothy Ko and Wai-yee Li each carefully read the manuscript in full and offered excellent suggestions and corrections. For this, for the highest creative standards set by their own scholarship, and for years of friendship, I will always be in their debt.

To the expert team at the University of Hawai'i Press, I'd also like to express my gratitude to Pam Kelley, whose enthusiasm and persistence deftly shepherded this book through its various stages, and to managing editor Cheri Dunn and copy-editor Margaret Black.

A very early pilot for this book was published in *Writing Women in Late Imperial China,* edited by Ellen Widmer and Kang-i Sun Chang. An earlier version of part of Chapter 3 was published as "The Return of the Palace Lady" in *Cultural Innovation and Dynastic Decline,* edited by David Wang and Shang Wei; a Chinese version of part of Chapter 4 was published in Chinese in *Tang Xianzu yu Mudan ting yanjiu,* edited by Hua Wei.

Finally, I have been lucky to have a brilliant intellectual family, each of whom is engaged in teaching, scholarship, or writing, and who have offered me support every step of the way: Ariel Zeitlin Cooke, Jonathan and Claire Zeitlin, Wu Yunming, Lida Wu, and above all, my extraordinarily generous and understanding parents, George and Froma Zeitlin. Both my sister Ariel and my mother Froma deserve special thanks for dropping everything to offer editorial suggestions at the last minute. My husband, Wu Hung, is of course in a class by himself: the first and best possible reader of each draft, whose erudition, creativity, visual acumen, and patience I have availed myself of time and time again. Our research has often intersected and traveled on parallel tracks. In the case of this book, our multiple visits together to historic ruins, temples, and tombs have greatly enriched this whole ghostly enterprise and made it come alive.

—Beijing, July 2006

Note on Citations and Abbreviations

I use a colon to separate a volume number and a page number and a period to separate a *juan* number and a page number.

To differentiate frequently used Chinese homonyms in the text, I sometimes use different spellings. *Gui* designates the character for "ghost," while *gui*[a] designates the character for "to return." *Qi* designates the character for "vital stuff," while *qi*[a] is used for "extraordinary" or "amazing."

Authors and titles included in the Bibliography are excluded from the Glossary. Unless otherwise indicated, all translations are my own.

The following abbreviations are used throughout the text (see Works Cited for complete bibliographic data).

CLEAR	*Chinese Literature: Essays, Articles, Reviews*
ECCP	*Eminent Chinese of the Ch'ing Period*
Guben xiqu I	*Guben xiqu congkan chuji*
Guben xiqu II	*Guben xiqu congkan erji*
Guben xiqu IV	*Guben xiqu congkan siji*
Guben xiqu V	*Guben xiqu congkan wuji*
Gudian xiqu	*Zhongguo gudian xiqu lunzhu jicheng*
HJAS	*Harvard Journal of Asiatic Studies*
Liaozhai or *LZ*	Pu Songling, *Liaozhai zhiyi (huijiao huizhu huiping ben)*
Shanben xiqu	*Shanben xiqu congkan*
TPGJ	Li Fang et al., comp., *Taiping guangji*
Xiqu xuba	Cai Yi, *Zhongguo gudian xiqu xuba huibian*

Selected Dynasties and Periods

Shang 16c.–ca. 1045 BCE

Zhou ca. 1045–256 BCE

Qin 221–206 BCE

Han 206 BCE–25 CE
- *Western Han 206 BCE–8 CE*
- *Eastern Han 25–220*

Six Dynasties period 222–589
- *Northern Dynasties 386–581*
- *Northern Zhou 557–581*

Southern Dynasties 420–589
- *Liang 502–557*
- *Chen 557–589*

Sui 581–618

Tang 618–907

Five Dynasties 907–960

Song 960–1279
- *Northern Song 960–1127*
- *Southern Song 1127–1279*

Jin 1115–1234

Yuan 1260–1368

Ming 1368–1644
- *Wanli period 1573–1620*
- *Chongzhen period 1628–1644*

Qing 1644–1911
- *Shunzhi period 1644–1661*
- *Kangxi period 1662–1722*
- *Qianlong period 1736–1795*

People's Republic of China 1949–

Long ago, when Cang Jie created writing,
Heaven rained millet and ghosts wailed in the night.

—HUAINAN ZI, *from the court of Prince Liu An (ca 179–122 BCE)*

When our ancestor invented writing, ghosts wept in the night.
When later people learned to read, their worries all arose.
I'm not scared of ghosts, and I'm also worry-free,
But at night as I amend this ancient text, my autumn lamp glows green.

—GONG ZIZHEN, *"Miscellaneous Poem, 1838"*

Introduction

THIS IS A BOOK about seventeenth-century Chinese literature, but the legacy of the stories, poems, and plays I explore in these pages still exerts a strong grip on the contemporary imagination. The 1987 hit Hong Kong film, *A Chinese Ghost Story (Qiannü youhun)*, directed by Ching Siu Tung and produced by Tsui Hark, is a case in point. Loosely based on a seventeenth-century tale from *Liaozhai's Records of the Strange (Liaozhai zhiyi)*, and a remake of a 1960 Shaw Brothers film, the movie retells the classic Chinese fantasy of sex between a female ghost and a living man.[1] At one extreme, such a union may be fatal, resulting in the man's debilitation and death; at the other extreme, the sexual power of love may be strong enough to reverse death, resulting in the resurrection or rebirth of the dead woman.

The movie principally recounts the romance between a sweet, hapless tax collector (Leslie Cheung) and a beautiful ghost (Joey Wong), but a prologue portrays the horrific fate that has befallen the other young men before him. The opening shots and soundtrack establish the setting: night at a spooky abandoned temple. The camera follows a leaf-strewn path blown by the wind to a lighted window. Inside sits a handsome young scholar, the traditional protagonist of Chinese romance, studying his books by lamplight. Suddenly the window flies open of its own accord. The scholar looks up and sees a beautiful woman in diaphanous garments performing a swirling dance to the strains of wordless, unearthly music. He is easily seduced. Her chiffon scarf wafts towards him. He picks it up and presses it to his nostrils, breathing in its perfume. As the woman pulls the other end of the scarf, he tumbles toward her, knocking the lamp into a bucket of water. Long strands of the woman's black hair nearly obscure her face as she places his hand inside the bosom of her robe. One thing inevitably leads to another. In the midst of their lovemaking, his hand accidentally brushes her anklet, which tinkles. Suddenly the scene cuts to a rope of massive bells outside, pealing wildly, and a rapid, low, tracking shot, enhanced by the discordant soundtrack, zips toward the window. Something creepy is coming. The ghost gently pushes the scholar back down on the bed. As his legs thrash, the scene cuts to his face, convulsed with horror at what he sees, and he screams. The climax of his pleasure morphs into death throes as the scene cuts back to the water bucket, where the spent flame of the lamp wick now expires. (See fig. 1.)

FIGURE 1 Handsome young scholar studies by lamplight; the ghost performs a swirling dance; the lamp falls into a bucket of water; the ghost makes love to the scholar. From *A Chinese Ghost Story (Qiannü youhun)*, 1987 Hong Kong film.

What did he see? Only much later does the film reveal the lethal form of the monster that the ghost is enslaved to: a giant tongue that instantly sucks dry all the life fluids of the victim, leaving only a desiccated skeleton.

This prologue owes much to the global conventions of the horror film—the spooky music and controlled point of view to enhance fear and suspense, the primal scream and unseen assailant. The gauzy soft focus of the lovemaking shots would likewise be familiar to any international moviegoer. But the prologue also skillfully draws upon an age-old symbolic code for a Chinese ghost: association with wind, disheveled hair, and the operatic whirling dance. The close-ups of the lantern falling into the water and the extinguishing of the flame make explicit the traditional cosmology underlying the sex-to-death sequence in which the fiery yang force of the living man is engulfed by the damp yin force of the female ghost.

At the end of the movie the tax collector fails in his attempt to revive the ghost, but he succeeds in liberating her from the monster and giving her a proper burial, thereby laying her spirit to rest and facilitating her reincarnation for subsequent sequels.[2] To the film producers and their audiences, even the premise of a murderous giant tongue must have seemed more plausible than the original ending of the seventeenth-century source tale, in which the hero marries the ghost and takes her into his household. There she becomes a model wife, faithfully serving his mother and bearing him two sons—and all this without even a formal resurrection. Now *that* sort of ending is totally unacceptable to a modern sensibility, even as fantasy.

Conversely, the source tale never describes the monster, an omission that is not explained simply by the predilection for brevity in Classical Chinese narrative. Rather, the literary ghost tradition is, on the whole, singularly uninterested in horror or suspense. Not that there are not exceptions.[3] But the ghost romance exemplifies the tendency of Chinese literature to displace fear back onto the specter, whose timidity and loneliness as an abject creature arouse instead feelings of pity and tenderness in her human benefactor.[4] One need not be a Freudian to detect projection at work here, that "operation whereby qualities, feelings, wishes, or even 'objects,' which the subject refuses to recognize or rejects in himself are expelled from the self and located in another person or thing."[5]

A passage from Shen Fu's early nineteenth-century memoir, *Six Chapters of a Floating Life (Fusheng liuji)* lays bare this logical process. After the death of his beloved wife, Shen Fu, a low-level clerk and artist, determines to remain in their bedchamber on the night when, local custom has it, the soul of the deceased will visit its former abode. He stations a friend outside the door as a precaution and sits up to wait alone, overcome with grief and longing for his wife. Suddenly he notices the candle flame turn green and shrink to the size of a pea, then leap up so high that it almost scorches the ceiling before shrinking back again. Uncanny behavior in a candle or lamp conventionally signals a ghostly presence, and although he ardently hopes for a sight of his wife's spirit, at this moment he is absolutely terrified. He tries to calm himself, but he cannot keep his limbs from trembling with fright. Just as he is about to call out to his friend, he stops himself: "I further reflected that her soul was so fragile and weak, I was afraid that it would probably be overcome by too strong a yang force in the room. Instead I softly called her name and prayed for her to come, but the room remained silent and nothing appeared. . . ."[6]

At the moment of his greatest fear, dreading to encounter what he most desires, he conquers his own weakness by imputing it to the ghost. Abetting this projection is the gendering of the specter. A shade who is a woman can be imagined as doubly shy and vulnerable; correspondingly, as a man and living being, he becomes doubly powerful and protective. The next morning, he reports, his friend admires his bravery, "not realizing that all the while I had simply been a fool for love."[7]

Since this episode is, after all, related in an autobiography, the encounter with the candle is the closest he gets to a glimpse of his late wife's spirit. In fictional tales, however, an uxorious husband is sometimes rewarded with visits from his dead wife's ghost in which they are able to find anew the pleasure they enjoyed when she was still alive. In such narratives of bereavement, as in the romance, congress between the living and the dead takes the form of sexual union.

Even today the hypersexual female ghost remains a source of fascination in East Asian media, including movies, TV, and novels, much as the vampire does in American and European popular culture. Whereas the sexually predatory vampire can be either gender, however, the erotic Chinese ghost is generally limited to female figures. This gender asymmetry and its complex roots and significance in Chinese literary history are a major focus of this book.

How is a ghost defined in Chinese writing? The earliest Chinese glossary, the *Erya,* probably compiled around the third century BCE, offers the following definition: "The character 'ghost' *(gui)* means 'to return' (*gui*[a])."[8] This gloss exhibits a favorite logic of ancient Chinese texts to define a word in terms of a homophone. The problem in this case is that the homophone is itself a complex and ambiguous term. In classical Chinese, *gui*[a] means, inter alia, to go to, to come back, to rely on, to swear allegiance to, to marry (for a woman), and to die.[9] Its most common meaning, however, is to return home, to return to one's roots or origins. But where is "home" for the dead? The multiple variations on the "ghost means to return" formula in different types of ancient writings show that there was a strong need to counter any ambiguity by specifying the direction of the return—away from the living. The *Ritual Canon (Liji)* therefore declares: "All living things must die; once dead they must return to the earth: this is what is referred to as a ghost."[10] Or as the *Book of Liezi (Liezi)* puts it: "When spirit and body separate [in death], each returns to its true [place or nature]. This is therefore what is referred to as a ghost. A ghost means to return, that is, to return to its true home,"[11] not to the "false" home to which the deceased clung when still alive, but to his or her "true" origins elsewhere. A ghost is therefore defined as what goes away and *does not* come back. The apotropaic impulse underlying these statements and, by extension, the need for the living to make sure the dead are well tended and have a proper place to go, were early on articulated in the *Zuo Tradition on the Spring and Autumn Annals (Zuozhuan):* "If a ghost has somewhere to return to, it will not become a vengeful spirit."[12]

Overall, the Chinese character *gui* has a broader spectrum of meanings than does the English word ghost.[13] The richness of the concepts associated with *gui* and other locutions for the spirits of the dead in Chinese literature will emerge more fully in subsequent chapters. Here a simple overview of the most important usages will suffice. As a noun, *gui* may denote any denizen of the unseen world, including ancestor, god, demon, or monster, but it is only in pre-Han texts (prior to second century BCE) that *gui* as a single character and not in a compound may refer to benevolent ancestors or gods.[14] Baleful connotations dominate the pseudo-etymology of the graph *gui* (鬼) provided in *Characters Explained (Shuowen jiezi),* a Han dictionary of the first century CE: "A *gui* is what a person returns to. The upper part (田) pictures the head of a *gui;* the bottom part contains two radicals: the radical for 'person' (儿) and the radical for 'not in the public good' (厶). It contains the second radical because the yin stuff *(yin qi)* of a *gui* is harmful and therefore goes against the public good."[15] In later expressions, *gui* therefore also became a derogatory term used as a curse or an insult. When used as an adjective, an early meaning for this character was foreign or distant, but over the centuries it acquired an array of extended meanings, including "cunning" (in the sense of both crafty and well crafted); "covert," "stealthy"; "unfathomable," "mysterious"; and "nonsensical." Nonetheless, from ancient to modern times, the primary meaning of *gui,* like the English word "ghost," has remained the lingering spirits of the dead; this understanding accordingly underlies my own framing of the subject.

Closely related to the concept of the ghost in Chinese thought is the term *hun* (soul or spirit). Early scholasticism posited the splitting of twin souls mapped onto a yin-yang grid to explain what happened upon death: the *hun* was a yang soul that flew up to heaven, and the *po* was a yin soul that descended into the earth. But as Ken Brashier has shown, most Han dynasty sources do not sustain the idea of multiple souls, and *hun* and *po* were frequently paired as a compound. Instead the dualism that most mattered and the split that occurred upon death was between body and soul *(hun* or *hun-po).*[16] This is emphatically the case in the ghost-story tradition, where the concept of a separate *po* soul is nonexistent (and the word rarely used except in a poetic context) but where a ghost is frequently represented as a disembodied *hun.* The notion of dual spaces for the spirits of the dead nonetheless persists in the literary imagination, since a ghost is sometimes represented as earthbound and residing in the tomb or underworld and other times as a weightless and airborne wanderer.

In Chinese literature the soul may split from the body not only upon death, but also in coma or dream when the body is similarly immobilized. As a shadow or reflection of an absent form, a disembodied soul is closely associated with dream, image, and illusion, and comes close to the English word phantom.[17] A major difference, however, is that in the Chinese imagination a disembodied soul may still have a corporeal aspect and even bear children. The term *hun* appears in many compounds referring to ghosts, *you*[a]*hun* (underworld soul), *you*[b]*hun* (wandering soul), *yuanhun* (wronged soul), *guhun* (lonely soul), but most central to this book is *huanhun*—the revenant, literally a "returned soul." In contrast to the verb *gui*[a] where the direction of return is ambiguous, *huan* means unequivocally "to come back," clarifying that the dead soul returns to the here and now to haunt the world of the living.

The revenant developed into one of the great themes of Chinese literature. Although a few fragmentary ghost narratives can be found in early histories such as the *Zuo Tradition,* the ghost tale proper first emerged in the literary genre of brief "accounts of the strange" *(zhiguai),* which developed in the fourth and fifth centuries CE during the Six Dynasties. Longer and more elaborate "tales of the marvelous" *(chuanqi),* often framed around verse, started to be written in the eighth and ninth centuries during the Tang dynasty. These "classical tales," so called because they were composed in classical rather than vernacular Chinese, continued to be written throughout the centuries. Some of the more famous tales were rewritten in the vernacular and eventually included in the story collections published in the late sixteenth and early seventeenth centuries. As northern drama *(zaju)* developed in the thirteenth and fourteenth centuries during the Yuan dynasty, play texts became another major form of ghost literature. With the flourishing of southern drama (also called *chuanqi*) in the sixteenth and seventeenth centuries, extant ghost play texts increase exponentially in length and number.

The revenant continued to preoccupy the Chinese literary imagination up until the early twentieth century, when the modern vernacular replaced Classical Chinese and the traditional system of literary genres collapsed.[18] The anti-superstition campaigns in the first decades of the People's Republic of China (PRC) nearly dealt a fatal blow to ghost literature and to ghost operas, at least on the Mainland.[19] In 1961 a new Peking-opera production of the seventeenth-century play *Li Huiniang* became the target of a political attack for daring to assert that "there's no harm in speaking of ghosts" *(you gui wuhai lun)*. This anti-ghost campaign, a prelude to the Cultural Revolution, seemingly hammered the final nail in the coffin. But ghosts have a way of returning. The political and economic reforms of the 1980s and 1990s in the PRC meant that formerly taboo topics like the occult, geomancy, and sex could once again be addressed in print, and remnants of the old ghost operatic repertory were again performed on stage. Repackaged collections and new compilations of old ghost stories as well as academic studies of ghostlore and ghost literature appeared in mainland bookstores to meet the pent-up demand.[20] As David Wang has demonstrated in his essay "Second Haunting," in the eighties and nineties some writers, not only in Taiwan, Hong Kong, and Malaysia, but even on the Mainland, began to experiment with new forms of ghost stories. [21] Still, the creative legacy of traditional ghost literature has been most readily apparent in the Hong Kong cinema and other forms of popular media.

The period from roughly 1580 to 1700, that is, the late Ming and early Qing dynasties, with which this book is centrally concerned, should be regarded as the high point of the literary ghost tradition. First, because of the well-documented publishing boom in this period, many older ghost tales and plays were printed, often for the first time, in a variety of accessible compilations that then went through successive reprints and repackaging. Some such editions were hack jobs, but others, such as Mei Dingzuo's *Records of Talented Ghosts* (*Caigui ji;* author's preface 1605), a compendium of tales with verse attributed to ghosts, were scholarly tours de force. Mei's compilation is one of the few to maintain an exclusive focus on ghosts, but many tale collections and even some poetry anthologies from the period include subsections on this theme. The publication of earlier ghost literature stimulated the production of new works on this subject. Accordingly, many anthologies, again exemplified by Mei's *Records of Talented Ghosts,* include contributions from both past and present.

The history of play texts followed a somewhat parallel trajectory in this period. With the exception of a single collection of libretti, our earliest extant editions of Yuan dynasty plays written in the thirteenth and fourteenth centuries were published during the late Ming, in the late sixteenth century. As a performance genre, northern drama had become obsolete by this period, so many of these plays were subsequently rewritten and expanded into contemporary southern dramas for performance and publication. The availability of the earlier ghost plays also stimulated the creation of many new southern dramas on the revenant theme that were enthusiastically staged and printed.

Second, ghost literature in this period stands out not only in terms of abundance and circulation but also in terms of quality and sophistication. In particular, this period witnessed the creation of three masterpieces in which the phantom heroine figures prominently: two southern dramas, Tang Xianzu's *Peony Pavilion (Mudan ting)*, completed in 1598, and Hong Sheng's *Palace of Lasting Life (Changsheng dian)*, completed in 1688, and Pu Songling's collection of tales, *Liaozhai's Records of the Strange*, written roughly between 1670 and 1700. These works, along with Mei Dingzuo's *Records of Talented Ghosts*, have inspired the core of my study.

Third, fueling much of the literary energy of the period was the widespread idealization of *qing*—love, sentiment, desire—as a passion capable of surmounting the gulf between life and death. *Qing* came to manifest its power above all through the figure of the female revenant, whose quest for love compels her to revisit the human world in search of her beloved and whose undying passion leads to her resurrection or rebirth, usually through the sexual agency of her male partner. One major purpose of this book is to explore how and why this cultural fantasy wielded such extraordinary influence.

Finally, this period witnessed the violent collapse of the Ming dynasty in 1644 and the Manchu conquest that led to the founding of the Qing dynasty (1644–1911). These historical events were traumatic not only because of the massive destruction, loss of life, and dislocation involved, but because seemingly overnight a whole world and way of life had vanished. Emotionally, for many, the overthrow of the old dynasty was experienced as a kind of death that demanded mourning. As a figure that embodies absence, melancholy, and the past, the revenant provides a key to the mood of nostalgia and loss that suffuses much of the literature produced in the first decades of Qing rule.

By concentrating on this historical period, I intend to move beyond the typological approach often adopted in previous studies of ghosts in Chinese literature, which emphasizes the classification and persistence of certain general patterns rather than the significance of drawing on this tradition at a particular time and in a particular literary context.[22] These classificatory efforts derive in part from the desire to impose some sweeping order and unity on the gigantic corpus of Chinese ghost stories and from the tacit recognition of the enormous influence that oral storytelling and folklore have played in shaping the literary ghost tradition. There is some early evidence that ghosts *(lingguai)* were one kind of subject matter that professional storytellers in thirteenth-century Hangzhou, the capital of the Southern Song, could specialize in.[23] But far more important was the practice of casual storytelling among friends, household members, or chance acquaintances. Many collections or individual tales refer to this oral context by including the names of informants or by describing the circumstances in which the story was told. At one extreme, this information is a literary convention meant mainly to enhance the impression of a tale's veracity; at the other, the attention to the storytelling context and the historical identity of each teller and listener grows so pronounced that the lengthy discussions of the tales often overshadow the tales themselves.

Ji Yun's late eighteenth-century collection, *Jottings from the Thatched Cottage of Careful Reading (Yuewei caotang biji;* henceforth *Jottings from the Thatched Cottage),* which is the primary example of the second extreme, includes one ghost tale that brilliantly debunks the trustworthiness of any oral storytelling frame.[24] A traveler falls in one evening with a group of strangers in a tavern, one of whom proposes telling ghost stories. The group takes turns spinning weirder and weirder tales until one of the men boasts that he has one that tops them all. The story he tells consists of a set of nested ghost narratives, each told as a story within a story by a successive interlocutor. The entire tale ends when one by one, in reverse order, the traveler discovers that each interlocutor in the chain of nested stories is actually a ghost, including the teller who began it, whereupon the entire group of strangers in the tavern vanishes like smoke.[25]

The practice of casual storytelling cut across class lines and was one way in which an oral folklore of ghosts was transmitted through time and space. But all the tales purporting to have been heard in such fashion were written down in Classical Chinese by elite authors for their own purposes. These authors had no interest in capturing the spoken quality of the stories they retold or any stake in authenticating the manner in which a narrative was recounted. The only case I have found in which the actual process of *telling* a ghost story is portrayed in detail occurs in a set of plays where the whole thing is staged as a comic hoax. In the scene an old flower seller, whom the audience knows has been hired for the purpose of deception, spins a long yarn about a haunted garden to frighten the hero into believing that his lover is really a ghost so that he will leave her and go sit for the civil service examinations.[26]

My book therefore examines the elite production of ghost literature in the seventeenth century and the complex set of concerns that the subject allowed men of letters to address. My working assumption is that it is impossible to peel off the layers of literary processing to arrive at some "popular" original version of a tale or the events described in it. When sources permit, and more than one written version of a tale from a short period of time exists, I have attempted to take into account the oral circulation of the story. I have not tried to ascertain which one is more "authentic" but rather to determine the varying meanings, aims, and context of each version.

Concentrating on a well-defined period also allows me to explore the interrelationship between different artistic genres, mainly narrative, drama, and poetry, in representing the ghost. When apparitions of the dead in Chinese cultural history have been studied as a literary or imaginative problem, attention has usually been confined to the ghost story, or, to a lesser extent, to ghost drama; scholarship in the one area has tended to work in generic isolation from the other. No one has addressed what is probably the most remarkable feature of the Chinese literary ghost tradition: the phenomenon of verse attributed to ghost writers—that is, by authors actually reputed to be spirits of the deceased—and the importance of lyric poetry in developing a ghostly aesthetics and image code.

This book deals extensively with all three genres, which are closely intermeshed in the representation of the ghost, especially in the Ming-Qing period. Verse is embedded and contextualized as "ghost-written" in tales or anecdotes, which provide a narrative frame; conversely, exchanges or displays of poetry set a ghostly mood and are often central to the action in stories. Tales furnish the core plotlines for plays; conversely, theater practices may have influenced the portrayals of ghosts in narrative. The poetic tradition provides the building blocks for the lyrics to the arias sung in plays, which contributed to the theatrical effect of a ghost on stage.

The case of dramatic literature's relationship to oral and popular culture during the seventeenth century raises a separate set of methodological problems. Plays were performed in a variety of venues and occasions, particularly on religious festivals and at ritual events. The full scope of what today is loosely called ghost opera *(gui xi)*, which would include the Buddhist Mulian plays performed at the annual "Ghost Festival" and masked exorcist drama *(nuo xi)*, lies outside the scope of the present study. Instead, although the issue of ritual is important to my analysis, I focus on play texts mainly composed during the seventeenth century while simultaneously foregrounding the specific performing context favored by the late Ming and early Qing elite, that of productions staged at banquets in private homes.

Historicizing the production and consumption of ghost literature is also necessary to counter the abiding influence of nineteenth-century sinologists such as de Groot or Doré, who, as Christian missionaries, read ghost stories indiscriminately as repositories of timeless religious beliefs or "superstitions" of the Chinese.[27] In their wake, many scholars have continued to mine this rich corpus as primary source material for popular beliefs about the afterlife, although a much more nuanced approach is now the norm.[28] For those committed to the modernist view of ghosts as backward superstition, an alternative strategy has been to rehabilitate this literature as social satire or political allegory whose supernatural content can therefore be dismissed as an expedient fiction. It is true that a distinct strain of ghost literature, particularly in the Qing, did exploit the bureaucratic image of the other world primarily to pillory the foibles of this one.[29] The problem has been the indiscriminate use of this interpretation to explain away the entirety of ghost literature simply as "fiction," here understood as the reverse of "belief." Even in sophisticated studies of individual works, debate over the literary value of ghosts has often continued to center on whether their presence should be taken as a fictional device and rhetorical embellishment or as a sign of an author's true belief in the supernatural.[30]

Belief as a category of scholarly inquiry has rightly come under attack by a number of anthropologists and historians. For example, Byron Good has argued that the adoption of "belief" as an unexamined analytic category in anthropology is partly the result of modern Christian biases mistakenly projected onto other cultures and colonialist assumptions of Western science's superiority over indigenous ways of explaining the natural world.[31] In a somewhat related vein, anthropologist James L. Watson has proposed that the notion of a belief system is unimportant in Chinese death ritual; practice instead is what counts.[32] In his study of ghosts in the deeply Christian Middle Ages, the social historian Jean-Claude Schmitt suggests moving from the use of "belief" as a passive noun to "believe" as an active verb in order to show the constant dialectical process of affirmation and contestation involved. Most important, he objects to seeing a belief in ghosts as something reified and immutable that exists for the historian of past cultures apart from the sources that he or she is using and their distinct "form of enunciation."[33]

My point of departure therefore is to shift the discussion of ghosts in Chinese literature from the question of belief or fictionality to the issue of representation and to explore the complex meanings, both literal *and* figurative, of these representations. What are the literary conventions for portraying ghosts? How and why do they change over time, in different genres, and in different contexts? After all, a ghost is by definition an otherworldly creature, invisible, inchoate, and intangible. A specter is always an image, culturally and historically constructed, and it therefore forces us to consider what it means to represent something in a given period and context.

This emphasis on representation does not mean that I treat the literary field as divorced from larger social concerns of the relations between the living and the dead. It would likewise be impossible for a study of ghosts to ignore the importance that death culture has wielded over the course of Chinese history.[34] Evidence of the weight accorded to posthumous matters is everywhere—in the complex and detailed prescriptions of degrees of mourning in the ritual canons, in the elaborateness of funerals and below-ground tomb architecture, in the variety of elegiac genres for commemorating the departed, in the maintenance of posthumous offerings in everyday life that was an integral part of ancestral worship, and in the elaboration of an underworld purgatory and rites to redeem trapped souls that were major contributions in the Chinese synthesis of Buddhism.

The richness and quantity of ghost stories, poems, and plays in the Chinese literary record is clearly bound up with this highly developed mortuary imagination. The literary ghost tradition amply substantiates two important points that Watson makes about Chinese death ritual: (1) the exchange between living and dead is seen as continuing after death rather than being severed by it, and (2) "the notion of gender, a cultural construct, survives in the Chinese afterlife."[35]

Nonetheless, as is common in much ghostlore across the world, the apparition of the dead in Chinese literature is always an anomaly, the sign of something gone wrong, whether with the death itself, with the mortuary ritual or burial, or with the mourning process of the survivors. From the point of view of Chinese religion, in Meir Shahar and Robert Weller's words, "ghosts are usually the departed souls of people who died prematurely, leaving no descendant kin behind to provide for them in the netherworld."[36] The demise of a young unmarried woman by definition disrupted the patrilineal, patrilocal structure of the normative Chinese kinship system. Not truly belonging to her natal family, she had no proper burial place, and without a husband and children, she had no one obligated to look after her posthumous worship. This problem in the kinship and ritual structure of society provides one explanation for why the female revenant returns so often in ghost literature.

Ever since Arthur Wolf's influential ethnography of Taiwan in the 1960s, anthropologists and historians of Chinese religion have been particularly concerned with delineating the boundaries between gods, ghosts, and ancestors.[37] The literary tradition mainly supports Wolf's pithy contention that "ghosts are strangers, other people's ancestors," in that very few stories center on a person's encounter with his or her deceased ancestors or other close kin.[38] The main exception is the apparition of a dead wife to her husband, and even here it is significant that there is no generational difference and that affinal ties rather than blood relations are involved.

In the complex history of the Chinese celestial pantheon, most gods are portrayed as occupying bureaucratic posts, and Arthur Wolf was by no means alone in observing that the hierarchical structure of the divine world offered a mirror image of officialdom in this world, with despised ghosts at the very bottom. (The literary subgenre of the ghost satire mentioned earlier is predicated on this symmetry.) But more recently scholars have emphasized that reified bureaucratic authority was not the only source of power for Chinese divinity, and that the boundary between god and ghost was actually very porous. "Many gods," argue Shahar and Weller, "share the kind of premature and violent deaths, often by suicide, that typify malevolent ghosts," and "draw upon the power of the margins, of death, and of the outside."[39] The ghostly origins of female deities are particularly pronounced because so many of them began as unmarried women who died untimely deaths.[40]

The female revenant in ghost literature clearly draws on the posthumous superhuman power of the disenfranchised. Despite the supposed fragility of such a disembodied soul, the impression is most often of her self-determination and initiative in contrast to living women and her dominance over her male partner. Death is what empowers her and frees her to act upon her own desires. Even in *A Chinese Ghost Story*, the beautiful ghost in the film, though pretending to be helpless, repeatedly rescues her human lover from the other demons in the temple. In short, the phantom is always the heroine of her own story; in any eventual resurrection or rebirth, she is always in large measure also the agent of her own liberation and redemption.

This book consists of four chapters and a coda. Each chapter focuses on one or more interconnected themes, which are often enunciated in certain genres. As I have emphasized so far, the interrelationship between love and death, sexuality, fertility, and disease is a fundamental concern of the ghost romance; accordingly, this set of corporeal issues, particularly as explored in the classical tale, is the subject of Chapter 1 ("The Ghost's Body"). But ghost literature is also an important place for probing the subjective experience of death and for testing the cultural notion of literary immortality that authorship promised. Here lyric poetry, as framed within tale and anecdote, is key and serves as the basis for Chapter 2 ("The Ghost's Voice").

This chapter excavates the foundational Six Dynasties and Tang texts that shaped the Ming and Qing production of ghost poetry, showing how this earlier tradition remained "alive" in the seventeenth century by being continually read and rewritten. The return of the past in the present, particularly in the political context of a new dynasty confronting an old one, is another major theme in ghost literature. Inspired by poetic meditations on the past, but revitalized by integration with the narrative romance, this type of ghostly encounter works through the memory of traumatic historical events and constitutes the heart of Chapter 3 ("Ghosts and Historical Time"). Imagining a ghost in the person of an actor in the context of a play sheds light on fundamental aspects of the theatrical experience. The dramatization of the ghost romance, particularly the elaboration of the phantom heroine *(hun dan)* role and the emphasis on staging doubles, is the focus of Chapter 4 ("Ghosts and Theatricality"). A final coda reads the ghost scenes in the historical drama *Palace of Lasting Life (Changsheng dian)* as a prism that refracts the major themes developed in the previous four chapters—the female corpse revived through sexual love, the imagination of mortality through the creation of a ghostly poetic voice, the mourning of the historical past by the present, and the theatricality of the split between body and soul—but which also transcends them.

1

The Ghost's Body

The affairs of the bedchamber can kill and they can give life.
—*Classified Medical Prescriptions*

Death is not personified in Chinese thought or rhetoric, and consequently death cannot be represented as a feminine figure as it is at many points in Indo-European traditions.[1] Yet the prominence of the female revenant and the frequent fantasy of her resurrection or rebirth is one of the most striking features of seventeenth-century Chinese literature. The taste for "phantom heroines" is part of the widespread fascination with the death of beautiful, talented women in the sentimental culture of this period, exemplified by the phenomenal success of Tang Xianzu's southern drama of 1598, *Peony Pavilion (Mudan ting)*, which was subtitled *The Soul's Return (Huanhun ji)*. The play was both the culmination of the late Ming glorification of *qing* (sentiment, love, passion, desire) and a primary vehicle for the promotion and dissemination of *qing* as a cardinal virtue for more than two hundred years. As Tang Xianzu defined it in his manifesto-like preface to the play: "Love *(qing)* is of origins unknown, yet it runs deep. The living can die for it, and through it the dead can come back to life. That which the living cannot die for or which cannot resurrect the dead is not love at its most supreme."[2]

The pivot of this often-quoted formulation is the ghost. *Qing* manifests itself on the borders of life and death, not simply as proof of the depth or sincerity of passion, but as the mode whereby an invisible force can be visualized and activated. With its mysterious origins, elusive movements, uncertain identity, and superhuman powers, *qing* is described in certain writings on the play almost as though it *were* a ghost.[3] In the words of Pan Zhiheng, a late Ming drama aficionado and friend of Tang's: "We know neither where desire *(qing)* originates nor where it ends, where it results in separation and where union, for desire is drawn to *the margin between presence and absence, distance and proximity, existence and nonexistence*. . . . Since we know not how or why desire comes into being, it becomes inexhaustible, and we ought not be amazed at the power of desire to make the dead live and the living die" (italics mine).[4]

Or as another late Ming connoisseur of dramatic verse puts it:

> As for this thing we call passion *(qing)*, it enslaves the senses and alters our reasoning, it makes us forget night and day and ignore hunger and cold; it can plumb the reaches of the empire and cross the remote territories of the earth; it can pierce metal and stone, move Heaven and Earth, and command all things. It is what keeps the living alive and what brings about the death of the dying, yet it is what can resurrect the dead and make the living perish. It can also prevent the dead from perishing and make the living forget life itself. *Far and near, floating and rippling, it vanishes and no one knows where it goes.*[5] (Italics mine)

Tang Xianzu's preface hails the heroine of his play, Du Liniang, as the perfect embodiment of *qing* because after dreaming of an imaginary lover and painting her self-portrait, she pines away and dies of desire. Three years later, she returns from the Shades as a revenant to consummate her sexual passion and be restored to life by her lover. Although in abstract terms, *qing* is conceptualized as a universal force of nature, in its embodied form, *qing* is a ghost and a woman.

In the long tradition of literary ghost stories that Tang Xianzu drew upon and which he in turn influenced, the woman who dies of desire only to be resurrected by a living man is a common scenario. This is not to say that men never die for love, or never materialize as ghosts in Chinese literature, but that male ghosts are propelled by motives other than sexual desire; female ghosts may also appear for a variety of reasons and are not always restored to life, but when they do revive, it is almost always in an erotic context. This distinctive pattern of imagination suggests some of the figural richness of ghosts with regard to gender, defined in its broadest terms as the cultural, social, and literary construction of male-female difference. The fixation on female ghosts also points to a seemingly paradoxical preoccupation with the materiality of the phantom's gendered body.

In an essay that establishes a basic typology of the Chinese literary ghost story, Anthony C. Yu points out that in accounts of what he calls "the amorous ghost," the revenant is virtually always female, the mortal lover virtually always male.[6] This asymmetry he contrasts with modern ethnographies of Chinese regions (mainly Taiwan), which report women having ghost lovers or husbands as well as the reverse. Yu attributes this imbalance to the fact that the literary tale was authored by men and represents male fantasies of woman as Other. Implicit in his argument is the notion that the literary record does not exhaust the range of beliefs, practices, or stories found in popular or folk culture. Thus he concludes: "The biases of culture and gender could not be more apparent."[7]

For the present study of the literary imagination of seventeenth-century China, ethnographies from an entirely different period, although they may be suggestive, cannot be relied upon as primary data. To support the argument that both sorts of ghost stories were in oral circulation, but that only the amorous female ghost developed into a literary theme, medical writings, which were published in great quantity during the late Ming and early Qing, provide a better foil. In fact, "dreams of sexual commerce with specters" *(meng yu gui jiaotong)* conceived as a type of possession, was an old medical syndrome for women, a counterpart to nocturnal emissions in men. This syndrome, recorded in Chao Yuanfang's *Etiology and Symptomology of All Diseases* (*Zhubing yuanhou lun;* comp. 610) entered the medical corpus early, but it is quoted and elaborated upon in subsequent writings, including late imperial medical encyclopedias. Case histories from the late Ming and early Qing further show that ideas about women succumbing to such illnesses continued to circulate in this period, even in elite discourse.[8] Indeed, when women are depicted as having love affairs with ghosts or other supernatural beings in literature, it is almost always in the context of illness, rather than in the guise of a romanticized erotic experience.[9]

Medical writings will play an important role in my approach to this chapter for several reasons. First, from antiquity, ghosts had been conceptualized as demonic agents capable of causing disease and death. To repeat a succinct definition offered by Wang Chong (27–97 CE) in the Han dynasty: "A ghost is a pathogenic influence" *(gui zhe, ren suo de bing zhi qi ye).*[10] As Yi-li Wu asserts, "In Chinese medicine, the *gui* always represented a noxious, evil, or heteropathic *(xie)* influence, which could invade the body of the living and cause disease."[11] Ample evidence for this view can be found in medical works throughout the ages, although by the late imperial period, ghosts do play a vastly diminished role in accounts of pathology. Nonetheless, late imperial medical compendia continue to include entries such as "haunting" *(xiesui)* and "possession or infestation by specters" *(gui zhu)* as standard nosological categories, and the relationship between ghosts and illness remained a matter of some debate among Ming and Qing physicians. In ghost stories, both of the anecdotal and the more elaborated sorts, the pathogenic potential of ghosts remains a given, whether as wisdom to be confirmed or as convention to be overturned.

Second, learned medicine was a written discourse that constantly interacted with folk or popular traditions and assimilated them into its own elite idiom. In this respect, medical literature bears a powerful resemblance to "accounts of the strange" *(zhiguai)* and "tales of the marvelous" *(chuanqi)*, the staple genres of the classical tale that purport to record in polished form stories being told in literati circles but that existed in a dynamic relationship to a common oral culture. Because physicians were often called upon to treat rare disorders and because anomaly helps establish the normative, accounts of the strange also sometimes figure in medical discourse but without the literary agenda of the classical tale.[12] Thus medical texts, particularly physician's casebooks, can provide an important alternative perspective to the occult subjects treated in Chinese literature.

Third, with the expansion of print culture beginning in the sixteenth century, medical reference books, which aimed to classify knowledge and make it available to a broader reading public, were increasingly compiled and published. This, too, has a counterpart in the proliferation of classified compendia of tales and anecdotes, published not only for entertainment but as sources of knowledge on a variety of subjects.[13] More important, medicine was not a purely specialist discourse read only by experts or practicing physicians but a branch of learning educated men were expected to be familiar with.

Lastly, one fruitful way to approach learned Chinese medicine is as a symbolic system mapping and figuring the experience of the body, construed more broadly as something like "embodied self." As Shigehisa Kuriyama has argued: "Desires and emotions figured centrally in traditional East Asian conceptions of disease, but they were never based in some disembodied psyche. They were invariably intertwined with somatic experience."[14] The tales to be explored in this chapter share a preoccupation with imagining the ghost's carnal body, the sexual and medical nexus that makes a phantom visible and tangible. In these stories I find strong connections between literary representations of corporealized ghosts and symbolizations of the feminine in Ming and Qing medical texts.

Feminizing the Ghost

The finale of *Peony Pavilion,* which sanctions both the phantom heroine's resurrection from the dead and her secret marriage to her mortal lover, defends these extraordinary events on cosmic grounds: "All obeyed the logic proper to the union of yin and yang."[15] On one level, this last phrase is a common description of both human reproduction and the creation of the world, and as such suggests the metaphorical potential for cosmogenesis present even in ordinary marriage. On another level, the wit of the passage depends on the multivalence of the terms yin and yang so that the values man and woman, to be expected in a nuptial context, can be overshadowed by those of man and ghost. Indeed, the interaction between female ghost and human male, especially when the result is rebirth or resurrection, inevitably suggests broader processes of cosmic decay and regeneration. From a certain perspective the phrase "female ghost" is even something of a tautology. To put it crudely, within the terms of yin-yang complementary opposites, a ghost is "super-yin," an intensification of the qualities or phases associated with yin as opposed to yang. Thus a ghost occupies virtually all points along the symbolic axis of yin (associated with cold, dark, moisture, earth, lower, death, femininity, etc.) as defined against the symbolic axis of yang (associated with warmth, light, dryness, heaven, upper, life, masculinity, etc.) As a story in the fourteenth-century collection *New Tales Told By Lamplight (Jiandeng xinhua)* balances the equation: "Man is the fullest flowering of pure yang, a ghost the noxious filth of deathly yin."[16]

Analogy affords another way to conceptualize the relationship between the two: ghost is to human as female is to male. The analogy emerges most neatly in Pu Songling's clever reworking of a line from a poem by Tao Qian (365–427) in the *Liaozhai* tale "Xiangchun." When the story's mortal protagonist hears the news that his young nephew, a child born in the Shades, will somehow be resurrected and join him in the world of the living, he reflects: "A ghost is not human of course, but as a comfort better than nothing at all" (*LZ* 10. 1324). The line in the original Tao Qian poem reads: "A little daughter is not a boy of course, but as a comfort better than none at all."[17] As both these lines reveal, though yin and yang are complementary and equally important, in a hierarchical culture and society, yang is also consistently prized at the expense of yin: ghosts are inferior to human beings in the natural and moral order of things, just as daughters are less valuable than sons.[18]

The symbolic reciprocity between woman and ghost makes the ghost the perfect site for imagining a purely aestheticized female ideal; consequently the specter comes to function in literary texts such as *Liaozhai* as a sign for something like "hyperfemininity." A brilliant writer such as Pu Songling enjoyed breaking down simple dualities such as yin/yang and ghost/man, particularly through the mechanics of the love triangle.[19] One of the clearest expressions of the ghost's super-yin function in his work emerges when defined not against a human male, but against a female fox-spirit. In the tale "Lotus-scent" ("Lianxiang"), a young scholar enters separately into clandestine love affairs with two beautiful women, willfully ignorant that one is a fox-spirit (whose name is Lotus-scent) and the other a ghost (whose name is Li). Even after each woman has secretly revealed the true identity of her rival, the scholar chalks up their charges to jealousy and refuses to believe them. Finally, after the scholar has failed to heed the fox-spirit's warnings to moderate his sexual conduct, and falls deathly ill from overindulgence with the ghost, both women appear together at his sickbed and launch into a heated and hilarious debate on ghost and fox lore.

> "I've heard that ghosts profit from a man's death because after he dies they can be together for eternity," said Lotus-scent. "Is that true?"
>
> "No," replied Li. "There's no pleasure at all when two ghosts meet. If it were pleasurable, do we lack for young men in the Shades?"
>
> "You fool!" said Lotus-scent. "To engage in the sexual act night after night is harmful with a living person, let alone a ghost!"
>
> "Fox-spirits can kill men. Through what art do you alone avoid this?" asked Li.
>
> "There is a type of fox that sucks away human breath, but I am not of that species," replied Lotus-scent. "So you see, harmless foxes *do* exist in this world, but harmless ghosts do not because their *yin qi* [yin stuff] is so abundant." As the scholar overheard them talking, he realized for the first time it was true that one was a fox-spirit and the other a ghost. (*LZ* 2. 225)[20]

This story pivots on the contrast between ghost and fox-spirit as intimated in their debate. Each supernatural woman is clearly marked as Other just as the male protagonist is marked as normative, but, as is often the case in *Liaozhai,* ghost and fox-spirit are not interchangeable. Lotus-scent is decidedly yang to the ghost's yin. The fox-spirit is associated with healing, laughter, warmth, and wisdom; the ghost with disease, melancholy, coldness, and infatuation (*chi,* a close correlative of *qing*). The story owes much of its humor to the fact that it is clearly a twist on the typical "demon story" as described by Patrick Hanan, in which an unmarried man unknowingly becomes involved with a demonic woman. Her dangerous identity is detected and eventually exorcised thanks to the ministrations of a Daoist practitioner.[21]

In "Lotus-scent," the fox-spirit herself, ordinarily just such a demonic creature, assumes the exorcist role, here (partly to enhance the comedy) recast as a learned physician, expert in both the requisite arts of pulse analysis and herbal prescription. It is the fox-spirit, then, who observes with alarm her lover's haggard appearance and who diagnoses his condition: "You are in danger! How is it you've grown still more fatigued and debilitated than when I saw you ten days ago? Surely you haven't taken up with somebody else? . . . Examining your overall vitality *(shenqi),* I find your pulse is erratic and disordered like tangled threads. This is a ghostly symptom *(gui zheng)!*" (*LZ* 2. 223).[22]

Medical cases collected in works such as Jiang Guan's *Classified Cases of Renowned Physicians* (*Mingyi leian;* 1549 preface) confirm that doctors might indeed diagnose sudden fluctuations in pulse as a symptom of a "ghost attack" *(gui ji)* or "haunting." In a Yuan dynasty case of "ghostly possession" *(gui zhu),* a man falls ill after he dreams of being struck below the ribs by a mysterious woman clad in green. The famous doctor, Zhu Zhenheng (1281–1358), who examines him, explains: "Your pulse at the median reading suddenly grows larger and smaller, and suddenly longer and shorter. This means your Blood and *qi* are unbalanced and a heteropathic *qi* is harming your orthopathic *qi.*"[23] In this passage, *qi* is employed in three different senses. "Orthopathic *qi (zheng qi),*" which Nathan Sivin defines as "what maintains and renews the measured, orderly changes that comprise the body's normal processes," is understood in relation to "heteropathic *qi*" *(xie qi),* which he defines as "what causes change that violates this normal order."[24] Unmodified *qi*—here meaning "vital stuff" and paired with life-giving Blood—denotes the primary and finite resources of the body.

In another Ming dynasty case in the same collection, a maiden suffering from amenorrhea and a bloated abdomen, turns out to have dreamt of having intercourse with a god after seeing his statue in a temple and feeling attracted to it.[25] The doctor who solves the case reveals that the maiden's anomalous mien and pulse provided the key clues: "The girl suddenly blushes and blanches: this is a sign of shame; her pulse suddenly grows bigger and smaller: this is a sign of being haunted."[26]

Like the medical authorities cited in these case histories, the fox-spirit in Pu Songling's story heals her patient through drug therapy rather than ritual exorcism, expertly doctoring him with rare herbal prescriptions to eliminate the ghost-induced "yin poison" *(yin du)* from his system.[27] In its rationalistic assimilation of ghosts as a medical disorder amenable to mainstream pattern diagnosis and treatment, this story may support—even as it parodies—Paul Unschuld's contention that during the Ming and Qing periods, demonology, which had previously been the purview of ritual healers such as Daoist priests or shamans, was increasingly integrated into elite medical discourse.[28] Alternatively, the fox-physician's practice here may provide playful evidence for Sivin's insight that "[m]agical remedies and what a modern doctor would consider empirical remedies both had to be translated into the abstract formal categories of classical medicine" and his contention that a medicinal drug prescribed by a doctor could also require a ritual form of preparation and administration to be efficacious.[29]

Again, humor in this story derives from the ordinarily insatiable fox-spirit herself mouthing the platitudes about sexual moderation and health common in Ming-Qing medical writings. Doctors, as Furth has described them, were "suspicious of erotic passion" and blamed "indulgence in the bedchamber for a variety of debilitating illnesses in both sexes."[30] Lotus-scent's medical / moral discourse of self-regulation, which exculpates foxes from inevitably bringing disease and death to their mortal lovers as ghosts do, helps erase any essential difference between foxes and human females. As she lectures the scholar:

> For someone of your years, if you desist for three days after making love, your Essence and *qi* will be restored. In this case, even if your partner is a fox-spirit, what harm would there be? But if you enter the fray night after night, a human lover will be worse for you than a fox! After all, surely all those poxed corpses dead from pestilence and the ghosts of those who perished from wasting diseases weren't poisoned by a fox's black magic! (*LZ* 2. 222)

Medical compendia of the period did indeed offer precise guidelines for how often a man should engage in sexual activity, adjusted for age and temperament. The numbers vary from text to text, but the fox's advice in this story corresponds perfectly to the interval recommended for men over twenty and under thirty in Wu Zhiwang's medical treatise *A Flourishing Yang (Jiyang gangmu)*.[31]

Implicit in Lotus-scent's argument is the common understanding that the amount of semen (Essence) and *qi* a man was endowed with was finite and needed to be used judiciously, not recklessly squandered. Intercourse with a demonic creature, particularly a ghost, was therefore seen as doubly injurious. As a Daoist exorcist lectures a young scholar in an eleventh-century demon tale:

> In general, when a man is young, his *yang qi* is plentiful and his *yin qi* is scarce; in his prime, his yin and yang are evenly matched; when he grows old, his yang is scarce and his yin is plentiful. When his yang is used up and yin is all that's left, then he dies. Now you are in your prime when your Blood and *qi* are just at their most robust, yet you are voluntarily pursuing a ghost, an alien creature of unadulterated yin. Squandering your *qi* in this fashion, you may expect your death any moment now![32]

In "Lotus-scent," the symbolic division of labor between the two supernatural women is reinscribed in the climactic healing scene at the scholar's bedside. Having anticipated the dire course of his illness with the foresight characteristic of both fox-divinities and famous physicians, Lotus-scent had long ago gathered the herbs necessary to compound a miracle drug.[33] But the treatment also demands the ghost's intimate cooperation. To be effective the prescription requires an activating agent based on the initial cause of the malady. For this reason, Lotus-scent dictates, the ghost must press her "cherry lips" against the scholar's mouth and spit drops of her "fragrant saliva" to wash the pill down his gullet. In effect, the deadly yin poison becomes its antidote, this reversal probably gaining in piquancy because in popular belief spitting at a ghost was supposed to make it disappear.[34]

This first step produces immediate results—the scholar's belly rumbles like thunder, a sign that often anticipates the body's evacuation of pathogenic impurities.[35] But mere purging is not enough. A second dose of the pill is required. This time the fox-doctor herself must give the scholar mouth-to-mouth resuscitation to build up his *qi*. "The scholar felt the fire in his 'cinnabar field' [the seat of sexual vitalities located somewhere beneath the navel] grow hot, and his energy and spirit *(jingshen)* blazed forth. 'You're cured!' cried the fox" (*LZ* 2. 227). This two-stage remedy hinges on the ghost's yin affiliation with dank bodily fluids and on the fox's yang affiliation with the fiery energy of *qi*. The effect of these therapeutic kisses is to eroticize medicine in general, but here it is the fox who supervises the cure, the ghost who is blamed for the illness.[36]

The inspiration behind the ghost's erotic contribution to the cure is surely also literary in origin. In the Yuan play *The Western Wing (Xixiang ji)*, which came to double as a handbook for lovers, the hero, lying prostrate with love and sexual frustration, shoots down the idea that his sickness will yield to any drug prescribed by a doctor. Instead, he says, if only he can swallow a drop of his beloved's fragrant, delicious, juicy saliva, he will instantly be cured.[37] In fact, the term "ghostly illness" *(gui bing)*, originally a term reserved for any weird or mysterious disorder, often ascribed to demonic causes, was transformed into a frequent synonym for lovesickness in the vernacular language of the medley *(zhugongdiao)* and the drama.[38] Thus the bedridden hero in *The Western Wing* makes the following self-diagnosis: "This ailment is due to a heteropath lust *(xieyin)*. My bones stick out like a corpse, invaded by a ghostly lovesickness *(gui bing)*."[39] He recovers immediately after receiving a love letter from his beloved proposing a rendezvous, which is coded as a prescription, with double entendres on the names of medicinal herbs.[40]

Throughout the first half of this story, Pu Songling plays on the double association between ghosts as invasive agents of disease and the symptoms of lovesickness. The fox-doctor's initial diagnostic reading of a pulse like "tangled threads" *(luan si*[a]*)* is also an obvious pun for "inextricable thoughts of longing" *(luan si)*. The play on words thus reinforces the complicity between the young man's internal psychological state and his disorder's external demonic cause. The ghost, far more than the fox in this story, is bound up with the mechanics of longing *(si)*, both as object and subject of desire. Her initial apparition is provoked by the scholar's "intense thoughts of longing" *(ning si)* as he sits up alone one night.[41] But as she later explains, she was compelled to haunt him as a ghost because even death could not sever the "lingering threads of her longing" *(yi si)*.[42] Thereafter whenever he fondles the tiny slipper she gives him and "thinks lovingly of her" *(ji si mu)*, she materializes in response, the manifestation of pure desire. The scholar's own fantasmatic thoughts and desires are thus responsible for his ghostly possession and the deterioration of his health, but the palpable existence of the specter is never in question; she is never simply negated as "a phantom of the mind."[43] Instead it is the free-floating longing of both sides that unites to produce the ghost in an economy that is best articulated in Feng Menglong's *Anatomy of Love (Qingshi leilüe):* "Long for it and keep on longing for it and you may communicate with gods and spirits. For longing [*si*] is born of love [*qing*] and gods and ghosts are likewise formed of love."[44]

The symbiosis between emotional states and the workings of the body was a basic tenet of Chinese medical thought. *Si,* which I have been translating as "longing," and which refers more broadly to any form of concentrated or obsessive mental activity such as worry or brooding, was classified as one of the major emotions, just as the Heart was conceptualized as the seat of consciousness. It was often used in medical discourse, as Sivin reminds us, to denote "excessive emotion that leads to illness."[45] *The Yellow Emperor's Inner Canon (Huangdi neijing),* the theoretical foundation of learned medicine, defines *si* as meaning "the Heart has something stored in it, a point to which consciousness keeps reverting; since the orthopathic *qi* stays put and will not move on, *qi* (primal vitality) congests."[46] The classification scheme of *The Inner Canon* correlates intense thought with congested *qi,* just as anger causes *qi* to reverse course and rise, or sorrow causes *qi* to waste away.[47] Congestion is a sign of serious disruption in a system where free circulation is taken as key to health; left unchecked or untreated, congestion can prove fatal. As early as the Six Dynasties, ghost stories describe a lovesick girl whose parents forbade her marriage as "dying of congested *qi.*"[48]

One of the most important and broad-based types of congestive disorder was stasis *(yu),* sometimes called static congestion *(yujie).*[49] In *The Inner Canon, yu* is pegged to the seasons and the Five Phases and has a basic meaning of blockage and obstruction.[50] An often-cited early Ming definition explains the term as a factor in nearly any illness: "*Yu* is something that accumulates and cannot dissipate. What ought to rise, rises not, what ought to descend, descends not; what ought to change, changes not. Therefore it is said whenever transformative processes lose their constancy, a static disorder will arise. Sometimes stasis persists and results in sickness; sometimes sickness persists and results in stasis."[51] Schemes identifying subtypes of *yu* proliferate in later medical literature, sometimes differentiated according to the organ system the stasis congests in, sometimes according to what creates or constitutes the stasis, such as Blood, phlegm, or food.[52] But *yu* also has a long history as a broad term for any emotional distress caused by suppressed grief, worry, rancor, or longing, and as such is often translated into English as "melancholy" or "depression."[53] *Yujie,* albeit in a nonmedical sense, is the very phrase the historian Sima Qian of the second century BCE employed in his formulation of literary creation as the crystallization of pent-up frustration and resentment.[54]

Late Ming medical encyclopedias increasingly stress the emotional etiology of *yu,* an innovation that surely reflects the heightened visibility of sentiment *(qing)* as a force in the culture and society of the period, but which can also be seen as part of a larger trend in medicine after the twelfth century to attribute the root cause of an illness to the emotions.[55] *A Complete System of Medicine Past and Present* (*Gujin yitong daquan;* 1556) defines static congestion as a disorder arising from the repression of the seven emotions; the affective origin of stasis is now said to explain its near ubiquity among patients.[56] Furth has argued that the dangerous emotionality long ascribed to women, coupled with the recognition of their social disempowerment, meant that they were considered particularly vulnerable to static congestion. She describes this as "a kind of melancholy syndrome of congealed blood associated with spleen system dysfunction. It was experienced as feelings of oppression and suffocation, pressure or tightness in the chest, languor and loss of appetite, all linked to pent-up resentments and repressed desires. Physicians knew that static congestion and [the] Liver Fire [of rage] were related, just as psychologists today know that anger and depression often mask each other."[57]

The strongest evidence I have found for the growing medical attention to the emotional roots of *yu* appears in the *Complete Writings of Doctor Zhang (Jingyue quanshu),* an influential compendium first published in 1624.[58] The physician, Zhang Jiebin, an expert on *The Inner Canon,* introduces what he identifies as a new category of stasis: *qingzhi yu,* "stasis related to the passions," which has its own set of symptoms and pulse readings, and which must be diagnosed and treated accordingly.[59] Within this category, he further distinguishes three manifestation types, all of which arise from the Heart: these are stasis from anger, anxiety, and longing.[60] Stasis from longing, which causes the *qi* to congest in the Heart and injures the Spleen system, was only likely to afflict two types of people: maidens and widows on the one hand, whose sexual desires could not be assuaged, and unsuccessful examination candidates on the other, whose ambitions were continually frustrated. In the case of a woman, stasis from longing could only be fully cured by gaining her heart's desire, but there was hope for a man if he could achieve a state of philosophical resignation.[61]

Despite Zhang's description of several types of emotionally based yu syndromes and his inclusion of male students among the types liable to develop stasis from longing, the two case histories he appends make clear that repressed female desire epitomized his view of the illness. The cases are credited to Zhu Zhenheng, but they were widely quoted in late Ming medical encyclopedias and lead the entry on *yu* in *Classified Cases of Renowned Physicians.*[62] In the longer case, a betrothed maiden is unable to eat and takes to her bed after her fiancé, a merchant, postpones their marriage by staying abroad for two years. Zhu diagnoses her illness as "the congestion of *qi* due to longing." It is as though her body had developed an internal obstruction to mirror the unwelcome impediment to her wedding, as though time could be frozen in the body as stasis. As he explains his clinical reasoning:

> "This is difficult to cure with drugs alone, but it can be dispelled if she is induced to cheer up; otherwise, make her angry. For the Spleen system governs longing. Excessive longing will cause *qi* to congest in the Spleen

and make someone stop eating. Anger belongs to hepatic Wood, which can overcome splenetic Earth.[63] If she grows angry, then her *qi* will move upward and smash open the congested *qi* in her Spleen." So he had them provoke her. She became furious and burst into tears. About three hours later, he had them comfort her and give her medicine. Then she asked for congee to eat. Zhu said: "Although the *qi* of longing has now been dispelled, she must rejoice if it is not to re-congest." So they lied and told her that a letter had arrived from her fiancé saying he was about to set off for home any day. Three months later her fiancé did return after all, and she finally recovered.[64]

The other less detailed case also involves a maiden suffering from fatigue and digestive ailments. After "something has gone against her wishes," presumably an affair of the heart, she develops static congestion in the Spleen and is unable to eat for half a year. She recovers after simply taking medicine prescribed by the doctor.

These medical cases of melancholy virgins display a close affinity to ghostlore, because blighted desires and unredressed grievances are precisely what compel the spirits of the dead to return as revenants. Had either of these patients actually died, she would have become a prime candidate for ghosthood alongside other victims of unnatural deaths—such as murder, execution, and suicide—joining the roster of unhappy "lonely souls" *(guhun)* with rancor against the living.[65] A young woman who dies unwed has ample cause for resentment; her death is by definition untimely and tragic: she has no proper place in the ancestral line and no descendants to look after her posthumous ritual.[66] And since she dies a virgin, she inevitably takes unfulfilled sexual desire to the grave; the force of this repressed desire can be measured inversely by the sexual insatiability imputed to her ghost.[67]

The concept of static congestion, a melancholic disorder arising from suppressed longing and resentment, which obstructs the normal processes of change, provides a symbolic key to the etiology of ghosts. The figures of congestion *(jie)* and dispersal *(san)*, which physicians deployed to describe *qi*'s somatic movement in the formation and alleviation of intense thought or stasis, are also the terms a philosopher such as Zhu Xi (1130–1200) used to explain the physics of ghosts in the natural world. Ordinarily, the spirits of the dead dissolve or disperse; what prevents this dissolution and causes a ghost to materialize is some force—*qi* in Zhu Xi's case, *qing* in Feng Menglong's—knotted up or congested inside it.[68] In this sense, a ghost literally becomes the outward manifestation and perpetuation of the invisible emotional and physical forces at work within the body before death. A ghost is a symptom of fatal blockage and congestion, an interruption of the natural cycle, the pathological return of something incomplete and unresolved. Here is an alternative route to Freud's theory of the uncanny as "the return of the repressed."[69]

The threat the female revenant poses to male health in the traditional demon story, however, is diffused or domesticated in sentimental versions of the scholar-virgin ghost romance such as "Lotus-scent" or *Peony Pavilion.* In such narratives, the melancholy of longing attributed to the ghost neutralizes the flipside of anger or the contagion of death. This suggests that the most important convergence between Ming-Qing medical images of women and literary representations of ghosts is the attempt to redefine and master the dangerous pollution assigned to both women and ghosts in common belief. As Furth contends: "Biology had tamed the powers of pollution associated with the borders between life and death, replacing them by a set of naturalistic symptoms controlled within a system of healing. . . . Threatening symbols of female sexual power were replaced by benign symbols of female generativity and weakness that moderated pollution taboos and permitted an interpretation of gender based on paternalism, pity, and protection."[70]

This process parallels the transformation the female ghost repeatedly undergoes in the Chinese literary tradition (particularly in the hands of Tang Xianzu, Pu Songling, and other late-imperial writers of a romantic cast)—from frightening, malignant, sexually predatory agents of disease and death to timid, vulnerable, fragile creatures in need of male sympathy, protection, and life-giving powers. Standing in for the figure of the doctor, the fox Lotus-scent's changing attitude toward her rival Li perfectly illustrates this shift in viewpoint: at first condemned as a dangerous, pathogenic carrier of yin-poison, the ghost becomes an object of pity who can be cured and rehabilitated. The concept of pollution is reinscribed in a moral framework and internalized by the ghost herself. Thus Li relates how, overcome with melancholy and guilt at having almost caused the scholar's death, she wandered far from her tomb in shame and despair at her body's "otherness" and "foulness" (*LZ* 2. 229). This self-consciousness marks her repentance and is the precondition for her reincarnation in a new body and her legitimate marriage to the scholar.[71]

In the classical tale, superlative beauty in a woman represents a rupture in the natural order and is almost inevitably interpreted as a mark of otherworldly status. For instance, in another story, upon glimpsing her rival, the wife of a man having an affair with a mysterious woman concludes: "Such unearthly beauty could not exist in this world: if she isn't a ghost, she has to be a fox" (*LZ* 2. 287).[72] In many stories, perfect beauty is absolute and simply functions as a free-floating signifier for otherness in general. In such cases, beauty masks any difference between ghost or fox, fairy or goddess, and poses an enigma: Who is she?

The confusion that undifferentiated beauty poses is skillfully exploited in "Lotus-scent," which repeatedly tropes on mistaken identity. The tale begins with a practical joke: When the scholar tells his next-door neighbor that even though he lives alone he is not afraid of foxes or ghosts, the neighbor sends over a courtesan who pretends to be a ghost. The gullible scholar is frightened out of his wits until his neighbor gleefully enlightens him. Thereafter when a real fox climbs over the wall and announces she is a courtesan, the scholar believes her. And when a real ghost also appears and tells him she is a girl from good family, he is likewise easily duped.

The practical joke's effect is to blind the scholar to the truth even when it stares him in the face, for the first part of the story takes pains to differentiate fox and ghost by elaborating a ghostly code of beauty in which a set of specific attributes—movement and expression as well as physical features and temperament—are signs of spectral identity.[73] From the beginning, Lotus-scent is introduced simply as an exceptional beauty, but Li is described in detail, an ethereal but insatiable virgin, with exceptionally tiny feet and a seductive floating walk, prone to feminine outbursts of tears and jealousy. Very young, with trailing sleeves and hair, she explains to the scholar on their first meeting why her hand is so cold: "Exposed to the frosty dew of night, how could this weak, juvenile frame of mine be otherwise?" (*LZ* 2. 221). When he later lifts her in his arms, he finds "her body as light as a straw effigy" (*LZ* 2. 227).

Casting the fox-spirit in the benign role of doctor further shifts the balance of the story's erotic weight onto the ghost. The embroidered pointed slipper Li gives the scholar as a love token is a magical talisman able to summon her at will, but it is also clearly meant as a fetish. She explicitly reminds him "this is something worn on the lower part of my body" (*LZ* 2. 221). The ghost's physical fragility and emotional vulnerability, however, are clearly only meant to contribute to her allure. The fox-spirit herself later confirms the attraction of this ghostly beauty: "Seeing such loveliness, even I have tender feelings, how much the more so would a man!" (*LZ* 2. 227).

In Li and a number of other virgin ghosts in *Liaozhai,* we find a powerful convergence between traditional representations of the ghost as a weightless, evanescent, mournful being, and new ideals of feminine attractiveness that emphasized qualities such as slenderness, sickliness, and melancholy, often in conjunction with literary or artistic talent and untimely death. In his *Sexual Life in Ancient China,* van Gulik charts a change in visual representations of the physical beauty of both sexes from fleshy and robust to elongated and frail, a change that he maintains is discernible during the late Ming, but really took hold in the Qing.[74] As an example of the literary type underlying this pictorial change, he cites "the ephemeral figure" of Dong Xiaowan (1625–1651), the talented, tubercular courtesan who became the concubine of Mao Xiang at the fall of the Ming: "Often ill and subject to attacks of fever at the slightest emotion, [she] foreshadows the type of very young, fragile, and delicate women that during the Ch'ing [Qing] period would become the ideal of feminine beauty."[75] A direct line leads from Pu Songling's ghost women to the brilliant, doomed Lin Daiyu, the adolescent heroine of the eighteenth-century novel *Dream of the Red Chamber.*

The aestheticization of physical frailty and delicate health as a specifically *ghostly* style of feminine beauty is most explicit in another *Liaozhai* tale, "Autumn Moon" ("Wu Qiuyue"). In this story, the adolescent hero is plagued by recurrent wet dreams in which he finds himself making love with the same beautiful young girl. Determined to catch this phantom in the flesh, he lies in wait one night with the candle lit; as soon as he shuts his eyes, he dreams she comes to him. Forcing himself awake, he quickly opens his eyes: "A young girl lovely as a fairy was still there in his embrace." After he finishes what she initiated, he learns that her name is Autumn Moon and that she died thirty years ago at the age of fourteen, but is predestined to come back to life and marry him. Lacking some of the *yang qi* required to revive her, but being too shy to approach him directly, she has taken cover in dream. Henceforth she comes to his bedchamber when he is awake, but she is still as incorporeal as a dream: "Blowing out the candle and climbing into bed was no different than with a living partner, except that after the girl got up, his semen would flow out and stain the bedmat and coverlet" (*LZ* 5. 669). The vaporousness of her body recalls the ghost of a peony-spirit in another *Liaozhai* tale, "Camelia" ("Xiangyu"). When the mortal protagonist embraces this flower phantom, "she feels insubstantial, as though his hand were clasping himself." As she sadly explains the change: "Before my death I was a goddess, so my body was dense; now I am a ghost, so my body is diffuse" (*LZ* 11. 1553). In these examples, the woman's physical fragility has become attenuated to the point of immateriality, her elusiveness also an elegant cover for male self-gratification.

In medical writings of the period, involuntary nocturnal emissions were considered a disorder, a sign of imbalance in the body, which resulted in squandering the precious, finite resources of *qi*.[76] Zhu Zhenheng divided this affliction into two categories: oneiric emissions *(mengyi)* and spermatorrhea *(yijing)*. The only difference between the two, explained the Ming physician Wang Kentang (1549–1613) was that the former was stimulated by dreams of sex with ghosts, while the latter was not. In practice, Wang maintained, the methods of cure for both were identical and so he grouped them as a single entity.[77] Case histories bear out that haunting by a ghost or demon in conjunction with sexual frustration or unrequited love was one possible cause, but that so was studying too hard or a weakened Kidney system.[78] Physicians such as Zhang Jiebin ascribed the root cause of the disorder to the Heart, for it was known that the Kidneys, which governed reproductive function, responded to emotional and mental stimuli by producing fluids. But erotic dreams could result equally from somatic as psychological imbalance—from the stirring of Essence or the stirring of amorous feelings—and so it was necessary to strengthen the Kidneys as well as purify the Heart. Zhang Jiebin believed that oneiric emissions were more likely to plague adolescents, the abstinent, and educated, quick-witted types.[79] The unmarried seventeen-year-old hero in "Autumn Moon" may be additionally vulnerable to this disorder because his betrothed has died before their wedding could take place, affiliating him with desires blighted by death. As the tangible sign of a physiological process whose stimulus is fantasy and longing, a nocturnal emission perfectly embodies the paradoxical realness of dreams, a theme which is developed throughout the story.

Much of the narrative action unfolds in dream. In contrast to the initial series of erotic dreams in which the phantom woman is presented as invading the man's dreams, in the second half of the story, the man deliberately harnesses his own dreams to undertake a journey to the land of the dead. There he rescues Autumn Moon from an underworld jail in a dream that likewise turns out to have the force of reality, since he finds her still beside him after he awakes at home. To escape apprehension from the netherworld authorities for his crime, he is obliged to raise Autumn Moon from the dead before her allotted time. After this premature resurrection, she is exactly the same as an ordinary woman except for her inability to take more than ten steps unassisted without swaying in the breeze as though she were about to topple over. "This physical infirmity actually added to her charms in the eyes of her beholders" (*LZ* 5. 671–672), in part, no doubt, because this fantastic difficulty in walking, here presented as a residue of ghostliness, is also clearly an exaggeration of the eroticized, crippled gait of bound feet that men so admired.

This intensification of the physical weakness and shyness of female specters is related to the lack of interest in horror evinced in the literary tradition of ghost stories, which becomes increasingly pronounced during the late Ming and early Qing.[80] The timidity and nervousness of virgin ghosts, already evident in Yuan plays, is inherited as a theatrical convention in Ming and Qing drama: for instance, the stage directions in *Peony Pavilion* instruct the female lead's ghost to "start at the offstage barking of a dog" and at "the sound of chimes in the wind." As she sings: "My heart suddenly catches in fear."[81]

From everything we know about the representation of ghosts in popular religion and ritual drama, this shift from frightening to frightened is an extraordinary transformation. In his introduction to Chinese religion, Laurence Thompson repeats the common view that "much of the popular religion was concerned with protection against . . . the malevolent ghosts, who sought revenge on mortals." And he cites as examples of this concern a long catalog of practices such as "charms, exorcism, communication through mediums, sounding of gongs and firecrackers, placing of spirit-walls to prevent entry of evil spirits through a doorway, offerings to placate them, the burning of incense, prayers, and fasting."[82] Writings on performances of Mulian ritual dramas in conjunction with the midsummer Buddhist festival of hungry ghosts describe the utter terror the ghost sequences in the play were supposed to have inspired in the spectators.[83] And practices meant to counteract ghosts as malignant forces spreading the contagion of disease and death are still easily discernible in the late imperial medical literature.

The supremely beautiful, sexually insatiable figure of the female revenant so ubiquitous in the literary ghost tale also circulated in Chinese oral tradition and folklore. Her invention cannot be chalked up simply to individual elite writers, although her transposition into the cultivated ideal of the "refined or elegant ghost" *(ya gui)* is clearly a hallmark of the classical literary tradition.[84] Her beauty may be translated into different social registers, coded positively or negatively, but its superlativeness remains constant, an attribute of hyperfemininity.[85] This yoking of death and feminine beauty puts us on territory explored by many Euro-American writers and theorists, including Poe, Freud, Lacan, and Elisabeth Bronfen. If the fears professed by the female revenant in late imperial literature are an inversion meant to displace and ward off the fright she potentially inspires, then we may also agree with Barbara Johnson's characterization of beauty as "the very image of death, castration, and repression which it is designed to block out and to occult."[86]

The unearthly beauty of the phantom heroines who populate these tales is only an imperfect, impermanent mask at best. In popular parlance, "to look like a ghost" signifies the very opposite of beauty. After a gorgeous courtesan in the *Liaozhai* tale

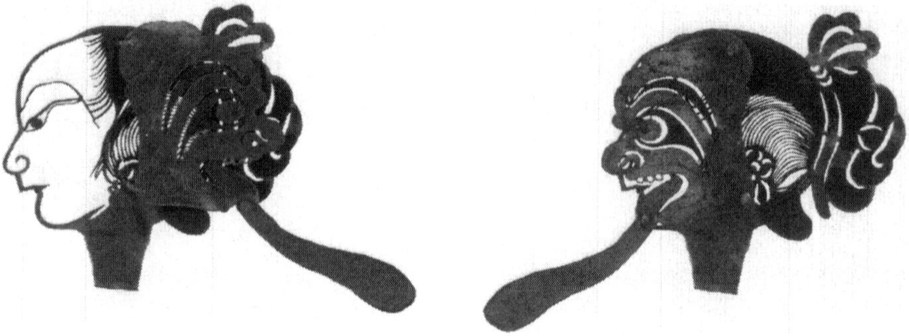

FIGURE 2 Shadow puppet head of a pretty woman on one side and a horrible hanged ghost on the other. Province unknown. Cowhide. Courtesy of Peter L. Rosenberg, Vallin Galleries. Photo provided by Nancy Berliner.

"Ruiyun" is stricken with a disfiguring skin disease, she is described as "looking as ugly as a ghost" *(chou zhuang lei gui)* (*LZ* 10. 1388). In another *Liaozhai* tale, "The Painted Skin" ("Hua pi"), the protagonist has the fright of his life, when, peeping through the window on his gorgeous mistress, he spies a hideous ghost *(ning gui)* with a green-blue face and jagged teeth calmly painting a human skin, which she then drapes over herself like a garment to turn back into a beautiful woman (*LZ* 1. 120). The terrifying transformation of beauty into its reverse was a trick of the shadow puppet theater, which fashioned an ingeniously crafted head that could turn from pretty woman to horrible hanged ghost with the flick of a wrist (see fig. 2). The constant here is the superlativeness of both beauty and ugliness, which reinforces the fact, quite literally in the shadow puppet example, that these seemingly opposite visual qualities are fungible, two sides of the same thing.

Male Potency and Ghostly Fertility

The hyperfemininity of the female specter naturally has repercussions on representations of masculinity. In certain *Liaozhai* tales, such as "Autumn Moon," the frailty and elusiveness of the ghost require a virile young man audacious enough to trap a wet dream and pull off a jailbreak from Hell; in this model, a surplus of yang compensates for yin's deficiency, highlighting the differences between the two sexes. More commonly, the hero, usually a talented literary type, is toned down to match the ghost, so that yang becomes more like yin, increasing the homology between the sexes. (This alignment may likewise be implied in medical discussions that join unsuccessful examination candidates to maidens as equally prone to the melancholy of stasis.) In the second scenario, it is sometimes necessary to supply an additional male figure to play the martial role on behalf of the hero. In the *Liaozhai* tale "Liansuo" (discussed at length in the next chapter), the shy and refined ghost heroine is coaxed into revealing herself to a gentle young scholar with poetic talent, but she apologetically refuses to exhibit herself to a second mortal admirer, even after he has vanquished her enemies in the underworld, because his fierce, martial style of manliness frightens her too much (*LZ* 3. 336).[87] The nonthreatening young scholar therefore occupies a somewhat ambiguous middle position in which he mediates between extremes of femininity and masculinity; the usual effect, however, is to push him further toward the feminine pole (like the *xiao sheng*, or young romantic male lead in the theater) and to reinforce the shifting, relational aspect of gender roles.[88]

Where female ghosts offer the most insight into constructions of masculinity in the cultural imagination of late imperial China, however, lies in the fascination with male generativity and bodily renewal, a realm that fiction and drama shared with learned medicine. Furth argues that sixteenth- and seventeenth-century medicine was intensely interested in fertility, and that while obstetrics went into decline, medical authors produced dozens of new tracts on the twinned themes of begetting descendants and attaining longevity or immortality by "nourishing life." The two are intertwined particularly through teachings on the male body of "inner alchemy" *(neidan)*, which drew upon and modified the old bedchamber arts. With the proper management of sexual and spiritual resources, male Essence could either be "released to father a son and produce new life or made to reverse course to rejuvenate the body and prolong life, even indefinitely."[89] The literature on inner alchemy's regime of hygiene and self-cultivation, which involves both occult Daoist precepts and esoteric medical practices, is complex and need not be gone into here. The point of chief concern for us is the creative power assigned to male sexuality, which could be harnessed for erotic, social, or cosmic aims:

> The male generative body, being linked to the alchemical body, incorporated sexual potency as significant as a sign of a body capable of transcending ordinary humanity. Male sexual powers are identified both with reproductive function that accomplishes the social mission of the family and with generative vitality that can replicate and extend the creative work of the cosmos at large.[90]

The generative male body of procreation is the explicit subject of a seldom-discussed *Liaozhai* story, "Ingenia" ("Qiaoniang"). Like "Lotus-scent," this tale involves a love triangle between a man, a fox, and a ghost, but the fox figure has been split into two, with the healing, maternal qualities now allocated to a middle-aged fox-woman and the amorous qualities allocated to her daughter.[91] Once again, the real erotic and romantic energy of the story centers on the ghost, as the manifestation of *qing*, rather than on the fox. Male reproductive dysfunction is the overt springboard for the plot. The adolescent protagonist has the misfortune to have been born a "natural eunuch" *(tianyan)*: "At the age of sixteen, his penis was only the size of a silkworm. His condition was known far and wide and no family would betroth their daughter to him" (*LZ* 2. 257). The natural eunuch figures in the discussion of human anomaly in Li Shizhen's *Classified Materia Medica (Bencao gangmu)* as the first of five types of "non-males," men deficient in *yang qi* who cannot father children.[92] In this scheme, potential fatherhood is what constitutes masculine identity, in both the sexual and social arenas. The prospect of the ancestral line being cut off, a disaster for the Confucian family, is a virtual fait accompli when the story opens, because the boy's father, who is already in his sixties, has only this one son.

One day, after having been delinquent at his studies, the boy decides to run away to avoid a scolding from his teacher. A few miles from his village, a beautiful woman (the fox) enlists him to deliver a letter for her, which brings him at nightfall to a distant, desolate area. A ravishing young lady appears (the ghost) and offers to give him shelter in what he later discovers is a tomb. She is only too delighted to have company, but, to his distress, insists on sharing her bed with him. "Ashamed at his body's foulness, he offered to sleep at the foot of the bed" (*LZ* 2. 256). The "body's foulness" *(xinghui)* is the same phrase the ghost in "Lotus-scent" employed to describe her own feelings of inadequacy and self-disgust.[93] The duplication of the phrase here suggests that more than plot exigencies have led the boy to the tomb; the shared sense of bodily filth and inferiority indicate his symbolic affinity with the world of both ghosts and women.

A hilarious scene ensues with the mortified boy curling himself into a ball and pretending to be asleep, as the sex-starved ghost, whose name is Ingenia, eagerly embarks on seduction. The discovery of the lack he has tried to conceal drives her to despair. The joke turns out to be that during her lifetime she had been married to just such a natural eunuch and had died of frustration. Her desire has only intensified in the underworld, and she laments the cruelty of fate that would play the same unfair trick on her twice. In tears, she instructs her maid to turn him out. Just at that moment, a middle-aged woman enters (the fox-matron), who also resides in the tomb, and the letter the boy has brought from her daughter is discovered. Eyeing him more closely, the fox-matron quickly divines the problem: "Oh, my clever lad, are you really female though male?" (*LZ* 2. 259).[94]

She leads the boy to her wing of the house and physically examines him. Presently, she produces a black pill, which she asks him to swallow. Then she leaves, instructing him to lie motionless. Wondering what ailment the medicine is supposed to cure, he drifts off to sleep. Some time before dawn, he awakens. "He felt a filament of hot *qi* from below his navel rise straight up into his genital region, and then he felt a wriggling sensation as though something were dangling on his thigh. He reached down, and lo! he now had the body of a powerful male" (*LZ* 2. 259).

The fox-matron craftily conceals the boy's miraculous cure from the ghost, reserving him instead for her own daughter, who soon returns home to instruct him in the art of love. He proves an apt pupil: "The sharpness of a blade fresh from the whetstone can be imagined" (*LZ* 2. 260). Although the foxes keep him under lock and key, he yearns to try out his new prowess on the ghost. One day when the foxes are out, he persuades Ingenia to release him and maneuvers her into restaging the original seduction scene; the result is a complete reversal of his former humiliation. "She playfully grabbed his crotch, saying: 'Too bad an adorable boy like you is so lacking here.' Before the words were completely out of her mouth, something brushed against her hand and filled her fist" (*LZ* 2. 262). The pair make love and secretly fall for each other, but afterwards the fox-matron is even more vigilant in keeping them apart.

Soon thereafter, the fox-matron sends him back home after requesting him to ask his parents to arrange his marriage to her daughter. His parents are delighted at his return but scoff at the idea of marrying him to a fox. "They left you alone only because you're a eunuch; that's why you managed to escape death and return alive!" (*LZ* 2. 262). The boy is too shy to enlighten them to the contrary. Instead, "itching to show off his new skills," he seduces the household maids. Gradually, he indulges himself with them even in broad daylight in the hope that his parents will hear of it. When his mother discovers the truth, she is beside herself with joy and speaks of her son's affairs to everyone she meets to advertise that he is eunuch no longer.

Despite the boy's gift for repartee, throughout the story he is afflicted with a peculiar muteness: he cannot use words to describe his body or express his desires. He can only speak directly through the body. Thus he cannot tell the ghost he does not want to sleep with her or warn her of his deformity; he can only express his reluctance through signs and gestures; he can only let her discover the truth by reading the lack inscribed on his body. He cannot inform the fox-matron who interrupts them how he has offended the ghost; instead he passively submits to a physical examination. After his recovery, he longs to tell the ghost of his changed circumstances, but he cannot articulate his desire; instead, he is compelled to eye her through a crack in the door "like a bird peering through its cage" (*LZ* 2. 259).[95] He must wait until the restraints to their physical proximity are removed to allow his body to speak for itself. After the ghost discovers the change, she asks in amazement: "How is it that something so tiny before has become so thick and heavy?" This is the only point in the story where he discusses his body directly; significantly, he speaks *as* his body, in the voice of the personified penis: "Before he was embarrassed at meeting a stranger, so he shrank back; now finding this ridicule and slander unbearable, he has puffed up with rage" (*LZ* 2. 261).[96]

Upon the boy's return home, he has no qualms describing to his parents his strange sojourn in the tomb or proposing an outlandish match with a fox, but he cannot tell them of his body's transformation. He can only demonstrate his new potency by debauching maids in broad daylight so that his body may be witnessed and spoken of by others—in that sense it is fair to call his sexual activities "performance" in both senses of the English word, as the successful completion of a task and as public exhibition.

The boy's verbal reticence with regard to his body no doubt stems from embarrassment and modesty, but within the context of the story, his silence highlights the anomalous position of the heterosexual male body as the object of such overt scrutiny.[97] This muteness also helps establish the body as the undeniable measure of truth in the narrative in contradistinction to language, with its potential for misrepresentation, irony, and deceit. (Linguistic duplicity is especially associated with the slyness of foxes.) The boy's physical condition is the pretext for numerous double entendres and ironic falsehoods in the story, but the naked male body itself can tell no lies.[98]

The boy's parents finally agree to his marriage with the fox-daughter, but he cannot forget his longing for the ghost. On his wedding day he asks what has become of her; his fox mother-in-law lies to him and tells him Ingenia has departed forever to enter the cycle of rebirth. He mourns her loss, but later hears reports of ghostly wailing at the old tomb site. The boy sets out at once in the hopes of finding Ingenia there. "Suddenly he saw a young woman with a babe in swaddling clothes emerge from the grave pit. Lifting her head, she cried bitterly, her face filled with boundless resentment. He, too, wept. Reaching toward the infant in her arms, he asked whose it was. 'This is your wicked legacy, born a good three months ago,' said Ingenia" (*LZ* 2. 263).

The tomb, ordinarily the site of death and decay, has become the locus of healing and birth. The boy's original sojourn there had the effect of reversing the loss of bodily integrity associated with death's debilitating influence and the decomposition of the corpse; the tomb has become instead a liminal zone of sexual and social regeneration, a space where bodily wholeness and potency can be miraculously restored. Although it is the fox who engineers his cure and her daughter who initiates him into sexual life ("the way of mankind" [*rendao*]), jointly transforming him from child to man, the setting is still the tomb, the funerary realm, which belongs literally and symbolically to the ghost.

Just as the fantasy of the ghost's dazzling beauty masks the hideous disfigurement of the corpse, so too the fantasy of getting a ghost with child blocks out the castration and barrenness inflicted by death. The return visit to the tomb makes clear that the ultimate proof of the boy's manhood is not his marriage to the fox or his seduction of the housemaids but his union with the ghost, because it bears fruit. Male deficiency is replaced by super potency, whose sign is the impregnated ghost. In the context of this astonishing feat of fertility, to engender new life is literally to reverse death's course, signaling yang's victory over yin. As in the medical literature on the body of internal alchemy, the tale's denouement links masculine power and pleasure with cosmic forces of creation and renewal capable of transcending the limits of human mortality.[99]

In terms of the social order, this birth in the tomb also reverses the patriline's death sentence by supplying the family with a male heir.[100] The hero, a boy no longer, takes mother and child home to join his ménage, where everyone lives in harmony; despite his origins, the child, who is healthy and plump and does not resemble "a wraithlike creature" *(gui wu)*, promises to be an exemplary scion (*if* he survives to maturity), passing the county examinations at the precocious age of thirteen.[101]

The conjunction of the two fantasies in this ending—begetting an heir and staving off death through the agency of the potent male body of generation—is where the story shows the strongest thematic parallels to the medical writings on nourishing life. To be sure, the anomalous circumstances of the boy's case permit Pu Songling to circumvent the dominant discourse of self-control, which regulates male sexual behavior for reasons of health, morality, and reproduction. In "Ingenia" the problem is singular rather than general: genital deformity rather than the finite resources of sexual vitality and lifespan; the cure is a miraculous intervention supplied by a female supernatural figure rather than a lifelong self-discipline of meditation and conservation; the result is not the rejuvenation or longevity of the male body but a projection of death-defying regeneration onto the body of the female Other, who is both doubly female and doubly other because she is a ghost. Despite these obvious differences, the concerns given narrative form in "Ingenia" and the advice literature on nourishing life are clearly emerging from the same cultural matrix.

Fruitful couplings between human men and supernatural women crop up in the Chinese literature on the strange, not only with ghosts and variations thereof, such as disembodied souls, dream visions, and painted images, but also with goddesses, immortals, and animal spirits. The potential fecundity of such unions, which Pu Songling's work particularly emphasizes, lends support to the thesis that in late imperial China, the erotic (as opposed to the pornographic) was strongly linked to reproduction, unlike modern constructions of the erotic as an entirely separate realm of pleasure.[102] The fertility of the ghost occupies a special place among such stories because it so neatly aligns the cosmic renewal of death onto a gendered axis.

The fantasy of a fertile union between human male and female ghost appears early in Chinese records of the strange and resurfaces intermittently throughout this literary tradition. We find two such stories attributed to the fourth-century collection by Gan Bao, *Seeking the Spirits (Soushen ji),* which were widely anthologized in the sixteenth and seventeenth centuries. In the first, a living man becomes the bridegroom of a young woman who has died unmarried; he resides with her in her deceased father's tomb for three days before returning home unscathed. Four years later, she returns to find him and tearfully hands over a little boy, the son she has borne him, then vanishes forever. As in "Ingenia," this "issue of a ghostly liaison" also enters his father's family and subsequently embarks on an official career, but here the ghost mother must regretfully return to the underworld, reestablishing the normative, impermeable boundaries between life and death.[103]

In the second story, an unmarried man is visited by a mysterious, beautiful young woman, who becomes his wife and bears him a son.[104] She warns him not to shine a light on her until three years are up, an injunction he inevitably disobeys. One night he gazes upon her sleeping form by candlelight: he sees a woman of flesh and blood from the waist up, a skeleton from the waist down. She rebukes him for interrupting the process of resurrection; had he been able to restrain himself one more year, she would have come back to life; now she must depart forever, leaving her son behind. From a psychoanalytic perspective, this figure yoking together a dead and living body is uncanny precisely because it is the lower half, with the organs of generation, that is pictured as the skeleton. But the image is also uncanny because it is hybrid and indeterminate: in freezing the cyclical process of rebirth midway, the scenario of death's conversion into life reverts to a palindrome for life's conversion into death. As in the first story, the loss of the ghost wife is required to balance the family's acquisition of a son, and the mood is predominantly one of sadness and mourning.

In both stories, the birth of a child emerges as the logical outcome of the rite of "spirit marriage" *(youhun/minghun)* between a dead woman and a living husband. References to a custom of arranging posthumous marriage for a son or daughter who dies unmarried are found in ritual texts, dynastic histories, and notation books spanning the two-thousand-odd years from Han to Qing as well as in modern ethnographies of different areas of China.[105] A little-known Jin or Yuan dynasty ritual manual called *The Secret Burial Classic of the Great Han (Da Han yuanling mizang jing)* includes a section on the "Rite of Spirit Marriage" ("Minghun yili pian"), which offers this rationale for the practice:

> With Heaven and Earth, there is the intermingling of yin and yang; with humankind, there is the relationship between husband and wife. In life, a couple shares a coverlet; in death, they share a coffin. But sometimes after a man has undergone the capping ceremony for coming of age, he dies before taking a wife; and sometimes after a woman has undergone the hair pinning ceremony to mark her maturity, she dies before being married off. Because it is not permitted to omit the "grand burial" for ancestors, in such cases, a marriage is made between two "pure souls" *(zhen hun)* to keep them from becoming lonely ghosts.[106]

Glen Dudbridge has noted that there is variation in virtually every detail concerning spirit marriage, even as he emphasizes "the continuity of *la longue durée.*"[107] He identifies as the most important variation whether the man married to the ghost woman is living or dead. In Dai Fu's *Great Book of Marvels (Guangyi ji),* the Tang collection of strange tales that Dudbridge has studied, the man must die before serving as a bridegroom in a spirit marriage; his one exception is also the only story in which a liaison with a ghost wife is fruitful, though even here the son dies before reaching maturity.[108]

Predictably, narratives of the strange, as opposed to the ritual manuals and accounts in official histories, are preoccupied with spirit marriage to address the needs of dead *women,* rather than dead men. It is not necessary to read these sorts of ghost stories simply as a repository for vestiges of a persistent cultural practice; rather, the interest of such narratives lies in their ability to animate ritual fictions, to play out the imagined consequences of ritual actions. In this respect, ghost stories inhabit the subjunctive space of *"as if"* or *"let it be so"* that anthropologists and historians following Victor Turner have suggested may be one of the best ways to understand the dynamics of ritual practice.[109]

In the case of ghost stories involving spirit marriage, the degree to which a ritual framework is explicit or implicit varies from story to story. Sometimes, as in the first tale from *Seeking the Spirits,* ritual protocol is emphasized: the marriage is formally arranged by the deceased fathers of the couple and the girl's given name is interpreted retrospectively as an anagram for spirit marriage, thereby inserting a specific reference to the practice into the text. Sometimes, as in the second story, the ritual apparatus is initially absent, but the aim of the ritual is clearly achieved. The story concludes with the discovery of the dead woman's identity; this enables a living father to call a living husband "son-in-law," thereby assimilating the volatile ghost into a stabilizing kinship network. In both stories, the existence of a son promises the ghost mother a secure place in her husband's family hierarchy and a male descendant to look after her posthumous worship, presumably resolving the problem that led her to materialize in the first place.

Among the many stories of spirit marriage in *Liaozhai,* we find both narratives that incorporate traces of a ritual context, particularly through the involvement of the dead girl's natal family, and those that do not.[110] In "Ingenia," a ritual framework is conspicuously absent because it is impossible: the anomaly of a boy who is neither male nor female is matched by the anomaly of the ghost's status, who, having been married to a eunuch during her lifetime, is neither maiden nor matron. Her situation in the tomb is doubly anomalous because she lives not alone or with ghost relatives but with foxes, who do everything in their power to thwart rather than to assist her marriage.[111] The birth of a son resolves both sets of blurred categories. But the story's focus is so much on the ghost solving a problem in the *male* descent line that when Ingenia enters her husband's family, she essentially disappears from the picture, and the story peters out with the proviso that Pu Songling's informant did not know how it ended.[112] Although an authorial commentary offering a final evaluation is often appended to tales in *Liaozhai,* no such comment is provided here. The effect of this ending, then, is a deliberate refusal of rhetorical closure, as though some essential contradiction were preventing a complete resolution.

The other notable tale in *Liaozhai* about a ghost bearing sons takes off almost exactly where "Ingenia" stops.[113] Entitled "Nie Xiaoqian," this story, the source for the film *A Chinese Ghost Story,* can, in many respects, be read as the inverse of "Ingenia." This moral fable about the domestication of the phantom Nie Xiaoqian, her transformation from harmful spirit to exemplary wife and her "progressive reintegration into the human community"[114] is only possible because the male protagonist maintains iron control over his sexuality. By resisting the ghost's advances at the beginning, he saves himself from the monster she is enslaved to, and is subsequently able to rescue her from the monster's clutches. Even after he takes the ghost into his household, he continues to abstain in deference to his mother's fears for his health. The oxymoron "ghost mother" is only possible in this story because moralized fate replaces biology as the main determinant of reproduction. As he explains to his mother, echoing contemporary debates, the number of a man's sons and daughters is endowed by Heaven rather than contingent on the physical capacities of father or mother.[115] For this reason, Xiaoqian argues, taking a ghost wife cannot adversely affect the continuation of the ancestral lineage. Just as the ghost gradually acquires the ability to eat and drink in the course of her moral rehabilitation, so she eventually develops the capacity to reproduce. He winds up with his predicted quota of sons, two by his ghost wife and one by a human concubine. Fertility is disassociated from both sexuality and death as childbearing becomes simply the final marker of the man's moral capital and the ghost's humanity.[116]

A brief tale explicitly entitled "The Ghost Mother" ("Guimu zhuan") is included in *The Magician's New Records (Yu Chu xinzhi),* an influential anthology of classical fiction and biography compiled by Zhang Chao and published in the late seventeenth century, during the period of *Liaozhai*'s composition. As Sawada Mizuho has shown, the story in *The Magician's New Records* is one of many written versions of a folktale that circulated in China from at least the Song dynasty up through the Republican period and which also made its way to Japan.[117] In its bare outline, the story concerns a woman who dies while still pregnant and is buried somewhere away from her hometown. Soon after, a mysterious woman starts frequenting a bun shop in the vicinity. Later the shopkeeper discovers that the coins she has given him to pay for her purchases have turned into the paper spirit money used to make offerings to the dead. His suspicions aroused, the next time this woman shows up, he tails her on her return route. To his horror, he sees her arrive at a grave and disappear inside it. When the coffin is opened, they find the remains of a female cadaver and a living infant beside it. Everyone marvels at a mother's ability to nourish her son even after death.

Sawada notes that the version in *The Magician's New Records* is the most polished and fiction-like of the written stories on this theme, by which he probably means that it is more assiduous than the others in supplying background detail and character motivation and in giving the narrative the shape of an exemplary tale.[118] In this version the pregnant woman who dies is the wife of a merchant who is forced to bury her temporarily en route. When her coffin is later opened, they find:

> The grave clothes and bones of the corpse had mostly turned to dust. The only living thing they could see was a baby boy. When the baby first saw them, he was still chewing on a bun in his hand, and he wasn't a bit frightened. Only after the number of onlookers crowding around him swelled and a noisy hubbub ensued, did he get alarmed and start to cry. Sometimes he looked in one direction and made as if he wanted to climb into his mother's arms; sometimes he looked in the other direction and made tugging motions on his mother's clothes. In fact, the boy still recognized this dead mother as his living one, and howled as though he were seeking refuge in her.
>
> Alas, this poor child! People ordinarily suffer at parting from the living, but this boy suffered at parting from the dead![119]

This exemplary tale goes even further toward rationalizing the fantasy of posthumous childbirth, effectively excising the father's role entirely from the miraculous event by having the mother die after conception but before delivery. Like the ghost emerging with babe in arms from the grave pit in "Ingenia," the configuration here is a mise-en-scène for the trope of death as the regeneration of life. But the exemplary tale's glorification of maternal love and filial piety as moral instincts transcending death helps counteract the residual uncanniness of the image.

In contrast to both "The Ghost Mother," which denies paternal participation in the miraculous conversion of death into birth and "Nie Xiaoqian," which downgrades the miracle by suppressing the biological aspects of parenthood, "Ingenia's" obsession with the sexualized male body serves to highlight the miracle. The hyperbolic trajectory from male anatomical deficiency to super potency, which rhetorically reinforces the upswing from death to birth, also works to keep normal reproductive functions continually in view. Here we may find helpful Bloch and Parry's anthropological insight into the logic of certain funerary rituals that stress the putrescence of the corpse to dramatize the renewal of life: "An emphasis on biological processes is used to darken the background against which the ultimate triumph over biology (and hence over death) can shine forth all the more brightly."[120]

Resurrection and *Qing*

The most common fantasy of male generativity in Chinese literature, however, is not begetting new life from a ghost, but bringing a ghost back to life. Although reviving the dead woman through the power of male sexuality is a theme with a long pedigree, it plays a central role in literature of the late Ming and early Qing, most famously in *Peony Pavilion*. In a finely nuanced discussion of *qing* as a philosophical concept in the contemporary discourse surrounding the play, Wai-yee Li characterizes the term as sometimes "synonymous with life-force."[121] Rhetorically speaking, in certain of the late Ming assertions glorifying the power of *qing*, the value *qing* is simply substituted for the more customary value *qi*, thereby conflating desire or love with primal vitalities equally capable, through the logical relationship of microcosm to macrocosm, of affecting the body and the universe at large. In a sensitive reading of key scenes in the play, Catherine Swatek demonstrates how recurrent natural images such as the flowering plum tree "suggest the procreative forces of nature" and the "creative force of human passion" by naturalizing Du Liniang's death and resurrection within a vegetative cycle of regeneration and renewal.[122]

Pu Songling's "Camelia" plays out this idea literally in horticultural terms. When the peony-spirit of the story is killed after someone uproots the flower bush of which she is the incarnation, her lover tenderly applies water and fertilizer to the spot. To his joy, the next spring, new shoots appear, signs of her regeneration and regrowth (*LZ* 11. 1554).

The association of chastity with coldness and death makes the virgin ghost the ghostliest figure of all, but the image almost irresistibly evokes the fantasy that she will be reborn through the generative power of male sexual love, given new ideological sanction through the elevation of *qing*. When Du Liniang reveals to her lover that she is really a ghost and seeks his help in resurrecting her, he exclaims: "How cold you must have been!" She replies: "Frozen body and soul in coldest chastity . . . [but] my cold flesh already / you have caressed to warmth."[123] Thanking him after her revival, she declares: "Having returned me to life, you are dearer to me than mother and father."[124]

Far more literal-minded than Tang Xianzu, Pu Songling medicalizes this scenario in "Liansuo." Lonely but virtuous, Liansuo, the phantom heroine of the tale, scrupulously refrains from responding to the sexual advances of the scholar who courts her for fear of doing him physical injury. As she explains: "These moldering bones from the grave are no match for the living. A liaison with a ghost only hastens a man's death; I could not bear to harm you" (*LZ* 3. 332). She haltingly reveals she has been dead for twenty years, having died of a sudden illness at the age of sixteen. "Slender and chilled, she shrank back as though she could not bear the weight of her clothes" (*LZ* 3. 331–332). Her extreme physical fragility elicits one of the most explicit descriptions of the female body in *Liaozhai*. The scholar, accepting that he cannot fully consummate his physical desire for the ghost, "playfully put his hand inside her bodice: the tips of her breasts were as tender as freshly shelled nutmeats; clearly she was a virgin" (*LZ* 3. 332). In a parallel but more oblique move, he then peeks beneath her skirt to inspect her tiny embroidered shoes and stockings, the fetishized, displaced locus of the female genitals in this period.

At the end of the story, the ghost-heroine comes to the scholar and begs his aid in reviving her, but warns him that to do so will cause him to fall seriously ill for a period of time. In accordance with the medical model of procreation, to be reborn she requires not only his semen, but his blood. Here the scholar completely takes over the generative function, supplying both male Essence and female Blood. The act of intercourse through which Liansuo loses her virginity and receives his semen is narrated in a single perfunctory phrase. It is the transfusion of blood as the masculine counterpart to her defloration that is described in detail: "'I still require a drop of blood from the living,' she said. 'Are you willing to suffer pain for the sake of our love?' The scholar took a sharp blade and stabbed his upper arm until the blood flowed; the girl lay on the couch as he let the blood drip into her navel" (*LZ* 3. 336). After instructing him where to find her burial spot, she vanishes.

The scholar's donation of his vital bodily fluids, which requires his willingness to endure self-inflicted pain and illness, is construed as proof of the depth and sincerity of a love able to tap into cosmic forces of creation.[125] The life-giving blood is imagined to drip into the ghost's body through her navel, mapped in medical thinking as the generative center in all bodies, but linked to the "conception tract" in women.[126] According to this symbolism, the new life the ghost gestates is her own. The aftermath of the act, however, reinforces the impression that simultaneously at work here is a medicalized fantasy of male conception. The scholar falls ill with pregnancy-like symptoms and is cured only by going through a process analogous to childbirth: "Over ten days later, his belly swelled up so painfully he wanted to die. After taking a remedy prescribed by the doctor, he excreted a foul substance something like mud. Within twelve days he had recovered" (*LZ* 3. 337).

His condition resembles accounts in the medical literature of a syndrome known as "phantom pregnancy" (*gui tai,* literally, "ghost fetus"), in which a woman, often a maiden, exhibits symptoms of false pregnancy: cessation of menses and an expanding belly.[127] Different explanations for the disorder are offered, which vary depending how literally or figuratively the "phantom" is understood. In Chen Ziming's (1190–1270) *Complete Good Prescriptions for Women (Furen daquan liangfang),* the culprit is weakened bodily defenses and psychic decline, which enable alien influences to penetrate the organ systems.[128] The case from *Classified Cases of Renowned Physicians* of a maiden who fell ill after dreaming of intercourse with a god's statue seen in a temple, which I discussed earlier as an example of a ghostly pulse diagnosis, is a classic narrative of "phantom pregnancy" literally construed, although the term is not actually applied there. A similar case is discussed under the rubric of "phantom pregnancy" in Yu Tuan's *Correct Transmission of Medicine* (*Yixue zhengchuan;* author's preface 1515). He glosses *gui* (phantom) as *wei* (false) and attributes the cause not to supernatural fecundation but to the woman's unbridled lascivious longings, which cause her own "liquid Blood and yin Essence" *(xueye yinjing)* to congeal into a lump and distend her belly as in pregnancy.[129]

Many later physicians shared Yu Tuan's skepticism. Zhang Jiebin, for example, held that phantom pregnancy was an internally caused disorder like a tumor rather than something provoked by an encounter with an external demonic force. "Surely it is not possible for a ghostly influence *(gui qi),* which is insubstantial and unreal, to penetrate a human womb in actuality and produce something that takes on a concrete form!"[130] Yet other seventeenth-century medical books such as *Fu Qingzhu's Medicine for Women (Fu Qingzhu nüke)* continued to attribute this disorder to dreams of intercourse with gods or ghosts provoked by a woman's illicit desires, which often ensued after an excursion to risky outlying areas such as temples or mountains.[131] Even in 1742, the imperially sponsored *Golden Mirror of Medicine (Yizong jinjian)* was still obliged to counter the supernatural view, attributing the cause of phantom pregnancy exclusively to the woman's repression of immoral desires, which congest the Blood and *qi* within the body.[132] Although varying combinations of drugs are prescribed as treatment in these medical cases, the desired result is uniformly to purge the body of the filth that ails it. "Excreting a foul substance" *(xia ewu),* the phrase Pu Songling employed, is the exact wording commonly found in such accounts. As *Fu Qingzhu's Medicine for Women* puts it: "Expelling the filth is of chief importance."[133]

After the scholar's convalescence, the resurrection takes a more conventional turn. He goes to the appointed place at the appointed time and exhumes the grave: "He saw that the coffin had completely rotted away, but the girl looked as though she were alive and seemed slightly warm to his touch" (*LZ* 3. 336). He takes her still unconscious body home and she revives at midnight.[134]

The relationship of ghost to corpse is an awkward and uncanny one, since they are doubles, not only of each other, but of the former living person whom they supplant.[135] In this story, as in *Peony Pavilion,* reanimation is a process mysteriously effected upon the ghost's body but registered on the corpse. As mutually exclusive images of the deceased, ghost and corpse cannot ordinarily coexist in the same time or space in the narrative. In an early horrific type of ghost tale reminiscent of vampire lore, phantom and corpse are for all practical purposes interchangeable. In these cases the exhumation of a grave and the discovery of an exquisite corpse—a cadaver that looks as fresh and lovely as in life—is proof that a malevolent ghost is abroad, and destroying or "killing" the corpse is sufficient to exorcise the specter.[136]

One fascinating exception is "Ainu" (*LZ* 9. 1191–1194), a *Liaozhai* tale that parodies the conventional division between specter and corpse. Here a man acquires a ghost named Ainu as a housemaid-concubine. To show his affection and esteem, he exhumes her grave so that he can rebury her remains. But when he opens the coffin, he finds that even though the grave clothes have rotted, her body is intact and looks "as though it were still alive." He therefore alters his plans and takes the cadaver home. As he is keeping a nighttime vigil by the body's side, Ainu's ghost suddenly comes through the door: "Is the grave-robber here?" she teases. Then changing her tone, she urges him to rebury her at once. He tries to persuade her to let her corpse be resurrected instead: "In antiquity, people dead a hundred years came back to life—now your fragrant body is as it was formerly, why don't you imitate them?" But she is unconvinced: "This is a matter of destiny. Besides, more than half the accounts of such miracles circulating are spurious." In the end she acquiesces, and we are treated to the unusual spectacle of a ghost stepping into the coffin and reemerging as an animated corpse. She is "as adorable as can be," except that when he takes her in his arms, she is "cold as ice or snow." The experiment proves to be a failure, however, because as a more material form than a specter, the corpse is also more vulnerable to decay. About a year later, after he drunkenly forces her to have a drink, she collapses, blood streaming from her mouth, and her corpse immediately rots.

If ghost and corpse are split images of the deceased, male desire is most often projected onto the mediating figure of the revenant, instead of directly onto the cadaver. It is the beautiful ghost, rather than the exquisite corpse of the Victorians, which dominates the late imperial Chinese imagination.[137] As Pu Songling quips in his final comment to "Ainu": "This is why I say an elegant ghost is better than a gorgeous corpse" (*LZ* 9.1194). Nonetheless, cases of necrophilia are found in Chinese narrative, particularly in stories of grave-looters, where the erotic spectacle of the stripped, immobilized female body often adds the violation of the corpse to the robber's already heinous crime of desecrating the grave.[138] In the vernacular story, "The Haunting of Pan's Wineshop" ("Nao Panlou duoqing Zhou Shengxian"), this double transgression results in the sexual reanimation of the corpse without the buffer of the ghost. Through a series of unexpected reversals, the story continually restages the problematic relation of corpse to ghost. And it is the missing ghost rather than the missing body that ironically proves responsible for the story's tragicomic climax.

The story was published around 1627 in Feng Menglong's *Constant Words to Awaken the World (Xingshi hengyan)*. Hanan dates the story to before 1450, the early period of the vernacular story, although he traces the plot material back to the Southern Song classical tale.[139] The heroine of the story falls in love with Pan, a young man whose brother runs a wineshop. She falls ill from longing, but her wealthy father categorically refuses the match when her mother broaches the subject. Upon overhearing their interchange, the girl is so shocked and upset, she falls dead on the spot. In remorse, her father ensures that her burial is richly furnished, which unfortunately attracts the attention of a professional grave-robber, who breaks into the tomb. "He proceeded to strip the girl of every stitch she had on, including undergarments, until she was stark naked. Seeing the girl's pure white body, a wave of uncontrollable lust came over him, and he raped her. You'll say it's amazing, but he saw the girl open her eyes and clutch him with both hands—how could he break free?"[140] To diffuse the horror of this moment, and in deference to the vernacular story's greater need for plausibility, the narrative adds a rationalizing explanation to convince the reader of this unlikely event: "It turned out that the girl had been wholeheartedly preoccupied with young Pan. When she heard her father yelling at her mother she had died of anger, but she hadn't been dead for many days. Now having received an infusion of *yang qi,* her soul revived and she came back to life."[141]

The grave-robber secretly takes the girl home as his wife, where he keeps her prisoner. Since no one else knows she has returned to life, however, she remains in a state of social death. One night she manages to escape and immediately makes her way to Pan's wineshop. Not surprisingly, he thinks she is a vengeful ghost, and terrified, tries to exorcise her by chanting, "Vanish! Vanish!" Since his words naturally have no effect, he throws a cauldron at her, which strikes her and this time *really* kills her. On the material evidence of the bloody corpse and the girl's empty coffin, he is arrested for murder and thrown into prison.

This ending is shocking because of the return of the corpse, which remains stubbornly present and inert. For Pan, the problem is that a ghost's body is immaterial, and ought not shed blood nor leave behind a corpse. For readers, the problem is that death has already been shown once to be reversible and so we expect the corpse to revive again. The repeated display of the corpse, which makes the story's beginning and end formally symmetrical, reinforces the story's cynical disassociation of romantic agency and the forces of life and death: the girl's corpse is revived not by her lover, but by a base criminal; and the girl is killed and returned to a corpse, not by the criminal but by her lover.

Appearing in print during the height of the *Peony Pavilion* craze, this story could easily have been read as a parody of the play, subverting the romantic trope of the woman who dies for love and is then revived through the beneficence of male sexual power. The story's unelevated social milieu and focus on the lowly corpse (instead of the refined ghost) contribute to the parodic effect. To mitigate against such an anti-*qing* reading, however, the story adds a dream interlude in which the girl's ghost, "splendidly attired," appears to her lover in prison to foretell his acquittal. "'So you didn't die after all,' he said in amazement. 'I died twice, both times only for you,' she said.... 'Now I've come specially to find you to fulfill my heart's desire.

Don't resist me, this too is clearly my underworld destiny.'"[142] He makes love to her ghost and receives her forgiveness. This dream interlude is precisely the passage in the story that Hanan suggests, on both linguistic and thematic grounds, was probably rewritten or supplied by a later author.[143] In "The Haunting of Pan's Wineshop," the apparition of the amorous ghost, missing in earlier classical accounts of the tale, is added to stabilize the unsettling corpse, and, by signaling the triumph of *qing* after all, makes the story conform, however perfunctorily, to the romantic ideology seventeenth-century readers would have expected.

The Ghost's Corpse

Jean-Claude Schmitt writes that the medieval rituals of *memoria* held in remembrance of the dead functioned in reality as a technique "to 'cool off' memory under the guise of maintaining it, to soothe the painful memory of the deceased until the memory became indistinct."[144] The apparition of a revenant in certain dream accounts becomes a way for Schmitt, as a social historian, to penetrate into what he calls "the heart of 'the work of mourning,'" into "the ambivalence of those who were in the clutches simultaneously of the obsessive remembrance of deceased loved ones and of the will to forget them."[145]

Chinese ghost stories on the theme of a bereaved husband longing for his dead wife likewise take us into "the heart of 'the work of mourning.'" It was Freud, who in his famous essay "Mourning and Melancholia," first conceptualized mourning as "work" that the survivor performed to "work through" his feelings toward the dead and to free himself of their psychic hold over him. The work of mourning normally ended, when, after a prescribed period, the mourner succeeded in detaching himself emotionally from the dead or fell into pathological melancholy if he did not.[146] Anthropologists (and historians such as Schmitt who are influenced by anthropology) have attempted to use Freud's insights into the mourner's psyche to understand the mechanics of death ritual in different societies.

In China, the proper observance of mourning ritual was considered of extreme importance, both to the family and to the state. The ancient ritual canons had set down extremely detailed rules for mourning observances, carefully differentiated by the degree of mourning to be observed. In somewhat simplified form, these ancient prescripts for mourning rites were incorporated into the Ming and Qing legal codes.[147] In keeping with the core Confucian idea of a man's greater obligation to his parents than to his wife, a man put on first-degree mourning and mourned his parents for twenty-seven months, but observed second-degree mourning for his wife, which lasted only for a single year. (By contrast, a married woman who had lost a husband observed first-degree mourning, but only second-degree mourning for her own parents.)[148] In the case of truly devoted couples, it is possible that the second-degree mourning prescribed for a bereaved husband may not have provided enough of a "cooling-off" period, the rituals inadequate to transform his feelings and memories of the deceased, particularly in conjunction with the frequently strong pressure from his lineage to remarry as quickly as possible.

The ghost story is one arena in which problems of this sort can be addressed. In tales about husbands who have lost adored wives to sudden death, the man's unresolved feelings of grief and longing are enough to conjure up her dead spirit. One brief narrative of this type in *Liaozhai* is entitled simply "The Ghost Wife" ("Gui qi"). Nie, the protagonist of this story, is an uxorious man whose wife dies unexpectedly. His grief is especially intense and therefore threatens to turn into a pathological form of mourning.

> Sitting up by day or lying down at night, Nie was so filled with grief and longing for her that he seemed to have lost himself. One night as he was sitting up alone, his wife suddenly pushed the door open and came in. "Where have you come from?" asked Nie in surprise. "I'm a ghost," she said, smilingly, "but I was so moved by your grief for me that I beseeched the Lord of the Infernal Regions to allow us a temporary rendezvous." Overjoyed, Nie pulled her down into bed with him, and everything between them was as it had always been. (*LZ* 8. 1044)

Things go smoothly between them for over a year, until Nie succumbs to pressure from his family to take a new wife so that his descent line will not be broken. On their wedding night, the first wife's jealous ghost suddenly appears in the bedroom to prevent the consummation of the new marriage, her smiles now transformed to curses, her loving embraces now replaced by tearing at his flesh with her fingernails.[149] Abused and terrified by this hideous apparition, Nie eventually hires an exorcist, who nails down her coffin with apotropaic peachwood plugs, and the haunting ceases. Nothing further is revealed of his psychic state, but his pathological investment in a dead love object, his inability to complete the work of mourning and forget the dead, have certainly been terminated by this demonic "shock therapy."

Such a psychological reading of "The Ghost Wife" is borne out by a case cited several times in late Ming medical writings as an example of an illness caused by the emotions that must be overcome through the emotions. The case involves a married woman who cannot get over her beloved mother's death and consequently falls ill from brooding. (The case of a married daughter longing for her dead mother is even less well served by Chinese death ritual and the kinship system; although she was entitled to assume second-degree mourning, matrilateral kinship ties, unlike those of the patriline, were seen as terminating with death.)[150] The doctor called in to treat the case realizes that this disorder cannot be cured by medicine and instead plots with the husband to hire a shamaness who will pretend to be possessed by the sick woman's mother. During the supposed trance, in which the shamaness convincingly takes on the mother's appearance and manner, the daughter breaks down in tears. Her "mother" starts screaming at her: "Don't you dare cry! Your life overcame mine, and so I passed away before my time. My death is all your fault! Now I seek vengeance upon you from the world below. Your lingering illness is all my doing. When I was alive, we were mother and daughter. Now that I am dead, we are implacable enemies." As intended, the daughter becomes enraged: "I fell ill on account of grief for my mother, yet she actually wants to harm me! Why should I long for her any longer?" And she recovers.[151]

In this case the hostility and aggression of the fraudulent ghost are as efficacious as that of the "real" ghost in the previous story. In both narratives the violent transformation attributed to the specter enables the mourner to get over the dead. But the argument that the above case is cited to support has nothing to do with ideas about psychosomatic illness, which assume a separation between physiology and emotion, or with debates on the existence or nonexistence of ghosts. Zhang Jiebin, for example, explains the case as a perfect illustration of classical medical theory, which taught that "Longing injures the Spleen, and Anger overcomes longing," a therapeutic principle that we have already encountered in Zhu Zhenheng's treatment of the girl who fell ill from longing for her absent fiancé.

The mourner's drama of ambivalence toward his dead loved ones is given full scope in the extraordinary "Zhang Aduan." This complicated *Liaozhai* tale also involves a love triangle, but between a man and two ghosts. The opening integrates the plot of the bereaved husband with the haunted house—another common scenario in the ghost tradition—linking the wife's sudden illness and rapid death to the place's infestation with ghosts.

> There once lived a young scholar named Wei Huiqi, who was cultivated and refined, but who possessed courage and fortitude in equal measure. At that time there was an enormous mansion belonging to one of the great clans, where ghosts could be seen even in broad daylight. Deaths ensued in rapid succession and the family wanted to sell the place cheaply. Attracted by the low price, Wei purchased the property as his residence. But the place was huge, and Wei had a small household. The eastern part of the garden was as overgrown as a forest, so he left the storied pavilion located there vacant for the time being. Members of the household were scared at night and kept kicking up a commotion about there being ghosts. After about two months, a maid died. Soon thereafter, the scholar's wife went to the pavilion at dusk and fell ill upon her return. Several days later, she too died. The household grew even more terrified and urged him to move elsewhere. He refused to listen, but he was desolate at the loss of his wife and overwhelmed by grief. The maids and servants kept bothering him with accounts of strange happenings. The scholar finally lost his temper, and in a fury, removed his bedroll to the abandoned building, where he lay down alone, keeping the candle lit to observe anything strange that might arise. (*LZ* 5. 627)

The bold protagonist of the tale combines a Confucian skepticism toward spirits with a bereaved husband's refusal to be reconciled to his wife's death. His mourning, understood in a Freudian sense as a libidinal investment in a dead love object, and in a late imperial sense as *qing*, takes the form of denying the existence of the ghosts who caused her death in the secret hope of calling them forth. He thus defiantly goes to sleep naked and alone in the abandoned building where the baleful influence is considered greatest, reinforcing his position as a mourner on the dangerous threshold between life and death. Predictably, ghosts do materialize in the haunted pavilion that night, including one lovely young ghost, who angrily demands to know what right he has to be there. "The scholar sat up with a chuckle. 'I'm the landlord of this building. I'm just waiting for you so I can demand my rent!' He leapt to his feet, stark naked, and tried to catch her. The girl immediately took to her heels." (*LZ* 5. 629) After he succeeds in cornering her and takes her in his arms, she laughs at him: "You lunatic! Aren't you afraid of spooks? I'm going to bring harm to you and make you die!" (*LZ* 5. 629). But the scholar is too busy unfastening her skirt and jacket to reply.

After they have made love, she reveals that her name is Zhang Aduan and that the cruelty and beatings of her wastrel husband had driven her to die of anguish twenty years before. The next night she comes again, and after their lovemaking, which is "even more pleasurable" this time, Wei asks if she can arrange a meeting for him with his dead wife because "the feelings of mourning are still unalleviated in my breast" (*LZ* 5. 629). This request reveals that Aduan does not represent a new love interest who replaces the dead wife, thus marking an end to the mourning period; instead, as double and surrogate, she recalls the dead woman and helps prolong his mourning. Moved by such a display of tenderheartedness, which forms such a bitter contrast to her own unhappy experience of marriage, Aduan agrees to help him.

The next night she indeed has Wei's wife brought to him. The couple's meeting is filled with tears and grief, but happily, when they climb into bed, they find that "their pleasure is the same as during her lifetime" (*LZ* 5. 629). Aduan is repeatedly called upon to devise strategies to extend the illicit reunion of living husband and dead wife, which contravenes the underworld's due process of rebirth. Eventually, Wei has Aduan sleep in the adjoining bed and spend the night along with him and his wife. "From dusk to dawn, they feared only their pleasure coming to an end" (*LZ* 5. 629). As the morbid passion and criminal complicity of the threesome escalate into manic joy, the liminal zone of the haunted pavilion becomes an ever more absorbing refuge from both the world of the living and the world of the dead. Finally, the ghosts do not leave even during the day; and the three of them barricade themselves inside, the candle kept perpetually burning. Time has stopped, obstructing both the finite protocol of mourning ritual and the natural cycle of change. Wei can no longer uncouple himself from the dead. Mourning has failed and become melancholia.

After more than a year of this, however, it is unexpectedly Aduan, not the mortal Wei, who suddenly falls ill. Wei's wife provides the diagnosis: "'This is a ghostly illness.' 'But Aduan is already a ghost,' he objects. 'How in the world can a ghost fall ill?'" (*LZ* 5. 629). Although Pu Songling employs the term *gui bing* elsewhere in its ordinary sense to mean a ghost-induced illness, here he exploits the ambiguity of the Chinese syntax to yield the unusual reading "the illness of a ghost"; the effect is close to the literalization of metaphor, a frequent device in the collection.[152] In fact, the implausible straightforward reading turns out to be correct: Aduan *is* suffering from a ghost-induced illness. Her symptoms include "trance and vertigo, anxiety and delirium, as though seeing a ghost" (*LZ* 5. 629).[153] Later she is also wracked by uncontrollable shuddering, terror, and the hallucination of a vengeful ghost whenever she closes her eyes. Again Wei's wife explains this conundrum. For losing her posthumous chastity, Aduan is being haunted by her dead husband, who has turned into something called a *jian:* "When people die, they become ghosts; when ghosts die they become *jian,* which ghosts fear just as people fear ghosts" (5. 629). Textual records show that the obscure character *jian* was apotropaic, inscribed as a charm to exorcise specters. Here it provides the inspiration for Pu Songling to imagine "the ghost of a ghost" *(guizhong zhi gui),* as it is glossed by one of *Liaozhai*'s nineteenth-century commentators.[154]

Unlike the rarified ghost syndromes in "Lotus-scent" or the medical casebooks discussed so far, Aduan is clearly suffering from a full-blown case of possession disorder, and her illness is not amenable to the pattern diagnosis and drug therapy of learned medicine. Medical experts themselves shared this view. The famous physician Xu Dachun argued that the "ghosts and spirits" of classical medical theory were not supernatural beings but heteropathic forces like wind, cold, damp, and heat that invaded a body with weakened defenses. He nonetheless admitted that in true cases of illness induced by wronged and vengeful ghosts, medicinal drugs were powerless, since such afflictions were the wages of sin or destiny.[155] It is plausible, as Wei's wife insists, that a ghost cannot be treated by a human doctor, only by a ghost, but this logic also offers Pu Songling a pretext to satirize the venal practices of fraudulent witch doctors. One such shamaness is called in, but predictably, her efforts fail. One day Wei overhears his wife weeping and discovers why: "Aduan had died upon the couch. Her discarded clothes were still there, and so he opened them: inside her bare bones were still evident. Wei greatly mourned her and buried her remains beside his ancestral graves according to the rites due a living person" (*LZ* 5. 630).

The ghost has paradoxically died a second death and left behind a corpse. But this is no ordinary cadaver, a frozen replica of flesh and blood, but bones wrapped in the garments of the dead. What kind of image is this and how should we interpret it? Both literary and pictorial evidence show that one possible way to represent a ghost was as an animated skeleton. We have already found a suggestion of this image in the Six Dynasties account of the resurrection that fails, in which the ghost wife's body is depicted as half flesh / half skeleton. In the fourteenth-century demon tale, "The Peony Lantern" ("Mudan deng ji"), a man's lover is revealed to be a ghost when someone peeps through the window and sees him supping with a "powdered skeleton," revealing the true horrific image of death concealed beneath a falsely beautiful exterior.[156] In "The White Falcon" ("Cui yanei baiyao zhao yao"), a vernacular story published in Feng Menglong's second story collection around 1624, the hapless protagonist, who stumbles into demon territory on a hunting expedition, spies his lost falcon in the hands of a skeleton, who is "tinkling the bell around the falcon's neck with one finger and cooing to it."[157]

In terms of painted images, the most striking is a mysterious Song dynasty painting in which a life-sized skeleton is shown manipulating a miniature skeleton marionette to an audience consisting of children and a nursing mother or wet-nurse (see fig. 3).[158] Our most extensive pictorial record of ghost images in late imperial China, however, are the sets of murals and hanging scrolls used in the Land and Water Rite (Shuilu zhai), a religious ritual performed for the salvation of dead souls in the underworld. Such rituals are conducted several times in *Liaozhai* tales, though no details regarding the ceremony are provided.[159] One possible way to depict a dead soul in extant Land and Water paintings (Shuilu hua) is as a skeleton. In the late Yuan murals in Green Dragon Temple in southern Shanxi, for example, we find a naked skeleton figure draped in chains amid a group of various kinds of ghosts who have died wrongful, violent deaths (see fig. 4).[160]

Since the ghost's clothes must be opened to find the bones in "Zhang Aduan," however, the image may not be that of a perfectly reconstructed skeleton, but a random pile of bones. If so, it is possible that the sudden appearance of the bones simply illustrates the common idea that upon death, illusion reverts to its true form, just as the corpse of a shape-shifting fox-spirit invariably turns back into a fox, or a mansion in the wilderness turns back into a tomb the next morning. But the revelation of metamorphosis is not really the point here. Instead, what is revealed is a logical relation: Bones are to flesh what ghost is to corpse.

The image in "Zhang Aduan" may well be that of a body disinterred after decomposition whose bones have been arranged in a natural order and placed in grave clothes in preparation for reburial. It is necessary to distinguish "reburial" here from what is known as "second burial." Anthropologists have long been fascinated with the practice of double burial as a routine part of the mortuary ritual involved in ancestor worship. The classic pattern as set forth in Hertz's 1905 study of Indonesia and Malaysia is a temporary burial of the corpse until the flesh has rotted away, disinterment, followed by permanent reburial of the bones.[161] The process is said to transform the volatile, dangerous, putrescent form of the corpse into the stable, beneficent, purified bones of ancestors. Parallel to the transformation the dead body undergoes is a gradual process of settling the soul and concluding the mourning process. Bloch and Parry argue that Hertz's symbolic themes—"the contrast between bones and flesh, the pattern of double obsequies . . . parallels between the state of the corpse, fate of the soul and ritual conditions of the mourners"—are particularly characteristic of southeast Asia, including southeast China.[162] Second burial was not the custom in North China, where *Liaozhai* was written, however, and in any event, would never have been performed for strangers and non-kin.[163]

In contrast, reburial, like the apparition of a ghost, is an ad hoc response to some abnormal disturbance in the settling of the dead rather than a routine part of normal mortuary ritual. A wide range of Chinese sources, including the ancient ritual canons, dynastic histories, law codes, anecdotal literature, and modern ethnographies mention the phenomenon of reburial, usually in response to a perceived problem with the first burial site or as a way to transfer someone's remains to his

FIGURE 3 Li Song (act. 1190–1230), *The Skeleton Puppet Master (Kulou huanxi tu),* Fan painting, ink and color on silk, Southern Song dynasty. *Songren huace,* pl. 58.

native soil.[164] Such reburials normally occurred after enough time had elapsed for the corpse to decompose. The apparition of a ghost to the living to request (re)burial of their bones is a common motif in Chinese literature and folklore. Although such ghosts may be kin to those they importune, more commonly they are strangers, and the reburial is performed as an act of propitiation and charity. Such episodes are sometimes provoked by a chance encounter with human bones, either accidentally exposed, or worse, never buried. Stephen Owen has written eloquently on the threat that such bones, "timeless, anonymous, without kin," pose to the individual who finds them in Chinese literature: "Bones without a commemorative marker represent a loss of identity, of one's place in time, and of the family whose purpose was to preserve the memory."[165] The resolution must therefore be found in the rituals of (re)burial and (re)commemoration.

As tokens of the absolute physical undifferentiation wrought by death, such bones are also threatening because they obliterate the fantasy of gender in death as represented by the female revenant or the exquisite corpse. Here the threat is particularly great because the bones are encountered not in the wilderness but on a human bed in a domestic space. For all these reasons, Wei's decision to rebury Aduan's bones is overdetermined. But the story says he had the burial performed "according to the rites due a living person," thus ritually denying its status as reburial. Ironically, performing a reburial as though it were a first burial becomes a mark of difference, a means to designate the rite as the burial of a *ghost's* corpse rather than simply the reburial of a decomposed body.

A similar logic of representation emerges in "Lü the Flawless" ("Lü Wubing," *LZ* 8. 1110–1118), an usual story that involves a ghost who is *not* beautiful as the main love interest. The heroine, ironically named "Lü the Flawless," is dark, with a pock-

FIGURE 4 Late Yuan mural in Green Dragon Temple (Qinglong si) in Jishan, Shanxi. Detail showing the ghosts of those who died violent deaths. Among them are a skeleton in chains, a drowned woman lifting her sleeve to her face, and a female soul with a white kerchief tied around her head. Photo by Wu Hung.

marked complexion, and from a poor family; accordingly she enters the scholar's household as a lowly maid servant. But she is "easily frightened" and her breath is "fragrant as lilies," so despite her homeliness, she gives the impression of loveliness, and the scholar eventually takes her as his concubine. She proves a faithful companion and an excellent stepmother to the living son of his dead wife. In the midst of a futile attempt to protect the boy from enemies in his father's absence, the phantom musters the last of her ebbing energy and appears to the scholar. She just manages to warn him of the danger before she falls weeping to the ground and vanishes, leaving no physical remains except an empty set of clothes and shoes. Deeply moved, the scholar takes up her discarded garments and buries them.

Early dynastic histories contain references to a custom of burying the clothes or personal articles of a deceased relative to replace a missing or irretrievable corpse. The practice was called "interments with evocation of the soul" or "burials of evoked souls" *(zhaohun zang)*.[166] This textual record may have sparked Pu Songling's inventiveness, much as in the case of the character *jian*. But in "Lü the Flawless," the absence of a corpse or any bodily remains is in itself a marker of a *phantom's* death. Burial of the ghost's clothes and shoes as a surrogate body is undertaken as a sign of gratitude and respect, which grants honorary human status even as it demarcates a difference from the regular burial of the corpse of a living person. (Since the ghost was already dead, even this surrogate interment must be understood as reburial.) To commemorate this paradox, the scholar erects a stele at the burial site with the inscription: "Grave of My Ghost-Concubine Lü the Flawless."

Ghosthood is most often portrayed in a Chinese context as an unstable and temporary state. Stephen Teiser has argued for the medieval Chinese invention of purgatory as an interim but finite phase between the stages of death and the next life.[167] As he puts it: "Ghosts are a species in transition. The dead person's *hun* and *po* souls are unstable, waiting to be assigned their next rebirth."[168] Impermanence is also a key point in Zhu Xi's philosophical discussions of ghosts. Thus he insists that although a person's *qi* may under certain circumstances linger after death, giving rise to a ghost, this *qi* will always *eventually* disperse, extinguishing the ghost.[169] The notion that ghosthood is prima facie a liminal stage also underlies the definition of a ghost provided in *A Complete Mastery of Correct Characters (Zhengzi tong)*, an important late Ming dictionary: "Every human being must possess the vital stuff of yin and yang for his body to take shape. When yin and yang disperse, then a person dies. When someone first dies, after his previous yin *(qian yin)* has ended but before his later yin *(hou yin)* has come, there is his so-called 'interim yin' *(zhong yin)*, which is what is commonly referred to as a ghost."[170]

In the same vein, Chinese literature and folklore abound with anecdotes about suicides or victims of unnatural deaths who must seek a replacement among the living before they can be released and reborn, again signaling the transitory conception of any ghostly incarnation.[171] Ji Yun's *Jottings from the Thatched Cottage*, which attempts to reconcile contradictory beliefs about the underworld, features one story in which a man meets a ghost who boasts happily of having been in a single place for three hundred years. The man suspiciously asks how he alone has managed to stay a ghost so long and avoid the normal processes of rebirth.[172]

The unorthodox burials in "Zhang Aduan" and "Lü the Flawless" both represent attempts to fix permanently the temporary status of a ghost through the commemoration of ritual. In both cases these burials accord honorary human status to the ghost in recognition of meritorious and loving service, redrawing the boundaries to expand the territory of what can properly be understood as humanity. But paradoxically, these rituals are able to do so only through the perpetuation of ghostly status, only by preserving the memory of the *ghost,* rather than that of the former living person.

In both stories, reburial is a response to the idea of second death. In many tales of the love between man and ghost, the vanishing of the revenant is experienced as parting and loss and her departure for rebirth is paradoxically experienced as a kind of second death. But "Zhang Aduan" presents an extraordinary case because the ghost is literally said to die *(bi).* Remarks the *Liaozhai* commentator Feng Zhenluan: "If it is possible to die again after death, when will dying ever end?" (*LZ* 5. 630). Another less sympathetic of the commentators grumbles: "This is total absurdity" (*LZ* 5. 631). Like the ghost of a ghost, second death implies the dizzying spectacle of endless doubling and repetition, an operation Susan Stewart has called "play with infinity." A prime example is looking in the mirror where "there is a splitting of subject and object, watcher and watched. . . . Yet there is also the terrifying possibility that the repetition will go on, that the splitting will occur in reverse and the self will break off towards infinity. And even more frightening is the possibility that all one will see in the mirror is another mirror, a doubling of reflexivity that cancels into nothingness."[173] Double death and the ghost of a ghost introduce the idea that death breaks off towards infinity, and since death is also a species of nothingness, this promises an infinity of nothingness. To pull back from this vertiginous move toward the infinity of nothingness, the rite of second burial is performed to stop death, to fix it once more in time and space.

But repeated death and the ghost of a ghost may also operate rhetorically as double negatives or double-nots, each term internally canceling the other out. This effect is intensified in this tale because Aduan is also structurally the double of another double, that of the dead wife's ghost. And this second ghost, too, subsequently undergoes a species of double death, which mirrors that of the first ghost.

Because Aduan is hounded by the vengeful spirit of her dead husband, her second death airs cultural anxiety and ambivalence about a widow's posthumous chastity: she is "killed" for her ghostly liaison with Wei even as she garners sympathy for it; and she must suffer at the hands of the *jian* until masses said for "the soul of her soul" hasten her rebirth. Aduan therefore also serves as a counterimage to deflect Wei's anxiety about his own wife, whose second death is instead refracted and redeemed through the ideology of *qing.*

For Wei's wife's ghost, to be a revenant means voluntarily choosing death and union over rebirth and parting; her ghosthood may thus be reevaluated as dying *posthumously* for love. But after three years, her transgression is discovered by the underworld bureaucracy, and she must leave him. Like Aduan, she, too, first falls ill, but the text is laconic, and no details are forthcoming. She tells him: "As someone in whom 'feelings are concentrated'[174] I originally hoped to die forever and found no joy in the idea of life. Now we must part for eternity—isn't this fate?" (*LZ* 6. 631). When he asks if she will suffer for her crime, she replies: "'A little. But the punishment for stealing life is great, for stealing death, small.' After she finished speaking, she became motionless. As he watched intently, her face and body gradually disappeared *(simie)*" (*LZ* 6. 631).

The choice of the compound *simie* reinforces the resemblance of this vanishing to second death. The graph *si* on its own means to die, to be used up; as a noun, it can even refer to a corpse; the more common graph *mie* also means to be destroyed or annihilated. But Wei's wife's double death is a shadow of Aduan's. Unlike Aduan's agonized second death, which left bones that could be reburied and serve as a physical marker, thus replacing the first death, the wife's peaceful second death leaves no stable image, only a gradual fading away, an absence and a diluted memory, so that the second death blends imperceptibly into the first death. Through the multiple restagings of loss, the husband's mourning finally is brought successfully to a close.

Bronfen has described mourning as a plot "having its trajectory in death," which often hinges on doubles of dead women: "For the purpose of mourning is to kill the dead by ceasing to reanimate psychically a body physically absent; by withdrawing one's libidinal investment in a lost love object, forgetting or preserving it as dead. . . . The killing of the revenant, a second killing of a corpse, a second burial, indicates the end of mourning."[175] Softened by *qing*, Wei's wife's revenant need not be violently killed, but dies a "natural" death. Although Wei still sometimes sleeps alone in the abandoned pavilion, hoping for another encounter with her ghost, it remains quiet, and the story concludes with the pronouncement: "And so the human heart found peace." Wei's work of mourning is finally over. In this formulaic ending, the phantoms of memory, like the household poltergeists, are finally exorcised and laid to rest.

2

The Ghost's Voice

> No excitement of pipes or drums is seen;
> weeping and grieving is all that's heard.
> In your lifetimes you knew not the duties of husband
> and wife,
> yet tonight your dead spirits will share a coverlet.
> On the yang path of the living, we hold a feast to celebrate
> your meeting
> but the yin road to the Shades is where you'll tie the
> lover's knot.
> — *Ritual prayer*

"PERHAPS THE MOST obvious thing about death," write Sarah Goodwin and Elisabeth Bronfen, "is that it is always only represented."[1] We can never truly know first hand what it would be like to be dead; we can only imagine it. This chapter is about a fantasy inside view of death. It is not an exposé of the topography or organization or activities of the afterlife, (although there are many Chinese stories that do this), but rather what it means to inhabit the subjective viewpoint of the dead. In contrast to the previous chapter, which was about imagining the Other's dead body, this chapter is about imbuing the ghost with a voice and confronting the self's mortality.

In the last chapter I concentrated on the ways in which ghosts were "embodied" in Chinese narratives of the strange, largely by being gendered female. My main interest lay in the medical and sexual construction of the phantom body, its often surprisingly physical, tactile, and fertile qualities. I emphasized the visual appearance of the face and figure manifested mainly as superlative beauty, although occasionally also as its opposite—supreme ugliness. Generally speaking, however, the acoustic manifestation of a phantom, often in disembodied form, is of equal importance in the Chinese literary imagination. No Chinese term for ghost involves sight per se. In contrast, the three most common English terms all have Latin or Greek root meanings pertaining to vision: "specter" (to look, to see); "apparition" (to appear); "phantom" (present to the eye).[2] A preoccupation with a ghost's *optical* dimension is deeply embedded in English and the Romance languages, but this one-sidedness may be a peculiarly European phenomenon, enhanced in recent years with the critical turn toward visuality and visual culture.[3]

The definition of a ghost as an "audition,"[4] not simply as an "apparition," is present early on in China. In his *Disquisitions (Lunheng)* of the first century CE, Wang Chong mounts several attacks against the belief that the spirits of the dead have consciousness. His arguments take for granted the idea that a phantom may assume either an auditory or visual form, and both components figure in his summaries of popular definitions of a ghost. As he writes in one passage: "If *qi* can resemble the human voice and wail, then *qi* should also be able to resemble the human form and be seen. Both of these are what the world takes to be a ghost."[5] Centuries later, Han Yu's (768–824) polemical essay "On the Origin of Ghosts" ("Yuan gui") accepts the existence of ghosts as a natural phenomenon but refutes the idea that they can manifest themselves to the living; a ghost is not only an invisible being, he asserts, but an inaudible one.[6]

Although these polemicists take it as a commonplace that the presence of a specter will be perceived through sound as well as sight, Six Dynasties accounts of the strange show a marked preference for the visual as the crux of an encounter. As Campany argues: "In all of these tales, the most important vehicle of contact with the dead is vision; the protagonist first and foremost sees the dead person or the realm of the dead, whatever other interactions may occur."[7] With the adoption of more sophisticated narrative techniques in Tang dynasty tales, a change Karl Kao has described as part of a new "esthetic of presentation,"[8] the reverse begins to happen: the protagonist of a story first often *hears* the dead person before glimpsing his or her specter. This artistic effect is skillfully utilized in two eighth-century ghost stories, both of which depict a man mourning the death of a beloved woman. In the first tale, "Li Zhangwu," the man sets out offerings of food and drink to his dead lover's spirit to solicit the longed-for encounter. The dead lover's apparition is first heralded by a strange rustling sound coming from the corner of the room, "as though a human form were slowly approaching."[9] In the second tale, "Tang Xuan," the artful use of sound preceding the visual materialization of a specter is even more effective. Unable to sleep, a man sadly recites a poem he has written mourning his wife's death. The response is almost instantaneous. "Suddenly in the darkness, he heard something that sounded like weeping. At first the sound was distant, but gradually it drew nearer."[10] As in "Li Zhangwu," a disembodied sound moving from far to near is used to evoke the ghost's journey from the unseen to the seen world. Even after the apparition of the ghost in these stories, the expressive use of voice continues to play an important role, most notably in the mournful poems man and ghost recite to each other. In certain other Tang stories or anecdotes, however, no sighting ever occurs, and the encounter with the phantom takes place solely in the realm of sound or words.

One such case is set in the years 679–680. This anecdote involves a traveler whose boat moors for the night at the perilous Gorges of Ba, where the Yangzi river flows eastward from Sichuan into Hubei. Suddenly, he hears someone chant a poem aloud:

> Yellow leaves fill the autumn path,
> Cold mars the roots of dew-drenched grass.
> The lone cry of a gibbon, then the sound breaks off.
> Layers of tearstains streak the traveler's face.

> The voice was high-pitched and intense, impassioned but mournful. And the chanting went on like this all through the night, dozens and dozens of times. When the man first heard it, he assumed it must be a traveler in another boat who couldn't sleep. But when he went to inspect at dawn, there was no other boat, only uninhabited mountains and rocky streams, with ravines remote and secluded. In the spot where the chanting had come from lay a human skeleton.[11]

An enigma is posed: Who is chanting? Five centuries earlier, Wang Chong had documented the belief that when parched human bones are exposed in the wilderness, "the sound of moaning will sometimes be audible, as though wailing could be heard in the night." As usual, however, he takes great pains to demonstrate that "although people say this is the voice of the dead, they are wrong."[12] The wordless, inarticulate moaning of the bones in Wang Chong's description has given way to poetry in this anecdote, the voice of the dead patterned in literary language and given aesthetic form. What I want to emphasize is not the persistence of certain beliefs about unburied bones in Chinese civilization but *how* the voice of the dead becomes imagined and articulated, particularly its increased embellishment and specificity. The expressive description of sound in a wilderness setting (the essence of the representation in Wang Chong) still plays an important role in the Tang anecdote, but it is far more complicated; the eeriness of the voice in the night is echoed by the cry of the unseen gibbon evoked within the poem, just as the impassioned but mournful tone of the chanting serves as a gloss to the emotional import the images in the poem are supposed to convey.[13]

Above all, the poem in this anecdote is an emanation of place, of this specific place, the Gorges of Ba, whose scenery struck medieval travelers as terrifyingly desolate and sunless rather than as sublimely beautiful. When the man first hears the poem, he assumes it must be a traveler like himself in another boat, partly because the quatrain is exactly the sort a traveler *would* recite at this very spot. Describing the Gorges of Ba at length in his *Commentary on the Classic of Waterways* (*Shuijing zhu;* late fifth-early sixth century), Li Daoyuan mentions the heartrending cries of the gibbons high in the cliffs overhead echoing through the deserted ravines, and he quotes a fisherman's song, which ends: "Three cries of the gibbon, and our clothes are soaked with tears."[14] A rhapsody by the Tang poet Xie Guan includes the line: "Late fall at the Gorges of Ba: five nights of grief as gibbons howl at the moon."[15]

Thus the quatrain the man hears recited over and over in this anecdote reworks a set of poetic images associated with the Gorges of Ba, a rendering of place so conventional it appears entirely natural, the emotions of sorrow it arouses seemingly automatic and effortless. The poem's participation in what Pauline Yu has called "a culturally shared lexicon within which correspondences of meaning were pre-established"[16]—in this case mapped onto a specific site—is what makes the voice overheard in the night so uncanny. It seems to externalize something in the listener's own mind and thus potentially to usurp the listener's own voice, especially since the last line of the poem explicitly keys in the "traveler's" response to the scene. It is this complicity between listener and chanter that makes the man first mistake the voice for a fellow traveler, an invisible double in an identical boat.

Yu argues that in Chinese poetics "imagery was not ultimately important for what it presented directly but for what it concealed and evoked in the reader,"[17] or listener, she could have added, since Chinese poetry was customarily composed and recited aloud. Explicit statement is foresworn and avoided so that, ideally, the latent intellectual or affectual meaning that inspired the poem will reappear and take shape in the reader's or listener's response. Repression—and the return of the repressed—may very well lie at the heart of this poetics, but with the important caveat that what is ordinarily suppressed in the poem is not always so much unknown to the poet as unspoken. In this anecdote, however, the pre-established cultural equation between the Gorges of Ba and the affect of grief is revealed to mask something deeper, something darker. What the night-long repetition of the quatrain in the darkness simultaneously "conceals and evokes" is the underlying fear of dying in this horrible place and not even getting a proper burial, a fear that is seemingly realized the next morning with the man's discovery of the skeleton at the very spot where the chanting originated.

Although the anecdote ends with the exposure of the skeleton and the solving of the enigma posed by the poem, there is no real resolution. Unlike most such encounters with human bones in Chinese writing, there is no reburial here; no ritual act of libation or mourning is performed to settle and placate the dead, to rectify his grievances and exorcise his ghost.[18] By implication, the Gorges of Ba will always be haunted; the quatrain will be chanted to eternity, an endless loop tape always ready to be heard by the next traveler passing through. This may be why the anecdote is entitled "The Inhabitant of the Gorges of Ba" ("Baxia ren").

The poem in this anecdote raises a number of themes central to this chapter. First, there is what I call "ghostly poetry," verse that creates a mood of intense melancholy and suppressed emotion mainly through a conventionalized set of natural images associated with a nocturnal, autumnal world of graveyards or uninhabited wilderness. The formative process through which these images became wedded to certain emotional effects, to the extent that we may speak of a ghostly style and aesthetic code, has a long history that I will trace in this chapter from its beginnings in the anonymous poems of the Han and the literary imitations of mourning songs in the Six Dynasties to its coalescence in the mid and late Tang, and finally its codification and classification in later anthologies.

Ghostly poetry often adopts the voice or viewpoint of the dead. It is thus closely linked to but nonetheless distinct from what I call "ghost poetry," in which a poem, whether chanted or written, is considered to have been authored posthumously by a ghost, understood as a communication from or a performance by a dead soul. A poem need not actually employ a recognizably ghostly style to be attributed to a specter; the status of the poem is determined mainly by the narrative frame that contextualizes it as "ghost written." More often than not, however, a ghost poem will incorporate potentially ghostly elements from the poetic lexicon and image code. In late imperial critical terms, the two concepts are occasionally differentiated as *gui jing* ("ghostly atmosphere") and *gui shi* ("ghost-authored poem").[19]

The phenomenon of poetry attributed to ghosts is more than an occult aberration or a literary curiosity; it is worth treating seriously because it magnifies aspects of mainstream Chinese poetics ordinarily hidden from view or taken for granted. The notion of ghost poetry is predicated on the intimate relationship between writing and death. This chapter will explore the larger implications of ghost poetry for the Chinese literary imagination: what deep-rooted assumptions about verse and writing facilitated this fantasy, and what this fantasy fundamentally tells us about the construction of authorship in the premodern period. Why ghost poetry was so readily amalgamated into the scholar-beauty romance, and why ghost poetry was so often attributed to dead *female* authors, is a subject I will take up in the later part of the chapter. Lastly, I demonstrate how ghost poetry became codified, historicized, and legitimated through its inclusion in mainstream anthologies.

The Graveyard Poem and the Invention of the Ghost Author

The graveyard poem appears at the very beginning of what was to become the dominant form of classical lyric poetry in imperial times, among the famous "Nineteen Old Poems" ("Gushi shijiu shou").[20] These poems were anonymous, formulaic, and loosely structured; the situations in the poems were vague and fluid, the images symbolic, the lyrics general and ambiguous enough to lend themselves to a variety of possible contexts and speakers. Composed most probably during the turmoil accompanying the collapse of the Eastern Han dynasty at the turn of the second century CE, their themes include loss and separation, the brevity of life, the irrevocability of death; their mood is correspondingly bleak, even when they sound the carpe diem theme to drink up and be merry.[21]

Poems XIII and XIV both depict someone going out the city gates of the capital Loyang and seeing before him the funerary grounds in the Beimang hills. The two poems, particularly the beginning of the first and the whole of the second, are so similar in tone and diction that some critics have found them to form a seemingly continuous whole or sequence.[22]

XIII

I drove my wagon out Upper East Gate
and gazed at far tombs north of the walls.
Winds whistled in the white poplars,
cypress and pine lined the wide lanes.
Beneath them lay men long dead,
fading far off into endless night.
They sleep under Yellow Springs sunken from sight,
and never will wake in a thousand years.
Shadow and Light move in endless floods,
our destined years are like morning's dew.

XIV

Each day those gone are farther withdrawn,
each day newcomers grow more like kin.
I went out the gate, stared straight ahead,
and all I saw were barrows and tombs.
The ancient graves have been plowed to fields,
their cypress and pines smashed to kindling.
Mournful winds fill the white poplars,
in their whistling a woe that destroys a man.
I long to turn back to my native town,
I wish to return, but there is no way.[23]

In both poems we find the whistling of wind in the white poplars, trees that, like evergreens, were typically planted in graveyards. Ever after the formula "wind, funerary trees: sorrow" will appear as a literary correlative for the emotions aroused by cemeteries. The tone of the two poems is simultaneously one of detachment, as befits the act of contemplation, and pain, as befits the theme of death.[24] As is characteristic of the Nineteen Old Poems, no personal pronouns are specified, and because abrupt shifts without overt transitions are common, it is impossible to say with any certainty who is speaking at any given moment. This indeterminacy enables the Qing commentator Wu Qi to suggest reading the final couplet of the second poem ("I long to turn back to my native town / I wish to return, but there is no way") as voicing the thoughts of the deceased buried in the graveyard, rather than as the thoughts of the man who seems to contemplate the funerary grounds at the outset.[25]

This alternative interpretation presupposes that we can discern in the second poem the outline of a set itinerary that begins at the city gates and that terminates in the graveyard.[26] The direction of the gaze at the beginning ("I went out the gate, stared straight ahead / and all I saw were barrows and graves") would then indicate the journey's final destination. In this reading, the cemetery shifts from "there" to "here," from a site to be visited to a place from which there is no return. Such a reading of the poem is predicated on the reciprocity between exile and death in Chinese culture, so that a longing for home can be understood equally as the impossible desire to return to one's native place *or* to the land of the living.[27]

What is important is not whether this reading of the couplet is "true" or "better"—Wu Qi himself concedes the validity of the straightforward standard interpretation as well—but rather that this particular Qing view of Old Poem XIV has clearly been conditioned by familiarity with a subsequent poetic development: the Six Dynasties vogue for literary imitations of burial songs as represented by the work of the poets Lu Ji (261–303) and Tao Qian (365–427). The early anonymous burial songs that still survive, such as "Village of Weeds" ("Hao li") or "Dew on the Shallot" ("Xie lu ge") and a few of the earliest imitations are brief quatrains, and no narrative or ritual sequence is discernible in them. In contrast, Lu Ji and Tao Qian's imitations each consist of a series of three burial songs depicting the ritual progress of a funeral, the procession outside the city for burial, and end by assuming the voice of the deceased, abandoned in the graveyard.[28] The experience of death as permanent dislocation and banishment is central to these poems. (Tao Qian's is typical: "I used to sleep in a high hall / Now I rest in the village of weeds. / We go out the gate one morning / The day of return will never come."[29]) But unlike the Nineteen Old Poems or the anonymous burial songs, these literary imitations use explicit personal pronouns in crucial places so that there can be no ambiguity that the dead are meant to be speaking. In Lu Ji's poem sequence, we have the staging of different voices—the deceased is apostrophized as "you" *(zi)* by the living mourners in the first stanza, then speaks directly for himself as "I" *(wo)* in the final stanza of the poem.[30] In Tao Qian's treatment, however, there is no such shift; the speaker throughout is the deceased narrating in the first person his experience of dying, of being mourned and buried.

Most disquieting is Tao Qian's famous final stanza about his coffin's journey to the graveyard:[31]

> How desolate the moorland lies,
> The white poplars whistle in the wind.
> There is sharp frost in the ninth month
> When they escort me to the far suburbs.
> There where no one dwells at all
> The high grave mounds rear their heads.
> The horses whinny to the sky,
> The wind emits a mournful sound.
> Once the dark house is closed
> In a thousand years there will be no new dawn.
> There will be no new dawn
> And all man's wisdom helps not at all.
> The people who have brought me here
> Will now go back, each to his home.

My own family may still feel grief—
The others will be already singing.
What shall we say, we who are dead?
Your bodies too will lodge on the hill.[32]

The macabre effect of this self-reflexivity is heightened because the "me" here is always taken as referring to the poet himself, rather than to some general ritualized persona of the deceased as in Lu Ji's burial songs. This traditional reading of Tao Qian's burial songs is reinforced by the fact that he also wrote a sacrificial elegy for himself ("Zi ji wen") in which he explicitly calls the deceased by his own proper name ("Master Tao") as well as by the pronoun "I." He is also responsible for the first autobiography in Chinese literature, an account in the third person that reads as though it had been written after the subject's death. Indeed following Tao Qian's model, the "autonecrology"—imagining one's own death and writing funerary pieces for oneself—became one of the main privileged spaces for autobiography in premodern China.[33]

Although Tao Qian narrates the ritual process of his funeral from the perspective of his dead self, no reader would ever take the poem literally, as having been composed posthumously by his ghost before being sealed forever in the "dark house" of the tomb. Because of the presumed nonfictional status of most Chinese poetry, however, many traditional critics have yoked his imitations of burial songs and his eulogy for himself to the historical occasion of the poet's death, maintaining that both must have been written on his deathbed.[34] Whether read in this specific light or more generally, the predicament of the living historical poet is foregrounded in these pieces, our attention drawn to a specific human consciousness in the process of imaginatively rehearsing his own death.

Wu Hung has argued for a fundamental shift in the concept of the mourner during the Six Dynasties. The underlying logic in each case is to force the mourner to undergo a process of psychological inversion that ultimately causes him to identify himself with the dead and to anticipate what it would be like to be on the other side, in the occult world. In this way "a mourner was not only a living person who came to a graveyard to meet a deceased Other, but also possibly a person who visited his own tomb to mourn for himself as the Other."[35] The liminal depiction of the deceased, as poised halfway through the gate of life and death, simultaneously looking backward and forward is found on stone sarcophagi from the period. In such images, someone is depicted twice, once facing outward in a frontal view, once moving inward, his back to the viewer. These "front and back images" provide the perfect visual correlative for dying, for the conflict between worldly activities and internal peace: "Again we find that lived experience ends at the point where someone turns inward, about to penetrate the solid surface of the stone."[36]

Both Lu Ji's and Tao Qian's burial songs end in silence, in the permanent snuffing out of the voice as the deceased turns inward. In Lu Ji's song, there is still the futile desire to speak and resentment at being silenced: "Beating my breast, I grieve my misfortunes; / Forever sighing, but never able to tell them." Tao Qian's stance is one of greater resignation. To quote A. R. Davis's prosaic translation of the final couplet, which has no pronouns in the original: "When a man has gone in death, what more to say / They have given his body to become one with the hillside."[37] The dead are mute now, either because they have been cruelly deprived of speech or because they have achieved a superior state of wisdom.

Beginning in the mid-eighth century, however, in the wake of the An Lushan rebellion (755–763), we find in the Tang anecdotal literature that such imitations of burial songs, what I call "auto-dirges," come to be attributed to the dead, rather than framed as imaginative projections by a living poet of his own death. In a number of tales the graveyard poem is now composed posthumously by a ghost, who can, after all, it seems, shatter the silence of the tomb and tell of his or her misfortunes. One such story from *The Great Book of Marvels (Guangyi ji)* concerns a district magistrate's wife named Wei Huang, said to have died between 758 and 759.[38] Her ghost returns home first simply as a voice in thin air, then by possessing a servant girl as a mouthpiece, who recites several poems dedicated to the dead woman's living relatives. The poem for her husband, which laments that the Underground Springs are her home now, bears a verbal signature: "By Wei Huang, Sojourner in the Tomb."[39] In the last mournful couplet of the verse to her sister, echoes of Old Poem XIV are unmistakable:

> Our span of years is fixed by fate,
>   and pomp and show unreal.
> Heart-broken in the Shades below,
>   My dark sorrow can't be fully told.
> Bitterly blows the wind in the white poplars,
>   At dusk a woe that can overcome us.[40]

In another example of an auto-dirge from *The Great Book of Marvels,* also strongly indebted to Old Poem XIV, the text of a poem from beyond the grave is conveyed not orally but in written form. In this tale a learned gentleman receives a letter on tattered paper from a reclusive stranger requesting to meet him. The recluse turns out to be the ghost of an educated man from the Southern Dynasties who had died roughly two hundred years previously and whose ancient tomb lies nearby. Attached to the letter is a poem:

> During my lifetime, I roamed from town to town,
> When I died, I was abandoned in a wasteland.
> Since saying goodbye to the human world,
>   I know not autumn or spring.
> Sheep and cattle have grazed here for ages,
>   How often have cypress and pine become kindling?[41]
> It's fine with me to have no traffic of horse and cart,[42]
>   I'm glad to group myself with fox and hare.

But whence comes this refreshing breeze?
  I'm fortunate to have a gentleman as a neighbor. . . .

The learned gentleman sends back a polite reply asking the recluse to visit him at home, and man and ghost strike up a satisfying scholarly friendship, removed from any burial context.[43]

The influence of Old Poems XIII and XIV, as filtered through Tao Qian's "Imitations of Burial Songs," is likewise strongly evident in the most remarkable of the Tang tales to feature a posthumous auto-dirge. The graveyard verses are the core of this story, not merely an embellishment or proof of the encounter between the living and the dead, as in the two examples above. Most important, the responses to these poems make explicit certain assumptions which encouraged the fusion of the concepts of author and ghost at this juncture in Chinese civilization.

The tale, which is likewise set in the latter half of the eighth century, survives in more than one version. The text of the verses is essentially stable; it is the order of the poems and the narrative frame contextualizing them that varies. The lengthiest version, from *Anecdotes about Tang Poems* (*Tangshi jishi;* compiled ca 1165), is based on an entry from a book no longer extant called *The Missing History of the Tang and Song* (*Tang Song yishi;* by 1067):[44]

> In the year 779, Li Daochang was serving as surveillance commissioner of Suzhou. One day, on Tiger Mound Hill, beyond the district city walls, two poems inscribed by ghosts emerged *(yin)* on a cliff.
>
> The first one went:
>
> In the green pines— so many doleful winds![45]
>   Their whistling is clear and sad.[46]
> The Southern Hills join dark grave mounds,
>   The dark grave mounds rear their barren heads.
> The bright sun shines to no avail—
>   No rays reach the Terrace of Lasting Night.
> Though I know about the joy of the living,
>   How could my soul ever come back?
> Especially when I remember my near and dear,
>   Painful tears come and my heart breaks.
> Painful tears—what more can be said?
>   Such grief, oh such grief.
>
> The second one went:
>
> No way to copy the immortals,
>   After the body's decay, the soul roams in vain.
> Bright sun gives me no dawn,
>   Green pines are now my gate.

Though the dead are divided from the living,[47]
    I am still mindful of my sons and grandsons.
How can this grief be banished?
    All things must return to their roots.
Send word to the men of your world:
    Don't tire of a fine brew before you.
About those questions Zhuangzi posed to the skull—
"The happiness of a king" is but empty words.[48]

Amazed at this miraculous event, the official submits a memorial to the throne and receives authorization to offer a funerary sacrifice *(ji)*, for which he writes the elegy himself. Several days after the ceremony, a new verse appears on the stone in response:

Though dead and living walk different paths,
    in the past, we devoted ourselves to literature.
If you want to know our burial place:
    north of the mountain lie two solitary graves.

Sure enough, the official later discovers two tomb mounds, thickly overgrown, but no one ever learns the names of those buried there.

Foucault has taught us to recognize that authorship is not assigned uniformly to every kind of writing in a particular civilization and what texts require an author may change over time. In the case of Chinese lyric poetry, the need for a firm attribution to an individual author emerged during the Six Dynasties but solidified during the Tang. Once the "author-function" had become required for lyric poetry, a development accompanied by the rise of occasional verse, it was no longer enough simply to know the author's name; it became imperative to know the circumstances behind the production of a poem. When these circumstances were not spelled out in the title or preface to a poem, they had to be discovered or invented. Hence the emergence during the Tang of a rich anecdotal literature to fill in the missing context behind a poem's composition. These sorts of anecdotes would play an important role in the "critical remarks on poetry" *(shihua)* that developed during the Song and proliferated throughout the late imperial period.

We can follow this transition in the development of the graveyard poem from the collective voice of the Nineteen Old Poems and burial songs to the literary imitations by specific poets such as Lu Ji and Tao Qian. Once poets stopped writing auto-dirges in their own name during the Tang,[49] the graveyard poem could not go back to being anonymous; instead it started to be attributed to stand-in ghost authors, their identity contexualized through a narrative frame. The story of the inscriptions at Tiger Mound Hill provides almost graphic confirmation of Foucault's thesis that in a civilization, once "literary anonymity is not tolerable, it is accepted only in the guise of an enigma."[50]

Most extraordinary here is how the enigma of literary anonymity becomes equated with the enigma of the anonymous dead. The hermeneutic structure of this story as it appears in *Anecdotes about Tang Poems* bears a marked resemblance to "The Inhabitant of the Gorges of Ba" discussed earlier. In that anecdote the origin of a disembodied verse chanted through the night is traced back to a set of exposed human bones; in this one, verses inscribed on a cliff face lead to the discovery of two unmarked graves. That the Tiger Mound Hill story is yet another variant on the old theme of the encounter with bones in the wilderness is underscored by the ending of the second verse, which explicitly refers to "those questions Zhuangzi posed to the skull." In a famous dialogue, the ancient philosopher Zhuangzi comes across a skull on the roadside and asks it a series of factual questions: How did you die and come to find your bones abandoned in this place? That night he has a dream in which the skull comes to him. Instead of answering his questions, the skull delivers a homily on the peace to be found in death. Unconvinced, Zhuangzi inquires whether the skull would not rather be brought back to life and return to its family and native place. "The skull frowned deeply, knitting its brows: 'Why do you think I would give up all the happiness of a king on his throne to return to the troubles of the human world?'"[51]

The two ghost inscriptions, full of grief, mindful of the joys and responsibilities of the living, refute the parable's ostensible thesis that the dead are pleased with their lot. In the text of his elegy, the official ignores Zhuangzi's final proposition to the skull; instead he follows in the vein of Zhuangzi's initial set of questions. But instead of asking "How did you die?" he asks "Who were you?" And not merely "Who were you?" but *"Who were you that you are able to compose poetry?"* This line of inquiry continues: "Whose son or nephew were you? What offices did you once hold? . . . In the loneliness of the Terrace of Night, you grieve for the bright sun. . . . You didn't sign your names, how can we determine your worthiness? Alas, what woe!"[52]

As a relic of the dead to be addressed by the living, verse has replaced skull. And without a signature, poems inscribed on a cliff outside the city walls become no less threatening than unmarked bones in the wilderness to a civilization founded on the commemoration and veneration of the dead. As the local representative of the state, Li Daocheng, who, according to the *Old Official History of the Tang (Jiu Tangshu)* became surveillance commissioner of Suzhou in 776, is aware of the threat posed by these anonymous but literary verses with their hint of political as well as personal grievances.[53] (The third couplet in the first poem, "The bright sun shines to no avail / No rays reach the Terrace of Lasting Night" is easily interpreted as political allegory, since the bright sun was a common metaphor for the emperor.) Thus it is in the name of the emperor that the official performs the propitiatory ritual. As the encomium to the elegy concludes: "Please be moved by our sovereign's offering this libation of clear wine / May you be reborn and serve an enlightened ruler."[54]

Within the story's terms, it is not only the poetic content and imagery that authenticate the otherworldly provenance of the inscriptions, but also the miraculous fashion of their manifestation. As the official remarks in his elegy: "Your words did not appear on paper, but emerged from within the hidden recesses of stone."[55]

The contrast drawn between stone, a solid material used for funerary architecture and memorial steles, and paper, a flimsy and ephemeral medium for ordinary communication, brings out the symbolic affinity of stone to death and eternity.[56]

In Tang China, poems were, in fact, not only written on paper or silk, but also on the surfaces of walls, trees, and rocks. The inscriptions on Tiger Mound Hill are easily recognizable as a species of verse called *tibishi,* poems written mainly on the walls of buildings or mountain cliffs.[57] Ordinarily a poet, often a traveler, would pen his words on plaster or stone with a brush; later, to preserve them, these verses might be copied and transferred to a stone or wooden placard placed at the site or engraved on the cliff face for subsequent visitors to encounter in situ. As graphic testimony to the fact that someone else once stood in the exact spot the viewer stood now, *tibishi,* perhaps more forcefully than any other literary subgenre, drive home the absence of the original writer, especially if the writer is believed to be dead. Partly for this eerie effect of absence, *tibishi* are one of the major forms of poetry attributed to ghosts in the anecdotal literature.

But in the case of these particular inscriptions, the claim of their otherworldly origin is strengthened because they are said to have emerged spontaneously from the stone.[58] The usage of the verb *yin chu* (which I have translated as "to emerge from hidden recesses") is curious here, but the same verb *yin* (minus the verbal complement *chu*) is also employed to narrate the mysterious appearance of the inscriptions in the tale's opening, so the usage is significant and deliberate. The implication is that the inscriptions have somehow "penetrated the solid surface of the stone" *but from within,* reversing the ordinary direction of engraving. The visual image of an inscription being produced from inside a stone surface seems a direct counterpart to the verbal device of a ghost writing his own funerary dirge.[59]

Conceiving the poetic process as a spatialized movement from inside to outside is an old notion in Chinese poetics. In the often-quoted line from the "Great Preface" to the *Book of Songs* (ca. 1st century CE), this logic is already clear: "A poem is where intent goes. In the mind, it is intent; emerging in words, it becomes a poem. When feelings are roused within, they acquire form in words."[60] Owen has emphasized that such a theory of poetry conforms to a fundamental Chinese paradigm of movement from inner to outer. In the traditional definition of a poem as the external discharge of powerful internal preoccupations, he sees a specific application of "the universal tendency of all things to move from latency to manifestation" in Chinese thought.[61] Elsewhere, Owen has elaborated on the implications of this idea for Chinese lyric poetry: "Literature is a gate for the latent and inarticulate to make itself manifest"; "A poem is an act of making manifest what is overlooked, lost, hidden"; or pithier still, a poem is "a verbal manifestation of an inner state."[62]

Although Owen does not comment on the occult flavor of his pronouncements, the psychoanalytic language of "manifestation" he draws upon originated from the vocabulary of the nineteenth-century Anglo-American spiritualist movement.[63] Cross-fertilization between ideas of the unconscious and the occult was ongoing in the early twentieth century. (Freud himself was interested in spiritualism, becoming a corresponding member of the London-based Society for Psychical Research and publishing an article on his theory of the unconscious in the Society's *Proceedings* for 1912.)[64] The fantasy in the Tiger Mound Hill anecdote of posthumous verse coming to the cliff surface from the hidden depths of the stone is partly predicated on the ghostly potential of the outer/inner paradigm in traditional Chinese poetics. But the fantasy is plausibly read in psychoanalytic terms as a mise-en-scène for "the return of the repressed," in which "ghost" and "the unconscious" (as the hidden, the prearticulate, the unknown) are synonymous terms, both discharging and manifesting themselves in the visible (or audible) exterior form of "poetry." Confucius is supposed to have said: "If a person does not speak up, who will know his intent? If his words are without pattern, they will not go far."[65] In this anecdote, the patterned language of poetry is indeed imagined to make words go far enough to penetrate the stone membrane separating the world of the dead from the world of the living.

The earliest extant version of this anecdote is attributed to *Communications from the Unseen World* (*Tongyou ji;* late ninth century).[66] In this version, however, there is no official, no state-sponsored ritual, no funerary elegy. Although the same three poems still materialize on a cliff on Tiger Mound Hill during the same reign period, no mention is made of their emergence from the interior of the stone. Instead, a Buddhist monk at nearby Tiger Mound Temple is said to have seen two figures clad in white disappear into one of the buildings the previous night. The inference is that the ghost inscriptions must have been left on the cliff face by these two mysterious visitors. Nor does an explicit hermeneutic sequence structure this version. All three poems appear at the same time, and the third poem, revealing the location of the two graves, is placed first, not last. Finally, the two graves are never specifically determined; the story simply ends with a pronouncement: "Ancient graves lay one after another in a cemetery ringed with trees; even today, the writing remains there still."[67]

In this version, however, the two auto-dirges bear titles, which furnish signatures for each other. The first is labeled "Shown to the Dweller in Dark Solitude," the second is labeled "Reply to the Resident of Darkness."[68] "Dweller in Dark Solitude" and "Resident of Darkness" are clearly generic substitutes for the unknown names of the deceased, but these "signatures," as we will see, seem to have sufficed to fill the cultural demand for an "author."

Like *The Great Book of Marvels* and other Tang collections of strange tales, *Communications from the Unseen World* was lost long ago. What stories and anecdotes from these books still survive have generally been preserved only in later compendia such as the imperially sponsored Northern Song encyclopedia, *Accounts Widely Gathered in the Taiping Era* (*Taiping guangji;* compiled 976–983 by Li Fang et al.). Remarkably, the Tiger Mound poems, stripped of any narrative frame, survive in another kind of source, which was completed during the Tang. This is the *Pine Knoll Anthology (Songling ji),* a collection compiled by Lu Guimeng (d. ca. 881) and Pi Rixiu (ca. 834–ca. 883), containing mainly the poems they wrote together.[69] Lu Guimeng, a native of Suzhou, was a poet from a prominent local family and a recluse associated with Maoshan Daoism. The poems in the joint collection were written primarily in 870 during the brief period Pi Rixiu was living in Suzhou.[70] This means that Lu Guimeng and even Pi Rixiu would have been in a position to know the local legends and miracles associated with Tiger Mound Hill.[71] Indeed, in this section of the *Pine Knoll Anthology*, these three ghost poems are bundled together with another set of supernaturally authored poems (attributed to a Daoist thousands of years old), also said to have originated on Tiger Mound Hill.

The quatrain mentioning the two graves and the first auto-dirge appear in the *Pine Knoll Anthology* under the title "Poems by the Lord of Dark Solitude"; the second auto-dirge is entitled "A Reply to the Lord of Dark Solitude" and is placed after them. Then follow two poems each by Pi Rixiu and Lu Guimeng written to match the rhymes of the Lord of Dark Solitude's poems.[72] Clearly the story that Pi and Lu knew basically accorded with the early version in *Communications from the Unseen World*, rather than with the later version in the *Missing History of the Tang and Song* and *Anecdotes about Tang Poems*. In this context, their private, purely literary ceremony of matching the poems by the deceased can be seen as a forerunner to the state-sponsored public ritual of the funerary sacrifice in the later version. Both are responses to the threat of the anonymous author; both aim to placate the unsettled dead by mourning the previously unrecognized literary talent and ethical merit revealed in their posthumous inscriptions.

Most remarkably, in Pi Rixiu's preface to this section of the *Pine Knoll Anthology*, we find articulated the first theory of the ghost author:

> Ah! When sages and worthies have intent that goes unfulfilled, they have no choice but to convey it to posterity in words. The greater ones produce canons and admonitions; the lesser ones produce songs and poems. Generally, those not entrusted with office in their own time will lodge a complaint with later generations. Or could it be that ghosts and spirits whose intent went unfulfilled in their lifetime do the same even in death?[73]

Pi Rixiu's theory is a logical extension of mainstream Confucian poetics, in which a poem is "intent" put into words, and intent is understood in a political sense as the desire to serve the state. But he is also drawing on an even more fundamental theory of literary composition, first articulated in the first to second century BCE by the great historian Sima Qian, which champions the written opus as conduit and compensation for unjust suffering and neglect.[74] One pours one's feelings and intent into writing so that they may be known by others and outlast one's own lifetime. This is how literature is supposed to grant immortality to an author—through his work, his name and his worth will live on after death. The novelty in Pi Rixiu's formulation lies in supposing that death may not put an end to "intent," but only intensify it; if so, the need to put it into words would not disappear but only be aggravated by the travails of the afterlife.

Li He and the Creation of the Ghostly Author

Pi Rixiu's preface of 870/871 is a milestone in the invention of the "ghost author"—a dead soul to whom is attributed the authorship of a poem. A parallel and related development of greater influence, however, had been set into motion some forty years earlier. This was the creation of the "ghostly author"—someone who pens verse in a ghostly style and is therefore doomed to die young—in the person of Li He (790–816/817). After his premature death at twenty-six, Li He became transformed into the "Ghostly Genius" *(gui cai),* the precocious man of talent with one foot in the grave. Although this specific epithet was not coined until the Northern Song, Li He's myth began to take shape within fifteen years of his death, in the preface the poet Du Mu wrote in 831 for the surviving poems of Li He.[75] Du Mu's preface begins dramatically, by recalling the circumstances in which he first learned about the existence of the manuscript:

> One midnight in the middle of October, from outside the house came the urgent cry of someone delivering a letter. I said: "Something strange must have happened," and hastily grabbed a light. When I opened the letter, it indeed *(guo)* turned out to be from the worthy scholar Shen Yazhi.[76]

Then follows the text of the letter, in which Shen relates that his late friend Li He, just before his death, had entrusted him with the poems written during his lifetime. Shen's letter continues:

> Tonight I woke up after a drinking bout and couldn't go back to sleep. So I began tidying up the papers in my trunk. Suddenly, I came across the poems Li He had given me earlier. Recollecting the past, all the conversations and outings we had together, every place, every season, every day, every night, every drink, every meal, came flooding back to me so vividly and so indelibly that unconsciously, my tears began to flow.

This discovery provokes Shen's fervent request that Du Mu write a preface expounding the work's significance and Du Mu's account of how he wanted to refuse, indeed had refused for several days, before finally relenting. This detailed account takes up more than half the preface, leaving only some 260 characters for Du Mu's actual compliance with Shen's request.

Going far beyond any ordinary display of polite deference, this narrative of how Du Mu was compelled to write the preface is crucial to the formation of Li He's ghostly image. The request arrives out of the blue, at midnight, in mid-autumn, during the hour and season associated with ghosts. It is surely unusual for a letter to be delivered at midnight, which is why Du Mu thinks it must contain something out of the ordinary. What kind of communication would be so urgent it could not wait until morning? Presumably, the announcement of a death or some other inauspicious event. When Du Mu opens the letter, his hunch is confirmed (as indicated by his usage of the adverb *guo,* indeed, or as expected). However, the letter does not convey news of a recent death, but of posthumous papers resurfacing many years after a death.

Shen Yazhi's accidental recovery of the poems that night also has an uncanny feel about it. As something created and bequeathed by the deceased, however, this manuscript is more than an ordinary relic of the dead. As something that mysteriously reappears after it was feared lost forever, the manuscript is very like a revenant. Li He, as someone cut off in his youth, who died without leaving any descendents, is a prime candidate to return as a ghost. And Shen Yazhi, as Li He's closest friend and confidante, who had criminally neglected Li He's only legacy, is a prime candidate to be haunted. "Since Ho [He] no longer has a family or children that I can support or sympathize with," wrote Shen to Du Mu, "I regret that all I have done up to now has been to think of him and enjoy his words as I recited them."[77] These feelings of guilt and obligation help account for the urgency and intensity of Shen's letter and Du Mu's inability to turn Shen down despite what seem like unfeigned misgivings.

This preface played a foundational role in the subsequent reception of Li He's poetry. The biography of Li He written by the poet Li Shangyin (813?–858), which was also influential in disseminating the Li He myth, begins by citing Du Mu's preface. The biography contributes an anecdote concerning Li He's anomalous methods of composition (tossing fragments of verse into a brocade bag) and the supernatural circumstances surrounding his death (the arrival of a divine emissary riding on a dragon; strange miasma and music outside the window). Li Shangyin strongly indicates that Li He's premature death was linked to his exceptional poetic talent, an outcome paradoxically explained as both reward and punishment.[78]

The view that writing poetry is an arduous, dangerous act, harmful to the poet's bodily integrity and material well-being, which underlies Li Shangyin's biography, is emphatically reiterated in a colophon on that biography penned by Lu Guimeng, whom we have already met as the coauthor of the *Pine Knoll Anthology*.[79] Shang Wei has demonstrated that the idea of poetic creation as a negative, transgressive force emerged during the late eighth century to early ninth century. This view was only one side of a more complex discourse about poetry at the time, which also included favorable assertions of the poet's power to master and even rival the mysteries of cosmic creation.[80] In contrast to this ambivalent but admiring mid-Tang picture of poetic prowess, later generations stressed only the negative side. Shang's earliest example for this change, however, is none other than Lu Guimeng's colophon (written between ca 858–880),[81] which blames the craft of poetry for the suffering of its practitioners: "How can one who reveals the secrets of life and death avoid being punished by the Creator? Li He died young; Meng Jiao was impoverished. Li Shangyin died without having been promoted to a position in the imperial court. All because of this. All because of this."[82]

Crucial to this negative view is a reversal of the causality inherent in the ancient expressive theory of literature: rather than being a medium to vent, relieve, and commemorate the writer's distress, the composition of poetry is now blamed as the *cause* of his distress. In his biography Li Shangyin quotes Li He's mother's cry of alarm at seeing her son's bag filled with lines of poetry: "This boy will vomit out his very heart before he's done!"[83] "To vomit out one's heart" (or one's heart's blood) came to have the figurative meaning "to work too hard at crafting a poem." In the context of Li He's early death, the phrase still retains the strong quasimedical connotations of the literal meaning. The idea that the expenditure involved in literary composition is injurious to the bodily economy and therefore responsible for cutting life short is bluntly put by Zhou Bida (1126–1206):

> In the past, it was said writing poetry could impoverish someone. Maybe this is not all it does; sometimes poetry can even a kill a person. For straining the guts and the liver to craft good lines already runs counter to the techniques for nourishing life. And besides, how could the flippant versification of all things in the universe bring joy to the Creator? The early deaths of Li He of the Tang and Xing Jushi of our own dynasty were most likely due to these factors.[84]

Although the self-torture inflicted on the internal organs undoubtedly should also be understood as a trope for the arduous labor of creation, the problem is not conceptualized exclusively in metaphorical terms but is always recognized to have real physical consequences.

The correlation between Li He's poetic output and his untimely death is also made on the basis of a cultural logic that has little to do with a bodily economy of psychic and physical exertion, or with a divine system of reward or punishment for poetic genius. From the Northern Song on, Li He's tragic fate was also specifically blamed on the inauspicious nature of the poetry he produced. For a line of poetry is not an ordinary utterance in premodern Chinese thought. As the externalization in patterned sound of unseen, unconscious forces, verse (like music, with which it was intimately related) was understood in the Confucian terms developed in the "Great Preface" to the *Book of Songs* as potentially diagnostic of the political health of a state. "The tones of a well-managed age are at rest and happy; its government is balanced. The tones of an age of turmoil are bitter and full of anger; its government is perverse. The tones of a ruined state are filled with lament and brooding; its people are in difficulty."[85] The border between the diagnosis of an existing condition and the prediction of a forthcoming one, however, is a thin one, and lines of verse, like dreams, often came to be interpreted as prophecies of the future. The model developed in the "Great Preface" is essentially a public and collective one, designed for a time before the individual author of poetry was fully established. Once the "author function" had been firmly attached to poetic composition, however, verse could now be interpreted as auguring the private fate of an individual writer, and was no longer restricted to auguring the public fate of the polis.

The predictive capacity attributed to an individual's poetry strongly fueled the creation of Li He's myth as the "Ghostly Genius." The fact of his early death was for later readers inextricably entwined with the macabre imagery of his verse. The life became the sign of the poems and vice versa. The poetry's inauspicious content was held responsible for precipitating the untimely death (according to the logic that to say something invites it to come true), and the knowledge of the untimely death was in turn read back into the poetry, making it even spookier and sadder.

The late Ming critic Wang Siren summed up this view in his influential preface to a seventeenth-century edition of Li He's poetry: "When someone's life is careening to a close, lovely scenery seems entirely pointless. That's why he set his disturbed and mournful thoughts to such an obscure tune. He liked to use words such as 'ghost,' 'weeping,' 'death,' and 'blood.' When someone's poetry is dark, chilling, and perverse, as a rule he will die young."[86]

To appreciate what it was specifically about Li He's poetry that fed his reputation for eeriness, I will consider in some detail one of his most famous compositions, "Criticism ("Ganfeng"), no. 3," which has been repeatedly singled out for its ghostliness by a succession of traditional and modern commentators.

> How mournful the Southern Hills!
> a ghostly rain spatters the barren grass.
> Halfway through a fall night in Chang'an,
> how many mortals [*ren*] has the wind aged?
> Dusk falls on the dimming path,
> Green oaks rustle along the road.
> Under the midnight moon, the trees' shadows straighten,
> and a white dawn envelops the hillside.
> Pitch-black torches welcome the new bride [*xin ren*].
> In the dark gravepit, the fireflies hover.[87]

This poem is disjointed and unsettling; no personal pronouns are employed, and there is seemingly no stable context to situate the perceiving subject's temporal or spatial position in the poem.[88] In these regards, this poem is no different from other famous pieces by Li He such as "Autumn Comes" ("Qiu lai") or "Amid the Fields of the Southern Hills" ("Nanshan tianzhong xing"), which it closely resembles in imagery and mood. In the case of "Criticism, no. 3," however, the pieces fall clearly into place once it is understood as a reworking of the old graveyard / auto-dirge poem. With the ritual procession of a funeral as a template, we can almost fit the poem into a coherent narrative. The Ming critic Zeng Yi aptly summarizes "Criticism, no. 3" as "relating the sorrow of being dead and buried."[89] The brilliance of this poem is that it does so without any overt display of mourning.

The poem begins with the familiar contemplation of a graveyard. The "Southern Hills" were the burial grounds outside the Tang capital of Chang'an, and by this time had replaced the Beimang hills as the generic name for a cemetery. The scene is suitably gloomy, damp, and uninhabited, but its ghostliness is made a feature of the empty and withered landscape, rather than attributed overtly to the consciousness of a perceiving eye. The next couplet moves us back to the city of Chang'an for the start of the journey and situates us in the usual season and hour of death. This couplet is a recognizable variation on a dirge's standard lament: how swiftly a human life passes! The wind that is always an element of the graveyard poem comes into play here, but it is made a precipitating cause rather than simply a natural attribute of a funerary scene or a response to it: this wind ages those it touches, pushing them headlong toward death. The sense of a journey is most strongly conveyed in the third couplet, which seems to be following something or someone down a path, presumably "the Spirit Road" *(shendao)* within a cemetery that leads to the tomb. The deadly wind of the preceding couplet now reaches its logical destination, stirring the green oaks along the path, as substitutes for the more standard white poplars.[90] The dimming light on the road is connected to night falling, but it may also suggest the gradual extinction of the faculty of sight the deceased would experience as described in Tao Qian's and Lu Ji's burial songs.

With the seventh and eighth lines, we return to the hills and arrive at the burial site. The achievement of these lines, as with the concluding couplet, is to create a new visual language for the conventional conceit of the reversal wrought by death. "Before I lived in a house of men; now I reside in the neighborhood of ghosts. Before I had a body six feet tall; today I have become ashes and dust," laments Lu Ji in his burial song, and sentiments such as these are a common refrain in the auto-dirge.[91] Here Li He flips day and night by substituting midnight for midday, through his jarring pairing of "noon" with the unexpected "moon," rather than the conventional sun. The trees also behave weirdly, casting their shadows as if it were midday, but as a result of the moon rather than the sun shining from its zenith. The effect of this imagery is to jolt the reader into realizing that for the dead, night *is* day.

"The Terrace of Lasting Night" is a common epithet for the underworld, which we have already encountered in the Lord of Dark Solitude's inscription. There the posthumous complaint that "the sun shines to no avail" elicits the response "Bright sun gives me no dawn" in the matching inscription. Both echo the sentiment voiced in the final stanza of Tao Qian's burial song: "Once the dark house is closed / In a thousand years there will be no new dawn." Morning does momentarily dawn in Li He's deathscape, however, confusing us until we figure out that this daybreak is a false one, an illusion. The point is that the only dawn the dead will ever see again can be nothing but a night when the moon lights up the sky. The pallor of this moonlit dawn is revealed to be only another color for death. As the traditional hue for mourning clothes, white is associated with funerals in China; as an attribute of a seasonal landscape, white connotes "bleakness, starkness, the absence of distinct coloration characteristic of late autumn," to borrow Maureen Robertson's formulation.[92] White—"the color of metal, of death, of specters, of stark dreamworlds"—is, as Edward Schafer notes, ubiquitous in Li He's poetry.[93]

In the original Chinese, this line conveys also a strong sense of desolation. (A more literal translation would read: "On the whole hillside, there is only the white dawn.") As Zeng Yi explains, this means that "from dusk all through the night, it is deserted without a single person present; all there is the whiteness of the hillside, which is called 'dawn.'" This means there have been no living mourners accompanying the funeral bier. And if there is no one present, the reader of a Chinese poem is conditioned to wonder, who is watching and describing the scene?

The final couplet clinches the suspicion that the vision is a preternatural one. The point of view shifts from that of some sort of traveling observer reaching a destination to that of old inhabitants beholding a newcomer. The terminology of this couplet's first line is chilling for it borrows the wedding rite of welcoming the bride into her new marital family. Because the norm in China was patrilocal marriage and multigenerational residence, a bride was quite literally the "new person" *(xin ren)* in her husband's household. The analogy between marriage and death drawn in so many cultures has particular force in the Chinese case because to become a wife by definition means to leave home forever and be exiled to the unknown.

The equivalence between death and marriage as the two main cultural forms of exile is the basis of a famous parable by Zhuangzi. Trying to reconcile the living to the fate of dying, he preaches:

> How do I know that to take pleasure in life is not a delusion? How do I know that we who hate death are not exiles since childhood who have forgotten the way home *(bu zhi gui*[a]*)*? Lady Li was the daughter of a frontier guard at Ai. When the kingdom of Chin first took her captive the tears stained her dress; only when she came to the palace and shared the king's square couch and ate delicious meats did she begin to regret her tears. How do I know that the dead do not regret that ever they had an urge to live?[94]

How do we know that in dreading our own death we are not as foolish as a young girl fearing matrimony with a king of a neighboring country? To bolster his point, Zhuangzi chooses the most traumatic form of marriage: the woman who is kidnapped and raped by the ruler of an alien state. But the symbolic reciprocity between death and even an ordinary wedding is deep-rooted in Classical Chinese. The word *gui*[a] (to return home, to swear allegiance to), which Zhuangzi uses in this passage for the exile who has forgotten how to go home, can be used to denote either death or a woman's marriage. The same term, as I discussed in the Introduction, plays a key role in the early punning definitions of a ghost: "A ghost means to return" *(gui, gui*[a] *ye)*. In both cases the logic is euphemistic or even apotropaic: the first, familiar home (life, natal family) is cast merely as a temporary abode, and the new, feared home (death, marital family) as the permanent residence to which one has always truly belonged. This must reflect the hope that the person who "*gui*[a]-s" (a dead soul, a daughter) will never come back to trouble those left behind (the survivors, the natal family).

There is no hint of fear or violence in Li He's portrayal of the dead soul's arrival at its final destination. But there is something wrong with this nuptial ritual, for the torches used to greet the newcomer are "pitch black," the oxymoron a figure for the will-o'-the-wisps or ghost fires, which were understood as transmutations of the dead. Poetic images for will-o'-the-wisps abound in Li He's poetry: elsewhere called "cold blue candles" or "ghost lanterns black as pitch."[95] Here the effect is again one of death as inversion, with the funerary procession morphing into a bridal procession and back again. Rather than the bride being welcomed to her new home with festive red lanterns, the dead soul is ushered into the glimmering darkness of a grave pit illumined by funereal glowworms or fireflies, another of Li He's favorite images. Both will-o'-the-wisps and fireflies signal the presence of ghosts as the denizens of the tomb, the last flickers of light before total darkness descends.

What makes this ending couplet so uncanny is the mutation of the word *ren* (human being) into its parallel opposite, *gui* (ghost). In Bronfen's discussion of Freud's famous concept *das Unheimlich,* she identifies such a blurring of semantic opposites as a central rhetorical strategy of the uncanny: "Because the word *unheimlich* refers both to the familiar and agreeable and to something concealed, kept out of sight, it comes to signify any moment where meaning develops in the direction of ambivalence until it coincides with its opposite."[96] Zeng Yi glosses the compound *xin ren* in Li He's poem (which I have translated "new bride") as denoting "a newly buried ghost."[97] And another Ming commentator praises Li He for opting to use "new person" *(xin ren)* rather than "new ghost" *(xin gui)* here.[98] A similar frisson is built into "The Inhabitant of the Gorges of Ba." Only after finishing the anecdote does the reader realize that the character *ren* in the title (which I've translated as "inhabitant") really means its opposite, *gui.*[99] In the ending of "Criticism, no. 3," the uncanny effect of converging opposites is heightened because the character *ren,* in its unequivocal sense of "person" or "mankind," has already appeared in the second couplet ("mortals aged by the wind" in my translation). Indeed, this is the only place in the poem that refers explicitly to living people at all. When the character *ren* recurs in the last couplet as part of the compound *xin ren,* the repetition spells out once again the poem's central trope of death's inversion: midnight for midday, funerals for weddings, blackened torches for beacons, ghosts for people.

In the ninth-century reception of the Tiger Mound Hill inscriptions, it was not only their morbid content and their proximity to a graveyard that facilitated their acceptance as ghost poems by readers such as Pi Rixiu and Lu Guimeng. In his preface to this section of the *Pine Knoll Anthology,* Pi Rixiu describes himself as "a lover of antiquity" who reads "the extraordinarily sad" poems by the Lord of Dark Solitude "with pleasure." Although he admits he does not know who wrote the "Reply to the Lord of Dark Solitude," he has included it anyway because it is "antique and mournful."[100] Pi Rixiu's editorial explanation suggests that the qualities he prized in a ghost poem were naturalness and plainness of expression, an old-fashioned period style, and the affect of grief.[101]

Pi Rixiu's qualification of ghost inscriptions as "antique" *(gu)* is predicated in part on the contrast between "old style" poetry and the new Tang style of regulated verse, but probably even more on the contrast between old-fashioned simple diction and the new brand of strange, arcane poetry favored by writers such as Li He. For admirers of this latest style, the "bizarre" *(guai),* which was not ordinarily a term of approbation in poetic discourse, became an epithet of high praise.[102] In terms of versification, Li He specialized in old style poems rather than regulated verse, but the kind of ghostly poetry he wrote was thoroughly modern, and the weird, intricate, and jarring style he adopted the antithesis of "plain" and "natural." One meaning of *gui* (ghost) is "superhumanly clever" or "exquisitely, devilishly wrought"; and indeed some critics have explained Li He's reputation as the "Ghostly Genius" partly on these grounds.[103] In the centuries after Li He's death, however, his individual style and lexicon became naturalized in turn and eventually superseded the "antique" and "plain" lament as the literary signifier for a ghost.

Writing in the 1960s, Li He's English translators, J. D. Frodsham and A. C. Graham, complained of his long neglect after the Song, mainly on the evidence of his omission from the conservative late eighteenth-century anthology *300 Tang Poems (Tangshi sanbai shou)*, which was instrumental in shaping late Qing and early twentieth-century taste.[104] In fact, although Li He always occupied an uneasy position in the mainstream poetic tradition, he was rarely absent from it because he filled such a distinctive niche. In a compilation of traditional criticism on Li He published in 1994, Wu Qiming demonstrates that a major issue for premodern readers of Li He was not neglect, but imitation.[105] The vogue for Li He imitations began soon after his death: Shen Yazhi, a close friend of Li He's, notes that "later scholars competed to imitate him."[106] In his famous remarks on poetry, the thirteenth-century critic Yan Yu listed "the Li He type" *(Changji ti)* as one of the possible individual author-based styles of Chinese poetry.[107] Reading Li He's style politically as "the tones of a ruined state," the Ming scholar Hu Yinglin (1551–1602) observed that imitators of Li He became especially frequent at the end of dynasties.[108]

Yagi Akiyoshi has noted a surge in Li He's popularity from the late Ming to the mid-Qing, as demonstrated by the quantity of newly annotated collections of his verse published during this period.[109] The quantity of Li He editions on the market must have inspired and been fueled by the enthusiasm for Li He imitations. Seventeenth-century critics noted this contemporary vogue, leading one of them to make the belittling remark that it was much easier to duplicate Li He's style than that of the greatest Tang poets. The same critic also lambasted the second-rate nature of contemporary Li He imitations for capturing only his ingenious, fantastic aspects but failing to equal his best lines.[110] And as the Qing critic Shen Deqian (1673–1769) warned: "Wang Shizhen [the famous Ming scholar-official] once said, 'Overdone, the marvelous becomes commonplace.' Imitators of Li He had better be aware of this!"[111]

By the late Ming, the conscious creation of a ghostly lyrical style was clearly understood to have originated with Li He. A circumscribed set of images, phrases, and literary effects, largely derived from or inspired by Li He, had become easily recognizable generic markers of "ghostliness." As the poet You Tong (1618–1704) wrote in the margins of the posthumous poetry collection of his closest friend, who had died young: "Entirely in the Li He style. The ghostliness of this poem is overwhelming."[112] The term "ghostly" *(you guiqi)* is employed in a range of seventeenth-century writings as an aesthetic evaluation associated with melancholy and foreboding.

As the Three Wives' commentary on *The Peony Pavilion (Wu Wushan sanfu heping Mudan ting)*, published circa 1694, observes of an aria Du Liniang sings upon her deathbed: "'The mournful chants of birds and bugs, the whistling of the wind-lashed rain': the ghostliness one feels in the words and between the lines is overwhelming. Reading this alone on an overcast night would be frightening."[113]

By the late 1780s, the ghostly poetic code based on Li He's work had become transparent enough to diagnose the authorship of a poem independent of context or signature. In his *Jottings from the Thatched Cottage*, Ji Yun relates that he had once found a piece of paper folded inside an old dictionary on which was written a poem. The poem included couplets such as "Blue will-o'-the-wisps, barely visible, emerge from ancient walls / Green moss eats through golden studs" and "The single speck of a damp firefly crosses the empty dike / Its dark gleam reflects the last of the red weeping." The stock images of ghost fires, dripping flowers, and decaying palaces, the intensive use of color, and the chiaroscuro effect of light flickering in the darkness are vintage Li He.[114] Certain phrases such as the "damp firefly" and "the red weeping" are lifted verbatim from Li He's work. These obvious linguistic clues are partly what lead Ji Yun to reject the attribution to an immortal appended to the poem: "I say this poem had to be composed by a ghost, not by an immortal."[115]

The Codification of Ghost Poetry

The standardization of ghost poetry conventions in the Ming and Qing dynasties was bound up with another notable development: the selection of supernaturally attributed verse from accounts of the strange for inclusion in anthologies of poetry and poetry criticism. When the first classified compendia of "remarks on poetry" began to appear during the late eleventh and early twelfth centuries, ghosts were already one subject heading. Ruan Yue's *General Source for Remarks on Poetry (Shihua zonggui)* devotes two chapters to "ghosts and spirits." A related compendium, Hu Zi's (1082–1143) *Remarks Collected by the Fisherman Hermit of the Tiao River (Tiaoxi yuyin conghua)*, includes two subsections labeled "ghost poetry." In both compendia, ghosts are only one possible conjunction of poetry and the supernatural. *A General Source* includes topics such as gods and immortals, poetic predictions, and dream poems, while Hu Zi's ghost poetry subsection follows on the heels of "miscellaneous anecdotes about gods and immortals."

The importance of gossip and story in remarks on poetry is flatly stated in the opening lines of the preface to *A General Source*: "Poetry imitates 'The Osprey' [the first poem in the *Book of Songs*] while 'remarks on poetry' are akin to the class of anecdote and unofficial history."[116] The evidence presented in such collections shows that their compilers were not only sifting through compendia of tales for specimens of ghost poetry, but that spirit verse had become the subject of conversation and connoisseurship in intellectual circles during the period.[117] Of these, Su Shi (1037–1101), also well known for exchanging ghost stories with friends and for his interest in the Purple Lady (Zigu shen), the patron goddess of spirit writing, is the most prominent cultural and political figure among the aficionados of ghost poetry.[118]

Hong Mai, the compiler of *Records of the Listener (Yijian zhi),* a massive collection of strange accounts, also combed the Tang anecdotal literature for poems composed by ghosts and immortals to augment his *Ten Thousand Tang Quatrains (Wanshou Tangren jueju),* which he presented to the throne in 1192. Hong Mai was addicted to collecting stories and poems on a large scale, but he was not interested in classifying the knowledge he amassed, and he does not compartmentalize ghost poetry in either of these compilations. To my knowledge, the ghost *author* appears for the first time as a separate category in Xin Wenfang's *Biographies of Tang Poets (Tang caizi zhuan;* completed in 1304). Whether because the compiler characterized such verse as the "absurd" product of "reflection and echo" or simply because the last pages of a book are particularly vulnerable to loss, no ghost poets are actually listed, however, and the ghost poet section remains appropriately a blank.[119]

The codification of ghost poetry as a distinct category during the late Ming was undertaken by Mei Dingzuo, bibliographer, playwright, and friend of Tang Xianzu's. His *Records of Talented Ghosts* expanded an earlier one-chapter work of this title into a sixteen-chapter scholarly tour de force arranged chronologically from Zhou to Ming. Several late Ming collectanea also credit Mei as the editor of the earlier *Records of Talented Ghosts,* which suggests the extent to which Mei was responsible for generating late imperial interest in this title and subject.[120]

Mei's sixteen-chapter work is the indispensable bible for anyone interested in ghosts and poetry, particularly for the earlier periods. (His chapters on the Ming are the least comprehensive.) The last three chapters of *Records of Talented Ghosts* are devoted to spirit writings from the planchette *(fuji),* a form of communication with otherworldly beings. The game of planchette was widespread among the elite, including Mei's own relatives and friends, which undoubtedly helped stimulate the late imperial interest in ghost poetry.[121] Like most anthologists before him, Mei included frame stories from a wide range of sources, mainly accounts of the strange and remarks on poetry, to contexualize the poems as ghostwritten. Indeed, in another of his anthologies, *A Garden of Old Ballads (Guyue yuan),* he defines ghost songs as another form of *zhiguai.*[122] There Mei asserts that not all such songs are necessarily forgeries, and he employs a stock defense found in prefaces to accounts of the strange: given the vastness and variety of the universe, nothing is impossible.

In his witty prefaces to *Records of Talented Ghosts,* however, he dismisses the problem of whether ghosts really authored the poems in his anthology as largely irrelevant. He does differentiate a few ancient accounts of poems by the dead communicated in dreams as "belonging to the category of talented ghosts," but he groups the rest as belonging to the category of "Mr. No-such and Mr. Non-existent," a common label for fiction. As he explains in his preamble: "It's exactly like Su Shi's requiring people to tell ghost stories—why in the world must one verify them? Just consider such things as literature and be done with it!" And in keeping with this outlook, the chief concerns Mei evinces in his anthology, such as bibliographic sources and textual variants, have nothing to do with the content or veracity of the stories and everything to do with establishing their literary history.

Despite the bibliographic bent of Mei's *Records of Talented Ghosts,* his work is also properly seen as part of the late Ming publishing boom in repackaging old compendia such as *Wide Gleanings from the Taiping Era* and reissuing them in the form of new story collections. Allan Barr is surely right to see Mei's work as a prime example of the classical tale collections on entertaining, specialized topics being produced for the mid-sixteenth- and seventeenth-century market.[123] In fact, Mei originally planned two additional collections of supernatural poetry, *Records of Talented Immortals (Caixian ji)* and *Records of Talented Gods (Caishen ji),* to make a trilogy, but these books were never published and probably never even compiled.

Based on the evidence compiled by Mei Dingzuo and other pre-nineteenth century anthologists of poetry, it is clear that women had always figured disproportionately high in the ranks of supernatural poets, especially compared with the meager number of works by actual women surviving prior to the Song. When comprehensive anthologies of women's poetry began to be published in the mid-sixteenth century, both reflecting and stimulating a late imperial surge in women's literary production, it is clear that the male compilers of these anthologies had trouble finding examples for the early period. Including works traditionally attributed to supernatural figures was a common solution to this problem (especially since such anthologies tended to copy from one another). General anthologies of old style poetry compiled in the late Ming, such as *A Selection of Old Poetry (Gushi gui*[a]*),* for instance, also included entries by legendary figures of both sexes from earlier dynasties. The increased output and publication of verse by women during the Ming and Qing meant there was less need for anthologists to use tale collections or anecdotal accounts as a major source for the late imperial sections. Some compendia of women's verse did indeed feature otherworldly poets more heavily in early period chapters and then taper off in the Ming and Qing chapters when the pickings were so much richer. But other compilations featured otherworldly poets from later dynasties too, and several anthologies of women's poetry with an exclusive late imperial focus happily include large supernatural sections. The picture is not uniform. Whether to incorporate ghost or immortal poetry became an issue that most anthologists of women's poetry had to address in their prefaces, if only to defend an editorial policy of excluding such material from their work.

The first crop of mid-sixteenth century anthologists inherited ghost poetry as a preexisting category, although they betray some uneasiness about this. As Tian Yiheng explained in his preface to *A History of Women Poets (Shinü shi):* "Poems by female immortals and ghost women certainly abound, but there are also quite a few forgeries. I am just including a few poems to furnish examples of this type."[124] In his *Remnants from Ladies' Writing Brushes (Tongguan yibian),* published around 1567, Li Hu rejected poems composed by the heroines of classical romances popular in his day as "not really being from a woman's hand," but he included some "elegant" and "credible" examples of poetry by supernatural women in a final appendix at the bottom of his hierarchy of female poets, after maid-servants and courtesans.[125]

A correlation between women, ghosts, and other supernatural beings was also encouraged by grouping them together in the last section of anthologies, which were classified according to the poet's social status. Qian Qianyi's influential collection of Ming verse, *Poetry from an Individual Dynasty* (*Liechao shiji*, published circa 1652) devotes a specific subsection to otherworldly authors, with anecdotes drawn from collections of classical tales and remarks on poetry replacing the biographies he included for other writers. Qian placed "poems by ghosts and spirits" at the back of the anthology, which was reserved for marginal figures, after monks, women, servants, and anonymous poets, but before Korean and Japanese practitioners of Chinese verse.

Although Qian Qianyi's own life and work show evidence of his involvement in a local spirit-writing cult, he presents the poems by ghosts and spirits without comment in his anthology of Ming poetry.[126] One of the anecdotes from an early Ming notation book included in this section, however, shows he understood how problematic it could be to correlate the poetic effect of the ghostly with the ghost authorship of a poem. As two men were strolling together after dark, the entry goes, one of them happened to think up this couplet: "Rain stops in the tall bamboo, / Flitting fireflies arrive after midnight." The man's initial pleasure swiftly turns to dismay: "These lines are too eerie; they're probably the type a ghost would compose."[127] In Qian Qianyi's anthology, as in the book he took the poem from, this anecdote is in fact offered as a comment on a preceding poem flatly attributed to a ghost.

The acclaimed female anthologist of women's verse, Wang Duanshu, was influenced by Qian Qianyi in her decision to include poems attributed to ghosts and immortals in her ambitious *Classic Poetry by Renowned Women* (*Mingyuan shiwei*; completed 1667), and there is some overlap between the two anthologies in these sections.[128] But she went beyond Qian or any previous anthologist in boldly labeling her section on supernatural poetry "illusion" *(huanji)*.[129] She clearly had fun compiling these chapters, which provided a rare opportunity to indulge her fondness for tales of the strange, an area women generally did not write about.[130]

Unlike Qian Qianyi or Mei Dingzuo's anthologies, *Classic Poetry by Renowned Women* is liberally laced with its compiler's literary judgments and personal observations. From these comments it is evident that Wang Duanshu's criteria for evaluating the merits of poems in the illusion chapters were primarily aesthetic and stylistic. For instance, she mentions that a contemporary girl from Nanjing was skilled at wielding the planchette, and that Yu Xuanji, a Tang dynasty courtesan, nun, and poet, was one of the immortal women who graced this girl's spirit-writing séances. Including one poem under the rubric of Yu Xuanji's name, Wang Duanshu remarked: "There's no need to ask whether this event really occurred or not. But the poem does have an immortal flavor, and doesn't seem like a fabrication by a later person."[131] Alternatively, she employs a Buddhist-inflected argument to defend a story about a late Ming encounter with the ghosts of Tang palace ladies: "All human beings are illusion and shadow, so there's no need to be amazed at these ladies manifesting themselves." But she concludes on stylistic grounds, that the verses these phantoms supposedly authored are probably not authentic: "They seem to have come from a single hand, so I suspect they are forgeries."[132]

By contrast, Wang Shilu (1626–1673), the compiler of the most ambitious early Qing project on women's writings, *The Lamp Oil Collection (Ranzhi ji),* decided to omit all materials from anecdotal or story collections. As the foremost proponent of applying the new methods of evidential scholarship to the history of women's writing, he was particularly rigorous about the nature of his sources and therefore ruled out supernatural authors. He explained:

> As for poems by ghosts or immortals, prior anthologists have sometimes included them in a separate appendix. I consider that many of this type are fictional inventions by men of letters. Making them the subject of witty conversation is permissible, but to record them formally in a silly fashion is nothing but a children's game. Someone remarked that Hong Mai's *Ten Thousand Tang Quatrains* stoops as low as insects and reptiles, not to mention immortals and ghosts. Now Hong Mai needed to fill a quota of ten thousand. Under the circumstances, he had to include superfluous material, but essentially, this is not the proper way to compile a work.[133]

It is not without a pang that he decided to pass up the fine poems by immortals or talented ghosts featured in previous anthologies, but he could not condone their inauthentic provenance. And so he resolves, "despite the brilliant literary quality of such pieces, to sacrifice what I love."[134]

Wang Shilu's exclusionary views on ghost poetry did not prevail among anthologists in his own day or even during the next century. *Complete Poetry of the Tang (Quan Tangshi),* one of the enormous scholarly projects commissioned by the Kangxi emperor, completed in 1707, devotes two chapters to poems written by ghosts, sandwiched between chapters of verse attributed to immortals and divinities and chapters devoted to the poetry of demonic spirits *(guai)* and dreams. (This whole section, as in Qian Qianyi's anthology, comes at the end of the book and follows chapters of verse by Buddhist monks, Daoist adepts, and women.) As anthologists before them had done for centuries, the editors of *Complete Poetry of the Tang* took the ghost entries from compendia such as *Wide Gleanings from the Taiping Era* and *Anecdotes about Tang Poetry,* but the decision to include such a large quantity of supernatural verse clearly accorded both with the imperial demand for encyclopedic comprehensiveness and the contemporary taste for such verse.

The rigid format of *Complete Poetry of the Tang* illustrates forcefully, even comically, the perils of ignoring Wang Shilu's cautionary words. Transposing a poem from its original context, downplaying the anecdotal frame, and adding a title turns a ghost into an author with a proper name. Due to the strict orthographic conventions of this imperial anthology, *The Ghost of the Gorges of Ba (Baxia gui)* or *The Ghost on the Other Side of the Window (Gechuang gui)* is placed in the slot reserved for authors and assumes the same "classificatory function" as the name of any other obscure Tang poet.[135] Accordingly, the proper name of an author no longer refers exclusively to a historical figure who lived and died in his or her own age. Within the pages of the anthology with its strict temporal guidelines, Xi Shi, the legendary beauty of antiquity, for example, is reclassified as a medieval author, based on the apparition of her ghost during the Tang dynasty.

The practice of including ghost poetry in the last section of anthologies classified hierarchically according to the poet's social and moral status continued into the Qianlong period. Both Lu Jianzeng's regional anthology *Shandong Poetry from Our Dynasty* (*Guochao Shanzuo shichao;* preface dated 1758) and Wang Qishu's compendium of women poets *A Nosegay of Verses* (*Xiefang ji;* 1773) conclude with poems attributed to ghosts and immortals. It is significant that the former, a mixed anthology, includes only two examples of supernatural verse, one by a woman, while the latter, which focuses exclusively on female poets, devotes two full chapters to this sort of stuff and is heavily indebted to literature on spirit writing. By this time, however, seventeenth- and eighteenth-century accounts such as *Liaozhai,* Wang Shizhen's *Occasional Chats North of the Pond (Chibei outan),* and Shi Zhenlin's *Random Records of West-Green (Xiqing sanji)* were supplying these anthologists with new source materials to fill these last sections. Only in the nineteenth century are ghosts and immortals finally banished forever from serious anthologies of women's poetry.

The Feminization of the Ghost's Voice in Later Imperial Times

Based on the evidence of poetry anthologies, the increased prominence of women in supernatural literature after the Tang, and the ascendancy of the cult of *qing,* it is possible to detect a feminization of both ghost poetry and ghostly poetry in the late imperial imagination. By the late Ming, most (though not all) of the negative and transgressive potential of poetry responsible for shaping Li He's ghostly reputation had been transferred to the figure of the beautiful woman of talent who dies young. As represented by the myths of the copycat deaths of the female poets and commentators associated with the reception of *Peony Pavilion,* the woman who succumbs to the dangerous allure of reading and writing poetry became the subject of intense cultural fascination in the seventeenth century.[136] Many of the strategies of interpretation originally applied to Li He's life and work were now applied to female poets. Reading a line of verse retrospectively as an unconscious cryptogram, an inauspicious omen of the poet's early death, is common in both biographies and fictional accounts of such women. For instance, Shen Yixiu's biography of her daughter Ye Xiaoluan (1617–1632), a gifted poet who died at sixteen on the eve of her marriage, recounts a line her daughter had composed spontaneously at the age of nine: "When the maple grows cold, the tumbled red withers." "At the time," she writes, "we were delighted with her cleverness and quick reflexes. . . . Sad, isn't it? Who would have thought in the end it would become a prediction of her early death?"[137]

The quasimedical argument that the labor of poetry is injurious to the Heart and other organ systems, and will sap the vitality and reduce the life span of the poet, worked particularly well when applied to women. In the late imperial argument that composing poetry was particularly dangerous to women's health, Furth sees evidence of the view that "a woman's literary productivity" was "deeply incompatible" with "a woman's work of reproduction" because "in the economy of the body the exertion of vital forces in writing / art must be at the expense of generative energies properly focused upon descendents."[138] Because the exchange of poems was the basic medium for conducting a love affair in romantic literature, the composition of verse by unmarried women (or sometimes courtesans) was easily read as a symptom of lovesickness and conflated with various melancholic disorders to which they were purportedly prone. The danger many arch-conservatives saw in a woman's writings circulating outside the household was partly due to fears of the seductive properties of poetry so well documented in fiction and drama; but the dangers of merely reading poetry were considered legion too because they could arouse unfulfillable desires, blocking the circulation of vital energies within the woman's body and afflicting her with a potentially fatal case of static congestion.

In the previous chapter I argued that the representations of the female ghost in the work of certain writers such as Pu Songling became aestheticized as a specific ideal of feminine beauty popular in the late imperial period. In the Chinese literary imagination, the sickly, slender, melancholy woman of beauty and breeding who died an untimely death was likely to have been an avid reader and writer of poetry during her lifetime. In stories that portray her as a revenant, the emergence of her poetic voice is often as crucial to the love affair as the materialization of her bodily form since both physical beauty and literary talent are so strongly linked in the Chinese romantic tradition. One such tale is "Liansuo," the *Liaozhai* tale in which the protagonist heroically offers up his bodily fluids of blood and sperm to resurrect the phantom he loves, thereupon falling ill with what I have diagnosed as a case of male "ghost pregnancy." This most physical of *Liaozhai* stories is also one of the most poetic and helpful for working out the late imperial aesthetic code of the ghostly. The heroine Liansuo is a perfect example of the hyperfeminine ghost type. Thin, shy, refined, mournful, and a devotee of palace-style poetry, she first attracts the attention of her future mate as a disembodied voice.

The tale opens with a description of the scholar's lodgings: "His study looked out onto a vast expanse of wasteland, and outside his window were many ancient graves. At night he could hear the wind whistling in the white poplar trees, the sound like stormy waves. Sitting up past midnight, with candle in hand, he was overcome with desolation" (*LZ* 3. 331). Suddenly outside his window a voice chants two lines of verse:

> In darkest night, a dismal wind
>   blows queerly backward.
> Flitting fireflies tickle the grass,
>   then stick to the curtains. (*LZ* 3. 331)

As he listens, the lines are repeated over and over; the mournful voice is faint and delicate like a woman's. The next morning he looks outside his window, but of course finds no trace of a human footprint.

It is as though the place itself has produced the couplet, the uncanniness of the effect enhanced by the couplet's compulsive repetition. The disembodied lines are both a projection of the loneliness and desolation the scene arouses in him and a response to those emotions. In this context, the opening description functions as a preface to the couplet, which becomes a perfect fusion of scene and emotion, an important aesthetic effect in Chinese poetics. The prose opening seemingly describes an actual scene, but here, folded into the narrative's prose description, the formulaic wind whistling through the white poplars operates as a naturalized allusion, shorthand to signal a ghostly atmosphere and to trigger a certain set of reader's expectations. As Feng Zhenluan notes: "From the very beginning a sorrowful wind fills the page, the gloominess *(yinyou)* is overwhelming" (*LZ* 3. 331).

The funereal sound of the wind the scholar hears alone in the darkness works like the bars of an overture to usher in the mournful melody of the chanting. Wind is then reprised in the couplet's first line, further blurring the distinction between the external description of the scene and the internal words of the poem. There the "dismal wind" blowing "queerly backward" suggests a whirlwind or some other freak wind pattern, a conventional sign of a ghostly presence. In the second line the eerie glow of the flitting fireflies recalls the will-o'-the-wisps or phantom fires that mark a spectral landscape. But the image is also coded as sexual, the nocturnal fireflies that flit through the grass replacing the customary diurnal butterflies and bees of Chinese poetry that frolic amid the flowers, then drunk with pollen fly into the bed curtains. The verbs "tickle" *(re)* and "stick to" *(zhan)* also lend the line a distinct erotic tinge. Taken together, the lines suggest pent-up emotion and unsatisfied desire, especially because there is no progression; the poem is stuck on the first two lines.

Night after night the scholar listens to the same disembodied lines chanted mournfully outside his window. His heart goes out to the author, although he realizes she's a ghost. She proves elusive, however, until one night, waiting for her outside, he recites a couplet of his own to continue the poem:

> What mortal glimpses this hidden desire
> and inner sadness?
> Kingfisher sleeves are thin against the cold
> at moonrise. (*LZ* 3. 331)

When he returns to his study, Liansuo materializes and the story proper begins. Here Pu Songling has adapted a device from conventional romances, in which an exchange of matching poems initiates a love affair. The scholar's couplet, which articulates "what the ghost wants to say yet is too shy to say,"[139] is both an expression of his sympathy for her loneliness and an invitation: if she appears to him, he will lend her his warmth in the cold moonlight. On another level, the linking of verse to complete the quatrain also foreshadows the union of the two lovers and the ghost's successful resurrection.

Liansuo's couplet shows the persuasive influence of Li He. The second line of her couplet bears a strong resemblance to a line in "Mawei Slope" ("Mawei po"), a poem Pu Songling wrote in explicit imitation of Li He's masterpiece, "The Grave of Little Su" ("Su Xiaoxiao mu").[140] Both the original and its imitation conjure up the glamorous ghosts of historical beauties, with Li He's Six Dynasties courtesan, Little Su, recast as the Tang imperial favorite Lady Yang (Yang Guifei) in Pu Songling's rendition. The seven-character line of Liansuo's couplet, "Flitting fireflies tickle the grass, then stick to the curtains" *(liuying re cao fu zhan wei),* simply expands the five-character line, "Damp fireflies stick to the dark grass" *(shiying zhan ancao),* from Pu's "Mawei Slope." In his study of Li He's influence on Pu Songling, Yagi Akiyoshi notes that "damp fireflies," a phrase lifted from another poem of Li He's, is used in several of Pu Songling's collected poems.[141]

The first line of Liansuo's couplet, "In darkest night, a dismal wind blows queerly backward" *(xuanye qifeng que dao chui),* is nearly parallel to Li He's line "Outside the curtains a hard frost flies backward" *(lianwai yanshuang jie dao fei).* Significantly, Li He's poem is entitled "At Night, Sitting and Chanting" ("Ye zuo yin") and depicts a woman alone in the darkness singing about her longing for an absent lover.[142] Other elements in the first line of Liansuo's couplet, such as the "dismal wind" (*qifeng*—a phrase that suggests Li He but does not actually appear in his work) also crop up in two other poems chanted by ghosts in *Liaozhai* ("A river full of wind and moon, cold and dismal"; "Dismal wind and cold rain fill the river town") to suggest the near formulaic character of such verse in Pu Songling's work.[143] We can understand why Feng Zhengluan commented approvingly on Liansuo's couplet: "The verse is ghostly" *(shi you guiqi)* (*LZ* 3. 331).

Particularly instructive on the formulaic nature of ghost poetry is an anecdote from Ji Yun's *Jottings from the Thatched Cottage:* "Before a certain young man's death, he was studying late at night, and in response to the scene a line suddenly came to him: 'When autumn enters the dark window, the lamp grows dim.' Suddenly a friend pushed his way through the curtains. The young man invited him to sit down and recited the line he had just thought up. His friend replied: 'Why don't you match it with the line "When a soul returns to his former town, the moon grows chill and dismal."' The young man asked in surprise: 'Why have you composed this ghostly line?' In a twinkling, the friend vanished whereupon the young man realized that he had not been a living being." Ji Yun explains: "This was because a declining *qi* manifests itself ahead of death, and ghosts, being moved by declining *qi,* respond to it. The young man did indeed die not long thereafter."[144]

The ghostly effect of Liansuo's couplet by no means derives solely from its Li He-like imagery and diction, however. The incessant chanting of the same verse by an unseen stranger throughout the night is an audible sign of a ghost in Chinese literature of the strange. But unlike the example of the Gorges of Ba that I discussed earlier, the compulsion to repeat is thematized as a *literary* problem in Pu Songling's tale. The ghost is forced to keep returning and repeating the couplet not because her bones are unburied but because she cannot finish the quatrain. Poetic composition is implicitly represented as a *cause* of this stasis rather than merely its symptom or manifestation. The scholar's completion of the quatrain is thus indispensable as the first step toward "curing" the ghost, a process of resolution that culminates in her resurrection and marriage.

A Song dynasty anecdote entitled "Continuing a Ghost's Poem" ("Xu guishi") posits a similar poetic ontology for a ghost. The story concerns a monk who composes a line of verse but dies before completing the couplet. "On nights when a dismal wind blew and a cold moon shone," the anecdote goes, this unfinished business compelled him to return as a revenant endlessly intoning the same line of verse, his ghost only nullified and spelled when a listener chanted back a matching line of his own to finish off the couplet.[145] The narrative frame surrounding the monk's verse is too schematic to say with any certainty what is motivating the repetition and return other than failed literary composition, the disturbing asymmetry of a dangling, vaguely inauspicious line.[146] It is clear, however, that as in Liansuo's case, such incompletion is strongly linked to untimely death.

The representation of ghosthood as a colossal case of writer's block translates into a poetic idiom certain definitions of the ghost I have already proposed: a fatal blockage or obstruction, an arrestation of the natural cycles of death and dispersal, the pathological return of something incomplete and unresolved. Following psychoanalytic theory we may say that the compulsive nature of the repetition is a sign of the act of composition's origins in the unconscious—here understood as "the meaning beyond the words" customarily suppressed in a poem, but which continuously erupts in the urgency and frequency of the chanting.

In "Liansuo," the conceit of a phantom's inability to finish a poem—thereby indefinitely prolonging a ghostly existence—is grafted onto the romantic trope of finding a perfect mate through the composition of linked or matching verse. In this gendered context, the repeated failure to continue a verse is a device meant to call attention to what is left unsaid, "the emotion all the more intense for being concealed."[147] Almost caricatured in this formulation is the foundational notion in Chinese poetics that "words don't exhaust meaning," and the concomitant faith that the proper reader will supply what has been left out.[148] The secret desire that is simultaneously inhibited and exposed in the woman's unfinished poem becomes the real underlying meaning, which must be acknowledged in any male response.

The romantic play of these issues is articulated in a Tang tale about an exceptionally beautiful girl who is always composing verse, but never gets further than the first two lines. When asked to explain this enigmatic behavior, she replies: "I can't help it. I'm entwined with feelings of longing; by the time I've reached the end of a couplet, I've lost my train of thought and nothing follows."[149] A handsome young suitor applies for her hand. Her father refuses at first because he wants to marry his daughter to an official, but he finally agrees on the condition that the young man is able to continue one of his daughter's poems and "fulfill her meaning" *(cheng qi yi)*.

The young man easily succeeds—it is the girl herself who is the judge, pronouncing, "This is the husband Heaven bore for me"—and she becomes his bride.

In such stories the exchange of verse performs a practical role in the plot to bring the lovers together; the initial couplet or quatrain usually encodes a symbolic message; the response signals that the message has been received and understood. But an important function of such poetic exchanges is not only symbolic—dependent on the words and imagery (the content) of the poems—but analogic—understood as an act that is performed. Matching a poem's rhymes and making two disparate entities formally parallel and coherent in meaning, corresponds analogically to the pattern of linking two people in marriage.[150] The idea underlying all romance that a perfect, predestined mate exists somewhere, just waiting to be found, also has a counterpart in a poetic theory, voiced by Su Shi, that every line thought up in the world, no matter how obscure, can be perfectly matched.[151] It is for these reasons, that the poetic exchange in "Liansuo" can be seen as enacting the plot in miniature.

But in "Liansuo," the romance always remains subsumed under the sign of the ghost, once again definable as a culturally designated "hyperfeminine." The plaint of the solitary woman so commonly featured in palace-style poetry is transposed in a ghost story like this from the boudoir to the outer reaches of the graveyard, thereby intensifying the familiar trope of feminine loneliness. As a phantom heroine sings plaintively in *Mistress and Maid (Jiao Hong ji),* a late Ming play influenced by *Peony Pavilion:* "This new bout of lovesickness *(gui bing)* is even worse than when I was alive."[152]

During the late Ming and early Qing, the always influential theory of poetry as the involuntary outlet for the author's suppressed emotion and pent-up resentment took on new importance to support women writing poetry. To justify women's composition of poetry as a natural and irrepressible act, Ming and Qing female writers not infrequently invoked Han Yu's famous dictum, "All things not at peace will cry out," which likened the human need to express feelings in writing to the natural force that impels plants to rustle in the wind or metal to ring when struck.[153] In his 1677 biography of a beautiful girl who drowned herself, You Tong did indeed borrow Han Yu's theory to account for the posthumous poetry written by her spirit: "Why should we marvel that she would project her spiritual glow and glamorous shadow as she amused herself in the mortal world in order to release her 'cry of not being at peace?'"[154] Or as the late Ming poet Chen Zilong imagined in his "Song of Purple Jade's Ghost" ("Ziyu ge"): "Human sorrow is truly to be pitied, but when will a ghost's sorrow ever end?"[155] For male literati, female ghost poetry has the potential to become the most involuntary and the most moving of all writing. As Liansuo explains to the scholar in *Liaozhai,* she is so lonely in the desolate wastes of the underworld that she has composed the couplet to express her hidden anguish and resentment. Her poem is a transposition of the ghostly wail, the pure articulation of sorrow.

3

Ghosts and Historical Time

We cannot repeat enough that the dead,
for whom history mourns, were once living.
—PAUL RICOEUR, *Time and Narrative*

IN THE PREVIOUS chapter I explored how the ghost was used in Chinese literature to stage a confrontation with mortality. Endowing the ghost with a voice capable of expressing subjective emotion, primarily through the vehicle of lyric poetry, opened a window onto the unknowable: what would it feel like to be dead, to be on the other side? Accordingly, these ghost stories represent death as an interior state of exile in which suffering and longing are intensified rather than annihilated. The paradigmatic sites of such stories are the cemetery, the unmarked grave, uninhabited wasteland; the paradigmatic poetic genres involved are the burial song and the auto-dirge. Only when the grievances fueling the phantom's manifestation are properly redressed can the emotional stasis of ghosthood be ended and the dead soul finally enter a cycle of rebirth or dissolve into silence and nothingness.

This chapter takes up another major concern of the ghost tale: not the self's experience of death, but the passage of collective time, the flow of human history. The themes of these two chapters are separate but clearly related. The central events in the Chinese construction of history are the rise and fall of dynasties. This formulation structures time linearly, imposing a clear sense of chronological progression and order. Because Chinese history is simultaneously conceptualized as the repetition of a single key pattern, the resulting grand narrative is also strongly cyclical, situating each collapse and conquest within a naturalized moral framework.[1] What Paul Ricoeur calls "historical time," which mediates between "the lived time" of the individual and "the cosmic time" of the universe,[2] was traditionally fashioned in China through the intermeshing of these two competing schemes.

As Jonathan Hay has reminded us, *wang*, the word most often used of a dynastic demise, means "to be lost," "to perish," "to die." Hay helpfully defines the concept as "the loss attendant upon death," and he consequently looks to late imperial death ritual as a way to comprehend the responses of Ming loyalists to the Qing conquest.[3] *Wang* can be applied equally to the demise of a dynasty or to the death of an individual; likewise, the term *bian* (change, transformation) becomes a euphemism for either the end of a human life or the destruction of a state. Without anthropomorphizing history in an overt or direct way, the polyvalence of such terms points to the powerful analogy between dynastic fall and individual death upon which the ghost story about historical time is predicated.

This chapter examines a specific type of ghost story, the historical ghost tale, by which I mean a ghost story about a traumatic historical event rather than a problem of individual mortality. The event is usually of a political nature, especially dynastic fall and conquest. This kind of historical narrative differs fundamentally from most of the historical fiction and drama so popular in late imperial times.[4] Although the historical ghost tale resembles a historical novel or play in attempting to reenact the past in the present, the ghost story never sets out to erase the difference between past and present through a vivid mimesis of bygone historical events. The ghost story about history is always explicitly framed through the perceptions of a living observer, who is placed in the position of contemplating the past reanimated in front of him. The narrative thus does not recreate the past in the present but dramatizes the present's encounter with the past. The ghost story about history never lets go of "the pastness of the past"; in the foreground is always the self-conscious awareness of loss, of a temporal distance that cannot be bridged, however much it is desired.[5]

In the historical ghost story, the past is always represented in some form as a loss to be mourned and lamented. Especially in tales that reflect upon violent events of the recent past, the course of history becomes the trauma that produces the ghost(s). This chapter focuses upon the cataclysmic turnover of the seventeenth century—the fall of the Ming and the Manchu conquest that established a new dynasty—and how the memory of these events was reconfigured and worked through in the early Qing ghost story. I first sketch the historical ghost tale's literary genealogy, thematic preoccupations, and spatial imagination. Next, I take up the legend of Lin Siniang, a famous early Qing tale haunted by the fall of the Ming, which circulated in multiple seventeenth-century versions. I argue that this set of narratives about the recent past participates in the cultural work of mourning, enabling the threatening memory of the old dynasty to resurface, to be tamed and rehabilitated, and finally put to rest and purged. The final part of the chapter deals with one exceptionally powerful ghost tale about the government suppression of a local rebellion during the early Qing. This tale, Pu Songling's "Gongsun Jiuniang," thwarts the easy panaceas proposed by the Lin Siniang narratives toward rehabilitating the victims of history and easing painful memories; instead, the historical ghost story is enlisted to capture the singular horror of this particular tragedy and the individual sufferers who must never be forgotten.

The *Huaigu* Ghost Story

There are many forms of rumination on history in Chinese literature, but the mode that shows the greatest affinity to the ghost tale is *huaigu*, "poetic reflections stimulated by visits to historic sites," to borrow Hans Frankel's formulation of this particular sort of "past-oriented poetry."[6] Such visits, Frankel and other scholars agree, can be imaginary as well as real, but the premise of a visit somewhere is important; what distinguishes the *huaigu* mode is the spatialization of time, the mise-en-scène of history envisaged in a specific place.[7] In ghost stories about encountering the past, it is most commonly the mortal visitor's presence at a historical site and the feelings the place stirs in him that provoke the apparition. Owen has outlined three of *huaigu*'s basic elements: "an ancient site encountered, the poet stirred by human loss in contrast to nature's cyclical continuity, and the outlines of absent shapes that hold the poet's attention and keep him from leaving."[8] It is not much of an exaggeration to say that the ghost story's fantasy of history is scripted according to just such a scenario.

The ghost story about historical time owes to *huaigu* not merely its setting (an abandoned, often ruined site), orientation (contemplation of the past), and mood (melancholy, sensuality, nostalgia), but something even more fundamental: the impulse to recall what has vanished from a place, to fill in what is missing or concealed from view at a spot. This emphasis on the imaginative work of memory, on recalling what is no longer visible, is particularly striking in the earliest instances of a recognizable *huaigu* sensibility. Both these well-known examples appear in formative Western Han sources; both examples take the form of an anecdote framing a poem whose meaning would be unintelligible without the anecdote. In the Mao commentary to the *Book of Songs,* a former high official of the fallen state of Zhou journeys past the site of the old capital and grieves to find that any remnants of the ancestral temples and palace buildings are completely buried beneath a thick growth of millet. Unable to tear himself away, he composes the following lament:

> There the millet is lush,
> There the grain is sprouting.
> I walk here with slow, slow steps,
> My heart shaken within me.
> Those who know me
> Would say my heart is grieved;
> Those who know me not
> Would ask what I seek here.
> Gray and everlasting Heaven—
> What man did this?[9]

In the version in Sima Qian's *Records of the Historian,* the narrative logic is the same: only the place, the grain, and the historical actors differ. The site is now the former Shang capital; the ruins are covered by a crop of wheat; and the poet is a prince of the overthrown Shang royal house. The main structural difference between the two is that Sima Qian spells out the scene's emotional affect in the anecdotal frame rather than in the poem: "Distressed, the prince could neither cry out nor weep like a woman. He thus composed the poem "Ears of Wheat" to express his feelings. . . . When the Shang people heard the poem, they all shed tears."[10] A perfect illustration of Sima Qian's theory of literary composition, the prince's verse is the product of pent-up anguish, a surrogate for tears. In this economy of sentiment, the poem operates as an ideal currency of exchange: in the response of the listeners, the grief initially displaced and transferred to the poem reverts back into tears.

Sima Qian's account refers to the abandoned capital as a *xu* (ruin), but there is no description, either in the frame or the poem, of the ruined buildings that once occupied the spot. This omission leads Wu Hung to assert that in these earliest *huaigu,* "it is the *site,* not dilapidated structures or artifacts, that crystallizes memory." Because there are no "external signs" marking the spot, a *xu* acquires "a subjective reality": "It is the visitor's recognition of a *xu*" that makes it "a site of memory."[11] It is precisely the concealment of these external signs of dynastic fall that lends the spectacle of ordinary fields of wheat and millet such extraordinary pathos. As the final resting place of a perished state, the unmarked ruin here, its architectural traces buried beneath vegetation, shares some of the same unsettling associations as an unmarked grave. Indeed, the root meanings for *xu* in early Han dictionaries are "a large mound" and "emptiness,"[12] both of which suggest a *xu*'s affinity with a graveyard. The unmarked status of the site in these earliest *huaigu* narratives is also what produces the need to commemorate the spot with a poem, and, for Sima Qian at least, to include the verse and the scene contexualizing it in his history.

As the meditation on the past developed into a poetic topos proper during the Six Dynasties and became codified as a poetic practice during the early Tang, the composition of *huaigu* began to find its way into "unofficial history" *(yeshi),* into the tales of the marvelous that proliferated in the eighth and ninth centuries. In such tales the *huaigu* impulse so emotionally charged in the originary Han examples could be considerably lightened, transforming the encounter with the past into a literary game. A perfect illustration is "Lu Qiao" (*TPGJ* 343. 2717–2718), a Tang ghost story set in the year 806, but written at least fifty years later:

> In the beginning of the Yuanhe period [806–821], there was a top degree graduate by the name of Lu Qiao. He was fond of composing poetry, for which he had accrued some praise. His home was in Danyang; his estate there was graced with terraces and ponds, and it was hailed as a scenic spot. Lu's family was wealthy and enjoyed a reputation for hospitality.
>
> One evening, as a refreshing breeze was blowing and the moon shone bright, there came a knock on Lu's gate. He went to see who it was and found a gentleman clad in a very impressive cap and robe, with a distinguished and graceful bearing. Lu invited him in, and the gentleman engaged him in conversation so brilliant and delightful that Lu was quite astonished. Lu esteemed him highly, considering no man his equal, and inquired his name.
>
> "Shen Yue," replied the gentleman. "I've heard that you are skilled at poetry, and so I've come to call upon you." (*TPGJ* 343. 2717)

Now Lu is truly astounded, for Shen Yue is the name of a major poet and statesman of the Liang dynasty (one of the short-lived southern regimes of the Six Dynasties) who died in the year 513. He recovers his aplomb quickly, however, and when Shen

Yue asks "Do you know my friend Grand Councilor Fan Yun?" Lu replies matter-of-factly: "Well, I've often read the *History of the Liang Dynasty*, so I've long been acquainted with his name."

The past has literally come knocking on the protagonist's door. This is the stuff of wish-fulfillment (or satire), especially when a renowned literary figure alludes to one's reputation as a poet. Shen Yue's ghost politely claims that his host's literary talent is what has drawn him hither, but the real clue is unobtrusively planted in the text: Danyang, the location of Lu Qiao's estate, outside present-day Nanjing. Shen Yue was governor of Danyang at one time, as was his first political and literary patron, the prince of Jingling, before him. These facts are easily available in Shen Yue's biography in the official *History of the Liang Dynasty (Liangshu)*, a book which Lu admits he frequently perused. As grand councilor of the Left, Shen Yue is yoked together with Fan Yun, the grand councilor of the Right, into a single biography in this work. In fact, with one notable exception, every detail the story provides about Shen Yue and his circle is lifted from this joint biography.[13] Read alongside the pertinent passages from the official history, then, the tale reveals itself to be a scholastic joke in which history books are imagined to come alive.

But the *huaigu* impulse that must have partly inspired the story in the first place is still worked into the narrative and expressed in poetic form. Shen Yue summons to the gathering the ghost of his ten-year-old son, whom he is teaching to write poetry. Shen Yue explains that he named the boy Scholarly Legacy (Qingxiang) because "I wanted to pass on my learning through him. Unfortunately, he predeceased me." The existence of such a son is the only significant detail about Shen Yue in the story not corroborated by the *History of the Liang Dynasty*. As an illustration of the boy's precocity and his own pedagogical methods, Shen Yue recounts this anecdote:

> This lad was with me and the grand councilor recently when we passed by the old palace, so I set him the task of composing "a lament on the past" *(ganjiu)*. He picked up his pen and was done in an instant. The result is really quite respectable.
>
> And so he recited the poem:
>
> By the old rivers of the Six Dynasties,
> how many centuries since their rise and fall?
> Their splendor now turned to desolation,
> Court assemblies were such hubbub before.
> A nocturnal moon on green-glazed water;
> spring breezes from a sky of eggshell blue.
> Grieved by time, I cherish the past *(huaigu)*,
> and shed tears before the capital gates.

Here we have a textbook example of a lament on the past, once it has become a conventional form of occasional verse. One reason this schoolboy exercise passes muster is because it sets forth with admirable simplicity a set of formulaic options for a *huaigu* as practiced in the Tang: the premise of a visit to an abandoned palace from the Southern dynasties; spring, the season of nature's yearly renewal, whose beauty drives home the absence of the grand mortals who once graced this spot; the contrast drawn accordingly between the permanence of the landscape and the transience of political power and human existence; and the poet's direct acknowledgment in the poem of the feelings the scene arouses in him, registered in outward displays of grief and tears.

The piquancy of this embedded moment is that it allows readers to imagine a *huaigu* on the demise of the Six Dynasties being recited posthumously by a major figure from the Six Dynasties. But the fantasy is undercut by the fact that the lament's composition is attributed to a representative from that dynasty too young to have really experienced that splendid past and too green to possibly understand the full import of his words. And the poem's affect is diluted further because the only emotional reaction to the sentiments voiced in the verse is postponed for several paragraphs. "'It's been four hundred years since the Liang dynasty,' sighed Shen Yue. 'The scenery, moon, and breeze are no different from then, but the people have all been replaced. How could we not be sad?'"

Lu Qiao himself objects to the blatant anachronism involved in the boy's *huaigu:* although ostensibly composed and recited by Liang dynasty ghosts, the poem is in the modern Tang style of regulated verse, which—Lu correctly points out—was not invented until the beginning of his own dynasty.[14] Shen Yue defends himself that since "the poem was composed in the modern age, it's written in the modern style." The twentieth-century critic Qian Zhongshu characterizes this exchange as a ploy meant "to deflect criticism and plug a hole in the argument."[15] But especially in conjunction with the earlier hint about the *History of the Liang Dynasty,* the tale's deliberate self-exposure of its own anachronism is surely a knowing wink to amuse the educated reader, whose knowledge of history is similarly derived from books.

This tale acknowledges the paradoxes involved in the ghost story's view of historical time. On the one hand, the paradigm advanced is of time constantly changing, registered through the evolution of literary forms. "Ghosts too keep up with the times" is how one eighteenth-century account refutes the frequently voiced objection to pre-Tang spirits composing regulated verse.[16] On the other hand, also offered is the opposite paradigm of time as frozen at the moment of death so that the ten-year-old boy never grows any older, even though 400 years have passed. Any pathos evoked by the *huaigu* in "Lu Qiao" derives from our awareness of the boy's having predeceased his father (reinforced by the irony of the boy's name, "Scholarly Legacy") and remaining for eternity a child doomed never to reach adulthood, a precocious poet doomed never to achieve maturity.

The Return of the Palace Lady

In "Lu Qiao" the ruins of the former dynasty are still implicit and concealed, remaining outside the story's visual frame of reference, whose narrative action is set instead on the grand estate of the present that has replaced the past. In both the *huaigu* poem chanted by Shen Yue's ghost and his flashback contextualizing it, the ruins of the old palace are still shadowy and unelaborated in the manner of the "originary" Han *huaigu.* But a poetics of visible ruins, particularly centered around the topos of a ruined palace, sometimes set within a ruined city, occupies a major position in post-Han *huaigu* literature. As the embodiment of both the splendor and the fall of dynasties, the ruined palace came to be signified by a set of standardized poetic images: vegetation run rampant, growing over collapsed or deserted buildings, moss creeping over and eroding every surface, will-o'-the-wisps, ill-omened wild beasts and nocturnal birds scampering in and out at will. The "powdered bones" and "buried fragrance" of the ladies who once inhabited this space are as much a staple fixture of the *huaigu* as these other images of defilement, decay, and abandonment. From Bao Zhao's rhapsody "The Weed-covered City" ("Wucheng fu") to the last act of Kong Shangren's *Peach Blossom Fan (Taohua shan),* laments for the grandeur of fallen dynasties inevitably conjure up the "faces of alabaster and vermilion lips" that "lie buried in these hidden stones."[17] It is this, in part, that makes the palace lady a natural magnet for ruin-sentiment in China and lends the *huaigu* poems on ruined palaces their sensual quality. And it is this, in part, that makes the return of the palace lady the most persistent kind of ghost story told about dynastic fall.

This type of tale also begins in the Tang, typically targeting the Southern dynasties or the short-lived Sui dynasty; the High Tang period, viewed retrospectively after the An Lushan rebellion that nearly destroyed the dynasty and permanently weakened it, also proved a favorite setting for such stories. In subsequent periods, return-of-the-palace-lady narratives were told about the falls of later dynasties, including the Song, Jin, Yuan, and Ming. Mei Dingzuo's *Records of Talented Ghosts* includes at least ten such stories and Feng Menglong's compendium *Anatomy of Love* begins its chapter on ghosts with a subsection devoted to "Famous Palace Revenants." Tales of encounters with the ghosts of palace ladies tend to evoke bittersweet nostalgia for a vanished glory; the mortal men who exchange poems with such glamorous ladies and sometimes bed them are granted the pleasure of possessing this past, if only fleetingly.

In the first story in the ghost chapter of *Anatomy of Love,* two friends are banqueting together one spring in the vicinity of Jinling (present-day Nanjing), when the misty southern riverscape suddenly clears.[18] The stereotypical elements for a *huaigu* are all here: site (a former capital of the Southern Dynasties, particularly Jinling); season (springtime); and occasion (a literati gathering with a panoramic view). Naturally, the two men begin to sigh over the flourishing and decay of dynasties. Just as we expect them to break into verse, peals of girlish laughter interrupt their reverie. A pretty maidservant suddenly appears and leads them to meet the ghost of Xi Shi, the palace lady whose fabulous beauty helped topple the ancient southern state of Wu. The *huaigu* impulse has magically conjured up Xi Shi, whose specter assumes carnal form to fulfill the men's ardent wishes for a meeting with the past. (A second palace-lady phantom conveniently materializes too so that men and women in the story are evenly matched.) In this streamlined and lighthearted fantasy, the men's frolic with the palace-lady revenants neatly replaces the production of any actual *huaigu* poem.

In other narratives, however, the ghost of the palace lady herself composes the lament for the past. One such story is "Teng Mu's Drunken Excursion to the Jujing Gardens" ("Teng Mu zuiyou Jujingyuan ji") from *New Tales Told by Lamplight*. In this influential tale set in 1314, a young poet named Teng Mu finds himself one moonlight night on the grounds of the old imperial gardens outside the former Southern Song capital of Hangzhou. "At the time it was already forty years after the fall of the Song. The garden buildings and terraces, such as the Hall of Assembled Fragrance, the Pavilion of Pure Radiance, and the Tower of Azure Light, all lay in ruins. Only the Cerulean Ford's West Porch still stood intact."[19] Before the poet has a moment to think up a *huaigu* to express the feelings the scene arouses in him, however, a palace lady materializes and does so for him, prefacing her poem with a sigh: "West Lake and the mountains surrounding it persist as in the past. The scenery remains the same, but the times have changed. How it makes one feel the sorrow of 'There the Millet is Lush!'" Then she chants this verse:

> The lakeside gazebo in the garden is so fine,
>   I remember my former haunts again.
> Here we asked for songs set to "Trees of Jade";
>   Here watched dances to the tune of "Lost Frontiers."
> Flowers still greet carriages along narrow paths,
>   Willows still brush boats on deep ponds.
> People of the past are all dead and gone—
>   With whom can I talk of romance? [20]

He rises to the obvious invitation by matching her poem, and they become lovers. Later she reveals that she had once served in the palace of Emperor Lizong (r. 1225–1265) of the Southern Song. After her death at the tender age of twenty-two she was buried beside the palace gardens. Thus the imperial ruins that the young poet finds himself in that night are also quite literally the palace lady's burial grounds and the site of her former pleasures, which her ghost still remembers and haunts.

The palace lady's opening poem weaves in two allusions to old tunes as instant markers of *huaigu* sentiment. "Trees of Jade in the Rear Courtyard" is the name of a song composed by the last emperor of the Chen, itself the last of the Southern dynasties before the Sui's reunification of the empire. The tune title immediately evokes whiffs of court decadence and imminent dynastic fall, neatly combining the twin functions of blame and prediction. A famous quatrain by the Tang poet Du Mu portrays the irony of singing girls continuing to perform "Trees of Jade" after the Chen dynasty's demise without comprehending the tune's deeper significance.[21] The palace-lady revenant, however, understands only too well the meaning of this allusion and the parallel reference to the tunes of "Lost Frontiers" ("Liangzhou[a]").

During the High Tang, "Liangzhou[a]" was a title of a grand song-and-dance performed at court; written interchangeably with homophonous characters, it denotes a tune of Central Asian origin from the northwest border region of Liangzhou[b], also popular at court. The awareness that the capital would be sacked, the emperor exiled, and his consort executed during the An Lushan rebellion again turns these melodies into signifiers for insouciant splendor encrypting its own destruction, for the self-conscious imposition of present knowledge on past history. Du Mu's singing girls are ignorant of history; the palace lady's return means she is not.[22]

These allusions are *meant* to be clichés. The point is that while the tale is set in a specific year, and situated among the vestiges of a specific regime and dynasty, the nostalgia that produces the ghost and which she vocalizes is also a free-floating one, independent of any particular historical moment. The structure of allusion, which draws analogies between past occurrence, present usage, and future repetition is not linear but circular. In this, allusion is the perfect literary figure for nostalgia, especially if we agree with Rey Chow's proposal that nostalgia may be "a feeling looking for an object," which moves in a "loop" rather than in "a straight line."[23] The circular syntax of a *huaigu* utterance therefore is perfectly encapsulated in the palace lady's opening couplet, when she says: "I remember again." Or as a poem attributed to the apparition of a Song palace lady in another Ming story puts it: "A new romance is a bygone romance."[24] In *huaigu*'s loop, one dynastic fall quickly rewinds and fast forwards into another. These stock allusions in the story jumble all former dynasties together as the specificity of history dissolves into the general terrain of the past.

In Li Zhen's *More Tales Told by Lamplight (Jiandeng yuhua),* published around 1433, two *huaigu* poems are cited in full at the very beginning of one story, "An Autumn Night's Visit to the Mandolin Pavilion" ("Qiuxi fang Pipa ting ji"), to illustrate the dashing young hero's poetic talent. In this tale set in the early Ming, these *huaigu* verses (with a somewhat intensified ghostly inflection) and the hero's fondness for touring ancient scenic sites to mourn the past are all it takes to spark a ghostly apparition when his travels bring him one night to the Mandolin Pavilion in Jiangxi province.[25] (The growth in tourist travel during the Ming was surely an important stimulus for the historical site-based ghost story in the two *Lamplight* collections.)[26] The hero thinks he is retracing the steps of the exiled Tang poet Bai Juyi and imagines that he overhears the ghostly strains of the tune performed by the old courtesan from the capital immortalized in Bai's famous ballad "The Mandolin Song" ("Pipa xing"). But he has gotten the plot and the dynasty wrong: the melody turns out to be sung by the much more recent ghost of a fourteenth-century palace lady buried in the vicinity. No matter. His seeking of the past still earns him the reward of her favors. This time the palace lady reveals herself to be a casualty of the civil wars at the break-up of the Yuan dynasty, a concubine of the warlord Chen Youliang, a contender for the throne, whom Zhu Yuanzhang had defeated when he succeeded in founding the Ming dynasty and crowning himself emperor.

"An Autumn's Night Visit," like "Teng Mu's Drunken Excursion" and several other stories in this vein, features an exchange of poems between the revenant and the mortal. (Typically, the lady initiates the sequence with a *huaigu,* while the man's poetic response primarily expresses his amorous interest in her.) The matching of poems in such tales clearly follows the logic of the romance I discussed in Chapter 2, in which linking verse serves both as verbal foreplay for the couple and an analogy for mating.[27] But in the *huaigu* ghost story, the act of matching poems also has an additional genealogy and symbolic function. One of the basic forms of poetic practice in late imperial times was imitating poems by dead masters. Such imitations were not only regarded as pedagogical exercises in the mastery of poetic craft but also as creative acts establishing a spiritual identification with specific past poets. Impressionistic copying of a predecessor's style or a poem was one possible form of imitation, but so was formally matching rhyme and meter as a response to a particular poem, allowing the later poet to participate in a game of communication across the borders of time and space, life and death. (In fact, "An Autumn's Night Visit" begins with the hero matching a poem by Sadula, a famous Mongol writer from the previous dynasty.)[28] This second mode is of particular relevance to the return of the palace-lady story, in which the fantasy of realizing a spiritual affinity with the past is first executed in poetic form, then repeated in sexual form.

The palace-lady ghost story frankly acknowledges the erotics underlying the proverbial Chinese veneration of the past. In *Remembrances,* Owen argues that as early as Confucius, the past became viewed as "an absence and an object of desire that had to be earnestly sought, its remains recovered, its losses lamented," a development he characterizes as pivotal in Chinese civilization.[29] The palace-lady ghost story nakedly represents the present's insistent backwards gaze as masculine, the yearned-for elusive past as feminine. The palace lady's chanting of a *huaigu* to initiate the present's amorous embrace of the past clearly reveals this desire. But the blatant wish-fulfillment involved in the lady's instantaneous materialization and solicitation of the earnest seeker of the past also suggests certain Ming and Qing fantasies of obsessive collecting, in which an object is moved by a connoisseur's appreciation and comes to him of his or her own accord, often in human form.[30]

The palace lady is not the only female figure to return to a destroyed historical site in a ghost story. Others include chaste martyrs and famous courtesans, the latter extending to a Hong Kong sing-song girl of the 1930s who returns as a revenant to the concrete highways and high rises of 1980s Hong Kong in Stanley Kwan's film *Rouge (Yanzhi kou).*[31] There are also tales about encountering the spirits of male heroes slain on the battlefield or in political purges.[32] The palace lady, however, is the most ubiquitous and important. One reason is the incorporation of the palace lady's bodily remains into the standard blazon of ruins in *huaigu* poetry. Hence the ghost story's frequent situation of her burial site alongside or amid the ruins. (Sometimes her tomb or her shrine *is* the major historical site in the tale, a focus pointing to the duality of a tomb as architectural remains of the past and as the dwelling place of the deceased.) The blurring of the boundary between the palace lady's physical remains and the geography of the site helps inspire the fantasy of her ghost reciprocating the tourist's own desire for "a spiritual meeting" with the past, as played out in the *Lamplight* stories above. Besides adhering to the customary logic of ghost narratives, the grounding of her burial at the site haunted by her spirit may also owe something to the practice of having palace ladies put to death and buried with their lord so as "to accompany him in death [*xun*]."[33] Other explanations include the palace lady's inevitable involvement in the historical paradigm of the last decadent ruler, whose overindulgence in carnal pleasures is blamed for bringing down his kingdom. (In one of the ghost stories about the ancient beauty Xi Shi, her specter appears a millennium later to refute the charge that she had brought about the kingdom of Wu's downfall.)[34]

Perhaps the most interesting reason the palace lady is so frequently invoked in ghost stories about historical time is because her person easily serves as an emblem of the past's inaccessibility. As a denizen of the inner quarters of the harem, the palace lady was supposed to be always off-limits and guarded from male view. Because of the palace's surplus of beautiful women, she was imagined to be deprived of male attention even as she was kept under constant surveillance. Entering a ruler's harem, even as a mere attendant or performer, was often regarded as a species of death because it cut the woman off from the ordinary world. Theoretically, death ought to erect another barrier around the palace lady, to put her still further out of a living protagonist's reach. But in such tales, death is represented as what *frees* the palace lady from the rigid confines of the palace and enables her to choose her contemporary lover.[35] The return of the palace lady holds out the fantasy of overcoming the past's inaccessibility, but in the end she is always made to vanish again, putting the past out of reach once more.[36] This is by no means always the case with the late imperial scholar-ghost romance, but it is always true in ghost tales about historical time—the gap between past and present can never be permanently closed, even in the imagination.

"Lin Siniang"

It is not surprising that "Lin Siniang," the most famous ghost story about the fall of the Ming, involves the return of a palace lady. What is more unexpected is that this tale is set in Shandong province, in Qingzhou prefecture. (Qingzhou is located on the main east-west road leading from the coast to the provincial capital of Ji'nan; see fig. 5). This means the tale is set in the North, but not, as one might expect, in the imperial capital Beijing, where the Chongzhen emperor hung himself in 1644 after Li Zicheng's rebel forces took the city, signaling the "official" demise of the Ming dynasty. When the Manchus turned around and occupied Beijing, making it the capital of their new Qing dynasty, they reconstructed their own Forbidden City on the ruins of the old Ming palace compound.[37]

Nor does "Lin Siniang" take place in Nanjing, another seemingly obvious location

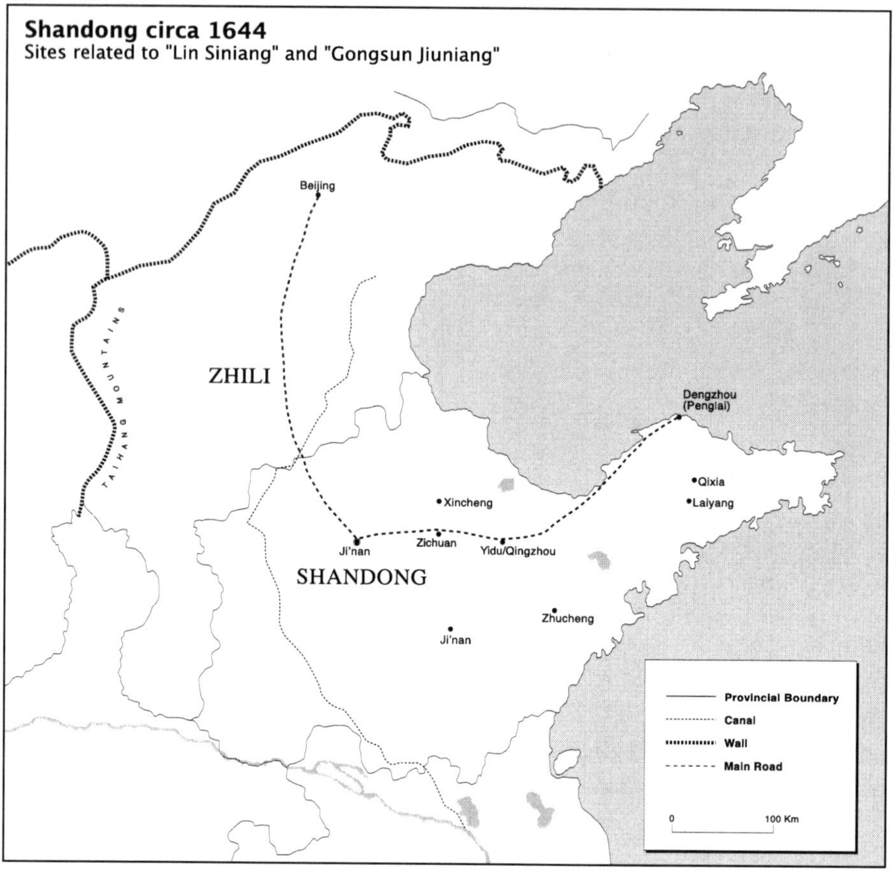

FIGURE 5 Map of Shandong province showing sites related to "Lin Siniang" and "Gongsun Jiuniang," including the location of Qingzhou during the Ming Qing transition; the proximity of Zichuan, Xincheng, and Zhucheng to Yidu; and the distance from Laiyang and Qixia to Zichuan and Ji'nan and Beijing. Courtesy of Roberto Marques.

for a ghost story of this sort. The original Ming capital had been in Nanjing before it was moved to Beijing in the fifteenth century. Nanjing was again made the capital of the short-lived Southern Ming regime and then destroyed when the Manchus conquered the city in 1645. Unlike its counterpart in Beijing, the old Ming palace in Nanjing was never reoccupied and rebuilt by the Qing but was left to molder until all vestiges of the ruins gradually disappeared.[38] As the former capital of previous short-lived Southern dynasties, Nanjing had long been a favorite subject for *huaigu*. The location of the Southern Ming's capital in Nanjing, a site already predetermined as a byword for splendor, decadence, and transience, thus offered multiple historical ironies, which Kong Shangren, for one, brilliantly exploited in centering *Peach Blossom Fan,* his drama of the Southern Ming's collapse, in this city.

The eastern region of Shandong, where Qingzhou is located, did suffer more than its share of violence and turmoil during the Ming-Qing turnover, however. Raids of Manchu troops on Qingzhou probably began by 1638. Although the Ming fell in 1644, first to Li Zicheng's rebel forces, and then to the Manchu conquerors, the region continued to be wracked by periodic popular uprisings against the Qing over the next two decades, only fully ending in 1662.[39] But "Lin Siniang" involves no famous atrocity or pivotal event in Shandong on the order of the Manchus' terrible massacre of Yangzhou as set down in "A Record of Ten Days in Yangzhou" ("Yangzhou shiri ji"). One important reason is that the ghost story lies at the opposite end of a spectrum from an eyewitness account like the "Record," which is almost journalistic in its emphasis on the vivid unfolding of chaotic events. Narrated in the first person, with virtually no tense markers, no structuring devices such as foreshadowing and echoing, and no authorial reflections with hindsight, "A Record of Ten Days in Yangzhou" seems to take place in the present. Such an eyewitness account attempts to depict the direct experience of traumatic events. The historical ghost story, on the other hand, is a new or secondary narrative that represents an attempt to come to terms with the recurrent *memory* of such trauma. This is why in a ghost story dealing with recent history, the haunting is almost always set some years after the precipitating events. In other words, if we understand a ghostly manifestation in a Freudian sense as "the return of the repressed," then enough time must have elapsed for something to be repressed and then resurface.[40]

Alternatively, if we adopt the insights of recent theorists of trauma, we may understand the interval of time separating the haunting from the traumatic event in the historical ghost story, not as "repression"—the suppression of unwanted feelings about an event which later provokes a repetition of the experience—but as "latency"—disassociation from an event as it occurs, so that the forgetting and repetition is built into the event and is what constitutes the experience of trauma. As Cathy Caruth explains: "It is this inherent latency of the event that paradoxically explains the peculiar temporal structure, the belatedness, of historical experience: since the traumatic event is not experienced as it occurs, it is fully evident only in connection with another place, and in another time."[41]

Qingzhou did, nonetheless, have a strong territorial claim on the ghostly imagination during the early Qing as the site of the ruined palace of the Ming prince of Heng.[42] The first prince of Heng, a son of the Chenghua emperor, was granted a fief in Qingzhou in 1487. In 1499 the prince built himself a palace in Yidu city, the seat of the prefectural government in Qingzhou, which he modeled after a princely residence in Beijing. The House of Heng remained enfeoffed in Qingzhou until the fall of the Ming in 1644–1645, when the palace in Yidu was destroyed and the last prince was taken north as a captive or killed.[43] The ruins inspired poetic laments by several Ming loyalists based in Shandong during the early Qing, including the famous Gu Yanwu.[44] Gu penned his *huaigu* on the prince of Heng's palace in 1658 when he passed through the city during his sojourn in the region.[45] The site remained a Qingzhou landmark throughout the next centuries, even as the last physical traces of the palace gradually disappeared. Today, all that survive of the palace are two stone entryways *(shifang)*, which have been incorporated into a public park in the modern city of Qingzhou.[46]

At least six accounts of "Lin Siniang" have come to light in late seventeenth-century sources alone; this suggests the extent to which the story struck a chord among conversationalists, readers, writers, and editors of the early to mid-Kangxi period (1662–1700). This group includes two cohorts: some were immediate members of the conquest-generation, but a larger group were those who came of age in the early Kangxi era:

(1) a tale by Pu Songling (1640–1715) in *Liaozhai.* Although the collection was compiled over a period of thirty years roughly from 1670–1700, this tale is surely an early rather than a late work.[47]

(2) a tale by Wang Shizhen (1643–1711), recorded in his notation book, *Occasional Chats North of the Pond* (*Chibei outan;* henceforth *Occasional Chats*); author's preface 1691; earliest published edition 1700.[48]

(3) the narrative preface to a ballad in Chen Weisong's (1626–1682) *A Collection by and about Women* (*Furen ji;* henceforth *By and about Women*), mainly completed by 1673. This account, though very different from the one in *Occasional Chats,* is also, I believe, by Wang Shizhen.[49]

(4) a tale by Lin Yunming (1658 *jinshi* degree), internally dated 1667–1668. The tale was published in Zhang Chao's anthology *The Magician's New Records* (*Yu Chu xinzhi;* ca 1684) and in two collections of Lin's work: *Wushan kouyin* (late 1680s) and *Yiguilou wenji* (1698).[50] (For simplicity, henceforth all called *The Magician*).

(5) an account by Li Chengzhong (1629–1700) in his unpublished anecdotal collection entitled *Notes from Genzhai (Genzhai biji);* completed in the period after 1691.[51]

(6) a brief entry by An Zhiyuan (1628–1701) in his manuscript *Qingzhou Anecdotes (Qingshe yiwen);* completed around 1700.[52]

Scholars have long been familiar with the first four versions, which are available in a variety of modern reprints,[53] but we owe the exciting recent discovery of the obscure fifth and sixth versions to Allan Barr.[54]

Each of these versions displays distinct differences in plot, detail, and emphasis, but they all agree upon three things: the time, the place, and the names of the story's two protagonists—a beautiful and talented female ghost called Lin Siniang, who haunts an early Qing official named Chen Baoyao after he arrives to take up an official post in Qingzhou. According to the 1859 edition of the Qingzhou prefectural gazetteer, Chen, originally a second degree holder from Fujian province, served as a circuit intendant in Qingzhou during the early 1660s, roughly twenty years after Ming rule had ended in Shandong. The 1907 Yidu county gazetteer gives the precise date of 1661 (Shunzhi 18) for the year Chen took office in Qingzhou.[55] Of the tales, *The Magician* is the only one to supply specific dates. Lin Yuming gives the year

1663–1664 (Kangxi 2) for Chen's arrival in Qingzhou and 1667–1668 (Kangxi 6) as the year he heard the story from Chen. External evidence confirms the two were acquainted.[56]

This early Kangxi temporal frame means that the stories of Lin Siniang's ghost are set at a time when memories of the violence surrounding the fall of the Ming in Shandong would have been rekindled by two contemporary events: the outbreak of the local Yu Qi rebellion in 1661 against Manchu rule in northern Shandong, which was brutally suppressed by the Qing government in 1662; and the news of the Southern Ming's eradication in 1662, when the execution of the Yongling emperor in Burma eliminated the last Ming claimant to the throne. The year 1661–1662 is also significant as the end of the Shunzhi emperor's reign and the formal beginning of Kangxi's reign. This moment is widely seen by historians as the turning point for the acceptance and legitimation of Qing rule.

Chen Baoyao was employed as assistant surveillance commissioner in the military and maritime defense division of the circuit *(bingbei haifang dao)*. This post was evidently his first, and this administrative unit was relatively new, having been established at the beginning of the dynasty.[57] The division offices were located in Yidu city, near the Qingzhou prefectural offices. The gazetteers are unanimous in locating the site of the prince of Heng's ruined palace to the southwest of the prefectural offices in Yidu (see fig. 6).[58] The geographical proximity of the circuit offices and the palace grounds is crucial for understanding the provenance of the Lin Siniang legend. Five of the six versions identify the revenant as a lady who served in the prince of Heng's palace. With the exception of the truncated version in *Qingzhou Anecdotes,* all of the loyalist versions include texts of a poem attributed to her ghost written from the standpoint of a palace lady. These palace poems contribute strongly to the nostalgia and sympathy for the fallen Ming dynasty, which, to varying degrees, suffuse each of these five narratives.

The Magician is the exception. Only in this version is the revenant not a palace lady but a talented girl of good family; only this version quotes no poem by her ghost; and only this version is devoid of loyalist sentiment. This version makes no reference to the dynasty's fall; however, even here Lin Siniang's death is specifically dated to the Chongzhen era, the last reign period of the Ming. I will consider the implications of the exceptions presented by this account shortly.

Lin Siniang's story was radically reconfigured when Cao Xueqin incorporated it into his novel *Dream of the Red Chamber (Honglou meng)* in the 1740s and 1750s during the Qianlong period. By this time the fall of the Ming had long ceased being regarded as part of the recent past and the last of those born under Ming rule with eyewitness memories of the fall would have been dead. Cao Xueqin's transformed version, "The Winsome Colonel" ("Guihua ci"), did away entirely with the ghost aspect of the story by pushing the narrative focus back to 1644–1645, imagining the scene of Lin Siniang's *death* rather than the scene of her *return.* This temporal shift also entailed eliminating Chen Baoyao, the early Qing official who encounters her ghost in the seventeenth-century tales. Instead, Cao turned the Ming prince of Heng

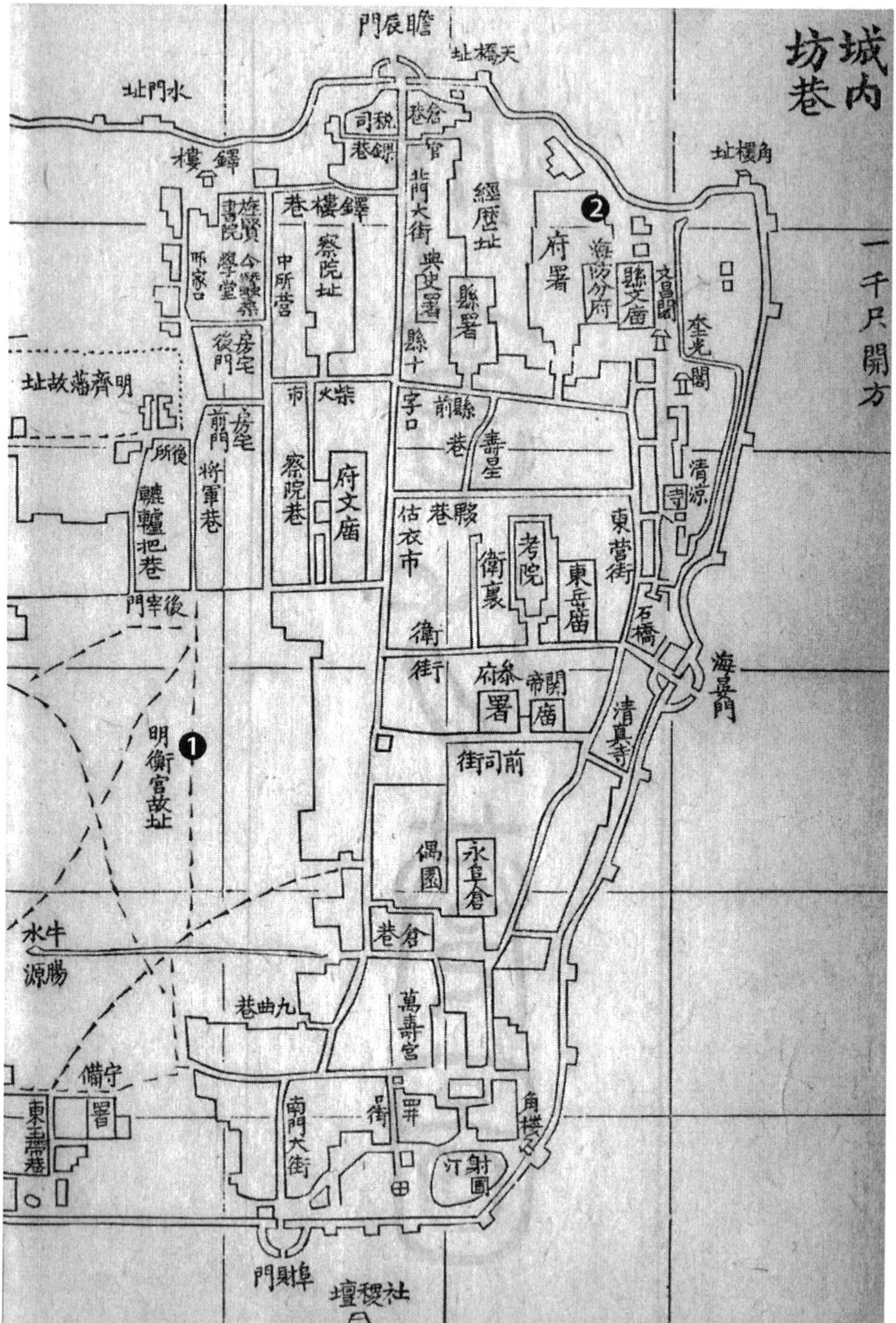

FIGURE 6 Map showing the proximity of the Qing prefectural offices (2) to the ruins of the prince of Heng's palace (1). 1907 *Illustrated Yidu County Gazeteer (Yidu xian tuzhi).*

into the major male character in the story, promoting him to military governor of Qingzhou and allotting both the prince and Lin Siniang heroic, martial deaths. Due in large measure to *Dream of the Red Chamber*'s extraordinary influence, it is this version of Lin Siniang that held sway thereafter and inspired the nineteenth-century plays dramatizing her story.

Whereas the seventeenth-century versions supply a series of vague, contradictory explanations for Lin Siniang's death and say nothing about the prince of Heng's fate, Cao Xueqin provides a detailed and unambiguous account: she and the prince were both killed defending Qingzhou against the popular uprisings that engulfed the Ming prior to the Qing conquest. Modern scholarship on the story has been largely concerned with determining the "true" history of Lin Siniang's death: was she killed at the hands of Ming peasant rebels, as Cao Xueqin says, or at the hands of the Manchu invaders, as the Ming loyalist mood of five of the six seventeenth-century versions seems to imply?[59] Scholars have tried to resolve the question by discovering what historical records say happened to the prince of Heng in Shandong, particularly whom he surrendered to in 1644–1645 but the sources are not forthcoming on the details or contradictory, and no consensus has been reached.[60]

The answer has mattered in the politicized debates of modern Chinese scholarship because it seems to hold the key to each author's "true" political intentions and allegiances in recording the tale. Read against Cao Xueqin's account, the discrepancies and vagueness among the seventeenth-century explanations for Lin Siniang's death have therefore tended to be interpreted as disguises or concealments of the truth, variously attributed to fear, ignorance, or censorship. (Exceptions are Xu Fuming's article on the subject and Wai-yee Li's "Women as Emblems of Dynastic Fall.") But as many scholars have now convincingly demonstrated, the immediate cultural responses to the Ming's overthrow and the institutionalization of the new Qing dynasty expressed in early Kangxi literature and art were far more varied, flexible, and complex than would be permitted later in the much less tolerant intellectual and political climate of the Qianlong period or within the stark either/or terms set by the anti-Manchu nationalist movement at the end of the nineteenth century.[61] To take Pu Songling as an example, since overt critiques of early Qing government brutality appear in other *Liaozhai* tales, fear of censorship cannot account for his reticence about the details of Lin Siniang's death.[62]

In my view, the reason for the contradictory accounts of Lin Siniang's death in the seventeenth-century materials is because how or at whose hands she died does not really matter in these narratives. What does matter is that she has suffered some sort of premature death and remains an unsettled spirit from the old dynasty who has not yet dissolved and can therefore still return to haunt a living representative of the new one. These conditions are satisfied in each of the six accounts. In *Occasional Chats* Lin Siniang says that she died young and was buried on the palace grounds; in *By and about Women* she merely remarks that she died in the prime of life. In Lin Yunming's version she confesses that she hung herself to prove her chastity to her father after he was released from jail. The *Notes from Genzhai* account, which is the least coherent of the six, offers no explanation for her death at all, contenting itself with the official's inference that the revenant is a "wronged soul," that is, the ghost of someone who died an untimely or unjust death. The *Qingzhou Anecdotes* entry, which is the most cursory of the narratives, asserts her identity as the ghost of a Ming palace lady three times, but makes no reference to her death at all. The *Liaozhai* version is the only one to hint strongly in the prose section of the tale at interdynastic violence as the cause of her death, but even here Lin Siniang simply confesses that "she died in a calamity."

Part of the problem in previous discussions of Lin Siniang, which have been mainly concerned with the topical issue of the Ming-Qing transition, is that there has been little attempt to contextualize the Lin Siniang story within the ghost tale tradition, to acknowledge the extent to which it is a recognizable story type. Although I'm in sympathy with Jean-Claude Schmitt's view that "what is important is not so much the age of a tradition as the currency of its uses,"[63] without a clear knowledge of a story's genealogy it is easy to misread what is significant in later permutations. The seventeenth-century Lin Siniang tales are not at all unusual in paying little attention to the details of the palace revenant's death. The early Ming tales "Teng Mu's Drunken Excursion" and "An Autumn Night's Visit," for instance, are similarly vague about the circumstances in which the palace ladies met their deaths and draw no direct causal links to the fall of the ladies' respective dynasties. (Indeed, in "Teng Mu's Drunken Excursion," the emperor the palace lady served was not even the last ruler of the dynasty.) The return of the palace lady is not a hagiographical tale about women who die resisting rape at the hands of foreign invaders or internal enemies of a dynasty. The palace lady's death does not metaphorically represent protest against the loss of national sovereignty;[64] instead her death stands in a metonymic relation to the demise of the entire dynasty, her ghost a pale remnant of what was once a vast corps of palace women.

The fact that we possess several different ghost stories about Lin Siniang in manuscript and printed sources datable to the last decades of the seventeenth century strongly suggests that this tale was circulating by word of mouth, at least in elite circles.[65] By the same token, however, the multiple retellings of this story within a relatively short time span are evidence of a powerful need to commemorate in narrative form the violent replacement of one dynasty by another. Here the work of the anthropologist Marilyn Ivy on the modern cult of the dead at Mount Osore in Japan is useful. She argues that the stories of ghosts at this site reveal that the memorial practices "aimed at ensuring the passage from unsettled, dangerous new death to stable, beneficial, settled death . . . are not always effective. . . . There are gaps in the edifice of memorialization, and through these gaps the unsettled dead appear: a ghost is a sign that memorialization is not fully adequate."[66] Along these lines, we may take the proliferation of Lin Siniang ghost stories in the late seventeenth century not only as a sign that the cultural work of mourning the Ming-Qing cataclysm was still incomplete but also as a sign that the memorialization process itself was still plastic and incomplete, the purview of unofficial local anecdote and legend, rather than an "edifice," dominated by a centralized, official version of events, as would occur in the eighteenth century.

The distinction between these two stages of memorialization can also be rephrased as the difference between memories of recent events that are still "live" and painful versus a past history that is "dead" and divorced from any actual remembrance or emotional investment.[67] This distinction is key to understanding the significance of Lin Siniang's metamorphosis in *Dream of the Red Chamber.* In chap. 78 of the novel, at a gathering of his literary friends, Jia Zheng brings up a report he has just read at the office of a forgotten heroine named Lin Siniang. He suggests that an account of her tragic death would make a grand topic for a commemorative poem. As Jia Zheng tells the story, one of the gentlemen whips out brush and ink and transcribes his words with only minor revisions, producing a short narrative preface for the poems that are to follow. But the gentlemen present are not asked to write on the topic. Instead Jia Zheng summons three junior members of the family, including his son Bao Yu, to compose the requisite poems. The remainder of the scene depicts the boys' efforts at public versification along with a critique by Jia Zheng and his friends. The episode emphasizes the stilted vapidity of a purely literary exercise memorializing a long-dead historical figure in order to sharpen the contrast with the heartfelt elegy Bao Yu writes in private in the same chapter to mourn the recent death of his beloved maid Qingwen.[68]

Jia Zheng makes it clear that his retelling of Lin Siniang's death is part of a larger government project to rectify the historical record by canonizing the deeds of obscure martyrs. When the gentleman hands over his transcription of the preface, Jia Zheng is prompted to recall the bureaucratic circumstances in which he originally learned the story.

> "It was a preface rather like this one that started off the discussion at our gathering. An Imperial directive was received at the Department yesterday asking for a search to be made in the records of this and the preceding dynasty for hitherto neglected instances of outstanding merit deserving some posthumous recognition. No class of persons was to be excluded: monks, nuns, beggars, women and girls—all were eligible. Wherever exceptional merit could be established, a brief account of it was to be forwarded to the Board of Rites for inclusion in the list of recommendations. The preface they were discussing at our gathering was a copy of the account sent in by our Department to the Board. It was reading that preface that gave those present the idea that they should write a 'Winsome Colonel' poem in commemoration of Fourth Sister Lin's [Lin Siniang's] heroic loyalty."
>
> "And very right that they should!" said the literary gentlemen smilingly. "But what is most admirable of all about this story is the tireless benevolence of the present Court which led to the unearthing of this forgotten heroism. Surely this is a thing unparalleled in any former age?"[69]

No involuntary return of the repressed here. Lin Siniang's "forgotten" story is duly dug up at the instigation of the central authorities as part of a magnanimous and self-aggrandizing gesture of largesse by the present regime toward a stable and safely buried past. Lin Siniang's ghost is banished in *Dream of the Red Chamber* because the Qing bureaucratic machine portrayed in the novel permits no gaps in the "edifice of memorialization" through which the unsettled dead from a previous dynasty could reappear.

With this renewed understanding, let us return to the seventeenth-century Lin Siniang stories. The discussion that follows will proceed from the assumption that there was no single "original" tale in circulation, no recoupable "true" accounts of the event surrounding either Lin Siniang's death or her apparition. My interpretation therefore treats the many odd differences and symmetries among the six versions not as evidence of the distortion of some essential reality but rather as opportunities for reading between the lines of individual accounts, of making sense of omissions or teasing out the full import of hints dropped but not developed in the narratives. Most important, these discrepancies provide points of entry into the individual strategies employed in each version to work through memories of the old dynasty's recent death and, with one exception, to confirm the legitimacy of a new imperial power.

PACIFYING THE GHOST: *THE MAGICIAN, BY AND ABOUT WOMEN,* AND *OCCASIONAL CHATS*

The most apparent discrepancy is the seeming anomaly of *The Magician*'s version, the only story that, on the surface at least, appears unrelated to the issue of dynastic fall and succession. Particularly jarring for readers accustomed to the elegant lady of the other "Lin Siniang" versions is the grotesque poltergeist who threatens Chen Baoyao and his staff in the first part of this tale. The infestation of Chen Baoyao's official residence, in the form of mysterious voices and sounds that go bump in the night, begins as soon as he arrives in Qingzhou. When one of the servants, fed up with the disturbances, attempts to drive the thing away with a spear, the failed attack provokes the first apparition—"a monstrous ghost, blue of face with ferocious fangs, standing there stark naked and looming so tall its head reached the rafters." The servant falls to the ground in fear and horror, but Chen Baoyao bravely rushes out to assert his authority: "This is a government office of the imperial court! What demon are you who dares to barge in like this without permission?" The poltergeist rudely snickers in Chen's face, so enraging him that he readies an armed guard of twenty men to lie in wait the next night. Uncowed, the poltergeist defiantly appears again. This time, however, "it was only three feet tall, but with a head as enormous as a wheel, a yawning mouth wide as a sieve, with eyes that flashed sparks as they opened and closed. As it came closer, dragging its feet across the ground, the coldness of its breath was overpowering." The poltergeist easily trounces the guards, who flee in fright. Chen next hires the services of an exorcist, but here, too, the poltergeist swiftly triumphs over its adversary, humiliating him in the bargain. After this, the offices are plagued day and night by falling tiles, flying firecrackers, walls that collapse of their own accord—the usual nuisances of a haunted building—but Chen is powerless to stop it.

At this point, a friend of Chen's named Liu providently stops in Qingzhou on his way to the capital and intervenes:

> "You've only yourself to blame for this trouble. There's a universal principle that where you have yang, you must also have yin. If you hadn't been so eager to drive this poltergeist out, it would never have wound up bothering you to this extent!"
>
> Before he was even done speaking, the poltergeist came out to thank him. Upon beholding the creature's hideous and terrifying appearance, Liu urged it to exchange this face for another. The poltergeist immediately excused itself and withdrew into a dark room. A little while later, a beauty of national standing emerged. Smartly dressed, her hair piled in an elaborate pompadour, she swayed daintily on her feet as she approached. Her clothes were fashioned of the finest mermaid silk, of the filmiest gauze, and betrayed no trace of a seam.[70] An unknown perfume of extraordinary fragrance swirled in her wake. She introduced herself as Lin Siniang. (*Yu Chu xinzhi*, pp. 90–91)

This dramatic metamorphosis of poltergeist to divine beauty here resembles nothing so much as a quick change of costume and mask offstage at the theater. Once Lin Siniang makes her entrance as a woman, her prior role of demon is abandoned for good. She quickly develops a close literary friendship with Chen, which consists not only of drinking and composing poetry at his parties but also of helping him with his government duties, including drafting documents and solving difficult cases. Thanks to her benevolent assistance, he earns an outstanding reputation as an official. When eighteen months later, she finally takes her leave of him forever, she retains a fond place in his memory.

The story *The Magician* tells in lieu of the palace lady's return belongs to another type of Chinese ghost story, which Glen Dudbridge has called "the tale of the haunted post."[71] Such a narrative typically begins with a new official arriving to take up his position, only to find that his government office or residence is haunted. A confrontation then ensues between the local spirit causing the disturbances and this incoming representative of the central government. Through various ritual actions, the official placates the spirit and succeeds in transforming it from a malevolent threat to him and his administration into a benevolent tutelary deity. Stories of this sort have a long pedigree and can be found not only in medieval anecdotal literature but also in dynastic histories and other documents, including stele inscriptions. By the Qing, as Rania Huntington has demonstrated, haunted-post tales involving fox-spirits, for instance, are so taken for granted that stories often depict incoming officials inheriting these now tame resident spirits along with other trappings of the office.[72]

The tale of the haunted post, which concludes with the unruly spirit's submission to (and even collaboration with) an agent of imperial authority, is easily read as enacting and resolving the perennial conflict between individual localities and the central power. On display is what Dudbridge identifies as an "official mythology, according to which a troubled episode in local affairs resolves into social and cosmic harmony under a wise and able administrator."[73] In tales that involve a hostile spirit from a previous recent dynasty, however, the underlying political conflict can be understood as pertaining not only to the issue of regional resistance to the center, but also to the legitimation of dynastic conquest and succession. One complex example involves the ghost of Jiong Yuchi, a general from the Northern Zhou dynasty (557–581), who during the 730s was said to have haunted the official residence of the Tang dynasty prefects of Xiangzhou. The story survives in several versions and in different kinds of Tang sources, and the whole legend and its historical background have been meticulously studied by Dudbridge.

Dudbridge is particularly interested in exposing the religious "vernacular mythology" of a local cult he detects buried beneath the overlay of "official mythology" in these materials, but his research also attests to the loyalist themes of the legend. The historical General Jiong committed suicide when the city of Ye fell to the armies of Yang Jian, the founder of the Sui dynasty, in a decisive battle that led to the demise of the Northern Zhou and the reunification of the empire. On a regional level, the battle resulted in the physical and political annihilation of Ye; the city was burnt to the ground, its population transferred elsewhere, and the prefectural and county government permanently moved to the nearby city of Anyang.[74]

The Sui dynasty in its turn proved short-lived, however, and after the Tang dynasty took power, the new founder, Emperor Taizu, granted General Jiong reburial and gifts in tacit recognition of the general's "loyal stand against the Yangs [the Sui emperors] whom he himself had replaced."[75] Despite these posthumous honors (or perhaps because of them since they called attention to the general's martyrdom), the potent and resentful spirit of the general remained unpropitiated, and stories of his haunting the prefectural post at Anyang persisted into the tenth century. In the most elaborate anecdotal version of the story from the eighth century, the general's ghost appears to the new prefect to request him to rebury the bones of his family that lie beneath the hall and delivers a lengthy, rhetorical speech detailing the historical events that led to his suicide and the massacre of his family. Proclaiming his heroic loyalism to the doomed Northern Zhou dynasty to have been an attempt "to restore the cosmos to rights and so maintain [the Tang founder] Emperor Taizu's heritage,"[76] the speech ringingly endorses the legitimacy and inevitability of the Tang dynastic succession. In response, the prefect reburies the bones and turns the hall into a memorial temple to the general and his lineage. In this version, the general's ghost shows his gratitude by extending personal guidance and protection to the prefect's family, but in a late ninth-century version, the ghost offers to repay the prefect by helping him excel in his administrative duties.

Despite the conspicuous absence of loyalist sentiment in *The Magician*'s version of "Lin Siniang," in its broadest contours the story does conform to the tale of the haunted post, as exemplified by the legends of General Jiong's ghost, in legitimating dynastic conquest and succession. The poltergeist who infests the official compound at Qingzhou and who openly rebels against the new agent of Qing imperial authority is identified as a *lie hun* (a martyred soul) from the last reign period of the Ming dynasty; her chaste suicide after her father's release from prison therefore coincides with the dynasty's demise. In this case, however, the wronged spirit is portrayed as having suffered under the previous dynasty's rule rather than at the hands of internal rebels or foreign conquerors of the regime. Thus Lin Siniang here occupies the anomalous position of being a *lie hun* from the fall of the Ming with no allegiance to the Ming.[77] She is therefore easily and swiftly appeased as soon as a little understanding and kindness are extended to her, her about-face from malevolent to tutelary spirit instantly signaled through her assumption of female gender and costume.[78]

At the end of the narrative *The Magician* mentions not only that Chen Baoyao was Lin Yuming's source for the story, but that Chen "commissioned" *(zhu)* him to record it. As the only version to represent itself as authorized by Chen Baoyao, *The Magician*'s account may come closer to representing an "official mythology" than the other Lin Siniang tales, which touch on more sensitive emotional territory and were recorded without Chen Baoyao's imprimatur.

One important point this story makes is that continuing to use force against victims of history is counterproductive to the consolidation of the new dynasty's rule and the reestablishment of social and cosmic order in a given locality. Similar wisdom is sounded in a brief *Liaozhai* tale called "Weeping Ghosts" ("Gui ku," *LZ* 1. 76), although much of the rest of the tale is satiric. In this case the ghosts are the victims of the Qing army's suppression of the Xie Qian rebellion (1646–1647) in Pu Songling's hometown of Zichuan in Shandong. The ghosts are infesting the house of a member of the local elite because so many of the rebels had been slaughtered there.[79] A minor official spending the night in the haunted house is so plagued by the sound of ghosts weeping en masse in the courtyard that he rushes out, sword in hand, to threaten them. His attempt at intimidation fails, meeting with nothing but ridicule from the ghosts, and the domicile is only rid of them after its owner holds a propitiatory Land and Water Rite to redeem their souls and provides food offerings outside to lure them from the house. Pu Songling, commenting as Historian of the Strange, draws a major lesson from this story: "When it comes to demonic creatures, only kindness can put an end to them." Thus although "Weeping Ghosts" and *The Magician*'s version of Lin Siniang are very different types of stories, underlying both is the basic idea that kindness and clemency, rather than persecution, is the only real way to lay a ghost and restore peace to a place.[80]

In his article on Lin Siniang, Xu Fuming divides the seventeenth-century narratives into two distinct branches.[81] In the first camp he places *The Magician* as the only version with no link to the prince of Heng's palace and with a strong Fujian connection: both Lin Yunming and Chen Baoyao, the protagonist of the story, whom Lin names as his informant, were Fujianese.[82] Lin Siniang is a native of Fujian in this version, as is the friend who intervenes with the poltergeist and the guests who later receive poems from Lin Siniang. The reason Lin Siniang gives for appearing to

Chen Baoyao is their shared native place of origin. In the second camp, Xu Fuming places the remaining narratives, which all involve a Ming palace lady who served the prince of Heng and which can all be traced back to Shandong writers living at one time in proximity to Qingzhou (Pu Songling in Zichuan, Wang Shizhen, and his older brother Wang Shilu in Xincheng).[83] (See map in fig. 5.) Naturally Xu Fuming was unaware of the *Notes from Genzhai* and *Qingzhou Anecdotes* versions, but they fit his typology quite well. The prince of Heng's palace occupies a prominent position in the *Notes from Genzhai* account, whose author, Li Chengzhong, a Shandong native and Ming loyalist, was from Zhucheng, a county in southern Qingzhou prefecture with a strong community of Ming loyalists.[84] The Qingzhou connection is even more explicit in *Qingzhou Anecdotes*. This collection was one of several local history projects on Qingzhou in which the compiler, An Zhiyuan, was involved.[85] The specifically Shandong identity of the story is brought out by Lu Jianzeng, when in the mid-eighteenth century, he ended his *Shandong Poetry From Our Dynasty* with a poem by "Lin Siniang of Qingzhou."[86]

The advantage of Xu Fuming's typology is that it explains the thematic difference between *The Magician*'s version and the others as a function of separate regional provenance. In particular, the absence in Lin Yunming's version of Ming loyalist sentiment (and therefore any *huaigu* poem to express it) can be chalked up in some measure to his own physical distance from the ruins of the prince of Heng's palace in Qingzhou. The disadvantage of Xu's typology is that it obscures the strong structural resemblance of Lin Yunming's tale to the version in *By and about Women*.[87] It also takes no account of Lin Yunming's own personal acquaintance with Wang Shizhen. The two men passed the *jinshi* exam the same year, in 1658, and subsequently worked together. Lin's published work includes the text of a letter he wrote to Wang in 1681, which reminisces about how the two of them used to scare each other telling ghost stories together some twenty years before.[88] Xu's typology also obscures the relationship between *The Magician*'s version and the *Notes from Genzhai* account. Both versions give the same name for one of the ghost maids accompanying Lin Siniang, and there are also some plot resemblances. Taken together, these facts suggest that we should not accept Xu Fuming's premise of two entirely separate regional branches for the story.

Of all the seventeenth-century collections to include a Lin Siniang narrative, *By and about Women* is the only one consistently loyalist and *huaigu*–oriented in aim, tone, and content. As I have argued in a separate study, this collection may be characterized as a private archive designed to preserve fragmentary traces from the former Ming dynasty, which at the moment of recording were already on the verge of disappearing.[89] The version of "Lin Siniang" in *By and about Women* is recognizably a watered-down variant of the haunted-post tale told in *The Magician*. It, too, begins with mysterious nocturnal disturbances that commence as soon as Chen Baoyao moves into his new official residence. Here again he reacts by mustering armed guards and ordering them to attack, and this effort at violent suppression also predictably fails. The main difference is that no hideous poltergeist ever manifests itself to confront Chen or his guards: the battle is one-sided, staged against an invisible foe. When the specter does put in an appearance several nights later, she skips directly to the elaborately costumed, beautiful Lin Siniang stage.

In contrast to the vague haunted-house thumps and voices in *The Magician,* the mysterious noises in *By and about Women* are clearly the sounds of a phantom banquet, an identification confirmed by a household staff member who glimpses the ghostly spectacle. Lin Siniang herself subsequently explains the reasons for this to Chen Baoyao in a speech heavily imbued with *huaigu* sentiment:

> In my youth I served the prince of Heng, but midway on my course I died. Just now I temporarily returned to the former palace, but I beheld the halls and towers had been destroyed by the authorities, and the flowers and bamboo buried beneath "an outgrowth of millet." I had with me some former companions from the palace. We deeply desired to converse together about the past, but we had nowhere to stop our carriages. And so I presumed to borrow your main rooms for a banquet space. I will certainly be unable to do you any favors, sir, but neither will I do you any harm. Would it be possible for us to enter into a friendship transcending ordinary bounds? (Chen Weisong, *Furen ji,* p. 33a)

The ghost acknowledges the official's rights over the property, and the only ritual amends she requests in return is the favor of his friendship, consecrated over a shared meal of food and wine. Chen assents only under duress at first, but for the next three months, Lin Siniang is a frequent visitor, on intimate terms with the womenfolk in the household and a generous entertainer of Chen and his friends at parties with poems and songs. As in the case of other haunted-post stories, a potential challenge to the territorial jurisdiction of the central government is defused and eliminated through personal ties formed between a local spirit and an officer of that government.

This message is also detectable, albeit much more faintly, in the minimalist *Qingzhou Anecdotes* account. The narrative contour of this version most closely resembles the one in *By and about Women.* Chen Baoyao's official residence in Qingzhou is plagued by nocturnal concerts performed by invisible musicians, a hint of the "disembodied-banquet" motif. After three or four nights a woman in her forties, costumed in Ming palace garb, enters to the strains of the music. Terrified, Chen enlists members of his household to attack the apparition, but to no avail. The next night the ghost comes again and quickly persuades him that she intends no harm. She merely wants to befriend him. She identifies herself as Lin Siniang, from the former palace of the prince of Heng: their friendship consists of her relating "former events" from the palace and of matching poems with him. When she takes her final leave of him, she predicts that he will not remain in this post long. Sure enough, soon after, Chen is promoted to a new position and leaves Qingzhou. Although no explicit causality is supplied in this flat and simple rendition of the story, the Ming palace lady's quick submission to this representative of Qing authority, her willingness to entertain him with reminiscences and poetry, prove beneficial to his official career.

The example of Lin Siniang's verse given in *By and about Women* is a generic palace-style quatrain sprinkled with a few ghostly markers such as green mist and moonlight.

> I stand for a moment on the marble steps, knitting my bashful brows.
> The moon gleams at twilight, turning the hazy mist green.
> Couches of gold and desks of jade will nevermore return,
> In vain, I sing the mournful tunes of this mortal world.
> (Chen Weisong, *Furen ji*, p. 33a)

A loyalist strain may be detectable in the last lines, where the possibility of temporary return for the revenant contrasts with the luxurious interior of the palace itself, which is gone forever.

The theme of displacement as an explanation for haunting is also prominent in the version of Lin Siniang in *Occasional Chats*. In this tale, however, the initial episode—the confrontation between the infesting spirit and the official typical of the haunted-post tale—drops out entirely. Instead, a beautifully attired Lin Siniang now comes in advance to request Chen Baoyao's permission to hold spirit banquets on his premises. The motivation given for this request is similar to that in *By and about Women:*

> A few years later [after my death], the dynasty was destroyed and the prince was taken north, but my soul still fondly lingers at the old site. Since the palace halls are overgrown and in ruins, for the time being I would just like to borrow your buildings to entertain my guests. This will certainly bring you no gain, but then neither will it bring you any harm. (Wang Shizhen, *Chibei outan*, 21. 513.)

Chen gives his consent, and an invisible but audible banquet swiftly ensues, thereby enlisting him and his staff as de facto witnesses to a gathering of Ming palace dead held on Qing government property.

Although in the *Occasional Chats* account these phantom banquets are officially authorized rather than trespasses, when read in light of the version in *By and about Women*, this motif suggests a residual affiliation with the tale of the haunted post. A separate note in *Occasional Chats* about what happened to former palaces of Ming princes in Shandong in the early Qing may help explain the prominence of displacement as a theme in both Wang Shizhen's accounts of Lin Siniang:

> After the chaos of the fall, "The Tower for Watching Spring" and "The Winding Pool for Floating Wine Cups" were still preserved at the former palace of the prince of Heng in Qingzhou. Above them was an ancient spreading umbrella pine that must have been several centuries old. When I picnicked there in

> 1656, there still remained dozens of tangerine trees and hydrangea bushes. Afterwards, when Governor Zhou Youde of Shandong built a new provincial yamen on the abandoned site of the former palace of the prince of De in Ji'nan from 1666 to 1667, he transported the trees and rocks from the prince of Heng's gardens for the construction. Once the complex was completed, it was magnificent indeed, but at the ruins of the prince of Heng's palace, nothing was left but a thick profusion of grasses.[90]

A brief story in *Liaozhai* about the haunting of a carpenter working and living on the construction site of the new official yamen in Ji'nan confirms that the conversion of the ruined palace of a former Ming prince into the headquarters of the Qing provincial government in Shandong was a stimulus to the ghostly imagination of the period. In this brief, inconclusive tale, which is entitled "Carpenter Feng" ("Feng mujiang," *LZ* 11. 1445), the carpenter enters into a loving sexual relationship with a young girl who mysteriously shows up one night at the site. After he discovers she is a ghost and starts to feel his energies diminishing, he seeks in vain to have her exorcised. Finally, one night, she comes to take her own leave of him because the allotted time of their liaison is up. The narrative never clarifies who this otherworldly woman is, but the tale's opening unobtrusively but unmistakably establishes a causal link between the demonic haunting and the governor's makeover of the former Ming palace into the chief seat of Qing power in the province.[91]

Although Lin Siniang is portrayed entirely as a decorous rather than menacing spirit in the *Occasional Chats* telling of her story, there is still one incongruous detail: a pair of daggers dangles from her belt, intimating a faint threat of violence. Influenced by the martial heroics of "The Winsome Colonel" in *Dream of the Red Chamber,* scholars have tended to read these daggers as clues to the manner of Lin Siniang's death, but might we not better understand them as weapons her ghost could potentially wield against the living? In *By and about Women,* where Lin Siniang's specter is similarly equipped with a sharp sword, the presence of this weapon helps safeguard her chastity against any assault by a living man. In the poem attributed to Lin Siniang's ghost in *Occasional Chats,* she describes herself as "[a] comely girl, too weak to be a vengeful ghost." But were there no underlying fear that her ghost might have cause to be hostile and take revenge upon the living, what need would there be to include this line?[92]

ROMANCING THE PAST: THE *LIAOZHAI* VERSION

In the *Liaozhai* version there are no intrusions of phantom banquets or dangling daggers: even these last slender links to the tale of the haunted post and the need to pacify the ghost are gone. All that remains to hint at the violent threat Lin Siniang's wraith might pose is the line "A comely girl, too weak to be a vengeful ghost," which appears almost unchanged in the poem she composes in *Liaozhai.*[93] (*Occasional Chats, Liaozhai,* and *Notes from Genzhai* all provide variants of the same twelve-line poem; *By and about Women* is the exception, supplying a textually distinct quatrain.) The theme of dispossession as a rationale for the haunting also disappears from Pu Songling's story, and the ruined palace only resurfaces in Lin Siniang's concluding poem:

> The palace has been locked tight for seventeen years.
> Who will "question Heaven" about our former dynasty?
> Trees grown so large they seal the palace halls.
> With weeping eyes, I gaze toward my prince turned to a whippoorwill.[94]
> Waves in the maritime region reflect the setting sun.[95]
> The smoke of war has stilled Han flutes and drums.
> A comely girl, too weak to be a vengeful ghost,
> Kind and brokenhearted, seeks answers in Zen.
> I chant prayers thousands of times a day.
> At leisure, read sections of the scriptures.
> Instead of crying, I sing songs of royal entertainment,[96]
> Inviting you to listen alone will make your tears flow too.
> (*LZ* 2. 288 289)

I will take up this poem in some detail below. For the moment it suffices to point out that the first four lines of the poem are a welter of loyalist clichés and that the first line in particular is almost formulaic in *huaigu* verse attributed to palace-lady revenants.[97] In such poems the palace lady becomes a synecdoche for what is being mourned and remembered, yet by venting her own feelings of loss, she also becomes both its chief mourner and the custodian of its memory. By performing her grief for the dynasty through music and verse, Lin Siniang enables her audience to share her sorrow vicariously and to participate in the work of mourning, enabling the repressed memories of the old dynasty to be effectively exorcised and banished.

In *Occasional Chats* and *By and about Women,* the spirit banquets Lin Siniang initially holds for her dead comrades give way to parties for Chen Baoyao and his friends at which her performance of mourning and nostalgia provides the main entertainment: "As she told of former events in the palace, she would be overcome with sorrow. Then she would sing to her own accompaniment and the sound would be filled with grief and resentment. The parties would always end with the entire company in tears" (Wang Shizhen, *Chibei outan* 21. 513). In *Liaozhai,* where the relationship between official and ghost is far more intimate (this is the only version in which the two are lovers), Lin Siniang's musical performances and recitations of the past are for his ears alone.[98]

> When he pressed her again, she finally bent her head, and beating time to the music, sang the tunes of "Lost Frontiers." The sound was mournful and delicate. As she finished her song, her tears fell. The magistrate, too, felt pangs of sorrow.
>
> Taking her into his arms, he comforted her: "Don't play the melodies of a fallen dynasty; it makes people too sad."

> The girl said: "Music is a means to express inner feelings. You cannot force a mourner to produce joyful tunes anymore than the joyful can be forced to produce mournful tunes."
>
> He then questioned her about former events in the palace. The girl told him all about them in vivid detail. When she reached the events of the fall, she became choked with sobs and could not continue. (*LZ* 2. 288)

Underlying most tales of palace-lady revenants is a crucial paradox: the ghost materializes in large measure to fulfill the present's impossible desire to interrogate a dead eyewitness of the past, someone with "living" firsthand memories of the now defunct palace, yet the content of these reminiscences is rarely, if ever, narrated.[99] In Pu Songling's rendering of "Lin Siniang" as well as in *Occasional Chats* and *By and about Women,* the revenant speaks of former events in the palace, but no details about the past are actually revealed. This absence of narration can be traced back to the Tang poet Yuan Zhen's influential quatrain about a former palace lady from the reign of Xuanzong, the Tang emperor Minghuang deposed during the An Lushan rebellion. In this quatrain, "The Emperor's Traveling Lodge" ("Xinggong"), the palace lady is an aged survivor rather than a ghost, but the principle is the same:

> How desolate is this emperor's traveling lodge of old,
> the palace flowers grow red, all alone.
> A white-haired palace lady is still alive,
> reclining, she talks about her late sovereign.[100]

Since this omission of content is common enough to constitute a pattern in palace-lady ghost tales, it cannot be chalked up to a failure of imagination alone, or even to the stereotyped nature of the revelations, which might invoke the narrative imperative to avoid what would be tedious if enumerated. This failure to provide any inside information about the palace is particularly striking in the version in *By and about Women* precisely because of the presence of other entries involving former palace ladies—live ones, not ghosts—which do supply concrete nuggets of gossip and reminiscence.[101] The absence of any content for the recollections of the past in the Lin Siniang narratives shifts the attention away from memory as a fixed object onto remembering as a ritual and iterative act. The point, as in much *huaigu* poetry, is the cultural act of remembering rather than what is being remembered.[102]

The performance of the past in the present is what is at stake in tales of the palace lady's return. But how to realize in narrative the fantasy of the past being contemporaneous with the present? In some form or other, newness must be shown breaking in on the old. This imperative is thematized in a variety of ways, but particularly through the playing of new music, the composition of new poems, and the flowing of new blood or tears.

In "Teng Mu's Drunken Excursion," the palace-lady revenant holds a banquet for the man she meets in the ruins of the royal gardens as a prelude to the consummation of their love affair. The lady instructs her maid, also a ghost, to sing a song for him; the maid requests permission to sing famous song-lyrics by Liu Yong (986–1053), the Northern Song poet, but the lady refuses because: "It's inappropriate to sing an old tune for a new lover."[103] Instead, she composes a new *huaigu* song on the spot, which her maid immediately performs.

The eruption of the new against the background of the old may also figure directly in the verse a ghost composes. In the ninth-century tale "A Journey to Zhou and Qin," the protagonist meets a hodgepodge of famous palace ladies from different dynasties, but ends up taking as his lover Wang Zhaojun, the Han palace lady tragically married off to a Hun prince. Before the ladies decide which of them will bed him for the night, each of them composes and recites a quatrain for him. Wang Zhaojun's opens:

> From my yurt in the snow, no glimpse of spring.
> My Han dynasty clothes are old,
> but the tears that flow are new.[104]

These lines fit the outline of Wang Zhaojun's original story as it was passed down. Sent off to suffer in the frozen wastes of the Huns, she is prevented from enjoying spring in the Chinese heartland. Within the symbolic economy of the ghost story, however, the couplet also signifies that as a wraith she is frozen in death and thus does not experience the yearly renewal of spring. The mention of spring, code word for amorous activity, already holds out the possibility that tonight she will be chosen to obtain a glimpse of it; the prediction is reinforced by the mention of new tears flowing, new bodily fluids being shed to interrupt the limbo of the afterlife.

The *Liaozhai* version of "Lin Siniang" most skillfully weaves together all these strands of making the past "present." As previously mentioned, this is the only one which makes the ghost and official lovers. Although the defloration of a virgin ghost is featured in several stories in the collection, only in "Lin Siniang," as Wai-yee Li has pointed out, does Pu Songling take pains to depict the blood flowing to stain the mat.[105] Here in his take on the return of the palace lady, the new graphically breaks in on the old, and by altering the past, present and past are, for a moment, in perfect synch. By deflowering Lin Siniang, the official is also, on one level at least, removing one of the ghost's grievances and redoing a historical wrong. Although Lin Siniang's redemption is overtly credited to her chanting Buddhist sutras, the generative power of male sexuality, common in other amorous ghost tales, may also be causally implicated, for in the course of the story Lin Siniang passes from frozen chastity to rebirth and reincarnation. In either case, Lin Siniang is released from the anomalous ghostly suspension of time she inhabits at the beginning and reabsorbed into the normative cyclical workings of time. The replacement of the dead by the living, the superseding of an old dynasty by a new one—the restoration and legitimation of these historical processes of time is embodied through her person.

A common paradox in the romantic ghost tale is that the prospect of rebirth for a ghost, which ought to be greeted with joy since it signals release from purgatory, is instead a cause of mourning since it means the lovers must now part for eternity. Rebirth is thus configured as a species of second death, a second parting. With the exception of the *Notes from Genzhai* version, the Lin Siniang narratives conclude with the ghost's coming to take leave of the official. In Pu Songling's version of "Lin Siniang," however, the requisite farewell scene is exceptionally dramatic and impassioned.

> She remained with him for three years. Suddenly, one evening, utterly wretched, she said good-bye. Alarmed, the official asked her what had happened. "In consideration of the fact that I lived a blameless life, and did not forget prayers and the sutras even during my death, the King of the Underworld has ordered me to be reborn into the Wang family. Our parting must be tonight. We will not meet again for eternity." Upon finishing what she had to say, she was disconsolate. The official too shed tears.
>
> But then he set out some wine and drank heartily with her. The girl passionately sang mournful tunes; with each word, her voice twisted and turned a hundred times. Whenever she reached a sad place, she became choked with tears so that she had to stop and start several times. After she finished the song, she drank, but could not find any solace.
>
> Then she stood up, and hesitated, intending to say farewell. The official insisted on detaining her, so she sat back down for a little while. Suddenly a cock crowed. "I must not stay here any longer. But you always reproached me for being unwilling to present you with one of my poor compositions; now that we are parting forever, I ought to write you a piece on the spot." She asked for a pen and completed a poem. Then she said: "I am sick at heart and my thoughts are jumbled. I cannot properly craft this poem. The tones are wrong and the meter is off. Please don't show it to anyone."
>
> Then she left, covering her face with her sleeve. The magistrate escorted her out the door and she vanished like smoke. He was beside himself with grief for a long time. When he looked at the poem, the characters were shapely and nice, and he treasured and preserved it. (*LZ* 2. 288)

The ostensible reason for the ghost's intensity of grief is the parting with her lover Chen Baoyao, but the loyalist message of the poem she bestows on him underscores that her sorrow is due primarily to the traumatic course of history. Especially through the descriptions of musical performance, repeated even within the poem, Pu Songling's version is one long mourning piece. It is cathartic, because it brings memory to the surface and works through forgotten or unwanted feelings, and because, in the end, Lin Siniang, as an innocent victim of historical forces, is rehabilitated and redeemed. Like the remnant subjects who finally decide to join the new regime and end their ritual mourning for the lost dynasty,[106] like the apparitions of the last Ming emperor and empress, who are sighted rising to Heaven at the end of *Peach Blossom Fan,*[107] Lin Siniang's rebirth helps mark the end of a period of national mourning and legitimate the new dynasty.

The final episode of Pu Songling's tale is taken up with introducing Lin Siniang's poem. In a decidedly awkward moment, she requests brush and ink and writes down the poem, rather than simply reciting it to cap her musical performance. The insistence that the poem(s) were written down is one constant that unites all six versions. In *Notes from Genzhai,* the poem is inscribed on the wall; in *Occasional Chats,* a manuscript of Lin Siniang's poetry is said to be in someone's possession. In *By and about Women,* Lin Siniang composes *huaigu* poems on the theme of the old palace, her brush moving at incredible speed. In *Qingzhou Anecdotes,* a one-volume manuscript of her poems is much in circulation among the Qingzhou elite. Even in *The Magician,* Lin Siniang is said to write down her verses, "though the poems she penned were so sad that no one could bear to read them."[108] This shared emphasis on Lin Siniang's poems as *written* documents is noteworthy because, as I showed in Chapter 2, ghost poems need not be committed to writing; they can also be chanted orally by a ghost character or overheard in the wilderness.

In the *Liaozhai* version, the flaws in the verse that Lin Siniang explains as signs of her emotional distress are counterparts of the choked sobs that interrupt her farewell song and earlier reminiscences of the fall, but the alleged breakdown in meter and rhyme also reinforce the conceit that the poem was composed extemporaneously, at this moment, for this occasion. Her unpolished verse is thus simultaneously presented as "new" and "authentic." But the poem also has to be committed to paper so that there can be a lasting trace of her once she "vanishes like smoke." In contrast to the ephemerality of her musical performances, the written poem is a tangible thing that can be "preserved and treasured" after she is gone to compensate for her absence. In the end the final production of a written poem, which can "outlive" and commemorate the ghost is a crucial part of the closure process through which the past dynasty is safely laid to rest.

RETURN TO RUINS: THE *NOTES FROM GENZHAI* VERSION

One major difference between the loyalist Lin Siniang tales and the early Ming stories of palace-lady revenants is that the protagonist does not visit ruins to seek out his fantasy of the past. Instead, the past abruptly comes to him, unsummoned and unwanted, as a sign of the old dynasty's dispossession. The main exception is the *Notes from Genzhai* account, in which Chen Baoyao, early in his tenure in Qingzhou, receives an official imperial order to open the former prince of Heng's palace:

> At that time the various halls and long corridors had been destroyed; only the retiring hall[109] and its courtyard were still under lock and key. The officer led a crowd to open the hall. They saw the courtyard filled with a mass of slithering snakes so dense there was no way to set foot inside. So they locked it up again for three days. When they returned, the courtyard was deserted; not a single snake was left. On the clothes racks the old gauze robes, exposed to the wind, turned to dust and flew off. In the bowls were sparrows' eggs the size of peas. It was exactly like something out of Yuan Zhen's "Ballad of Lianchang Palace" ("Liangchang gongci"). Inscribed on the walls were three quatrains, still wet and dripping ink.[110]

The text of the verses—the same as the poem in *Liaozhai*—is then given.[111] The ghostly author in the *Notes from Genzhai* account is never identified, but the content of the verses, particularly the opening quatrain, make it plain that she is meant to be a palace lady.[112] The image of an abandoned palace fastened tight reoccurs in verse attributed to palace-lady revenants, but only *Notes from Genzhai* takes the image literally and weaves it into the narrative so that the condition of the spectral poem's discovery is actually the unlocking of the palace.

Chen Baoyao's encroachment on the palace proves to be the equivalent of opening Pandora's Box, however, for that very night, back at the office, the haunting begins, and we are back on the now familiar terrain of the tale of the haunted post:

> Sitting in his chambers, he heard the sound of plaintive weeping. It had to be a wronged soul, he thought. So he ordered it to appear before him. It said: "I have no clothes, so I dare not come out."[113] So he gave it clothes, but still it wouldn't appear. Then it said: "You must personally burn some spirit money at the main gate to welcome me." So he did as it asked, but in the end still nothing appeared. Later he got a bit fed up and tried to intimidate it with firecrackers, but it wasn't scared in the slightest. It then manifested itself lying on the roof. It was exactly the length of the roof but too faint for anyone to figure out what it was.[114]

Subsequently a mysterious girl dressed in a crimson robe with kingfisher-blue sleeves who calls herself Lin Siniang appears, not to Chen Baoyao himself, however, but to his younger brother. The story ends with Chen Baoyao's recall from office because of his mother's death and the unexplained death of his younger brother.[115]

The *Notes from Genzhai* story is an unusually disjointed account of several anecdotes that makes no attempt to put the pieces together to create a degree of narrative coherence. Indeed without prior knowledge of the other Lin Siniang versions, it would be difficult to make sense of the story altogether; without this knowledge, we might not even be justified in taking these anecdotes as comprising a single story.[116] With the other Lin Siniang stories as a template, however, we may infer that the author of the verses on the prince of Heng's palace wall, the wronged soul who confronts Chen Baoyao in his official residence, and the woman calling herself Lin Siniang who visits his younger brother are one and the same. And based on the logic of ghost stories in general we may construe the ill-fortune that befalls Chen Baoyao and his brother as a direct result of their encounter with the ghost of Lin Siniang, and their failure, for whatever reason, to appease her spirit through ritual amends.[117] But *Notes from Genzhai* itself never specifies any of this so that the narrative remains rudimentary, depending entirely on juxtaposition and sequencing for any internal connections.

With this provisional reading of the story in mind, let us reexamine the opening anecdote, the second unlocking of the palace ruins. The mysterious infestation of yin snakes has been replaced by a scene less horrific perhaps but much more eerie: a garment crumbling to dust when a tomb is disinterred and a coffin is opened is a common motif in ghost stories.[118] No signature accompanies the verses on the wall, but none is necessary: their author is clearly designated a ghost in the story, for who else could have penetrated a sealed hall guarded by a plague of snakes? The discovery of a freshly written inscription in a ruined setting that has been sealed off for years is an established way of indicating a "ghostly autograph" in Chinese tales of the strange.[119] The verses inscribed on the wall, however, are not only fresh, but "dripping wet." Particularly in conjunction with the opening quatrain about "my prince turned to a whippoorwill," this image connotes not only ink, but blood.

Allusions abound in Chinese verse to a mythical king of Sichuan who metamorphosed into a whippoorwill after his death and wept tears of blood, but they are particularly favored in Ming loyalist poetry to commemorate the dead emperor and princes of the deposed royal house. The loyalist poet Chen Zilong, for instance, wrote an entire ballad on this topos, which includes these impassioned lines:

> One cry of the whippoorwill cracks fissured stone.
> Looking up at Heaven, it weeps blood
> and stains the white clouds.

And the poem ends in despair with the image of fresh writing on the wall:

> All one can do is take the Nymph of Mount Wu by the hand:
> On the walls of the Qu ancestral temple,
> a set of "Questions to Heaven" is dripping wet.[120]

Chen Zilong's final couplet employs another powerful loyalist trope, the legend of Qu Yuan, the courtier and poet of the ancient state of Chu who, after his unjust banishment, was said to have written his "Questions to Heaven" ("Tian wen") on the walls of the state ancestral temple to vent his bitterness and anguish.[121] The same reference figures in the opening of Lin Siniang's poem in *Liaozhai:* "Who will question Heaven about our former dynasty?"[122] The identical line appears in *Notes from Genzhai,* but here, even more appropriately for the allusion, this verse lamenting the Ming's demise in Qingzhou is discovered written on the wall of the prince of Heng's ruined palace.

Kang-i Sun Chang astutely observes that this whole ballad "is built upon the image of blood, symbol of political tragedy and human sacrifice and of death itself."[123] The final image of ink dripping wet likewise evokes blood and ties the last line into the rest of the poem's symbolic framework. In certain anecdotes from the period about poems written on walls, the writers of the verses are even said to have used blood rather than ink to convey the sincerity and despair of their feelings. As in *Notes from Genzhai,* the point of the ink / blood not having dried yet in Chen Zilong's poem is to juxtapose two conflicting temporal orders, superimposing the unspent and unresolved force of the present onto the ruined but not yet vanished architecture of the past. Lacking a proper narrative, however, the fragmented *Notes from Genzhai* account could not, unlike the other Lin Siniang tales, reconfigure the traumatic memory of the fall and provide closure for readers of the early Qing.

"Gongsun Jiuniang": Victims of History

In contrast to the multiple retellings of "Lin Siniang" in Kangxi period sources, "Gongsun Jiuniang," Pu Songling's commemoration of the victims of the 1662 suppression of the Yu Qi rebellion, stands virtually alone in the literature responding to the Manchu conquest and consolidation of power. Unlike "Lin Siniang," "Gongsun Jiuniang" was not the result of an oral story making the rounds in elite circles. Rather, so far as we can tell, this tale, though thoroughly steeped in the literary ghost tradition, is the singular product of Pu Songling's imagination. "Gongsun Jiuniang" is singular in yet another regard: it is not about an infinitely reenacted cycle of dynastic fall and succession but instead attests to the horror of a specific historical event unassimilatable to comforting generalities.[124] The tales of Lin Siniang's specter, as I have shown, are predicated in large measure on the absence within the narrative of any concrete details concerning the demise of the dynasty, the "originary" historical trauma that produces the ghost. This fuzziness is essential to suffuse the phantom with the romantic glow of the past and to turn Lin Siniang's return and rebirth into simply the latest local instantiation of an eternal pattern of change. The specificity of the past disappears as this palace lady becomes every palace lady, this dynastic turnover a repetition of every previous and future one. Living memory fades and the standard narrative of history is back on track as the cosmic time of the universe and the finite time of the individual are once again in perfect realignment. As a ghost story recounted repeatedly in both oral and written venues at a specific moment in time, however, we may also understand the intertwined commemoration of the dead individual and the fallen dynasty involved in the Lin Siniang narratives as "a form of collective memory," which Jean-Claude Schmitt perceptively explains, is actually "a social technique of forgetting."[125] The palace lady returns in the Lin Siniang narratives so that she can carry out anew the ritual of separation between the living and the dead botched during the chaos of the fall and lay the memory of the old dynasty properly to rest.

But "Gongsun Jiuniang" denies the possibility of ever achieving any full closure to the trauma of history. The protagonist's encounter with ghosts in this tale, rather than providing catharsis and healing, instead constitutes a reliving of the trauma. The exact circumstances of the local historical events responsible for producing the ghosts are thus crucial in this tale in a way that they are not in the Lin Siniang narratives. Moreover, Pu Songling himself, who was only four when the Ming fell in Shandong, but in his early twenties when the Yu Qi uprising came to a head, was, in a much more immediate sense, a "survivor" with close-hand knowledge and experience of this later tragedy.[126] The brutal quelling of the rebellion took place in the eastern counties of Laiyang and Qixia in Shandong, around the rebel base of Sawtooth Mountain, but the capital sentences meted out to those arrested, which included large numbers of innocent people, were carried out in Ji'nan, the provincial capital and seat of the prefecture to which Pu Songling's hometown of Zichuan belonged (see map in fig. 5). No immediate relatives or friends of Pu Songling's perished in this incident, as far as we know, but many members from the Shandong local gentry, his own social group, were unjustly rounded up and put to death.[127] For all these reasons, the psychological, moral, and literary imperative for Pu Songling to document these particular atrocities must have been acute.

"Gongsun Jiuniang" is therefore prefaced forthrightly with a chilling account of the mass executions undertaken by the Qing government in reprisal for the uprising:

> In the crackdown that followed the Yu Qi rebellion, the largest number of people implicated and sentenced to execution were from the Qixia and Laiyang districts in eastern Shandong. On a single day, several hundred people were arrested and massacred in the military parade ground. The earth ran with the "jasper blood" of the martyred and stacks of bones stretched to the heavens.[128] Out of compassion, senior officials donated money for coffins; as a result, the workshops of Ji'nan were entirely emptied of lumber. This is why most of the poor souls [*gui*, literally "ghosts"] from the eastern counties were buried on the southern outskirts of the city. (*LZ* 4. 477)

This brief opening does more than provide the necessary background and set the proper mood: the philanthropic acts performed by the officials in the provincial capital that enable the slaughtered victims, the would-be ghosts, to receive a decent burial anticipates the structure of the narrative proper, where a personal act of generosity toward the memory of the dead twelve years after the massacre sets the events of the story in motion.

In 1674 the protagonist of the tale, a scholar from Laiyang, comes to Ji'nan and, remembering the friends and relatives who had perished there, purchases some spirit money and makes a libation to their souls in a deserted field. It is important that within the context of ancestral worship, the scholar was not *required* to look after the posthumous ritual for these relatives and friends, but that it is a *voluntary* act of compassion and charity. The very next night he receives a visit from the ghost of an old friend from his hometown, who had died in the rebellion. The scholar's initial act of remembrance does not absolve him of the past but rather entangles him in an ever-escalating web of ritual obligations to the dead. The friend's ghost, surnamed Zhu, has not come to thank the scholar for his attentions. Instead he seeks the scholar's help in arranging a posthumous match between himself and the scholar's unmarried niece, who, after the death of her mother in childhood, had resided for a time in her uncle's household.[129] The niece had later been arrested and brought to Ji'nan during the crackdown, where, upon learning of her father's execution, she had expired of grief and shock. Although the scholar initially resists shouldering further obligations to the dead,[130] he follows Zhu back to the underworld, to a large, newly established village "with hundreds of families," which is populated solely by ghosts of the rebellion's victims. There the scholar has an emotional reunion with his niece at her humble cottage:

> He saw a desolate courtyard half a *mou* wide, with two small rooms set side by side. In tears, his niece came to the door to greet him, and he too wept. A lamp glimmered in the room. The girl's face was as lovely and fresh as during her lifetime. Staring at him and blinking back the tears, she asked him about each of her aunts and cousins in turn. "They're all in fine health," he said, "except for my wife, who has passed away." The girl then sobbed again. "Aunt brought me up as child, and I have still never repaid her one bit. I never expected I'd be buried first. I feel such pangs of regret and remorse. Last year, my cousin took my father away, leaving me without a thought.[131] Hundreds of miles away from home, I'm lonely as a swallow in autumn. You, uncle, have not forsaken me even though I'm a dead soul. I have already received the gifts of money you sent." (*LZ* 4. 478)

During his visit, after he, as a senior male relative, authorizes his niece's marriage to Zhu, he falls in love with one of her ghost neighbors, the talented and beautiful Gongsun Jiuniang. His niece detects his feelings and offers to speak on his behalf to Jiuniang's mother, that is, she says, "if you're not put off by the filth and dirt of the underground." On his next visit to the village of ghosts a few days later, he finds that his niece and his friend are already happily married and cozily ensconced at Zhu's place. His niece has meanwhile arranged for him to take Jiuniang as his bride, and here the story enters the familiar terrain of the scholar-ghost romance. There is one stipulation, however: because in her loneliness, Jiuniang's mother cannot bear to part from her daughter, her only relative in the village, the scholar must reside with them for the duration of the marriage.[132]

Although the traditional Chinese marriage system is ordinarily patrilocal, under certain circumstances a husband sometimes agreed to marry into the wife's family; these uxorilocal marriages were generally regarded as lower in status and considered somewhat degrading for the man. In narratives where a living bridegroom enters into a marriage with a ghost in the tomb, it is perforce conceptualized as an uxorilocal arrangement, because the underground world of the tomb is represented as her abode. Sometimes, as here or in "The Bridegroom" ("Xinlang," *LZ* 1.95–96), the ghosts' dead relatives insist on this condition for the match, thereby naturalizing the ritual framework of the spirit marriage between a living man and a dead woman. In such cases, the polluting aspects of a union with the dead are conjoined with the humiliation of an uxorilocal arrangement.

There are many tales that situate an amour between man and ghost exclusively in the tomb or underworld. Often the interior of the tomb is experienced as a sumptuous mansion or palace while the man resides with the ghosts, but when he finally leaves and turns around for one last look, the palace has reverted into a grave mound. The architectural space of the dead is not always depicted in luxurious terms in a ghost story, but the extensive description of the humble domestic circumstances of the phantom village in "Gongsun Jiuniang" is quite unusual.[133] Coupled with the story's acute attention to the intimate texture of everyday life, the naturalistic portrayal and modest level of the afterlife depicted here is *unheimlich* in both the contradictory senses of the German term singled out by Freud: uncanny *because* something ordinarily concealed from outside eyes turns out to be so homey and familiar.[134]

One of the early anonymous burial songs from the Han dynasty calls the graveyard a "village of weeds" *(haoli);* later commentators said this dirge was sung at the burial of common folk, rather than of the high and mighty:

> What man's land is the Village of Weeds?
> It is the crowded home of ghosts,—
> Wise and foolish shoulder to shoulder.
> The King of the Dead claims them all;
> Man's fate knows no tarrying.[135]

In ghost stories that take place inside the abode of the dead, however, the mortuary unit is ordinarily the individual tomb, or at most a small complex of family graves.[136] Depicting the social world of a full-fledged graveyard is exceedingly rare. In "Gongsun Jiuniang," portraying an entire community of ghosts—"a large village with hundreds of families"—is a deliberate device to convey the scale of the executions and hence the size of the graveyard in which the victims were buried en masse. Jiuniang explains to the scholar that her village is called by the portmanteau name of "Laixia" because "it is mainly populated by new ghosts from the two districts of Laiyang and Qixia" (*LZ* 4. 481). A cemetery in Ji'nan combining the names of these two counties is mentioned in the Laiyang county gazetteer of 1935. The gazetteer concludes its account of the rebellion and its suppression by noting that nowadays in front of Yu Qi's former base of Sawtooth Mountain in Laiyang, "there's a hamlet called Blood-Bath Pavilion (Xueguan ting), while outside the southern gate of the provincial capital is an untended graveyard called Qi-lai Village (Qilai li). From these names, one can realize how cruel and terrible the slaughter was."[137] Although the appellation Pu Songling coined in "Gongsun Jiuniang" combines the syllables differently, the relationship of his village of ghosts to this mass burial field is clear and the horror evoked by it the same.

An essential feature of "Gongsun Jiuniang" is the doubling of the plot through the development of two parallel victims: the niece and Jiuniang, both virgin ghosts, who, first orphaned then robbed of life during the crackdown, enter into posthumous marriages. In the case of the niece, the narrative carries through the comforting fictions that survivors can intervene in the misery of the dead, that ritual practices by the living can ameliorate the lot of the deceased, and that victims of a mass killing are not alone in the next world because they have one another. The domestic happiness the niece finds with Zhu holds out the possibility that the scholar's nuptials with Jiuniang may produce a similarly favorable outcome. But sorrow, not joy, accompanies their union from the beginning, and the survivor is denied this easy panacea.

On their wedding night, after the consummation of the marriage, the scholar learns the tragic circumstances of his bride's death for the first time: she and her mother had been arrested after the rebellion and were being sent to the capital, Beijing. When they reached the city of Ji'nan, her mother died of distress. Jiuniang then slit her own throat. "Recalling the events of the past as she lay beside him on the pillow, she was choked with sobs and could not sleep. So she recited two quatrains of her own composition":

1.
My gossamer gown of bygone days has turned to dust;
In vain I behold my previous karma and resent my former life.
After ten years of dew chilling moonlit maples,
Tonight I first encounter spring in this painted chamber.

2.
Wind and rain surround the white poplars by my lonesome grave.
Who'd imagine clouds of love gathered again over Sunlit Terrace?[138]
All at once I open the gold-stitched casket and peer inside:
The stench of blood still soils my old gossamer skirt.[139]

The first quatrain ends with a beginning: after ten years of despair frozen in ghostly limbo, she has finally encountered the fecund thaw of spring. The coming of spring, which ordinarily signifies a sexual relationship, doubles as a common metaphor for resurrection in ghost poetry. In the Tang tale "Zhang Yunrong," a man finds himself making love to three female ghosts and is told that only one of them is fated to revive from his amorous attentions. "He makes a sprig of spring bloom in the dark valley," chants the fortunate one. "Tonight's bright spring will merely turn to fall," chants an unluckier one.[140] In "Teng Mu's Drunken Excursion," the ghost herself spells out the significance of this metaphor after she invites the visitor to become her lover: "Anyway, just now your poem with the line 'I'd like to . . . make spring bloom once in the dark valley' means you've already agreed."[141]

Jiuniang's physical initiation into love holds out the prospect of rebirth, a suggestion also implied in the opening of the second quatrain. There we find stock poetic signifiers of ghostliness: white poplar, wind, rain, grave. In conjunction with the clouds gathering in the next line, the rain also helps spell out "clouds and rain," the most common poetic euphemism for sexual intercourse. Read against the phrase "lonesome grave," Sunlit Terrace (literally, "Yang Terrace") also connotes the cosmic union of ghostly woman and mortal man. Up to this point, the lines Jiuniang chants are a pastiche of common ghost poetry elements that suggest revival and deliverance.

But the final couplet of the second quatrain unexpectedly takes a violent turn. The "stench of blood" soiling her old gossamer skirt instantly turns the nuptial image of the gold-embroidered dowry casket back into a coffin, shattering any further promise of rebirth or redemption. The refinement of a ghostly beauty is abruptly exposed as the morbidity of a corpse. The horror of history has reclaimed the pleasure of fantasy. As part of a verse chanted on the occasion of her wedding night, the blood staining her dress takes on a double meaning, superimposing defloration and suicide, linking blood not to rebirth as in "Lin Siniang" or resurrection as in "Liansuo" but to decay and annihilation. Jiuniang's defloration becomes the triggering mechanism that, in the manner of trauma victims, abruptly compels her to reexperience the shock of her own suicide.[142]

In contrast to the straightforward physicality of the ghost's body in many other tales, Jiuniang's body is shrouded, evoked only indirectly through the ephemeral material of her clothes. Anticipating the last line of the final quatrain, the opening line of the first verse also begins with a textile image: "My gossamer gown of bygone days has turned to dust." And when it is time for the scholar to leave the village of the ghosts forever, she sadly makes a final request: "Be mindful of the gratitude owed even for a single night of marriage and gather up my bones to take home with you. Bury them beside your family graveyard, so that a hundred generations from now, I will still have a secure resting place, and though dead, I won't have perished" (*LZ* 4. 481–482).[143] Then she presents him with one of her gossamer stockings as a parting keepsake. An intimate piece of female apparel, the stocking, like the shoe is a frequent lover's token in *Liaozhai,* but in this tale it registers additional meaning.

Stricken with grief, the scholar promises to do as she requests, but once he returns to the world of the living, he discovers "he had forgotten to ask for the inscription on her grave marker." When he returns that night to the southern outskirts of Ji'nan, where the victims of the Yu Qi rebellion are buried, he finds more than a thousand graves; try as he may, without more specific indications, he cannot locate her grave and fulfill his promise. "He took out the stocking she had given him. The moment the fabric caught in the wind, it turned to dust" (*LZ* 4. 482). The image echoes the opening of the first quatrain, lending the poem in retrospect a predictive force, intimating the irrevocability of her body's decay and the obliteration of her name. The stocking's disintegration also signals the rupture of any possible lingering attachment between ghost and man, the end of any hope even for ritual amends.

The scholar moves back east, but still cannot rid himself of her memory. About half a year later he revisits Ji'nan, longing to find her again. As night falls, he rides once more through the burial ground. This time, however, the atmosphere has changed: "The myriad graves stretched endlessly before him, their desolate wastes blurring his sight, the ghost fires and howling foxes striking terror into the human heart" (*LZ* 4. 482). At this moment, the prelude to a horror tale, he sees a girl who looks remarkably like Jiuniang walking alone amid the tombs. He tries to speak to her, but she flees "as though she doesn't recognize him." When he tries to approach her again, "a look of anger came over her features. She raised her sleeve to screen her face. As he called out her name, she vanished like smoke" (*LZ* 4. 482).

A ghost also covers her face with her sleeve before disappearing forever in other tales, including the *Liaozhai* version of "Lin Siniang," but in these instances, the gesture is part of an amicable farewell and has the effect of a gentle fadeout.[144] In such cases, raising the sleeve to the face, as though to wipe away tears or cover the mouth, is also a persistent gesture of grief for ghosts. In a remarkable Tang tale from the ninth century about an infamous political purge in 835, when the ghosts of the victims, all former loyal officials, hear a poem commemorating the tragic history of their deaths, "they each raised their sleeves to cover their faces, as though they were about to weep. . . . Then they mounted their horses and vanished like smoke."[145] In Pu Songling's day, the same gesture is also described by Kong Shangren to evoke the anguish experienced by certain members of the audience at performances of his *Peach Blossom Fan:* "But amidst the music and lavish display, now and then some spectator would cover his face with his sleeve; he would turn out to be a former official or aged loyalist from the last dynasty."[146] Some pictorial representations of ghosts may also depict this veiling gesture of sorrow. The famous Yuan dynasty handscroll of Little Su's ghost shows her partially covering her mouth with her sleeve (see fig. 7). In the Land and Water mural of ghosts in Green Dragon Temple, a drowned female ghost similarly raises her sleeve to her lips (see fig. 4), as does a late Ming woodblock illustration of Mulian's mother as a dead soul in the underworld (see fig. 8).

But only in "Gongsun Jiuniang" is raising the sleeve to block the face a hostile threat, a menacing gesture: Leave me alone or I'll avenge myself on you. The abruptness and theatricality of the gesture here suggest that the stage may have offered Pu Songling additional inspiration. When Du Liniang appears midway through *Peony Pavilion* for the first time after her death, the stage directions read: "She enters wailing as a ghost, and hiding her face with her sleeve." And when she exits, the stage directions indicate that she do so also "wailing as a ghost." In the final scene of this tale, however, Jiuniang is mute and cannot even vent her bitter feelings in a ghostly wail. Communication between man and ghost is no longer possible; there is only the void, as she vanishes like smoke. Jiuniang's veiling herself with her sleeve just before disappearing also recalls the unstable textile images—the crumbling gossamer gown, the disintegrating silk stocking—used earlier to shroud her body and adumbrate its decay. In this sense, the disembodiment of Jiuniang's presence throughout the story reminds us, in Marjorie Garber's words, that "the ghost—itself traditionally often veiled, sheeted, or shadowy in form—is a cultural marker of absence, a reminder of loss."[147]

The extent of what is lost in "Gongsun Jiuniang" emerges clearly in contrast to "Lin Siniang," where, after the ghost's departure, the lover is left with something to remember her by that still bears the traces of her hand.[148] The written text of the poem she leaves behind is a bulwark against her total disappearance. But Jiuniang never transcribes her verses anywhere, and the flimsy keepsake she does bestow upon her lover soon disintegrates. Having forgotten to ask for the inscription on her gravestone, the scholar from Laiyang has ensured that, for all practical purposes, any written sign of her presence is gone forever. Owen discusses the need to have a written marker to commemorate the deceased in Chinese culture: "To weep for a particular man rather than for the anonymous dead, there must be a stele of writing, a mediating fragment that marks the name and the specific spot."[149] Nie Shiqiao and Deng Kuiying are right that the great achievement of "Gongsun Jiuniang" is

FIGURE 7 Liu Yuan, *Sima Caizhong's Dream of the Courtesan Su Xiaoxiao.* Handscroll, ink and color on silk, Yuan dynasty. Detail depicting the ghost of Little Su, appearing in Sima Caizhong's dream and raising her sleeve to her face. Courtesy of the Cincinnati Art Museum.

FIGURE 8 Mulian's mother as a dead soul appearing in her son's dream, raising her sleeve to her face. Zheng Zhizhen, *Mulian Rescues his Mother (Mulian jiumu), Guben xiqu* I, no. 67.

to individualize the mass of ordinary innocent people who perished in the executions.[150] Nonetheless, without the transmission of the inscription on Jiuniang's tombstone, ritually, in the context of the narrative, she must remain one of the anonymous dead, buried in the frightening expanse of an untended mass graveyard, rather than in the protective confines of ancestral tombs. That is part of the horror of the ending, an outcome that no one, however good-intentioned, can ever change. This includes not only the scholar from Laiyang, the survivor in the story, but the author of the tale, who bears witness to the historical event.

The narrative proper ends abruptly with Jiuniang's refusal or inability to recognize her husband; the scholar's response to this rejection, this heartbreaking proof of the dead's ultimate estrangement from the living, goes unrecorded. But the Historian of the Strange's final comment on the story shifts back to the scholar's point of view:

> When the loyal courtier Qu Yuan drowned himself in the Bolo River, hot blood flooded his breast. And when Prince Shensheng, the faithful son of Duke Xian, received the pendant worn at Dongshan telling him not to return, his tears soaked the sandy soil. These are cases of filial sons and loyal ministers from antiquity, who, even in death were never pardoned by their father or sovereign. Could it really be because the scholar failed in his mission to move her bones that Jiuniang's resentment was so implacable? One cannot tear one's heart from one's breast and show it to others. How unjust! (*LZ* 4. 483).

The reason the scholar fails in his mission to move Jiuniang's bones, the reason he fails in the obligations he incurred to the dead is because he has forgotten to ask for the inscription on her tombstone and therefore cannot locate her grave. In other words, the reason the story ends badly is because something was forgotten. The narrative "blames" him for forgetting to ask, but it could have equally blamed Jiuniang for neglecting to tell him. (To guard against just such a contingency, in "Liansuo," or *Peony Pavilion*, the ghost volunteers the precise information necessary to recognize her grave when she requests her lover to exhume her bones and then nags him not to forget.) Since the scholar has been assiduous throughout the story in extending kindness to the ghosts, the rhetorical question posed in the commentary raises further doubt as to the meaning of the ending: "Could it really be because the scholar failed in his mission to move her bones that Jiuniang's resentment was so implacable?" If the scholar's ostensible offense was in fact rather trivial, then what is the reason for Jiuniang's "implacapable resentment"?

Nie and Deng dismiss the importance of the Historian of the Strange's postscript, which seems to shift the blame onto the scholar, and argue that the true cause of Jiuniang's anger and bitterness is resentment against the Qing authorities responsible for the massacre.[151] Allan Barr finds greater significance in the comments, as expressing not so much sympathy for the misunderstood scholar, as commiseration with the injustice suffered by all those who died: "In his postscript, by alluding to classic historical cases of faithful allegiance spurned by royal distrust—Qu

Yuan and Prince Shensheng—Pu Songling dignifies and ennobles the victims of the 1662 suppression and at the same time emphasizes the depth of his sympathies for their tragic demise."[152] The problem with Barr's reading is that contrary to what one would expect, the parallel drawn is between these classical exemplars and the *scholar,* rather than between them and *Jiuniang.* By empathizing with the scholar's rather than the ghost's predicament in the postscript, Pu Songling, in his role as Historian of the Strange, conveys the survivor's feelings of guilt and anguish at the memory of his impotence to save the Yu Qi rebellion's innocent victims.

Yet Barr is also right that the Historian of the Strange's sympathy and indignation in the postscript, which ends with the ringing cry "How unjust!" must also extend to Jiuniang, and through her, to the rest of the slain. Although narrative and authorial comment usually have separate rhetorical divisions of labor in *Liaozhai,* shared imagery sometimes helps bridge the disjunction between the two.[153] In the case of "Gongsun Jiuniang," the formal parallelism of the postscript's style gives rise to a chiasmus between the lines "hot blood flooded his breast" *(xue man xiongyi)* and "his tears soaked the sandy soil" *(lei ze nisha)* to give us "hot blood soaked the sandy soil" and "tears flooded his breast." In this fashion, the postscript's use of language not only evokes the tears shared by survivor and victims throughout the story, but also recalls the earth running with the jasper blood of the martyred in the story's opening and the stench of blood that stains Jiuniang's gossamer skirt at the end.

In his passionate meditation on time and narrative, Ricoeur asserts that in reconstituting the past, "everything takes place as though historians knew themselves to be bound by a debt to people from earlier times, to the dead."[154] The great problematic of the Chinese literary ghost story is what obligation the living owe the dead who have no prior lien of kinship or acquaintance on them. This is why the crux of the dilemma the scholar faces in "Gongsun Jiuniang" concerns Jiuniang, initially a stranger, rather than his niece or his old friend; and this is why the scholar-ghost romance, which binds a living man to a dead stranger he previously owed nothing to, is so prevalent. In a ghost story that takes as its subject the commemoration of a local historical tragedy and the obscure victims crushed by it, which opens up a space for commemoration that no other literary form could provide, these two debts—the obligation the historian owes to the past and the obligation the living survivor owes to the dead—converge. This is why the scholar from Laiyang's offense was not trivial at all. His crime is forgetting, and the entire point of "Gongsun Jiuniang" is the injunction to remember, not to let the sufferers of history pass into oblivion.

4

Ghosts and Theatricality

There is likewise always something ghostly or haunting about an actor.
— MICHAEL GOLDMAN, *The Actor's Freedom*

THE YEARS FROM 1580 to 1700 witnessed an explosion of ghosts in writings for the stage. In part, this increase stemmed from a general proliferation of new plays, for this was the heyday of the southern drama *(chuanqi).* As the playwright Yuan Yuling (1592–1674) declared: "There's never been such a superabundance of plays as nowadays."[1] This surge had as much to do with the late Ming boom in publishing as with the passion of literary men for the theater. The lengthiness of southern drama play texts—thirty or forty acts was average, but fifty acts was not uncommon—meant that these plays were much more likely to be read than performed in their entirety. The printed versions that have come down to us—many complete with scholarly prefaces, lavish illustrations, and marginal commentaries—bear all the hallmarks of works destined for the desktop rather than for use on the stage.

In his essays on the art of the theater, the playwright and impresario Li Yu (1611–1680) adopts the viewpoint of contemporary actors fed up with overly bookish plays when he expresses the wish for another First Qin Emperor to arise, who would torch "the editions of plays published by literary men," leaving only the "hand-copied versions made by actors."[2] Li Yu's hyperbole notwithstanding, it is largely the published editions rather than the hand-copied versions that have survived today and that are therefore our main source for theater in this period.[3]

The prevalence of ghost themes in seventeenth-century plays stems in part from the importance playwrights and their public placed on the quality of *qi*[a]—amazing, novel, marvelous—in the composition of southern drama. Since this word figured in the name of the genre—*chuanqi* (literally, "passing on something amazing")—it was natural for Ming and Qing writers to indulge in wordplay on the term. As Xu Xianglin, quoting a common saying in the period, asserts: "Especially during the late Ming and early Qing, playwrights followed the trend 'if it's not amazing, it can't be passed on' *(fei qi*[a] *bu chuan).* The figure of the ghost and the ghost story perfectly fit this idea of the amazing, and so the apparition of a ghost in southern drama became all the rage in theater circles at the time."[4]

During the late Ming and early Qing, *qi*[a] was prized as an aesthetic category in many realms, including poetry, painting, calligraphy, and personality, but when applied to drama it had a specifically theatrical application. As Guo Yingde makes clear, what many seventeenth-century drama critics meant by "amazing" or "novel" had less to do with the *content* of a play than with the *mode* of constructing a plot. In other words, what make a play "amazing" or "marvelous" are not ghosts or supernatural elements per se, though these may contribute to the effect, but the twists and turns that provoke surprise and wonder in the audience. Of these, Guo singles out the devices of "mistaken identity" *(cuoren)* and "breaking up the match" *(pohuai)*.[5]

This emphasis on *qi*[a] was in large measure a function of the southern-drama form itself. By convention, this theater was a genre of romantic comedy, featuring star-crossed lovers who are reunited in the end. As in romantic comedy the world over, the need is to forestall the permanent union of the lovers, to devise ingenious ways of keeping the lovers apart or unmarried until the grand finale. In the southern drama, again as in romantic comedy elsewhere, the imperative to delay leads to the proliferation of disguises, false identities, and doubles, and to the continual manufacture of obstacles, real and feigned, thrown in the lovers' path. What distinguishes the southern drama, however, is the favoring of a scenario, exemplified by *Peony Pavilion,* in which the dilation necessary to romance is accomplished by killing off the heroine in the first half of the play and then bringing her back as an amorous ghost before her eventual revival and marriage to the hero. There are multiple variants of this plot type, but in each case the introduction of a female revenant opens the door to a whole range of comic impersonations and misidentifications, producing impediments and complications enough to satisfy even the lengthiest play.

In a letter to Yuan Yuling, Zhang Dai (1597–1684), the theater connoisseur whose memoirs of the Ming entertainment world are such an important source, protested the absurdities of the contemporary stage:

> Nowadays the penchant for the strange and fantastic *(guaihuan)* in the southern drama has gone over the top. No sooner has the male lead made his entrance, than he starts thinking about changing his name; no sooner does the female lead appear on stage, than she wants to put on a disguise. In both cases, there's no rhyme or reason to it, and no logical connection. Playwrights are just after some noisy excitement *(naore)*, so they don't bother with the why or wherefore. They just want to make something amazing happen and don't care about their writing making sense.[6]

Zhang Dai's letter is a polemic against playwrights such as his friend, whose most recent play strives so hard to dazzle the audience that it neglects the richness of everyday life and loses sight of basic logic, relying instead on easy tricks of the trade such as special effects and spectacle. One of Zhang's chief complaints is the overuse of supernatural display unmotivated by story line or dramatic necessity: "Playwrights nowadays want to dazzle the audience from the start, so in the prologue they have the actors costumed as gods and ghosts playing devilish tricks and wreaking havoc. After this bout of noisy excitement, when the male lead makes his entrance in the first act proper, if his self-introduction is at all long, then it feels terribly tiresome."[7] Thus in his estimation, the superfluous insertion of gods and ghosts in a play works against rather than towards the playwright's desire to amaze.

It is well known that in late imperial China public theatricals open to members of all social classes were presented on ritual occasions and at religious festivals.[8] The most famous of these are the operas that depict the Buddhist saga of Mulian rescuing his mother from Hell. These lengthy productions, which can be traced back to at least the twelfth century, were typically performed during the mid-summer Ghost Festival as part of the rites to propitiate lonely souls and hungry ghosts, and featured a terrifying panoply of demons inflicting tortures on the dead in the underworld. Zhang Dai's memoirs describe one particularly elaborate seventeenth-century performance, financed and orchestrated by his uncle, which ran three days and three nights on a stage erected in the local military training ground.[9]

During the late Ming and Qing, spectacles with actors costumed as ghosts and gods were common not only at religious festivals, which were usually held at temples or other public spaces, but as part of the entertainment at the private banquets hosted by the wealthy elite, where theatricals were de rigueur. As Zhang's letter suggests, a chief attraction of supernatural spectacles in a banquet performing context was the opportunity they afforded for "noisy excitement."[10] Li Yu also complained about his contemporaries' penchant at parties for "filling the stage with ox-headed demons and serpent gods,"[11] but what he most objected to was the inappropriateness of offering this sort of fare at private celebrations: "Ah, for a living person to see a ghost is an inauspicious omen. Even more so on a festive family occasion, how could bringing out demons and monsters be conducive to longevity?"[12]

Although there is no indigenous Chinese term that corresponds to the English word "theatricality" (a word only coined in 1843 and covering a wide range of meanings), I agree with Tracy Davis and Thomas Postlewait that "its denotations and connotations connect it with terms, concepts, and practices that have a long history in many cultures."[13] Zhang Dai's and Li Yu's complaints about the overuse of gods and ghosts in the private performances of their day shed light on the first of three interrelated concepts of theatricality central to this chapter. On the most basic level, in my usage, theatricality refers to everything that differentiates representation in drama from that of other literary genres, notably the tale and poetry. Inherent in this notion of theatricality is the dual perspective in drama of text and performance. Zhang's critique argues from both perspectives, literary and experiential: too many ghosts too soon violates his definition of a well-made play; excessive deployment bores the audience. Li Yu's critique, on the other hand, adopts solely the perspective of performance, in which a play is a theatrical event, whose meaning and affect are above all contingent on context, occasion, and audience. The dangerous power that he ascribes to the performance of a ghost in the wrong setting underscores the close link between ritual and theater in his world even on ostensibly secular occasions.

The second concept of theatricality important to this chapter includes the entire sensorial experience at a performance of a play for which a play text is only a blueprint at best. Underlying this notion of theatricality is the overall importance of mise-en-scène, understood to encompass not only the visual and acoustic spectacle, the construction of stage space, and the bodily deployment of the actor, but the entire range of stage practices and acting conventions through which a specter is realized in the theater. Taken collectively, these practices and conventions constitute a semiotic code of ghosts in drama.

My third concept of theatricality refers to the capability of the theater to reflect upon its own status as performance. In this metatheatrical sense, the fact that plays frequently incorporate direct or indirect references to the conventions of their own enactment allows us to read plays as statements about the nature of theater. It is my contention that scenes in which the soul is shown splitting from or rejoining the body, or in which the body of one woman is possessed by the ghost of another woman, or in which a corpse is revived and resurrected, lend themselves especially well to metatheatrical interpretation because they lay bare the most fundamental convention of theater, that of the actor's doubleness—the experience of playing another and bringing this character to life on stage.

Rather than investigating all late Ming and early Qing drama in which a ghost or demon makes an appearance, this chapter will explore how the female revenant was staged in southern-drama play texts and what, by extension, this staging tells us about how phantoms were represented and conceptualized in the period. These play texts were composed by literary men and were largely intended to be staged as banquet entertainment, though they were not restricted to any single performance context.[14] A chief aim of this chapter is to understand how the ghost romance was translated into the dramatic conventions of a play text and the histrionic conventions of the stage during the highpoint of the southern drama. As I will demonstrate, the art of representing the revenant in these plays is closely connected with the central question of how to manifest invisibility and visibility on stage and with the fundamental theatrical values of showing and hiding, appearance and disappearance.[15]

In the first part of the chapter I attempt to reconstruct the histrionic code of the female revenant and her affect, highlighting the importance of role type and stage directions, the dramatic and symbolic threshold of entrance and exits, the sensorial cues of sound and movement, and the manipulation of costume. The second part examines two sets of interrelated late Ming revenant plays, which, though heavily influenced by *Peony Pavilion*, feature more than one female lead and must therefore propose alternative solutions to the theatrical problem of a dead woman's desire.

The Phantom Heroine

The most fundamental division in traditional Chinese theater is that of role type. Yet, as Liu Chuhua has argued, the ghost never developed into an independent role category but was instead assigned to a number of already existing role types.[16] In the case of a female revenant, the part is overwhelmingly assigned to the *dan* (the female lead) and only occasionally to another role type such as the *tie* (a supporting young female role). For this reason the most common term for the female ghost role is *hun dan*—the female lead's soul—which I translate as "phantom heroine." Although the term is most commonly applied to the spirit of a dead woman, death is not an absolute requirement: *hun dan* may refer to any soul that is detached from a body—whether in a coma, or in the guise of an image, such as a likeness in a portrait or a reflection in water or a mirror.[17] All of these resemble a ghost in being conceived as "shadow or reflection without form,"—as a secondary representation, a double of a missing original.[18]

This "secondary" aspect of the phantom heroine is crucial to understanding why despite the importance and elaboration of this part in dramatizations of the ghost romance, it could not develop into an autonomous role type. The term *hun dan* appears on no list of role divisions, late imperial or modern, with the exception of contemporary Sichuan opera, which is famous for its ghosts.[19] At the same time, a specter must also be recognizably different on stage from an ordinary human or divine being. This necessity helps explain why the phantom heroine developed into a distinct sub-role with its own special gestures, dance movements, costumes, formulaic lyrics, stage business, sound effects, and probably distinctive vocal styles. The presence of this sub-role in Ming and Qing theater required playwrights to have a basic contour of the role in mind when they scripted their plays, performers to have received the appropriate training to specialize in such parts, and audiences conversant with the stylized conventions of such roles. The presence of at least some of these conventions in a play text easily allows us to identify a character as belonging to this subcategory even when, as in the case of You Tong's *Celestial Court Music (Juntian yue),* the playwright foregoes adding the prefix *hun* and instead uses the term *dan* indiscriminately to refer both to the living heroine and her ghost.

The phantom heroine first coalesced as a leading role in Yuan drama, where it pertains equally to a wronged ghost in pursuit of redress and to an amorous revenant in pursuit of love. No phantom-heroine play is among the only extant edition of plays published during the Yuan, however, so we have no way of knowing Yuan textual conventions for this part. The earliest sources to include such plays, which date from the late sixteenth and early seventeenth centuries, couple the terms *hun* and *dan* to designate the role, but the syntactical order is not uniform.[20] The earliest usage of *hun dan* appears in the late Ming editions of Zheng Guangzu's Yuan play *The Disembodied Soul (Qiannü lihun),* where the term is employed to differentiate the heroine's disembodied soul from her body immobilized in coma, which is designated as the "principal female lead" *(zheng dan).*[21]

The comparable term in Yuan plays for a male revenant (most often a slain warrior) is simply *hunzi;*[22] using the proper name of the character rather than a role-type designation, especially for an historical figure such as General Guan Yu or the demon-catcher Zhong Kui, is also common. Judging from our corpus of extant Yuan plays, male ghosts outnumbered female ghosts on the Yuan stage by a considerable margin.[23] In late Ming and early Qing southern drama, we find a not unexpected reversal: the ratio of female to male ghosts on stage becomes much higher, in keeping with the general trend toward the increased "feminization" of the supernatural in later imperial times, which the romantic orientation of the theater in this period reinforced.[24]

One important characteristic of the phantom heroine is that the role is always conceived in tandem with a living heroine and therefore always represents a kind of theatrical doubling, since one performer ordinarily played both roles. In Yuan northern drama, as in the case of *The Disembodied Soul,* such doubling is mandated since only one singing role is permitted per play. But it is carried over into Ming southern drama, where no such restrictions apply, and where generally speaking the two leads—the *sheng* and the *dan*—did not engage in the extensive doubling that other role types did.[25] The continuation of this practice in southern drama suggests that it was not simply due to the peculiar exigency of Yuan dramatic conventions. To the contrary. One appeal of the ghost romance for the southern drama was precisely the opportunity it afforded for doubling the female role, both for thematic reasons and to showcase the skills of the performer.

The immediate stimulus for the profusion of phantom-heroine roles in the late Ming and early Qing was the sensation caused by *Peony Pavilion* and its female protagonist, Du Liniang. *Peony Pavilion* includes five scenes featuring Du Liniang in the *hun dan* role (one as a dead soul in the underworld and four as a revenant in the garden where her body lies buried).[26] With the exception of the underworld scene, none of the revenant scenes became part of the late eighteenth-century repertory of opera excerpts, which shaped the performing canon that has come down to us today.[27] Some recent productions of *Peony Pavilion* have attempted to revive these missing scenes with mixed results.[28] Although the revenant scenes in *Peony Pavilion* clearly fell out of favor with later performers and theatergoers, the number of extant seventeenth-century plays that adopt the formula of a phantom heroine and her revival strongly suggests that playwrights were catering to a contemporary audience that expected and relished such episodes.

The intensity of the seventeenth-century response to *Peony Pavilion,* particularly among female readers and spectators, has been the subject of a number of recent studies.[29] Among male playwrights of the period, however, the play's influence was arguably even more far-reaching. First, several prominent literary figures in the theater world, including Shen Jing (1553–1610), Zang Maoxun (1550–1620), and Feng Menglong, drastically rewrote and abridged the play text and even published their revised editions.[30] Their alterations involved the rearrangement of certain scenes and plot elements with significant changes in the staging, including the revenant and resurrection portion of the play. Their ostensible aim was to make the play more performable by reducing the number of arias and by altering the lyrics to make them better conform to the prosodic requirements of *kunqu* (*kun*-style opera, so-called because it originated in Kunshan, outside the city of Suzhou), which had become the reigning musical mode of performance in elite circles. But as Catherine Swatek shows in her study of *Peony Pavilion*'s performance history, the reasons behind the revisions were much more complex and were also intended to correct perceived violations in logic, decorum, and dramatic convention.[31]

Second, many new plays were written to showcase the phantom heroine, both by playwrights considered followers of Tang Xianzu, such as Wu Bing (1595–1648), and by those considered Tang's opponents, such as Shen Jing. Some of these new creations mechanically copied *Peony Pavilion,* but others sought to revitalize the formula by adding all sorts of novel complications. Still others, such as Meng Chengshun's *Mistress and Maid* greatly expand a phantom-heroine interlude that is a mere tangent in the novella the play is based on.[32]

In several of these new plays the influence of *Peony Pavilion* is explicitly acknowledged, not only in marginal comments, but even incorporated into key arias or dialogue.[33] For example, in Wu Bing's *Lady in the Painting (Huazhong ren),* when the servant (played by a clown) prepares to dig up the heroine's coffin as part of his master's plan to resurrect her, he complains: "There's never been such a thing in the world! Where did he come up with this notion? I expect it's from having misread *The Soul's Return,* so he thinks there really was a Du Liniang who came back to life. My master is truly an idiot!"[34] The clown's wink at the audience notwithstanding, the crazy scheme does succeed, precisely as the well-known scenario promises.

In this climate, Yuan plays on the ghost-romance theme, which had influenced Tang Xianzu in his creation of Du Liniang, gained new currency. Meng Chengshun's 1633 anthology of Yuan plays chose *The Disembodied Soul* to head the collection, a placement Patricia Sieber attributes to Meng's conviction that this play was the main source for *Peony Pavilion.*[35] The corpus of new plays stimulated by *Peony Pavilion* included rewrites of these Yuan northern dramas into southern drama form, which entailed expanding a concise four- or five-act play into a capacious one of thirty or forty acts. Although none of the southern-drama rewrites of *The Disembodied Soul* are extant, an excellent surviving example of this trend is Fan Wenruo's (1588–1636) *Intoxicating Dream of Flowers* (*Menghua han;* henceforth, *An Intoxicating Dream*), completed around 1632, which was based on the Yuan northern drama *Emerald Peach Flower (Bi taohua).*[36] The playwright's preface recalls that during his childhood, this play had already been adapted for the southern drama and was being widely performed, but declares that his own specific point of departure was *Peony Pavilion.* As he explains: "Now I have written up my own new version of this play, because while the plot subtly resembles *Peony Pavilion,* in terms of occult marvels, spine-chilling glamour, twists, turns, and reversals, I think this one surpasses it."[37]

In affect and presentation, the phantom heroine differs from the two other common types of Chinese stage ghosts—painted face roles *(jing)* such as Zhong Kui and the judges of the underworld, or the colorful demons and ghosts in their infernal entourage played by clowns or extras. Underworld settings and characters provided the kind of noisy excitement and spectacular display that Zhang Dai and Li Yu scoffed were so popular among their contemporaries. For this reason, no doubt, the comic underworld scene "Infernal Judgment" ("Ming pan") in *Peony Pavilion,* where Du Liniang's dead soul is granted a temporary reprieve to return to the land of the living, was widely copied in subsequent phantom-heroine plays, and was, as I have mentioned, the only ghost scene from the play to remain in the later performing repertory.

As befits a romantic female lead, the phantom heroine of the theater is ordinarily portrayed as the superlative beauty familiar to us from the classical tale. As such, she has little in common with the grotesque denizens of the netherworld whose antics aroused so much amusement or terror in spectators. Only once in the sixteenth- and seventeenth-century ghost plays I have studied does the phantom heroine transform herself on stage into a monstrous being. In *Lady in the Painting,* the spirit of the portrait, (who in Wu Bing's convoluted plot is also the revenant of a dead woman), is about to be raped by the villain. To rescue her, the play text inserts a striking bit of stage business: "The female lead suddenly assumes ghost/demon form *(hu bian zuo gui xing);* the villain flees in alarm at the sight; the female lead pursues him a while, then exits."[38] Confronting the villain again in a subsequent scene, the stage directions similarly instruct the female lead to "suddenly change to a ghost/demon face" *(hu bian gui lian).*[39] No contemporary source I have seen offers any corroborating description of how such an effect might have been achieved on stage. It is tempting to imagine that it might have involved a mask.[40] However, since another scene in *Lady in the Painting* explicitly has a clown "don" and "remove a ghost mask" *(dai/luo gui mian)* to scare a charlatan exorcist, it may be more likely that the dramatic transformation from beautiful woman to terrifying demon in this play would have been mimed, relying simply on the performer's facial and body technique.[41]

A leading attraction of the phantom heroine role for sixteenth- and seventeenth-century dramatists was the scope it afforded for the expression of feeling, the all-important quality of *qing* that *Peony Pavilion* explored in such depth, and which its imitations and spin-offs pursued so avidly. Even the few vengeful female ghosts in late Ming plays are still presented basically as *qing gui*—revenants who are compelled to return as much or more for love and desire as for a thirst for revenge. In Xu Zichang's dramatic version of *Outlaws of the Marsh* (*Shuihu ji;* 1590), for instance, in a scene that is performed today as "Taken Alive" ("Huo zhuo"), the courtesan Yan Poxi refrains from haunting her murderer, returning instead to reclaim her clownish lover and drag him down to hell with her.[42]

Although lighthearted elements and comic effects are still often incorporated into phantom-heroine scenes (usually at the expense of the hopelessly naive male lead, but occasionally at the expense of the boorish clown), the lyrical power of the stage ghost stems from the arias she sings. In Wu Bing's *West Garden (Xiyuan ji),* an exemplary aria juxtaposing the passion of desire with the melancholy of death is sung by the phantom heroine as she makes her entrance, en route to the hero's study for their first ghostly tryst:

> *(sings to the tune "Tenderly Painting Brows")*
> Clad in the garments I wore in life,
> jade dangling at my waist,
> I'm lovely as before.

Don't say my make-up has melted away
    or my bones are no longer sweet-smelling.
The feelings I have now as a ghost
    are still capable of affection,
    exactly as a human being's are.
It's just that since my death I can't shake this malady:
    when a desolate wind blows,
    I love to walk in cold places
    beneath a broken sliver of moon.[43]

The fusion of scene *(jing)* and feeling *(qing)* so prized in Chinese poetics takes on additional urgency in dramatic arias because of the usual absence of visual scenery in the theater. Time and place must be established through word pictures sung by the characters onstage, which become imbued with their own subjectivity. This aria serves multiple purposes then: it paints a cold, wind-blown nighttime vista, dimly illumined by a crescent moon—a properly ghostly scene—and it identifies the singer as a revenant, compelled to walk night after night, her longing intensified by the loneliness around her. The "malady" *(bing)* she is suffering from is the usual lovesickness of the amorous ghost: though her bones have decayed, her feelings are "still capable of affection," and the jade pendants dangling from her waist adumbrate a body ready for love. Most important, the aria is sung directly to the audience, rather than overheard by a character within the play.

In ghost plays, as opposed to ghost stories, the phantom heroine's own experience and feelings are foregrounded so that they equal or even surpass those of any mortal protagonist. This represents a major departure from the literary convention of the ghost story. Following the generic affiliation of accounts of the strange to unofficial history, most Chinese ghost stories claim to be based on hearsay or eyewitness reports, and play on the border between credulity and incredulity. For this reason, as we have seen, the ghost story inevitably presents a ghost as other from an external narrative perspective, filtered through and framed by the experience of the human witness who encounters the specter. Access to knowledge and point of view are therefore restricted for the reader, who is usually placed in the same blinkered position of ignorance vis-à-vis the ghost as the story's mortal protagonist(s). In such tales the ghost's identity becomes a mystery that the reader must solve. By contrast, the theater offers the possibility of unmediated presentation, for the ordinarily elusive specter to be fully present on stage in the physical person of the actor, who directs what the audience sees and feels. At issue in drama therefore is not the existence or reality of ghosts, nor even the power of illusion. On stage, the ghost is no longer an enigma.

The feelings that the phantom heroine in *West Garden* sings about upon her entrance are not meant simply to be experienced by herself as an autonomous character in a play, but by an external audience of spectators, listeners, and readers. Again we must understand *qing* in a specifically theatrical context. The strong point of the theater, emphasized again and again by seventeenth-century writers, was its ability to invoke emotion in the audience. Scripted by the playwright, invested in a character, embodied by an actor, and sung to music, *qing* could be seen as more central to the theater than to any other artistic or literary form. It is no coincidence that *Peony Pavilion,* the most important work to champion *qing* expressly, was a play, or that the height of the southern drama, when new plays were being produced in greatest number, was also the era when the cult of feeling was, ideologically speaking, at its hottest. The female ghost, as I have argued throughout this book, was conceived as the best way to give *qing* an external form with the power to induce corresponding feelings in an audience—much as an actor does in the theater.

Stage Directions

I have mentioned that many long southern plays in this period were probably only read in their entirety, but playwrights naturally hoped that their works would be staged, at least in abridged or excerpted productions, and wrote them accordingly. Being able to imagine how a work would be staged was considered a fundamental part of the playwright's craft, and there developed a strong consciousness that while the lyrics to and arrangement of the arias were paramount, they alone were not sufficient to carry a play. An anonymous critique in a late Ming edition of Tang Xianzu's first play *The Purple Hairpin (Zichai ji)* makes this point clearly:

> A southern drama should have arias, dialogue, stage directions, and gags. Now *The Purple Hairpin* only has arias; the dialogue is especially awful, and though there are gags occasionally, they don't make anyone laugh. As for the so-called stage directions, even in his dreams, the playwright never envisaged any! . . . For a playwright, the arias are the flesh, the stage directions are the sinews and bones, the dialogue and gags are the facial expressions. But when it comes to *The Purple Hairpin,* flesh is all there is, so how could it move? Isn't it just a corpse of flesh? [44]

Imagery based on a medical mapping of the human body was common across a range of aesthetic discourses in China, including calligraphy, painting, and poetry, but less so in drama criticism, so that here the somatic metaphor still retains a polemical freshness and wit.[45] The choice of "flesh" *(rou)* as an analogy for the lyrics to arias is particularly apt because "flesh" was also used as a metonym for the human singing voice.[46] As such, the oxymoron "corpse of flesh" recognizes that a play text conceived solely as words to be sung will be inert and dead. Lyricism must be yoked to action for a play to "move." The passage's conceit also picks up on a recurrent notion in late Ming drama criticism, that a good playwright reincarnates his characters, bringing dead figures from the past to life with his brush and reanimating them on stage.[47] The problem in this case is that the corpse stubbornly remains a corpse, a lifeless dud.

What is particularly noteworthy in this passage is not simply the implication that the theater is about "animating" a written text, but that the capacity to be animated must be present from the start in a play text. In an essay on Baudelaire's failure as a playwright, Roland Barthes calls attention to a paradox: theatricality, as he defines it, is "theater-minus-text,"—that "density of signs and sensations built up on stage starting from the written text," but it must also be an embryonic quality, a potential present in the play as written—"a datum of creation, not of production," as he phrases it.[48] Although Barthes is discussing nineteenth-century France, and assumes a much closer alignment between play text and staged production than would have been the case in sixteenth- and seventeenth-century China, his insight is nonetheless helpful for approaching the lengthy plays of the southern drama, which in essence were written simultaneously for two art forms, for circulation as reading material and for adaptation as performance.

For reconstructing how the mise-en-scène of ghosts was imagined in the southern drama of this period, stage directions in extant play texts are crucial, since contemporary sources offer neither detailed descriptions of actual performances nor prescriptions for the performance techniques involved, while modern stagecraft, though an important reference point, has changed too much over the centuries to be any reliable indication for sixteenth- and seventeenth-century practice.[49] Broadly conceived and defined, stage directions consist of everything in a play text that falls outside the lyrics to arias or the words to dialogue—those written instructions pertaining to exits and entrances, role types, gestures, sound effects, costumes, and props.[50] Occasionally information provided in the stage directions (say, regarding costume or sound effect) is also incorporated into the dialogue or alluded to in the arias. Because stage directions ostensibly offer instructions to performers and owners or managers of troupes, it is easy to misconstrue the elaboration and proliferation of such cues in a text as the sign of a script for production or a record of what transpired on stage. In fact, the history of stage directions in Chinese drama suggests that the opposite is true. Along with increased dialogue and the addition of illustrations and commentary, the expansion of stage directions can be strongly linked to the wide-scale publication of plays and emergence of a reading public for drama that solidified in the late sixteenth century.

In discussing the transformation of Yuan northern drama by late Ming editors, Stephen West argues that "as these texts were published and as the manuscripts were fleshed out, they changed in nature from scripts (or at least production-based texts) to a fully rationalized narrative form."[51] Although West does not address stage directions per se, the increase and gradual standardization of stage direction notation was part of the same editorial process that facilitated the reading of plays as narrative literature. In the case of southern drama, although no systematic study has been done, my impression is that hand-copied versions of plays that may show closer ties to staged performances tend to have sparser stage directions than do published editions.

Throughout the seventeenth century we find an increasing tendency to include ever more detailed and complex stage directions in imprints of southern drama, culminating in Hong Sheng's *Palace of Lasting Life,* which is the subject of the coda to this book. Naturally, the elaboration of stage directions varied from playwright to playwright or even within a single playwright's oeuvre. You Tong, for example, provided only perfunctory stage directions in *Celestial Court Music,* his sole contribution to southern drama, which was performed and published around 1665. Tang Xianzu, on the other hand, seems to have taken to heart the criticism of his *Purple Hairpin* as being insufficiently theatrical, because his next play, *Peony Pavilion,* goes to the other extreme in notating the staging. The elaborateness of the stage directions is yet another respect in which we should regard *Peony Pavilion* as a landmark in the history of Chinese drama.

In his *Dictionary of the Theatre,* Patrice Pavis notes a somewhat analogous phenomenon in the expansion of stage directions in eighteenth- and nineteenth- century European drama.[52] As in Chinese imprints, stage directions in these European texts enabled the reader to supplement the direct discourse of the characters to fill in psychology, action, and plot. But with the exception of tense, European stage directions basically utilize the same narrative voice and language as the novel.[53] By contrast, in Ming and Qing play texts, the language of stage directions remained deliberately distinct and histrionic. Characters are referred to by role type, rather than name, actions are labeled as stage gestures, and so on. In this regard the imaginative reading process for Chinese drama may have always retained some more indissoluble link to the stage.

The presence of detailed stage directions in southern-drama play texts, then, is simultaneously a sign of drama's coming of age as a form of narrative literature for readers *and* of the playwright's or editor's recognition that an attentiveness to mise-en-scène was required for a play to succeed both on the page and in the theater. It is important to underscore that the sixteenth- and seventeenth-century playwrights and editors whose identities we know were intimately acquainted with actors and the stage. The wealthiest had their own private household troupes; others collaborated with or advised actors; still others worked with professional troupes; and all would have been frequent spectators at performances, often as invited guests at banquet entertainments. As such, we cannot dismiss stage directions in published plays simply as literary devices divorced from any experience of contemporary staging and performance. These printed notations for staging—even in the case of plays or scenes that may never have been performed—still required the playwright's familiarity with the basic building blocks and conventions of stage technique, which could then be rearranged, elaborated, or experimented with at will.

ENTRANCES AND EXITS

In previous chapters I have shown how games with appearance and disappearance or visibility and invisibility figure in Chinese ghost stories. The manipulation of these effects is of a different order of importance in drama, however, because a ghost must always be imagined in the person of an actor occupying real time and space on stage. To put this another way, in drama the vanishing and reappearing acts of a revenant must always be translated into a specifically histrionic code of exits and entrances. For Michael Goldman, a theorist of Western drama who has focused on the actor, these issues strike at the heart of what constitutes theater. As he declares: "The art of the theater—and the nature of its appeal—cannot be separated from the mechanism of appearance and disappearance. Theater is exits and entrances. Resurrection and rehearsals, the dimming of lights, curtain calls, the curtain itself, the structure of the scene, wings, traps. . . . Wherever we have theater, we have hiding and surprise, appearance and disappearance."[54]

The control of entrances and exits may be fundamental to theater the world over, but it is of paramount importance in traditional Chinese opera, which was performed on a stage devoid of scenery and visual scene changes, without front curtains or modern lighting, and which was free from any Aristotelian strictures governing unities of time and space.[55] Zhou Yibai has characterized the absolute weight placed on entrances and exits to construct the stage as one of the basic features uniting Chinese drama performed in all periods and regions. As he asserts: "Beginning from writing the script, the entrances and exits of the actors is the hinge upon which the whole play hangs. This includes changes in time and space, the arrangement of the characters, shifts in staging, whether an actor is in motion or at rest, and the pacing of individual episodes. . . . To put it another way, the stage in Chinese drama *is* the entrances and exits of different characters."[56]

It is not surprising therefore that Chinese drama developed an elaborate vocabulary of specialized entrances and exits that Ming and Qing playwrights could utilize to convey the manifestation and vanishing of specters on stage. One staple was the "stealthy" or "silent" *(an)* exit or entrance, which involved omitting the customary fanfare used to call attention to the formal entrances and exits of major roles.[57] Another important resource was the "empty" *(xu)* exit or entrance, employed when a character has to leave and return in quick succession, but when the performer has no time or finds it too awkward to physically exit and reenter the stage. The actor effectively becomes invisible to the characters in the scene during the duration of the empty exit, a convention that the audience, for whom the actor is still visible, readily accepts.[58] Another frequent device is the sudden and unusually rapid "flash" *(shan)* entrance or exit; occasionally the "rushed" *(ji)* entrance or exit is used.[59] The evocative but cryptic stage direction "to exit, as a shadow" *(zuo ying xia; ying xia)*, probably meaning to hide and exit, is even found twice in *An Intoxicating Dream*, but may simply have been the playwright's invention, since I have not seen it elsewhere.[60]

Such specialized entrances and exits provided one technology for enhancing the speed, secrecy, and suddenness of a revenant's movements to and from the stage. But the significance of exits and entrances for understanding how a phantom heroine was conceptualized in late Ming and early Qing theater goes beyond a simple list of specialized types and requires some understanding of how the stage was actually constituted in this period.

The easily improvised and flexible nature of Chinese theatrical space facilitated banquet performance, the venue with which this chapter is most concerned. During the late Ming and early Qing, although permanent stages in private residences were not unheard of, at a minimum all that was required to establish a stage was a rug, with an area to the back or sides to serve as a combination backstage / greenroom from which actors could make their entrances and exits.[61] This backstage / greenroom area was commonly called the "play room" *(xifang);* in at least one Ming source it is also called the "back room" *(houfang);* Zhou Yibai suggests that during the Ming, it was also called the "inner stage" *(neichang),* a term which in Peking opera today refers to the visible upstage portion of the stage.[62] What most concerns us is a name frequently used in Ming and Qing times for the points of transit between the play room and the stage: "ghost doorway(s)" *(gui men dao* or *gui men).*

The earliest definition of this term appears in a drama song formulary by the early Ming prince Zhu Quan (1378–1448):

> Ghost doorways are the places in a theater from which someone exits and enters the play room. The reason the word "ghost" is used is because those whom the actors dress up as are all people from the past. Because a drum is placed by the doors, the ignorant and vulgar call them "drum doorways" *(gu men dao*[a]*),* but this contravenes the principle involved. They are also called "ancient doorways" *(gu men dao*[b]*),* but this too is incorrect. Su Shi's poem, which goes 'Performing events of then and now / Through ghost doorways, they come and go,' refers precisely to this.[63]

This often-cited passage raises almost as many questions as it answers for historians of the Chinese stage. Liao Ben, for example, points out that the couplet the prince attributed to Su Shi appears in no other source of this famous poet's work, and therefore may not be a reliable indicator for Song dynasty theaters. Liao argues that surviving visual representations of Yuan dynasty stage performances suggest that a backdrop was used to separate the backstage area from the front of the stage and that there may have been no set openings; actors simply raised a corner of the backdrop to enter and exit. He therefore speculates that the prince may actually be describing a modification in the early Ming theaters of his own time that involved establishing formal openings of some sort to serve as stage doorways.[64] Che Wenming's exhaustive survey of extant temple stages demonstrates that it is not until the early sixteenth century that the addition of a wall made of wood or brick to separate back from front stage is evident. He further notes that such partitions were equipped with two doorways flanking the stage for entrances and exits.[65]

Because of the weight accorded entrances and exits to constitute the stage, it became important to keep the two functions formally and visually distinct. As Che Wenming's evidence confirms, by at least the mid-Ming, and earlier according to other theater historians, it was customary to leave an opening on either side of the stage, the left one (stage right) ordinarily reserved for entrances and the right one (stage left) for exits.[66] This is still true today. Such stage practices were maintained in banquet settings and other improvised performance spaces. Although it was possible in a banquet hall to screen off part of the performance area facing the spectator-guests to serve as a makeshift backstage, historians of Chinese theater think that in many cases one or two side rooms off the main hall doubled as play rooms; the side-room exits would then have functioned as stage doorways for the actors.[67]

To return to the term "ghost doorways," the historical accuracy of the prince's etymology need not concern us. The coexistence of several phonetically close terms for the same thing suggests, as so often in the history of the theater, an oral provenance for words that are only subsequently assigned written characters and whose origins remain fertile ground for speculation. The term "ancient doorways" *(gu men)* is used in the sixteenth-century court manuscripts of Yuan northern drama that are our earliest sources for these plays; both "ancient doorways" and "ghost doorways" are used in Ming and Qing southern drama play texts ("drum doorways" rarely, if ever, appears). By the late eighteenth century, the term "ghost doorways" prevails, a usage that lasted into modern times.[68]

The prince's advocacy of "ghost doorways" over the rival written terms stems above all from a fundamental conception of the actor and stage space. Stage doors are the thresholds through which an actor crosses from a hidden zone reserved only for players to the public domain of the stage and its spectators. Actors are ghosts, he says, because they impersonate dead figures from the past. While stories about history constitute one of the great sources for Chinese drama, and the association between history and the stage is frequently asserted in traditional discourse on the theater, the conflation of actors and ghosts, of offstage with the world of the dead and the past, and front stage with the world of the living and the present, runs deeper.

The Japanese theater historian Tanaka Issei speculates that the appellation "ghost doorways" may derive from what he believes is the precursor of theater in China, namely, sacrificial rituals involving the staging of salvation for lonely souls and other spirits of the dead.[69] It has been commonplace in modern writing on the Chinese theater since Wang Guowei's pioneering work in the early twentieth century to attribute the origin of Chinese theater to impersonation of the dead in ritual sacrifices.[70] But as Tanaka and other scholars have shown through historical research and contemporary fieldwork, exorcistic and ritual functions have been important throughout the history of Chinese drama in various performance contexts, particularly rural society and the court.[71] Even if we nowadays reject a primordial origin for theater in ritual sacrifice, it is still clear that for Ming and Qing playwrights and their publics the analogy between actors and ghosts remained a powerful conceptual undercurrent.[72]

There is a piece of evidence that during the seventeenth century the play room itself, by extension, could be referred to casually as the "ghost room" *(gui fang)*. In his memoir, Zhang Dai recalls having attended a matinee given by a professional acting troupe in the Nanjing pleasure quarter some time prior to fall of the Ming. One of the courtesans in the audience was so impressed that she went into the "ghost room" to question the actors as to why their performance that day was so much better than usual.[73] Zhang Dai does not gloss the term "ghost room," implying that it was in common currency in his time, at least in the Jiangnan area.

In his study of the semiotics of theater architecture, Marvin Carlson notes how easily utilitarian and symbolic functions become conjoined. Offstage areas, which arise to serve the practical need of providing a place for actors to change costume and from which to enter and exit the stage also come to serve the dramatic need of signifying a fictive "elsewhere." His point of departure is the offstage skene house of the ancient Greek theater, which, "in addition to its practical service, provided a tangible sign for the hidden 'other' world of the actor, the place of appearance and disappearance, the realm of events not seen but whose effects conditioned the visible world of the stage."[74]

Ming and Qing authors of phantom-heroine plays were closely attuned to this "otherworldly semiotic" of offstage space. In *West Garden,* for instance, in "Invoking the Spirit" ("Hu hun"), the male lead literally calls forth the heroine's ghost from "the other side" as represented by the interior, unseen space of backstage. He calls her name repeatedly, when suddenly, to his amazement, "from within comes a faint response." Again he calls her name and again comes the reply from backstage. Now the sound cue for wind stirring up is given, and then the "phantom heroine enters, making a ghostly wail," crossing over at last into the world of the living, to the front of the stage visible to the audience. The identification between offstage and the underworld is made explicit in her opening lines: "I am the ghost of Wang Yuying. From the shades below I suddenly heard a human voice calling me. My spirit gave an uneasy start, exactly as though I were abruptly awakening from a dream."[75]

Certain other plays consciously exploit the ghost doorway's specific semiotic properties to pinpoint the moment of the revenant's passage from the world of the dead to the world of the living. The resurrection scene ("Hui sheng") in *Peony Pavilion* is an excellent example. Liu Mengmei, the male lead, accompanied by Sister Stone, the nun-custodian of Du Liniang's shrine, is supervising the exhumation of her grave by a servant boy (mimed, as all such stage business would be). When the boy's hoe finally strikes her coffin the female lead "moans from within." With astonishment the company cries: "Her living ghost breaks the silence!" They then "crouch facing the ghost doorway as the business of opening the coffin is performed." The tension is broken by Sister Stone cracking a bawdy joke about the "clouds and rain" of their union having rusted the nails on the coffin; then once again "moaning comes from within." Now the stage directions cue the male lead "to perform the actions of seeing the female lead and physically supporting her" as he announces: "The young lady is truly here!"[76]

Although the exhumation of Du Liniang's grave is acted out on stage in full sight of the audience, the reanimation of her dead body takes place entirely offstage. Kneeling in the direction of the ghost door calls attention to this offstage space, the unseen physical source of the moaning, and to the miraculous process of revival that must be imagined taking place there. This bit of stage direction heightens the dramatic tension by leading the audience to anticipate the performer's momentary entrance but it also abruptly reinfuses the ghost door with a literal significance that the conventional theatrical usage of the term usually masks. In this context, stepping through the ghost doorway enables the actor symbolically to enact the transition from death to life, to move from ghost to living person, from the role of phantom heroine back to female lead proper. The fact that no cue is given for her formal entrance onstage, but instead Liu Mengmei is directed to assist her because her newly revived body is still too weak to stand alone underscores his creative agency in her resurrection, as did Sister Stone's earlier quip about "clouds and rain."

The exploitation of the ghost doorway for dramatic and symbolic effect is not confined to a single scenario or significance, of course. The most striking use of this theatrical device in a late Ming phantom heroine play to highlight the performer's suspension between two worlds occurs in a rewrite of the "Spectral Disputation" ("Gui bian") scene from Zhou Chaojun's *Red Flowering Plum (Hongmei ji)*. One of the many plays influenced in part by *Peony Pavilion, Red Flowering Plum* survives in several early seventeenth-century editions, testifying to its popularity in this period. The story of Li Huiniang, an entertainer belonging to the vicious Song dynasty official Jia Sidao, whom he beheads after she makes a single admiring remark about a young man, is only a subplot. She is therefore played by a *tie*, a supporting female role, rather than by the female lead, but the scenes involving her are the ones that remained alive in the later performing repertory and for which the play was attacked in 1961.

After Li Huiniang's perfunctory burial beneath a clump of peonies in the garden, she returns as a revenant to consummate her desire for the young man and to save him from Jia Sidao's thugs, who have been ordered to murder him too. Furious to learn of the young man's escape, in the "Spectral Disputation" scene Jia Sidao assembles his harem and begins savagely interrogating them under the whip. It is at this point that Li Huiniang's ghost appears to own up to the "crime" and denounce Jia Sidao to his face. In the scene as originally written, the phantom heroine enters unseen by the characters on stage and narrates the scene she overhears as a series of arias in the manner of a Yuan northern drama, where only one role is allowed to sing in any given play. When she finally makes herself visible and confronts Jia Sidao, he fails to recognize her and no one on stage realizes she is a ghost until she suddenly vanishes.

There is evidence that some contemporary critics found this treatment of the scene profoundly dissatisfying. Several late Ming editions of the play published under different titles and by different publishers share the same commentary, which is spuriously attributed to Tang Xianzu or Yuan Hongdao, both famous literary figures whose name publishers used to boost sales. The commentary is quite scathing about this scene's deficiencies, which it denounces as "slack," "dull," "hard to perform" and "illogical" because what should be a lively and busy group scene is reduced to a long sung monologue, while postponing the revelation that Li Huiniang is a ghost until after her exit deprives the scene of any dramatic excitement.[77] Consequently, the rewrite of the scene consciously set out to rectify these shortcomings.[78]

In the rewrite, rather than slipping onstage undetected by the other characters, the stage directions instruct the supporting female role who plays Li Huiniang's dead soul "to stand in the ghost doorway, her head wrapped in red gauze" as she recites her first lines.[79] The rewrite borrows the costume indication given here from Li Huiniang's first appearance as a revenant in an earlier scene ("Spectral Rendezvous") where she enters "making a ghostly wail and crying out her misfortune."[80] As will become clear later in this chapter, what is unusual in this text is not the headgear itself but specifying the color red. Color has symbolic functions in Chinese theater, but the symbolism is not fixed. Red is an especially complex color in Chinese culture.[81] Among other things it is a yang color, associated with good fortune and marriage. Jo Riley emphasizes the exorcistic associations of the color red in China, which "'brings happiness' because it keeps the bad things away," especially during perilous moments of transition.[82] The color red is not infrequently associated with a female revenant. A detail in Luo Pin's 1797 handscroll *The Ghost Path (Guiqu tu)*, for example, depicts an amorous ghost couple: the female phantom is clad in a red jacket, her sleeve intertwined with that of her lover, who is offering her a flower (see fig. 9).[83] Luo Pin's 1781 portrait of the ghost of Little Su provides her with a red dickey from which hangs a red cord, tied in a lover's knot, over her heart.[84] In the case of Li Huiniang, the color red may be intended to ward off her malignant influence.[85] As a murder victim with a serious grievance, Li Huiniang is inherently much more threatening and dangerous, and consequently also potentially more powerful and inauspicious, than a Du Liniang type who pined away for love.

With the ghost doorway cue, we are on more solid ground because the meaning of this stage cue is actually written into the dialogue. The villain Jia Sidao "listens and then says to himself: 'Hey! There seems to be someone talking in mid-air.'" He

FIGURE 9 Luo Pin, *The Ghost Path (Guiqu tu)*. Handscroll, ink, and color on paper, dated 1797. Detail showing a pair of ghost lovers in a miasma of black *qi*. The female ghost wears a diaphanous red jacket with one sleeve hanging down; the other sleeve is intertwined with that of her male companion, who is embracing her with one hand and offering her a flower, perhaps an orchid, with the other. Blocking them stands a mocking Wu Chang demon in a tall white cap holding a fan. The theatricality of their gestures is palpable. Xubaizhai collection. Courtesy of the Hong Kong Museum of Art.

gives the order to have the women he has been interrogating dismissed. Only then is the cue for Li Huiniang's entrance given. After her first aria, he responds: "At first I could only hear a human voice, but now I gradually make out a human form. Its head is draped in red and the clothes it wears are blue. What kind of demon is it, I wonder?"[86] From Jia Sidao's reaction it is clear that, in this scene at least, the actor standing in the ghost doorway makes the character visible to the audience but invisible to the characters on stage. Only after the actor makes his or her formal entrance—that is, steps through the ghost doorway—does the specter also become visible to the other characters present.

DISEMBODIED SOUND AND WIND

From the above examples it is evident that a primary stage technique for representing the invisible presence of a phantom was the use of disembodied sound, that is, sound emanating from offstage space, whose cause was unseen. In these cases the audience is primed to expect that the bodily source of the sound will be revealed momentarily, and, as such, the technique is strongly associated with the theatrical entrance. It is not difficult to see how this acoustic device translates to the stage certain sound effects employed in the early ghost story, in which, for instance, the protagonist of a tale first hears the strange rustle of a human form slowly approaching before the specter comes into his visual field.

A ghostly wail or cry uttered by the actor performing the ghost is another important acoustic technique used to convey ghostliness in the theater.[87] It is sometimes cued upon entrance, but more frequently upon exit, reasserting the character's spectral identity at the moment of disappearance and reminding the human protagonist in the scene that he (or she) has indeed been dealing with a phantom. The ghostly wail may have been especially effective upon exit, however, because the vibrations would have reverberated in the performer's wake, causing the sound to linger on stage after its maker had departed for the unseen world of backstage, once again signifying a ghostly presence through absence and disembodied sound.

The split essential to theater between actor and character means that a performer need not be secreted backstage to be invisible for dramatic purposes. For instance, in the "Invoking the Spirit" scene from *West Garden,* once the phantom heroine makes her formal entrance and comes into full sight of the audience, she still remains invisible but audible to the male lead who called her forth. His endeavor to locate the mysterious source of the sound is the pretext for some comic stage business—his opening the window and her darting in, his attempt to shine a light on her and her blowing it out—that are fairly routine in scenes of this nature.[88] Again, as in ghost stories, the odd behavior of lamps, candles, or flames, are routinely taken as optical signs of an otherwise invisible ghostly presence. The stage drew on such conventional associations, but conveyed the imagined visual effects through mime and dialogue.[89]

A sudden gust of wind is the most frequent auditory signal for the imminent entrance of a specter, the cue occasionally sounded to signal a specter's exit as well.

(Sometimes the sound cue is even coupled with stage business involving lamps and candles being blown out right before a phantom's entrance or exit.) In a scene from *Mistress and Maid,* the male lead, who has just been warned that he is being haunted, is awaiting nightfall and the arrival of his phantom lover with trepidation. So fixed is the significance of the cue "wind rises from within" that here it is immediately followed by the direction "the male lead performs the gesture of alarm." And to spell it out even further, right before the phantom heroine makes her entrance, he exclaims:

> The leaves on the trees are rustling; at the foot of the wall, the dirt is stirring—isn't that a ghost approaching?
>
> *(sings)* See how a frigid gust of dank [yin] wind pierces the casement,
> Chilling me right to the bone.[90]

In previous chapters we have seen how closely the whistling of the wind—particularly a cold and damp yin one—came to be associated with the production of a ghostly atmosphere in the Chinese literary code. As a prime example of a thing that has sound but no form, as something that can be heard but whose origin is unseen, wind had a categorical affinity with ghosts that the stage understandably drew upon.[91] The stage directions in *Palace of Lasting Life* fortunately explain how the sound cue for wind worked: "From within, a gong is struck to produce the effect of wind rising" *(nei mingluo zuo feng qi ke).*[92]

Wind itself might be formless, but its effects are very much visible to the naked eye. On the Chinese stage the wind's power has above all been conveyed through the movements of the actor.[93] The performance of wind provided an ideal showcase for set kinetic routines and dance. It is likely that training for the phantom-heroine role in southern drama involved mastering a special kind of ghostly glide that could convey an eerie impression of weightlessness and floating. Ghost walk routines are still performed in various Chinese opera traditions upon a phantom heroine's entrance, including the Sichuan opera and recent *kunqu* stagings of the underworld scene from *Peony Pavilion* and the "Taken Alive" scene from *Outlaws of the Marsh.*[94]

To my knowledge we find no explicit stage directions or descriptions of ghost walk technique in Yuan, Ming, or Qing sources. In both northern and southern drama play texts, however, the phantom heroine's opening arias and spoken lines frequently depict her preternatural lightness and speed as she traverses the stage, often in conjunction with wind. For instance, in *Lady in the Painting,* upon the female lead's first appearance as a ghost, she "enters, walking" and sings: "As light as paper, I'm carried along by the wind / In a twinkling, a thousand peaks rolled up by evening waves."[95] A woodblock illustration of this scene pictures the phantom heroine gliding across the room, with cloud-like lines obscuring her feet (see fig. 10). Since none of the phantom-heroine scenes featuring a ghost walk became part of the later repertory of extracts, we do not know exactly how this "walking" was performed, but it presumably involved something akin to the ghost-walk routines still seen in the theater today.

Textual and visual evidence from Ming play texts strongly suggests that the ghost walk on the seventeenth-century stage involved dangling both arms so that the long sleeves of the costume would hang down over the hands. In Zang Maoxun's revision of *Peony Pavilion,* in the "Spirit Wandering" scene, Du Liniang's ghost is instructed "to enter with her arms hanging down" *(chui shou shang).*[96] Indeed, Shen Jing's *Peachwood Amulet (Taofu ji),* a southern drama rewrite of Zheng Tingyu's northern drama *Flowers in the Rear Courtyard (Houting hua),* has his characters poke fun at precisely this stage convention. Judge Bao has just warned the male lead to expect a visit from a female ghost that night. When the phantom heroine shows up as predicted, the male lead accuses of her being a ghost, which she denies.

FIGURE 10 Woodblock illustration of the phantom heroine performing a gliding "ghost walk." Wu Bing, *Lady in the Painting (Huazhong ren),* scene 21, in his *Canhuazhai wuzhong.*

MALE LEAD: If you're not a ghost, then why are both your arms always hanging down?

PHANTOM HEROINE: Do you mean to say you can't make your arms hang down?

MALE LEAD: What? You mean, I can also make my arms hang down? Let me try and see.[97]

Peachwood Amulet survives only in manuscript versions and the stage directions are not very detailed, but undoubtedly in performance these lines were followed by some comic business where the male lead mimicked the heroine's ghostly pose.

Generally speaking, the illustrations accompanying Ming and Qing printed plays make little attempt to render scenes as they might have looked on stage. It is possible occasionally, however, to detect traces of theatrical influence in the gestures of some figures.[98] Two excellent examples are found among the late Ming illustrations of phantom-heroine plays. The first (see fig. 11) is a rendition of Act 2 of *The Disembodied Soul* from an edition of Zang Maoxun's *Selected Yuan Plays (Yuanqu xuan),* published in 1616. In this act, upon her entrance, the phantom heroine sings of the swift, silent journey she makes on foot to catch up with the male lead's boat. Weng Minhua has speculated that such lyrics allow us to imagine the special poses and dance movements that would have accompanied the vocal performance of the aria on the Yuan stage.[99] This seems exactly what the illustration to this scene does. By the early seventeenth century, however, Yuan northern drama was rarely if ever performed, and so the illustrations in Zang's edition, if anything, would have reflected the theatrical practices of his own time. The picture shows the phantom heroine gliding over the bridge that separates her from her lover, who is seated in a boat moored beneath a willow tree, playing his lute—a quite unexceptional romantic scene. What arrests the eye are the female figure's sleeves, which are fully extended, covering the hands and dangling forward as though blown by the wind. The sleeves are disproportionately prominent (nearly as thick as the figure's waist) and the slightly hunched stance also contributes to the impression of forward movement and the overall theatrical effect.

The second illustration (see fig. 12) is a depiction of scene 23 ("Invoking the Spirit") from a late Ming edition of *West Garden.* Again, the overall composition is quite standard for a romantic play. In the upper part of the picture, the hero is visible through a round cut-out window sitting in his study, a candle lit beside him to show it is night, while the phantom heroine stands outside below, bending her face toward him. What is unusual is the theatrical way the female figure's gestures and stance convey a ghostly effect of being windblown.

A comparison with other Ming pictures is helpful here. A composition similar to "Invoking the Spirit" but without a ghost can be seen in a woodblock illustration from Min Qiji's color album of *The Western Wing,* in which the living heroine Yingying stands outside listening to her lover's nocturnal serenade on the lute (see fig. 13). A striking difference between the two figures are the exaggerated scalloped sleeves

FIGURE 11 Woodblock illustration of Act 2 of *The Disembodied Soul (Qiannü lihun)* showing the phantom heroine standing on a bridge with her sleeves hanging down as she listens to her lover play the lute. Zang Maoxun, *Yuanqu tuxuan,* facsimile reprint of 1616 edition.

of the phantom heroine in *West Garden,* which are fully extended and dangling forward, the movement echoed by the hem of her skirt. It is true that a painting of a lovelorn beauty or river goddess skimming the waves, such as Qiu Ying's *Woman in Spring Longing* (sometimes identified as the *Nymph of the Luo River*) (see fig. 14),[100] may depict the female figure as windblown by having her sway slightly to the right with sashes streaming to the left, but again, such figures are not depicted as the revenant in *West Garden* is, with her sleeves hanging down in such an odd manner, as though the wind were blowing her from behind and propelling her forward.

FIGURE 12 Woodblock illustration of scene 23 from Wu Bing, *West Garden (Xiyuan ji)*. The phantom heroine stands outside the male lead's study, her dangling sleeves blowing in the wind. Chongzhen edition.

FIGURE 14 Qiu Ying, *Woman in Spring Longing*. Hanging scroll, ink and color on paper. Early sixteenth century. Detail. Courtesy of the National Palace Museum, Taiwan.

(Facing page)

FIGURE 13 "Yingying listens to Student Zhang play the lute." Illustration for Act 8 of *The Western Wing*. Min Qiji edition (1640). Museum für Ostasiatische Kunst, Köln. Photo: Rheinisches Bildarchiv, Köln.

The dangling arms are still part of the ghost walk routines preserved in certain Chinese opera traditions, including Sichuan opera and *kunqu*. A book on the twentieth-century performing technique of the *dan* in Sichuan opera compiled by Yang Youhe, a male performer born in 1913, lists under "Walking" something called "phantom steps" *(guihun bu* or *hun bu),* which involved "pinning the upper arms against the body, with both arms hanging down behind a little (sometimes dangling left, then right). The body is held stiffly and sways a little; then taking quick steps hunched forward, the body sways a bit to the left, the eyes full of aggrieved feelings."[101] There is some resemblance to a recent description of the ghost walk technique for Yan Poxi's ghost in the *kunqu* version of "Taken Alive," where "upon coming out on stage, the performer's face is full of sorrow and resentment. Both arms hang down immobile while only the heels touch the ground."[102] A photograph of contemporary *kunqu* diva Liang Guyin shows her costumed as Yan Poxi, with her arms dangling down in appropriately ghostly fashion (see fig. 15).

In certain cases something more than the performance of ordinary wind was required for the phantom heroine, and a play text calls for a whirlwind to be acted out. As a cosmic anomaly, the advent of a whirlwind had from Han times been associated with the supernatural, portending political chaos and destruction. However, just as a whirlwind represents the most terrifying potential of wind—its velocity, violence, and freakishness—so, too, in the theater, the whirlwind is often, though not always, associated with the most threatening and dangerous sort of ghost—the victim of murder or execution.[103] In *Flowers in the Rear Courtyard,* the ghost of a murdered woman manifests herself to Judge Bao to seek his intervention in her case. The stage directions, which appear even in our earliest sixteenth-century recensions of the text, specify that "her soul enters, performing a whirlwind" *(dan hun shang xuanfeng ke).* In his spoken lines and aria, Judge Bao immediately recognizes the whirlwind as the sign of a ghost in broad daylight and orders it to return that night when his court will be in session. The ghost utters not a word, but obeys instantly, again, as the stage directions indicate, "performing a whirlwind" as she exits *(xuanfeng xia).*[104] In *Injustice to Dou E,* the heroine, who has been wrongly executed, returns as a ghost to the human world to appeal to the official reviewing her case (who happens to be her father). Although no specific stage directions are provided, upon her entrance she sings: "Slowly I pace in darkness / And quickly I am borne along by the whirlwind; Enveloped in fog and clouds, / I come fast as a ghost."[105] It is therefore conceivable that here too a whirlwind might have been performed.

Dancing the swift, swirling motion of a whirlwind must have been something of a tour de force on stage in Yuan and Ming times, as it is today.[106] Once again, the rewrite of the "Spectral Disputation" scene from *Red Flowering Plum* provides our most specific indication for seventeenth-century performance practice. The stage directions call for Li Huiniang to "dance up a whirlwind, as she lets out a ghostly shriek." A woodblock illustration of the scene imagines her riding into the room on a thick black cloud with a swirling tail (see fig. 16). In the play, the whirlwind is not just the sign of a wronged soul or a vague force propelling a revenant on and off

FIGURE 15 A photograph of contemporary *kunqu* diva Liang Guyin costumed as Yan Poxi, with her arms dangling in ghostly fashion. Photograph courtesy of Lu Eting.

the stage or in and out of the underworld, but a deliberate weapon that she wields to immobilize her enemy, Jia Sidao, after he attempts to strike her with his sword. Again the text spells out the desired dramatic effect: "The villain acts out attempting to go forward but falling back. He shouts inside: 'Come quickly! There's a ghost! . . . a gust of wind is holding me fast. I can't take a single step!' And the phantom sings: 'With this whirlwind I pinion you. . . . Please allow yourself to acknowledge me a little longer / I'm about to take this bloody head of mine and ram it against your heart.' The villain performs the business of trying to dodge her and waving his hands in a panic. The phantom continues singing: 'Now you'll believe in the might of Li Huiniang's ghost!'" The villain promises to call in a top monk the next day to conduct

FIGURE 16 Illustration of Li Huiniang riding on a black whirlwind in the "Spectral Disputation" scene. *Dangui ji,* scene 17. Facsimile reprint of Wanli edition. *Guben xiqu* I, no. 99.

rites for her soul's salvation if she stops haunting him. She tacitly acquiesces but inflicts one last act of aggression as she quits the scene, ramming him as she exits so that he falls to the ground.[107]

Staging the Land and Water Rite

The above scene ends with the exhumation of Li Huiniang's makeshift grave and with Jia Sidao's orders that the corpse (which "still looks as though it were alive") be properly reburied. The ritual to propitiate her soul he puts off indefinitely, thereby obviating the need to depict it onstage. Such rites are indeed seldom acted out in late Ming drama, but two contemporaneous plays do add a final scene representing the elaborate salvation rites family members hold for a phantom heroine. These scenes especially deserve close attention for the way in which they portray invisibility and visibility in the staging of the ritual and its outcome.

The plots of these plays are closely related. The first, Fu Yichen's *Man/Ghost, Husband/Wife* (*Rengui fuqi;* 1642 preface) is based on a vernacular story by Ling Menchu published in the 1620s and again in the 1630s, which, in turn, retells a famous early Ming classical tale entitled "The Golden Hairpin" ("Jinfeng chai ji").[108] The second, Wu Bing's *West Garden* (published between 1628–1644) is not technically based on either the story or tale, but follows the overall contours of the narrative and was probably influenced by an earlier dramatization of "The Golden Hairpin," Shen Jing's *Dropped Hairpin* (*Zhuichai ji,* completed ca. 1607).[109]

"The Golden Hairpin" tells of a girl who was affianced in childhood to a boy whose family moved away; when he fails to return to carry out the marriage, she pines away and dies. She is buried with his betrothal gift, a golden phoenix hairpin. Soon thereafter he shows up, but it is of course too late. During the Qingming grave-sweeping festival, he picks up a golden hairpin that he is led to believe her younger sister has dropped by mistake. Visited that night by its true owner—the older sister's ghost, who passes herself off as the younger sister—she forces him to elope with her. When after a year's time they return, he enters alone to beg the parents' forgiveness for absconding with their younger daughter. Amazed, the parents protest that all this while she has been lying ill in a coma. He produces the golden hairpin as proof; they immediately recognize it as the older sister's burial good. The younger sister then arises from her sick bed and, possessed by the older sister's ghost, prevails upon them to marry the living sister to the dead sister's bridegroom. After the wedding he sells the golden hairpin to pay for rites to ensure salvation for the older sister's soul, who appears in a dream to thank him.

Both *Man/Ghost* and *West Garden* depict only the final stage of the much longer ritual process for her salvation: the seventh day of a "sacrificial service for the dead" *(jian wang gongde)* in the former; the forty-ninth day (seven times seven) of a "Land and Water Rite" *(Shuilu daochang)* in the latter. Structurally and symbolically, the conclusion of the ritual is made to coincide with the finale of the play, the fulfillment *(yuanman)* of the ritual period aligned with the theatrical grand reunion *(tuanyuan)*. Both scenes open with the ritual specialists—a group of Buddhist monks—who announce that they have carried out the preceding stages. They now prepare the way for the family members of the deceased who have commissioned the rite—the dead girl's parents and the newly wedded couple—to enter for the final part of the ceremony.

Although *Man/Ghost* does not specifically call the ceremony it depicts a Land and Water Rite, this play, even more strongly than *West Garden,* invokes key elements of this grand Buddhist ritual for the deliverance of the spirits of the dead from suffering and their ascension to paradise or Heaven. The performance of the rite by Buddhist monks for a lay clientele can be traced back to at least the Southern Song, but the practice became especially popular during the late Ming, when these two plays were written. Although it was a rite of universal salvation, in practice, as Daniel Stevenson asserts, it quickly became assimilated as "a technology for the postmortem transition of deceased kin as well as the pacification of malevolent ghosts."[110] The rites staged in *Man/Ghost* and *West Garden* combine these last two functions. Both plays share a fixation on the moment of transcendence, which confirms the efficacy of the ritual and completes the exorcism, but only *Man/Ghost* shows the ritual technology that effects the passage from one state to the other.

The culminating moment of the rite in *Man/Ghost* is the crossing of the "bridge of immortality" *(xian qiao)*. The male lead bears the dead woman's "soul banner" and the second female lead carries her "spirit tablet" as the two first circle and then walk across "two benches placed on stage and pushed together to make a bridge."[111] Husband and wife are part of a larger entourage making the crossing, which includes the lead monk, who performs the ritual gesture of knocking on the gates of Heaven and Earth with his staff midway across, and his acolytes.

The motif of a bridge that the deceased crosses to reach transcendence in a celestial realm is longstanding in the Chinese mortuary imagination. A recently excavated Northern Song tomb from the year 1108 includes two painted scenes that show just such a process.[112] The first scene (see fig. 17, upper register) portrays a procession of figures carrying a soul banner and crossing a bridge borne aloft by clouds. The object of their destination is depicted in the adjacent scene: a palace emitting rays of light, which is likewise floating on a bed of clouds (see fig. 18, upper register). A symbolic bridge of immortality also figured in the Land and Water Rite. According to a major 1823 ritual handbook, during the rite "a bridge of immortality" (also called "the pure path") made of a bolt of cloth was suspended in the courtyard outside the inner altar.[113] As one small component of a long, complex, costly, and multi-site ritual centered on the distribution of food to the dead, this bridge of immortality, as far as I know, does not seem to have played a major role in the overall proceedings of the rite. Its great value as a dramatic device capable of conveying the gist of the ritual and its desired effects, however, is displayed not only in *Man/Ghost* but in a roughly contemporaneous play completed around 1650 by the Buddhist monk Zhida.

This remarkable proselytizing work, entitled *Mirror of the Return to Origin or The Transmission of the Lamp (Guiyuan jing/Chuandeng lu)*, is a hagiography of three Buddhist monks across time written in the form of a southern drama. The third, and only contemporary figure among these monk protagonists, Yunqi Zhuhong (1535–1615), had produced the key liturgical tract on the Water and Land Rite, which is still in use today. The play ends its portrayal of Zhuhong's life on earth with his performance of this rite in a scene entitled "Bringing Universal Salvation to Souls in the Underworld" ("Puji youhun"). As befits the theme of universal salvation, no individualized character is mourned or redeemed; instead four classes of souls—officials, warriors, beautiful married women who have died young, and victims of suicide and violent death—are invoked and assembled by Zhuhong to be fed, ferried from the sea of suffering in the underworld, and escorted across a bridge by the Bodhisattva Guanyin. The minimal stage directions do not explain how the bridge would have been represented on stage, but after the procession has crossed it, they indicate that Zhuhong "strikes the table" (presumably representing the altar) and

FIGURE 17 Scene from a mural in a Northern Song tomb in Pingmo, Shanxi, showing a procession carrying a soul banner and crossing a bridge borne aloft by clouds. *Zhengzhou Song Jin bihua mu,* p. 48, pl. 64.

FIGURE 18 Scene from a mural, adjacent to that in Figure 17, showing the procession's destination: a palace emitting rays of light, which is likewise floating on a bed of clouds. *Zhengzhou Song Jin bihua mu,* p. 48, pl. 63.

the group "soars up to the clouds, ascends to Heaven, and exits."[114] With that the ritual is concluded.

A woodblock illustration of the scene from one of the early seventeenth-century editions of the play shows a procession of ghosts representing the four classes of souls crossing a bridge, which looks exactly like a bolt of cloth suspended between two tables since it has no volume or depth (see fig. 19). At one end Zhuhong presides over an altar; on the other altar, food offerings are displayed, which two hungry

FIGURE 19 Woodblock illustration of the scene "Bringing Universal Salvation to Souls in the Underworld" from Zhida, *Mirror of the Return to Origin ([Yifang bian jingtu] Chuandeng lu Guiyuan jing)*, scene 39. Facsimile reprint of 1789 edition. *Guben xiqu* V, no. 68.

ghosts are eagerly snatching. Below, some unfortunate souls are still mired in the sea of suffering; above, Guanyin and other gods preside from their celestial clouds. This picture bears no resemblance to any of the paintings or murals used in the Land and Water Rite; it illustrates a "theatrical" representation of the ritual as it would look in a reader's imagination, not as it would have looked on stage.

A comparison of this scene from *Mirror of the Return* with the finale from *Man / Ghost* reveals the extent to which *Man / Ghost* has eliminated any specific Buddhist content from the ritual, emphasizing instead a simple mortuary context and syncretist message of transcendence from the perspective of the family members who have sponsored the ritual. What *Man / Ghost* shares with *Mirror of the Return* is the exploitation of the dramatic medium to act out in full view what could only be imagined in any actual ritual: the dead soul(s) crossing the bridge. In *Man / Ghost*, the passage of the ghost is effected by human agents carrying ritual substitutes for the deceased—the soul banner and spirit tablet—over the bridge. These props are meant not simply as symbols of the dead but as talismans for the dead, designed to draw the soul forth. As the male lead sings: "Follow my patterned banner, which leads the way." What makes this scene so interesting is that the articulated ritual desire is fully realized: the symbolic procession is shadowed by the "real" ghost following in its wake.

The phantom is at first visible only to the audience and is unseen by the characters in the scene. The stage directions are quite explicit on this point. After the male lead and second female lead take up banner and tablet, but before they approach the bridge, the stage directions read: "Covered in a spirit kerchief and her arms hanging down, the female lead follows behind the second female lead." After the company has crossed the bridge and the couple finishes singing of their hope that "the root of immortality be firmly protected and her spirit reach the celestial gates," the stage directions immediately instruct the female lead "to remove the kerchief and act out making herself visible."[115] The amazed living couple quickly put down the ghost's ritual surrogates—the banner and tablet—to embrace the "real" thing. Father and mother are quickly called on stage for the grand reunion as the female lead makes her final tearful good-byes and confirms the efficacy of the ritual. She reveals that as a former immortal banished to earth, she has now received a dispensation to return to Heaven, thanks in part to their piety in holding this rite. The scene ends with the female lead "performing a whirlwind dance and exiting," as the company sings with astonishment at seeing her fly up into the clouds and reach the heavens.

One important detail in the staging of this scene deserves further attention—the "spirit kerchief" or *hun pa*, which the phantom heroine dons and removes in the course of the action. Based on the evidence of play texts, a piece of fabric covering the head and sometimes all or part of the face, called a *hun pa* or simply a *pa*, had entered the costume repertory for the phantom heroine by no later than the early seventeenth century. Undoubtedly, the use of this costume device for dead souls or revenants had developed earlier in theatrical practice; its appearance in play texts signaled that the device had become sufficiently conventional on the stage to be attended to by playwrights. One of its primary functions was to serve as a sartorial marker enabling an audience to distinguish at a glance an actor playing a phantom from an actor playing a living being, which was especially important when the same actor played both roles. In all extant texts of *The Disembodied Soul,* at the beginning of Act 2 when the phantom makes her first appearance, the stage directions instruct that the "principal female lead enters costumed differently as a disembodied soul," but offers no further information as to how this sartorial difference was to be conveyed.[116] The manuscripts in the *Mowangguan* collection append costume lists used in the early Ming court for many Yuan plays, though not, unfortunately, for *The Disembodied Soul* or other phantom heroine plays. The closest thing to a *hun pa* on the *Mowangguan* costume lists is a *hunzi yi*—a "ghost garment," which offers no greater degree of specificity than *The Disembodied Soul.*[117]

It is clear that the *hun pa* was one of several theatrical signs of a revenant meant to be immediately perceptible to an audience in addition to the sound cues of wind and ghostly wail, the kinesthetic cues of the ghost walk and whirlwind dance, and the ghostly imagery of the lyrics to the arias. In a recent study of premodern Chinese stage costume, Song Junhua speculates that the *hun pa* may derive from a custom of covering the face of the deceased with a handkerchief before burial, but gives no source or details. Song is primarily interested in the ubiquity of the *hun pa* assigned to ghosts on the costume lists for the grand supernatural pageants in the nineteenth-century Qing court, however, and unfortunately does not explore the emergence of this sartorial device in earlier plays or performance venues.[118]

Cloths used to cover and/or represent the dead figured in Chinese mortuary ritual. It is therefore reasonable to imagine that the image of some cloth buried with the deceased may have fueled the adoption of the *hun pa* in the theater, something along the lines of the sheets or shrouds in which European ghosts frequently reappear.[119] However, in Chinese ghost stories, we find nothing like the *hun pa;* it remained a purely theatrical device. No evidence has yet turned up to link the *hun pa* with Yuan or earlier stage practice. As far as I can tell, it entered the textual record in the late Ming with phantom-heroine plays and became a standard feature distinguishing ghosts from other supernatural beings in Qing theatrical practice. In *kunqu* and Peking opera today, the *hun pa* survives as a piece of long gauze, usually black, worn mantilla-fashion over the head and down the back (see fig. 15).[120] I have found the color of a *hun pa* specified only twice in seventeenth-century play texts—black in scene 3 of *Man/Ghost* and red for the vengeful ghost of Li Huiniang in *Red Flowering Plum.* The latter also stipulates that gauze was the fabric "covering" *(meng)* and "wrapped around" *(dou)* her head.[121] Both verbs of covering (such as *meng* and *gai*), and verbs of wrapping or winding (such as *dou* and *guo*) are used in seventeenth-century stage directions to modify the *hun pa,* which suggests that how the *hun pa* could be worn on the head varied. It may not have always resembled the modern mantilla, but could have also been worn as a simple kerchief tied around the head, perhaps something along the lines of two ghosts pictured in the late Yuan Land and Water murals in the Green Dragon Temple in Shanxi (see fig. 4) or in the illustrations of Mulian's mother (see fig. 8) and Du Liniang as dead souls in the underworld (see fig. 20).

Alternatively, it is possible that the *hun pa* may have been adapted from headgear worn by mourners.[122] As a verb, the character *pa* (pronounced *mo*) means "to wind," "to wrap around," and is most frequently applied to cloth wound around the head. The ritual treatise in the *New Tang History (Xin Tangshu),* for example, employs this verb in a funerary context to dictate that on the day the coffin is laid out, the chief mourner and all the sons of the deceased should remove their hats and "wrap" their heads with a mourning cloth.[123] If such a derivation for the *hun pa* has any merit, then we would find once again the cultural logic of representation by which the practices and sentiments of mourning are reflexively projected onto the figure of the ghost, so that a ghost mourns itself.

Whatever the origins of the *hun pa,* it is clear that what may have begun in the theater as a simple sign of a ghost assumed a more complex array of semiotic functions for late Ming playwrights. Chief among them, as we have just seen in *Man/Ghost,* was a whole set of operations related to the fundamental theatrical values of hiding and showing so important to the representation of ghosts on stage. In this respect the *hun pa* resembles nothing so much as a veil, an apparatus that both conceals and reveals. Tang Xianzu did not deploy the *hun pa* in his *Peony Pavilion;* instead when Du Liniang first enters as a revenant in the "Spirit Roaming" scene, the stage directions instruct the phantom heroine to "enter making a ghostly wail and hiding her face with her sleeve." In Chapter 3 I discussed raising the sleeve to screen the face as an ancient gesture of grief and noted its conjunction in ghost stories with the act of vanishing like smoke to reinforce the instability of a phantom. In a theatrical context, especially upon first appearance, screening the face with the sleeve above all suggests the visibility of the invisible, something obscured, shrouded, present only through absence—all attributes of the ghost.[124] In Zang Maoxun's revision of *Peony Pavilion* published in 1618, one of his changes in this scene is to replace the sleeve-screening gesture with the *hun pa* so that the phantom heroine now enters "covered by a *pa,* with her arms hanging down."[125] One reason for the change could be that raising the sleeve is incompatible with the dangling hands of the ghost walk; another is that the light fabric of the *hun pa* swirling along with any dance steps would have enhanced the graceful effect on stage. But above all the replacement suggests the interchangeability of the raised sleeve and the *hun pa* as a veiling mechanism.

The idea that the *hun pa* could be adjusted to vary the degree of invisibility or visibility emerges especially clearly, as we have seen, in *Man/Ghost.* The business with the *hun pa* in the finale echoes the earlier use of the device in scene 3, "Union in the Shades." After the male lead has picked up the hairpin and gone to bed, when the phantom heroine makes her first entrance in the play and sings her opening aria to the audience, the stage directions specify that "her head is wrapped in a black *pa* revealing about half her face as her arms hang down."[126] Once she enters the male lead's room and shows herself to him for the first time, the stage directions indicate that she "removes the *hun pa.*" In the final scene the phantom heroine's face is com-

FIGURE 20 Woodblock illustration of the "Infernal Judgment" scene from *Peony Pavilion*. On the right stands Du Liniang as a dead soul in the underworld raising her sleeve to her mouth and with a white kerchief wrapped around her head. *(Continued on next page)*

Above her, the Flower God enters on a burst of clouds. On the far left sits the underworld judge sentencing some dead souls to reincarnation as bugs and birds. In Tang Xianzu, *Mudan ting huanhun ji*. Wanli edition published by Jinling Wenlinge. Photo by Julia Orell.

pletely covered with the *hun pa* in order to be fully invisible to the other characters as they cross the bridge.

In a study of stage props in Euro-American theater history, Andrew Sofer argues that the crucial feature distinguishing the prop from other material objects deployed on stage, such as costume and furniture, is *motion:* a prop is an object that is "visibly manipulated by an actor in the course of performance."[127] In most cases in late Ming and early Qing play texts, the *hun pa* functions not only as part of a costume, but as a prop according to Sofer's definition. The lightness of a gauze fabric would certainly have facilitated such manipulation in performance. This means that the stage business of removing the *hun pa* (and, less often, putting it on) also helps produce meaning in the play. To be sure, removing the *hun pa* may have also served a practical function. In Zang Maoxun's revision of the "Spirit Roaming" scene from *Peony Pavilion,* Du Liniang is led on stage by two little ghosts, who remove the *hun pa* for her before exiting. A marginal comment notes that having the ghosts remove the *hun pa* and take it away makes the later ghost tryst scene with Liu Mengmei more "convenient," suggesting perhaps that despite its lightness, the *hun pa* may have been awkward for the actor to wear all the time on stage.[128]

In Shen Jing's play *The Dropped Hairpin,* when the older sister's dead soul appears before the underworld judge, his first words are: "Remove the *hun pa.*"[129] And after she is granted a travel permit to return to the living world and is about to be led from the court, two attendants first "wrap the *hun pa* around the principal female lead's head."[130] Aside from marking her as a phantom, why is the *hun pa* necessary in this scene?

A Patchwork of Scenes (Zhui baiqiu), published in 1789, helps shed light on this question. The same business of removing the *hun pa* also appears in the underworld scene from *Peony Pavilion* in this edition. In fact, since the underworld scene in *The Dropped Hairpin* is highly derivative of *Peony Pavilion* and since the extracts in *A Patchwork of Scenes* are considered to be closer than full play texts to stage performance practice, at least in the eighteenth century, it is possible that the removal of the *hun pa* was a bit of staging first used in seventeenth-century stage performances of the *Peony Pavilion* scene, which then made its way into the manuscript copy of *The Dropped Hairpin.* Whatever the case, in *A Patchwork of Scenes,* after Du Liniang's *hun pa* is removed, she cries: "How frightening!" as though she were suddenly able to see the uncanny spectacle of the underworld court for the first time.[131] Her reaction suggests that in this scene the *hun pa* is still related to seeing and concealment, but rather than serving only as a cloak of full or partial invisibility that hides the ghost from the gaze of others, it operates also as a blindfold that prevents the ghost, as a prisoner transported in the underworld, from seeing what surrounds her.

If wearing the *hun pa* is above all a visual marker of ghostly identity, then its removal on stage can become a powerful means to signify the shedding of that status. Zang Maoxun uses precisely this symbolic tool in portraying Du Liniang's resurrection in his revision of *Peony Pavilion.* In the original play, as we have seen, Tang

Xianzu downplayed much of the scene's dramatic potential by having the female lead come back to life offstage. Zang rewrote the scene to enhance the spectacle so that the female lead is resurrected onstage in view of the audience. The stage directions in his revision call for the female lead "to crouch under the table, wrapped in a *pa*."[132] Zang had already taken the precaution of reintroducing the *hun pa* in the previous scene, in which Du Liniang reveals to Liu Mengmei that she is a ghost and extracts his promise to exhume her coffin and marry her. After her exit, as in Tang's original, she almost instantly makes a second entrance to warn Liu Mengmei to act quickly and threatens him with her implacable resentment in the underworld if he reneges on his promise; she then exits again, this time making a ghostly wail to add substance to her threat. Zang adds the detail that she reenters "wrapped in a *pa*" to reinforce her ghosthood, as does the ghostly wail, but also to signify visually the barrier that now exists between them, which Liu Mengmei must remove.[133] In the resurrection scene he does precisely this. After Du Liniang is led out from under the table, the stage directions instruct Liu Mengmei to "remove the *pa*," signaling the exact moment of her resurrection and his agency in the process.[134] Like all robing or disrobing on stage in a play, which calls attention to the costuming of the actor, the removal of the *hun pa* here is also supremely theatrical because it refers to the conventions of the theater's own enactment.

Read against Zang Maoxun's revised staging of the resurrection in *Peony Pavilion*, it becomes clear that in *Man/Ghost* the manipulation of the *hun pa* in the bridge sequence also spells out the meaning of the ritual. The female lead removes the *hun pa* after the crossing not only to make herself visible to the human participants but to prove the efficacy of the rite: having now been assured her ascent to the celestial realm, she is ghost no longer. This reading of *Man/Ghost* in turn sheds light on the handling of the *hun pa* in the finale of *West Garden*, even though the ghost salvation ritual is conceived and staged in an entirely different fashion in this play.

In *West Garden*, the older sister's ghost intercedes directly with her lover, the male lead, to urge him to marry the younger sister (scene 29). After the wedding the phantom heroine appears once more to the male lead to reveal her true identity as a ghost and to bid him a final farewell (scene 32). As a true man of *qing*, he refuses to relinquish her, exclaiming "Even if you really are a ghost, who cares?" and then breaking into song: "Hold me tight while I embrace your cold bones; there's still a glow in those banked embers."[135] But no lovemaking can induce resurrection here. She is fated to return to the underworld to be cut off from him forever, she tells him. And with that, as the stage directions indicate: "she lets out a ghostly wail, wraps the *pa* around her head, and exits straightaway."[136] This whole scene is deeply indebted to the "Spectral Vows" scene in *Peony Pavilion*, but this bit of stage business closely resembles the new staging adopted in Zang's revision of the scene.[137] As in Zang's staging, the phantom heroine's assumption of the *hun pa* reconfirms her spectral identity at the moment of farewell and visually reinstates the barrier between the ghost and human worlds. Structurally, too, the donning of the *hun pa* anticipates its removal in a subsequent scene, but as in *Man / Ghost,* since there can be no return to life, the lifting of the *hun pa* takes place after the completion of the ritual held for the ghost's salvation.

Although the finale of *West Garden* borrows the Buddhist setting, trappings, and linguistic referents of the Land and Water Rite, no part of the ceremony is staged in detail as it is in *Man / Ghost.* Instead the scene focuses on an addendum to the ritual: the lead monk has told the family that on this final night of the ritual period the dead girl's soul is expected to return home for a visit. It is to pray for this eventuality that the parents and the nuptial couple enter and bow to the Buddha and then spend part of the night in the ritual chamber.[138]

In *Man / Ghost* the theatricality of the ritual represented in the play—that is, its distinction from the performance of a real ritual, its status as an illusion being simultaneously confirmed and disavowed—is accentuated by framing the scene within the comic riffs of a monk played by a clown, who disrupts and deflates the solemnity of the ceremony. In *West Garden,* the theatricality of the ritual is instead conveyed by structuring the whole scene strongly through the subjective and highly sentimental perspective of the phantom heroine, for whom the rite has been staged. The primacy of her feelings and vision is mainly expressed through the lyrical arias she sings, but it also appears in the multiple entrances and exits she makes that frame the appearance of each group of living participants in the scene. It is first the noise of the monks' chanting and music and the scent of the incense that draws the phantom heroine onstage. There she catches sight of an embroidered spirit banner and wonders for whom this sacrificial service is being held in West Garden, her former abode. Only by reading the placard with her name does she realize the service is for her.

Although this opening resembles the "Spirit Roaming" scene in *Peony Pavilion,* where Du Liniang's ghost returns to her shrine in the garden and finds a ritual offering of flowering plum set out by Sister Stone, in *Peony Pavilion* the phantom heroine and the nuns never appear onstage together in the scene. In *West Garden,* by contrast, the phantom heroine watches and listens to her sister and her former lover as they pray for her, but when she tries to greet them, to her consternation, they "make no response and exit straightaway." She then realizes that this is because "ghost and human are cut off from each other. It's not surprising they couldn't see me."[139] Only later do we realize that the reason she was invisible is because she was still wearing the *hun pa* that she had put on in the previous scene, and which now represents the unbreachable membrane separating the ghost from the human world.

This understanding of the *hun pa* only emerges afterwards when the family retires to the ritual chamber and the phantom heroine enters again. As she tries to approach them, she finds she cannot bear such "an abundance of human *qi,*" but she rejoices that "[t]he candles are starting to burn out, the lamp is about to die down; I'll lift the *hun pa* that conceals me."[140] Now that darkness is falling, the *hun pa* is no longer necessary to shade her from view. The family acts out falling asleep and the phantom heroine can now address them under cover of dream. She thanks them for sponsoring the ritual, which has already succeeded in delivering her from the sea of suffering and granting her rebirth in Heaven. As in *Man/Ghost* then, the removal of the *hun pa* in *West Garden* also operates symbolically and visually as a sign of the ritual's efficacy. As in *Man/Ghost,* too, this ritual of salvation and exorcism successfully brings to an end the family's mourning period, effecting that "cooling off" of the memories that bind the living to the dead. The need to effect a permanent separation between the two and to imagine the ghost's ascension to an immortal land outside the familial mortuary realm is especially important because as an unmarried woman she has no place in the ongoing rites of the ancestral cult. Through the fictional mechanism of theater, these sentiments are voiced by the dead to the living and given heightened force in song:

> Father and Mother, there's no need for you to remember me any longer. You have another daughter close by to look after you in your waning years and seek your happiness. Brother-in-law and Little Sister, you must believe that "The dead are distant but the living are intimate." How would I ever want to disturb the felicity of your marriage?

And with that, she exits. Because this is after all opera, and because the heroine's renunciation of life and love for the good of the family deserves reward, she makes one final entrance in order to be escorted offstage for her final exit by a bevy of immortal ladies holding a spirit banner and musical instruments to signal her ascent to Heaven. Only the audience can see the procession, but the ascent is ratified on earth by the family members onstage, who hear invisible music and smell the scent of invisible incense. Again like *Man/Ghost, West Garden* ends with the elimination of the threat the dead sister poses by staging her ascent to Heaven.

Doubling and Splitting the Phantom Heroine

The challenge of representing the female revenant on stage articulates most eloquently the doubleness of the actor's body. That split is not only enacted as the drama between the body's effacement and visibility, the audience and the actor's consent, but also as narrative contemplations on the question of the female body and female desire. Such doubleness, as we have seen, is built into the role of the phantom heroine, in which a single performer ordinarily played both the regular female lead and her ghostly self.

Man/Ghost, West Garden, and *The Dropped Hairpin* constitute one set of plays that enhance the theatricality of the revenant not simply by splitting the female lead into the regular *dan* and her phantom but by adding a second full-fledged female lead played by another performer. *Man/Ghost* and *The Dropped Hairpin* cast the principal female lead *(zheng dan)* as the older sister and the secondary female lead *(xiao dan)* as the younger sister. In *West Garden,* where the two girls are not technically sisters, the roles are reversed so that the *xiao dan* plays the girl who dies, the *zheng dan* the girl who lives. The plotline of these plays pits the two female leads against one another as rivals and doubles, not merely because the ghost of the first *dan* usually passes herself off as the second *dan* in her post mortem trysts with the male lead, but above all because the life and marriage of the one requires the death of the other. In this kind of play the easy remedy of resurrecting the heroine, as in *Peony Pavilion,* or of reuniting the heroine's body and soul, as in *The Disembodied Soul,* no longer fully resolves the split between body and soul that the phantom heroine's appearance initiated because there is one dead woman too many. The surplus of female leads and the asymmetry of their fates produce a disturbing imbalance in the economy of life and death, and this requires a more complex series of theatrical solutions.

This dilemma is thrown into relief in the possession scenes staged in *The Dropped Hairpin* and *Man / Ghost.* These plays adopt opposite strategies to represent the disjunction between the body and soul of the two female characters, and in so doing foreground two different aspects of the uncanny relationship of actor to role. In *Man / Ghost,* the possessing force is invisible, internalized within the body of a single performer. When the male lead learns from his in-laws that he has been cohabiting with a ghost, while his supposed wife has in fact spent the last year ill in bed, the "real" younger sister (the *xiao dan*) enters and, to the amazement of all, assumes the identity of the older sister (the *zheng dan*). She demands that her parents "continue the match" by marrying the younger sister to the male lead, because then, she says, "Even though I am dead, yet will I still live, so that it will be possible to shut my eyes forever in the brown dirt below."[141] After the parents agree, she bids farewell to the male lead, imploring him: "Once you have wedded my little sister and celebrate your love with your new bride *(xin ren),* do not forget me, the former bride *(jiu ren).*"[142] With that the *xiao dan* falls to the ground; upon gradually coming to, she resumes her own identity.

It has been a trend among Euro-American theorists of world performance keen to recover the lost ritual origins of their own theatrical tradition to liken the actor to a shaman because he or she appears to be possessed by another. Richard Schechner, for example, discusses the model offered by trance possession, of the performer being "'added to,' becoming more or other than s / he is when not performing," "doubled" in "Artaud's sense of the word."[143] For David Cole, it is the "public impression" of possession—"that of a body being rather (spookily) lived by a life not its own" or "that of a body alive with alien life"—that shows the clearest parallels to acting.[144] Both Schechner and Cole are specifically interested in religious performing traditions of deliberately induced possession, but the supremely theatrical nature of the possession scene—as a performance requiring an audience—emerges also in the kind of ad hoc pathological situation represented in *Man / Ghost.* In aligning the stage audience's perspective with that of the family members witnessing the possession, *Man / Ghost* highlights the spectator's metatheatrical awareness of watching an actor perform the role of another.

By contrast, *The Dropped Hairpin* stages the possession scene in a way that seems to play out the performer's own experience of acting. In this version, when Qingniang, the younger sister, makes her entrance, the stage directions indicate that the ghost of Xingniang, the older sister, "enters, following her." The phantom heroine remains present but silent for the duration of the trance, visible to the audience, but invisible to the characters in the scene. The father observes, "How strange! The body is Qingniang's but the voice is Xingniang's!"[145] Although the line comes from the source tale, it carries much greater force if we imagine the actor playing the older sister's ghost standing onstage along with the actor playing the possessed younger sister. On the one hand, the visible presence of the second actor, by revealing the hidden possessing force, contrives to dispel for the spectator much of the uncanny sensation that the possession invokes in the father. On the other hand, because the main female lead stands by silently, in effect watching the second female lead perform her, this staging of the possession scene makes concrete and explicit the kind of "double existence" or "consciousness of doubleness" that any number of Euro-American theorists of performance have posited characterize the actor's experience on stage—of being split into two parts, one speaking the lines and performing the gestures, the other observing itself doing so.[146]

Of course, the underlying assumption in this scene is that the phantom heroine is not simply an onlooker but the agent who is controlling her proxy. Considerable effort is made throughout *The Dropped Hairpin* to make the ghost's invisible agency observable to the audience, by bringing the phantom heroine onstage to shadow the second female lead or by splitting the part of the female lead into two performers. In the other versions of the story, both narrative and dramatic, how exactly the golden hairpin drops from the younger sister's carriage at the male lead's feet is left rather shadowy, the frisson enhanced because we do not know precisely how this buried object has suddenly resurfaced from the grave. In *The Dropped Hairpin,* the stage directions indicate that the phantom heroine "enters alongside the second female lead's carriage." Remaining on stage after the younger sister exits, she simply "throws down the hairpin" before making her own exit.[147]

Even the earlier moment of the older sister's death is staged so that the normally invisible process of the soul departing the body is played out in full view, and the actor playing the female lead is twinned or shadowed. The unusual stage directions here read: "The principal female lead dies; the *mo* (an older male role) plays her disguised soul and emerges weeping from under the table; the earth god leads him offstage."[148] The same desire to enact the split between body and soul on stage at the moment of death for a future phantom heroine is also evident in Wu Bing's *Lady in the Painting,* but here the roles are reversed: it is the principal female lead who plays the soul and exits, and an extra who plays her dead body.[149]

As in *Man / Ghost,* the bout of possession in *The Dropped Hairpin* concludes with the possessed woman falling to the ground in a faint, but the invisible hand behind the action is again displayed dumb-show fashion, as the stage directions indicate that the phantom heroine "pushes the second female lead down before exiting."[150] The push is unseen by the other characters in the scene, who fear the fainting away of the younger sister may be an actual death and who greet her sudden coming to as a true coming back to life. The older sister's push makes visible to the audience the reason for the younger sister's fall, but it also reveals itself as a naked act of aggression. Recall that in the rewrite of the "Spectral Disputation" scene from the *Red Flowering Plum,* Li Huiniang's ghost employs a similar hostile gesture when she rams into her murderer and knocks him to the ground as she exits.[151]

One of the striking features of both "Golden Hairpin" plays is that at the very moment the identities of the two sisters are finally sorted out, the possession intervenes to blur them all over again. The ghost who had previously impersonated her sister now becomes her, inhabiting her body and designating her as a living surrogate for the dead. The ambiguity of this fusion is best conveyed through the possessed woman's statement in *Man/Ghost:* "Even though I am dead, yet shall I still live." Grammatically the space of difference between the two sisters collapses, holding out the threat that the distinction between them will be entirely eliminated and prove fatal rather than life-giving to them both.[152]

Despite the protective sentiments and benign intent the ghost voices through the mouthpiece of the sister, the danger the dead woman poses to the living woman who is to supplant her remains close to the surface. In *The Dropped Hairpin,* the ghost's request to the parents is couched as a direct threat: If they acquiesce, their living daughter will recover completely; if not, her very life will be at risk. The threat has teeth because it is now clear that the *gui bing,* the mysterious sickness the younger sister has been suffering, has been inflicted upon her by the older sister's ghost (and is therefore literally a "ghost illness"). *Man/Ghost* explicitly links the onset of the illness to the girl's visit to her dead sister's grave during the Qingming festival.

In both plays, despite the ghost's insistence that the younger sister marry the older sister's bridegroom, the hostility of the ghost toward the nuptial couple remains a lethal threat, grafting as it does the jealousy of one woman vying with another for the same man onto the presumed envy of the dead toward the living. In *The Dropped Hairpin,* the last line voiced by the ghost in the possession scene, before the phantom heroine pushes the second female lead to the ground, is addressed to the male lead: "How can I bear to leave and give you up?"[153]

This jealousy theme is explicitly developed at some length in *The Dropped Hairpin.* In an underworld court scene modeled on *Peony Pavilion,* the main female lead is granted a one-year reprieve to return as a revenant to the human world to consummate her marriage with the male lead. The reprieve is finite, the underworld judge tells her, only because her sister is fated to marry him later. "Ah, sister, my sister, your fate is really so superior to mine!" she cries. The judge admonishes her not to envy her sister, and then explains that although she cannot come back to life, all three of them—both sisters and their joint husband—are fated eventually to become immortals. To which she bitterly retorts: "My sister will be alive and I will be dead. How are these comparable in any way?"[154]

Borrowed Corpses

In "The Golden Hairpin" plays the ghost possessing the living woman quits her in the end; redemption in the celestial realm exorcises her, leaving the happy couple in peace. The new bride may be a designated substitute for the dead woman, but she is still alive and well. But what happens if the first woman's ghost never quits the second woman's body? What if she usurps it for good in what amounts to permanent possession? Such a scenario, which requires killing off the second woman who is to serve as the substitute, is the premise of a second set of phantom-heroine plays involving a surplus of female leads.

Each of the three plays in this group begins by following the basic story line of the ghost romance epitomized by *Peony Pavilion:* a young unmarried woman dies prematurely and, after an interval of time, returns as a revenant to consummate her predestined love for the male lead. Her ghost is granted a reprieve from the underworld court to return to life and marry him, but here the *Peony Pavilion* model breaks down, for the phantom heroine's "fleshly body" has already decomposed and is therefore unavailable. The solution is for her soul to return in the body of a second woman who has died recently and whose corpse revives expressly for this purpose.

The first of these plays to enact "borrowing someone else's corpse to come back to life" *(jieshi huanhun)* as this folkloric motif is called, is the Yuan northern drama *Emerald Peach Flower.* As in "The Golden Hairpin" plot, the principal female lead who dies is the older of two sisters; the man the phantom heroine has the liaison with was her promised bridegroom before death; and the prospect of the family's marrying the younger sister to the male lead to "continue the match" is already being discussed before the ghost's identity is revealed. Dramatically, the greatest difference is that the younger sister is not developed as an independent entity in *Emerald Peach Flower.* She appears on stage only after the older sister's soul has already taken over her reanimated corpse and erased any difference between them. The advantage of this staging is that it follows the rules of Yuan drama, which allow only one main singing role per play, so only a single female lead is permitted.

But neither this convention nor the concise form of Yuan drama fully explains the omission of the younger sister as an autonomous character. The lead role frequently doubled other parts in Yuan plays; in fact, in *Emerald Peach Flower,* the female lead also plays the matchmaker in another act and presumably could have played the younger sister before that. Rather, this complete absence of the second sister from the stage also makes possible her perfunctory treatment as a mere double of the first in the resolution of the play. Only in this way can the second death be presented solely as a rebirth. There is therefore no mourning for the younger daughter voiced in the play, still less are any ceremonies mentioned for the settling or salvation of her soul. Ironically, it is the complete disembodiment of the second girl—her lack of corporeal presence as a character on stage—that allows the play to gloss over the gross inequity in the fates of the two sisters, in which—though sanctioned by predestination and underworld fiat—the older sister effectively causes the death of her younger rival and replaces her.

The second of the plays is Feng Menglong's revision of *Snow-Sprinkled Hall (Saxue tang),* a southern drama based on an early Ming novella from *More Tales*

Told by Lamplight.[155] The play was written by Mei Xiaosi around 1628, but only Feng's revision, which he published, survives.[156] In keeping with the source story, the asymmetry of the two girls' fates is mitigated somewhat by making the pair complete strangers rather than sisters. With the more expansive form of the southern drama, the second girl is now given her own stage identity—she is cast as a *tie,* a supporting female role—and her sudden death is treated in a separate, properly sentimental scene (scene 35), so that she has already been introduced as a living character before her body is annexed by the first girl.

The inherent arbitrariness and unfairness of the body-swapping, however, is addressed comically in the next scene, which is set in the underworld (scene 36). There the female lead is offered a choice of bodies to borrow from a line-up of the recently dead, played by a clown, a painted face role *(jing),* and, of course, the *tie.* The clown quips: "You can borrow mine to use as long as you return it." "No!" corrects the underworld judge. "What would be borrowed is *your* corpse; what would return is *her* soul." "Then how about I borrow *her* corpse and let *my* soul return?" "Stop talking nonsense!" roars the judge.[157] When the female lead selects the *tie* on the grounds that she is the prettiest, the *tie* objects and tells her to go pick someone else's body. The female lead even attempts to persuade her that the arrangement will actually be in the *tie*'s own best interest, arguing that "it's better to have your body and name occupied by someone else than to end up like a heap of collapsed tiles or a puddle of melted ice."[158]

The underworld judge finally puts an end to all this arguing, and the revival proceeds as planned. In scene 37, which is set in the *tie*'s family residence, the female lead first enters, makes one circuit of the stage, and then exits. The *tie* then immediately rushes on stage. In terms of the plot, the female lead returns to life in a body of her choosing and gains her heart's desire, but theatrically the performer is eliminated, since this exit signals the end of her role in the play. The *dan* may replace the *tie* in the narrative, but the *tie* replaces the *dan* on stage. The change of bodies is physically enacted through a shift in performers, which is played out as a tour de force of acting along the lines of the possession scenes in "The Golden Hairpin" plays: the body is that of the living woman, but the voice and manner are those of the dead woman.

Since the *tie* prevails on the stage, it is the theatrical and ritual problem of the female lead's absent body that is raised in the play's grand reunion finale (scene 40). This scene, which stages the wedding ceremony of the *tie* and the male lead, assembles relatives from both families, principally those of the female lead, whose family has, as it were, won "custody" of the reborn girl, but also those of the *tie,* who maintains their claim. After the ceremony the new bride is still troubled by one thing—what is to become of the corpse of her former self, which lies in a coffin temporarily lodged at a temple? Not to worry, assures her bridegroom. He would "never dare forget" about these material remains. He will have the coffin shipped home with them, so that at the end, the three of them can be buried together in the same grave.[159] A ritual solution for the disposal of the surplus female lead's body is thus proposed, while a reunion of the three principals missing from the final scene is simultaneously promised and deferred.

An Intoxicating Dream, Fan Wenruo's southern drama rewrite of *Emerald Peach Flower,* is the last of the three plays and by far the most convoluted. The playwright's claim in his preface that his play surpasses *Peony Pavilion* in terms of plot twists and reversals is no idle boast, since every possible dramatic cliché related to the female double is piled on: not only phantoms, real and feigned, but portraits, dream visions, reflections in the water, and personified flowers.[160] Likewise, the comic possibilities for disguise, mistaken identity, and jealousy are exponentially increased by designating not just two female leads, but *three:* a principal female lead (the *dan*), who plays the girl who dies initially of lovesickness and returns as a phantom; a secondary female lead (the *xiao dan*), who plays her adopted younger sister and rival for the male lead's affections and who temporarily becomes a Daoist nun after she is stranded on the road; and a third female lead (the *cha dan*), a stranger to the other two, whose corpse the female lead will use to come back to life. Fan's borrowing of the term *cha dan,* an obscure role subcategory from Yuan drama that did not ordinarily figure in Ming southern drama, suggests how rare it was, even for the lengthiest comedy, to feature *three* young romantic female leads in a single work.[161]

As this promotion of the body surrogate into a leading role suggests, *An Intoxicating Dream* goes far beyond *Snow-Sprinkled Hall* in developing the part into a full-fledged character and foregrounding the pathos and absurdity of her existential predicament. Even before her death she is granted two major scenes (scenes 20 and 23), and great effort is made to reinforce not just her physical identity but her symbolic identity as a double and imitation of the main female lead. In her dream-like death scene (scene 25), for example, the *cha dan* finds herself, like the famous tragic heroine Xiaoqing, gazing and calling out to her own reflection in a pool; but at this moment the female lead enters and stands behind her so that the *cha dan* can see the female lead's reflection supplant her own. After her death, in keeping with her dying wishes, the *cha dan* is to be buried beneath an emerald peach tree. The family servant is sent ahead to excavate the burial site (scene 29), where, to his surprise, he discovers the skeleton and grave marker of the female lead already occupying the spot; at that very moment, news of the miraculous revival of the *cha dan*'s corpse is reported. The split-second timing of the two events—the exhumation of the bones and the revival of the corpse—implies a causal relationship between them. It also suggests an uncanny simultaneity, a sleight of hand by which the revival of the *cha dan*'s body appears not simply as a rebirth of the female lead's soul but as the resurrection of her skeleton.

As in *Snow-Sprinkled Hall,* once the revival has taken place, the performer playing the revived corpse replaces the female lead on stage for good.[162] Having previously developed the surrogate into a full-fledged character, however, enables *An Intoxicating Dream* to make a radical turn here. The former self of the *cha dan*—the body's original soul—does not disappear entirely from the play. Instead, in a remarkable scene (scene 32), the *cha dan* returns briefly as a lovesick phantom heroine to haunt the male lead. How are we to understand this second iteration of the phantom heroine, which amounts to the doubling of a double, the copying of a copy?

Like "the ghost of a ghost" discussed in Chapter 1, this proliferation of phantom heroines places us within the logical terrain of the "play with infinity," one of the basic operations linked to repetition and reversal that Susan Stewart has identified in the making of nonsense. If the soul of a borrowed body can return as a revenant, then why not have this soul reborn as well in yet another borrowed body, and so on ad infinitum? If death can be made not to count once, why not undo it again and again and again? [163]

The dizzying prospect of an infinite chain of revenants at loose ends and borrowed corpses coming back to life drives home the point that within a play the resurrection of a phantom heroine is not only a sentimental instantiation of the triumph of love over death but a game played with mortality in which death can be reversed and canceled at whim. Tang Xianzu well understood the profoundly ludic impulse underlying resurrection on stage, which is one reason he wrote the revival scene in *Peony Pavilion* as a comic one, in which any high drama is undercut by deliberate anachronism, puns, bawdy jokes, and general clowning.

The appearance of a second lovesick phantom in the same play pushes the whole trope firmly into the realm of a joke. After all, a ghost is not simply regarded as a figure of fear or suffering in Chinese folklore and speech but as a figure of fun. The phrase "ghost talk" *(gui hua),* for instance, means "nonsense"; to "do a ghost" *(dao gui)* means to "play tricks."[164] This humorous side was very much part of the seventeenth-century fondness for ghosts in the theater, as Zhang Dai's and Li Yu's complaints about their contemporaries' penchant for this sort of noisy excitement indicate. Even the romantic phantom heroine, as *An Intoxicating Dream* shows so clearly, was not exempt. The scene in which the *cha dan*'s ghost returns is entitled "Hun hua," which literally means "soul talk," but which makes sense only as a play on the phrase *gui hua* to mean "nonsense." In fact, both the phrases *gui hua* and *dao gui* are employed in the scene's dialogue to underscore this meaning. Although both phrases are commonly uttered in phantom-heroine plays to point up the fun, this sort of word play appears with unusual frequency throughout *An Intoxicating Dream.*[165]

But what of the secondary female lead—the adopted younger sister temporarily turned nun, who contrives to marry the male lead as well in the end? (Polygamy exponentially increases the possibilities for happy endings in romantic comedy; the marriage of the male lead to two female leads is a common finale in southern drama.) Alone of the three female leads, she does not die, but she too is implicated in the ghost economy of the play by being mistaken for a phantom. The comedy of the false female ghost, where the male lead is tricked into believing that a living woman is really a specter, was a well-established subplot in Yuan northern drama that late Ming playwrights eagerly seized upon.[166] In phantom-heroine plays involving more than one female lead, such as *West Garden,* the comic possibilities are increased because the male lead can not only mistake a living woman for a ghost but a ghost for a living woman.[167] In this respect, too, *An Intoxicating Dream* deliberately pushes repeated misunderstanding over the top into absurdity.

After the primary female lead's death (*dan* no. 1), the male lead unknowingly becomes involved with her revenant (scene 15); later he also becomes involved with the little nun (*dan* no. 2), who warns him that her rival, whose name is Xie Qiantao, is a ghost (scene 18). He is naturally terrified when he meets *dan* no. 1 again, but she lies, assuring him that she is really Feng Cuiliu (the name of *dan* no. 3, the *cha dan*) and therefore alive; it is dan no. 2 who is really the ghost. Confronted by *dan* no. 1 and *dan* no. 2 together on stage, each of whom shrilly accuses the other of being a ghost, the male lead is forced to decide who is right. Naturally he chooses to elope with the "wrong" woman, that is, with the "real" ghost (scene 21). Later, he loses track of *dan* no. 1 and again meets *dan* no. 2, who now pretends to be a ghost; he subsequently hears news of the *cha dan*'s death but not of her revival. It is understandable, therefore, that by scene 32, when someone knocks on his door in the middle of night and he finds another woman standing there—the phantom of the "real" *cha dan*—he is a touch confused: "Are you an immortal? A human? A ghost? A dream vision? A painting spirit? Are you Xie Qiantao? Feng Cuiliu? The little nun? Please explain yourself clearly."[168] She persuades him she really is a revenant, and to prove it she exits, "giving a ghostly wail." He now begins shouting: "A ghost! A ghost!" when who should enter but *dan* no. 2. "Oh, no! Here comes another ghost!" he cries.[169] She tells him she has only pretended to be a ghost to trick him and that she is really a living woman.

The predicament the male lead finds himself in comically illustrates Marjorie Garber's insight that a major source of the uncanniness aroused by a ghostly apparition is "its manifestation as a sign of potential proliferation or plurality and to its acknowledgement of the loss of the original—indeed, to the loss of the certainty of origin."[170] The boundaries between life and death and between impersonation and identity have blurred so often in this play that they have become meaningless. As the *cha dan*'s father puts it: "Truly it's hard to distinguish between the living and the dead, and to tell fake from real."[171] But in the theater the logic of reversal underlying masquerade and resurrection is the same. Just as a disguise can be removed and proper identity restored, so too death can be undone and a corpse returned to life. No death is ever real on stage, where, as Michael Goldman puts it, "all losses can be restored."[172]

Still, the conundrum posed by the reborn corpse's identity is such that in the finale the great Judge Bao must be brought in to adjudicate (scene 34). Even he is stumped at first, but finally pronounces a compromise verdict: the girl will be recognized as the daughter of the *cha dan*'s father and the goddaughter of the *dan*'s mother. Meanwhile, the second female lead has entered, claiming to be the *cha dan*'s soul reborn in the little nun's body. The *cha dan*'s father is understandably skeptical: "Her daughter is in my daughter's body, while my daughter is now in the little nun's body. I don't believe it."[173] Sense has been reestablished by the authority of Judge Bao, only to be undermined again by a bogus repetition of a borrowed corpse's rebirth. Although the audience and most of the characters in the scene are aware that the little nun is an imposter, the father throws up his hands, recognizes both girls as his daughters, and agrees to marry both of them off to the male lead. This ending reinforces the fundamental notion that the truth status of an event—or a ghost—is never really at stake in the theater, where what unfolds on stage is always simultaneously confirmed and denied.

Comedy rather than ritual, therefore, furnishes the solution to the surplus of female leads in *An Intoxicating Dream*. Through blatant sleight of hand and lies, the second female lead compensates for the loss of the third and shares in the happiness of the first. An orphan and a nun, she is indeed returned from social death and thus "reborn." She is essentially a place keeper, in the numerical sense of the term. Stewart notes that the "sameness of the integer" makes it possible to put anything in a series, because each thing is still "one" regardless of what it actually is.[174] The interchangeability of souls and bodies paves the way for the interchangeability of all the daughters. As the *cha dan*'s father, who gets all the best lines, sums up the mathematical equation through which loss is overcome in the play: "My son-in-law dreamt of only one beautiful woman, but obtained two. I lost one daughter to death, but got two daughters returned to life. Isn't this a joyful thing?"[175]

Coda: *Palace of Lasting Life*

Hong Sheng's masterpiece, *Palace of Lasting Life,* has long been acknowledged as one of the two last great works of the southern drama, representing both the culmination and the virtual endpoint of the literary playwright's creative engagement with this form of theater.[1] Begun in 1679 and completed around 1688, after nearly ten years of work, this fifty-act play is also important as one of several early Qing plays to reflect upon the fall of the Ming in 1644 and the memory of its loss.[2] This occurs on several planes in *Palace of Lasting Life.* On the narrative level, the play recounts the splendor and collapse of an imperial court, displaced to another historical period. On the level of mood, the second half is suffused with absence and regret. And on the literary level, the play reworks many of the theatrical motifs favored by late Ming playwrights to fit a more introspective and nostalgic early Qing sensibility; prominent among these are the phantom heroine and her resurrection. Because Hong Sheng's ghost scenes reprise but pull in new directions many of the major themes traced in the previous chapters—the female corpse revived through love, the imagination of death through a ghostly poetic voice, the mourning of the historical past by the present, and the theatricality of the split between body and soul—a close reading of *Palace of Lasting Life* also provides a fitting endpoint for this book.

The play was an immediate and lasting success, both on the page and in the theater. Hong Sheng's foreword says that his work quickly became publicly known through his associates who read the manuscript and through the actors who borrowed his script and performed it.[3] A "gala performance" in Beijing the following year during what turned out to be a period of imperial mourning became a famous scandal that resulted in Hong Sheng's being stripped of his status as a stipendiary student in the National Academy and kicked out of the capital.[4] Nonetheless, the scandal seems to have only increased the reputation of the play rather than suppress it. *Palace of Lasting Life* continued to be in demand on the stage, and it was partly to counteract "vulgar" alterations in the many productions of the play that Hong Sheng published his own authorized version of the text, Volume I in 1700 and Volume II in 1704.[5] Before his death that same year, Hong Sheng attended a full-length performance of his play staged by Cao Yin, textile commissioner of Nanjing (and grandfather of Cao Xueqin, the author of *Dream of the Red Chamber*), which lasted three days and three nights. This is the only complete performance on record.[6]

The play retells the famous tragedy of the Tang dynasty emperor Minghuang's love for his concubine Lady Yang (Yang Guifei or Yang Yuhuan). When An Lushan rebelled in 755 and took the capital Chang'an in 756, the emperor and his retinue fled to Sichuan. En route, his soldiers mutinied at the Mawei courier station and murdered the hated prime minister, Yang Guozhong, a cousin of Lady Yang's, and then forced the emperor to acquiesce to Lady Yang's execution at the site. Although the rebellion was eventually quelled, the emperor was forced to abdicate in favor of the crown prince and go into exile, where he lived out the remainder of his days in grief and remorse, pining for her. This is the historical nucleus of the story.

According to legend, a necromancer later revealed to the emperor that in a former life Lady Yang had been an immortal banished to earth, and that after her death, she had achieved apotheosis and rejoined the immortal realm. This legend is considerably elaborated and expanded in *Palace of Lasting Life.* The play's action alternates between two worlds, the sublunar realm of human affairs and the lunar realm of the immortals. The happy ending mandated for southern drama is achieved by staging the posthumous reunion of the emperor and Lady Yang, now both immortals and together for eternity, in the celestial domain of the Moon Palace.

Like most southern drama play texts, *Palace of Lasting Life* has a bipartite structure and is divided into two volumes of equal length, a practice that facilitated complex patterns of echoing and cross-reference. The disjunction between the two parts is especially pronounced in *Palace of Lasting Life,* however, because the major historical events that furnish the real dramatic action in the play all take place in the first part, which ends climactically with the overthrow of the emperor's rule and Lady Yang's death, by suicide rather than execution in the version of the story that Hong Sheng chose to follow. This is not to say that the distinction is between a this-worldly, historical Part I and an otherworldly, mythical Part II. Scenes set in the human and immortal spheres are distributed across both volumes, though to be sure, historical episodes are more densely clustered in Part I, mythical ones in Part II.[7] It is rather that once the emperor has been deposed and exiled, his fate is decoupled from that of the empire. Consequently, in the second half, the love between the emperor and the now-deceased Lady Yang no longer affects the larger course of history as it did so emphatically in the first half of the play. The three historical action scenes in Part II, which recount the battles fought to retake the capital and defeat An Lushan, are therefore reduced to filler tying up loose ends, because they have no organic relationship any more with the dramatic thrust of the emperor and Lady Yang's story.[8]

Instead, the split between the two halves of the play is better characterized as that between events and memory. In the first part, our sense is that of history—in both its public and private dimensions—ineluctably unfolding before our eyes. In this respect, *Palace of Lasting Life* succeeds admirably in the most basic goal of historical drama, that of bringing the past to life for the present. The energy in Part II, by contrast, is mainly channeled into the recollection, mourning, and commemoration of the events enacted in Part I, particularly Lady Yang's death. As Liu Yanjun observes:

"The second half is completely submerged in a strong mood of loss and uses memory, dream scenes, the immortal world, and all sorts of nonrealistic methods to intensify the subjective feelings of grief."[9] For the emperor and Lady Yang, memory is mainly staged as an introspective process of private remembrance and expiation. Private remembrance is also the subject of a scene where Lady Yang's former palace attendants set out a ritual offering to the spirit tablet of their former mistress (scene 39). In two further scenes the emperor performs his commemoration in public rituals, consecrating an effigy statue of Lady Yang in a temple he has dedicated to her (scene 32) and exhuming her body for reburial (scene 43). The play also includes two outstanding scenes of what may be termed "collective memory"—the group viewing of a stocking that once belonged to Lady Yang, now a relic on public display for a price (scene 36), and a temple fair performance by a former court musician of a ballad recounting the tragedy of the emperor and his lady (scene 38). These collective-memory scenes, with their vulgar gawkers and fairgoers, are also practically the only ones in the unusually somber second half to introduce any of the comic elements normally required in southern drama. These scenes are also the principal moments in the play where the two temporal orders of historical drama—the past of the story being told and the present of the playwright and audience—are superimposed to ironic effect.

The overall orientation of Part II toward remembrance partly explains why Hong Sheng inserted a cluster of scenes featuring Lady Yang's revenant (scenes 27, 30, and 37). The last of these scenes culminates in the resurrection of her corpse as a precondition for shedding the bodily constraints of mortal existence and achieving apotheosis and happiness. This ghost interlude has no real counterpart in the abundant previous treatments of the saga—historical, poetic, fictional, and dramatic—that Hong Sheng consulted and reworked into his play. There are of course minor exceptions. In the Tang tale "A Journey to Zhou and Qin," the male protagonist encounters the specters of famous palace ladies from several different dynasties, including Lady Yang, who is the most recent, but she is not the one he chooses to bed, and in any event, she is simply part of a general jumbling of the past's bygone glamour momentarily made accessible to the present.[10] Closer in time and genre, *The Startled Swan (Jinghong ji),* the main late Ming southern drama to treat Lady Yang's story and a major influence on *Palace of Lasting Life,* has the necromancer summon her spirit on stage for the final reunion scene (scene 39). This play demotes Lady Yang to a supporting role (the *tie*), casting Lady Mei, a legendary rival of hers, as the female lead (the *dan*), who becomes the emperor's living consort. Although the scene is entitled "Grand Meeting of the Dead and the Living" ("Youming dahui"), Lady Yang is not, in fact, represented as a ghost. The stage directions indicate that "she enters wearing Daoist garb and carrying a whisk" (a theatrical prop signifying Daoist status) to reinforce the main purpose of her hasty apparition: to announce the news of her having become an immortal to the happy couple (see fig. 21).[11]

The addition of an interim ghost phase between Lady Yang's death and her attainment of immortality, therefore, is essentially Hong Sheng's innovation. These

FIGURE 21 Woodblock illustration of the necromancer summoning Lady Yang as an immortal to greet the emperor and Lady Mei in the final reunion scene. *Jinghong ji,* scene 39. Late Ming edition. Photo by Jeehee Hong.

scenes, particularly scene 27 "Infernal Pursuit" ("Ming zhui") and scene 37 "Release from the Corpse" ("Shi jie"), contain some of the most inventive writing and ingenious staging in the play. The scenes fully support Wang Jilie's claim that "in terms of stagecraft *(paichang)* in southern drama, nothing tops this work."[12] Because of the experimental staging and the inauspiciousness of such subject matter unleavened by comedy, but above all because this interlude departs from the contours of the well-known story, the ghost scenes dropped out entirely from the performing repertory of excerpts that has come down to us from the eighteenth century.[13] Indeed, with the exception of the final reunion in the Moon Palace, none of the otherworldly scenes have remained part of the stage tradition.[14]

Hong Sheng's desire to showcase Lady Yang in the role of the phantom heroine clearly shows the profound influence of *Peony Pavilion* and marks the endpoint of the seventeenth-century vogue for phantom-heroine plays. The initial publication of *Palace of Lasting Life* underscores the closeness of the ties linking it to *Peony Pavilion.* Hong Sheng's authorized edition was published in collaboration with his close friend and publisher, Wu Yiyi, who also furnished a preface and an extensive commentary.[15] Hong Sheng's preface praises the commentary for having captured the author's intent, and he recommends Wu Yiyi's twenty-eight-scene abridgment, which is no longer extant, for "those seeking brevity and ease in performance" ("Liyan," pp. 1–2). About a decade earlier, Wu Yiyi had published his Three Wives' annotated edition of Tang Xianzu's play, entitled *Wu Wushan's Three Wives' Combined Commentary on Peony Pavilion (Wu Wushan sanfu heping Mudan ting).* Hong Sheng's daughter, Hong Zhize, contributed a colophon to this edition in which she reminisces about the frequent discussions her father and Wu Yiyi held on *Peony Pavilion.*[16] Comparisons with *Peony Pavilion* crop up both in Hong Sheng's prefaces to *Palace of Lasting Life* and in Wu Yiyi's commentary on Hong's play. On the whole their remarks, while acknowledging *Peony Pavilion*'s influence, strive to differentiate *Palace of Lasting Life* from Tang's play, to stress the way the copy diverges from the model.[17]

The ghost interlude is one of the most powerful examples of *Peony Pavilion*'s influence, yet it is also an area in which Hong Sheng departs particularly radically from his predecessor, for the traditional template of the ghost romance fits rather badly with Lady Yang's story. Ordinarily, as we have seen, when an innocent girl dies of lovesickness before her marriage can take place, her return as a revenant to find her predestined lover is a way of restoring, if only temporarily, the pleasure that death had cheated her of. Typically in such romances, ghosthood becomes a phase of freedom that liberates the disembodied soul from social convention and the physical constraints of time and place, enabling her to pursue and consummate her desires to the fullest, if only temporarily.

But for Lady Yang, as a mature woman and violent suicide, who dies not from unfulfilled longing but from an excess of love, ghosthood becomes an ordeal of suffering and repentance, rather than a stage of freedom and enjoyment. What justifies considering the interlude as an extension of the ghost romance is the play's overpowering ideology of *qing*. It is the weight of Lady Yang's undying love that prevents her *qi* from dissolving into nothingness, as it should upon death, and causes her to return as a revenant. As she sings upon her first entrance as a phantom in scene 27:

> Time is up,
> His oath forsaken,
> My body fouled.
> Only drop after drop of foolish love undestroyed.
> I fly toward the Yellow Springs,
> Holding fast to my burden. (p. 142)

Ghosthood erects an unbreachable barrier between Lady Yang and the emperor, rather than facilitating posthumous contact with him as it ordinarily does in the ghost romance. She is never permitted to meet the emperor in phantom form, not even under cover of dream. In this regard, *Palace of Lasting Life* deliberately departs from another of its great predecessors, the Yuan northern drama *Rain on the Pawlonia Tree (Wutong yu)*, where the final act grants the disconsolate emperor a brief dream of Lady Yang's apparition one rainy, dismal night.[18] Hong Sheng rewrites this famous act by splitting it into two scenes. In the first, scene 29 ("Hearing Bells"), during a stormy night on the road to Sichuan, the emperor takes refuge in a pavilion, where he is denied the solace of sleep, much less of dreams. Tormented by memories of her death, the grief of this bereaved husband conjures forth no spectral visit or vision. Instead, he is compelled to imagine her ghost enduring this horrible night alone at Mawei. As he sings:

> In such a heartrending place,
> I recall her desolate grave all the more.
> As white poplars whistle and rain blows sideways,
> her lonely soul must be so bleak and cold there,
> amid the chill gleam of ghost fires
>   and grass-drenched fireflies.
> How I regret betraying you in haste! (p. 156)

The set language of ghostly poetry worked into the emperor's aria—the windblown funerary trees from the "Nineteen Old Poems," the cold, wet gleams of will-o'-the-wisps and fireflies from Li He's verse—are familiar to us from the history of the ghostly image code traced in Chapter 2. The specific placement of this scene within the ghost interlude, however, makes the emperor's aria especially poignant. Since the audience has already "witnessed" Lady Yang's ghost at Mawei, the emperor's imaginings partake of a reality and concreteness that is nonetheless completely inaccessible to him. He can encounter her ghost only through poetic language, driving home the extent of her absence and their separation.

In the second scene derived from *Rain on the Pawlonia Tree* (scene 45, "Dreaming in the Rain"), the bereaved emperor, now exiled in Sichuan, does fall asleep, but even in dream, Lady Yang remains hopelessly unattainable. His dream begins with the joyful news that she had actually escaped death at Mawei and is waiting for him there. But when he arrives, to his dismay, the station is deserted. (Unbeknown to him, she has already joined the immortal world; her death has been undone and her soul has departed from Mawei; in this sense, the dream is "true.") Suddenly, in a rapid, unexplained scene shift so characteristic of dream experience, he finds the station has disappeared and that he is back at the old Winding Stream Imperial Garden outside the capital. He notices that the garden walls have fallen into decay, but no palace lady materializes in the ruins. Instead, out of the surging waves of the Winding Stream a monster in chains suddenly leaps out at him. The emperor flees in terror and is saved only because supernatural sentries in gold armor abruptly appear and haul the monster away. The emperor's anxiety dream has turned into a full-fledged nightmare. His return to Mawei and the ruined pleasure garden thwarts his yearning to undo the past; instead he is forced to relive the trauma of history. He does not find Lady Yang even momentarily (as in the original Yuan play), but instead is attacked by a "monster," a thinly disguised allegorical figure for An Lushan.[19] What the emperor most desires has been replaced by what he most fears.

The pursuit of the emperor by Lady Yang's ghost is similarly fruitless and painful. In scene 27, when her ghost flies out of Mawei station, her first thought is to rejoin the emperor's speeding carriage, which she spies in the distance. But though she possesses all the traditional attributes of a disembodied soul—weightlessness and the ability to fly with the wind—try as she may, she cannot catch him. As she sings:

> Soundless, my soul light as a leaf,
> Swift as the shuttle of a loom, his cavalry.
> No sooner do I complete one turn through the air,
> Than the tip of his turquoise pennant is swallowed again
>   by the mist on the trees. (p. 142)

Throughout the ghost interlude, Hong Sheng contrives to weave into the scene's action the repertory of stage techniques associated with the phantom heroine, particularly the ghost walk and whirlwind dance. Sometimes these routines are implied in the lyrics of the arias, as in the example above; sometimes such movements are also reinforced by explicit stage directions, as in the example below.

Just as it seems she is about to reach her goal and overtake the emperor, a gong suddenly sounds offstage, and she finds her way blocked by a preternatural black wind, which blots out everything in her path, including the emperor's carriage. She stands by, forced to witness the agonies of her sister Lady Guo and her cousin the prime minister as their wraiths are savagely hauled off to hell by underworld ghouls. As she weeps, aware now that her love for the emperor has led to her family's destruction, and overwhelmed with remorse, she realizes that the miasma of *qi* that surrounds her is also a product of her own guilt. As she sings:

> No wonder I'm enveloped in every direction by clouds of sorrow:
> All have been puffed into being from my thousand cries
> and resentful breath *(yuan qi)*. (p. 143)

The implication is that the black wind is not simply an inauspicious harbinger of her relatives' apparitions or the result of the "clouds of sorrow and fog of suffering" (p. 143) that surround them, but an external manifestation of the state of her own soul.

Such is the didactic lesson presented in the sixteenth-century edition of the Buddhist play *Mulian Rescues His Mother (Mulian jiumu)*, from which Hong Sheng may have drawn inspiration. In a scene entitled "Visiting the Terrace for Gazing Home" ("Guo Wangxiang tai"), the soul of Mulian's mother in the underworld is led onto this terrace with the expectation of glimpsing her relations and former home. To her horror she finds that a black mist has descended, obscuring her view entirely. The ghost attendant with her explains that the mist is not heaven-sent, but has arisen from her own "black heart," from the bad deeds that she had done when still alive.[20]

This scene from *Mulian Rescues His Mother* suggests a far deeper parallel with the ghost interlude in *Palace of Lasting Life,* that it serves as a de facto state of purgatory for Lady Yang. The notion of an interim state, in which souls of the dead were tormented in the underworld while awaiting rebirth, arose from medieval Buddhism.[21] The understanding that efforts of the living could ameliorate the lot of souls in the underworld continued to stimulate the popularity of rituals like the Land and Water Rite throughout the late imperial period. But self-reflection, emotional suffering, and penitence are what redeem Lady Yang in *Palace of Lasting Life,* not the emperor's attempts at commemoration and reburial or other rituals performed by the living on her behalf. The inner process of self-redemption, carried out from her viewpoint and within her subjectivity, takes on overwhelming weight in the ghost scenes. Zeng Yongyi has noted the intricate musical structure of scene 27, which is composed of arias alternating northern and southern tunes. Such a mixture is commonplace in southern drama. What is unusual here is that only Lady Yang's ghost sings northern tunes; all the other characters who come on stage sequentially (the emperor, the ghosts of Lady Guo and the prime minister, the local Earth God of Mawei) sing southern tunes. Formally, at least, this musical structure sets Lady Yang's subjective viewpoint apart from that of the other characters, thereby reinforcing the primacy of her vision throughout the scene.[22]

Most brilliantly of all, Hong Sheng situates Lady Yang's stint in purgatory not in the underworld but on earth, in the major sites of her life and death.[23] Condemned to haunt these places of the past, she is repeatedly forced to confront her unwelcome memories as part of the expiation process. After the black wind effaces any forward path, she has no choice but to head back to the Mawei station. As she circles back on stage, she sings of her dread at returning there: "The tumult of sparrows returning to their glade at evening/I still mistake for the cries of mutinying soldiers" (p. 144). Back at Mawei she catches sight of some characters inscribed on a tree: it is her epitaph, marking the spot of her temporary grave. Although in *Peony Pavilion* Du Liniang's ghost returns to the garden where she is buried and discovers her memorial shrine and spirit tablet, she does not confront the actual grave mound; moreover, for Du Liniang, the garden is a place of remembered delight, not a killing ground.[24] The violence surrounding Lady Yang's suicide makes her coming face to face with her grave all the more wrenching. Imagining the "sloughed off remains of the corpse" lying beneath "the cold earth and desolate mound" that serves as her final resting place, she calls out to her body: "Yang Yuhuan! Your soul is here!" (p. 145). In this moment of high dramatic pathos, she finally grasps the split that death has wrought between the soul as self and the body as other. Confined to the Buddhist chapel where she had hung herself on a pear tree in the yard, the events of her forced suicide linger before her eyes: "Crossing once more the courtyard where my life ended / I see how tearstains still foul the foot of the tree" (p. 145).

Lady Yang's purgatory is structured with clear symbolic markers signaling her progress toward redemption. At the outset of scene 27, she appears "with a strip of white silk tied around her neck, costumed exactly as in the previous scene of her death" (p. 142). A rare illustration of Lady Yang's death scene from *The Startled Swan* shows her with a white strip of cloth tied around her neck, dangling from the tree in the chapel yard as soldiers patrol the outer wall (see fig. 22). Appearing with a white strip of cloth tied around the neck was a conventional sign of a hanged ghost, not only in the theater, but in ghost stories and in pictures associated with the Land and Water Rite (see fig. 4).[25] At the end of scene 27, the local Earth God of Mawei enters to inform Lady Yang that she is really a banished immortal and announces

FIGURE 22 Woodblock illustration of Lady Yang's death scene, showing her corpse hanging from a tree in the chapel yard with a white strip of cloth around her neck. *Jinghong ji*, scene 27. Late Ming edition. Photo by Jeehee Hong.

the heavenly order releasing her from the consequences of a wrongful, violent death. The word used for "release" is *jie*[a], which also means to "untie"; the phrase *yuan jie* is employed for "wrongful death," where *jie* also has the meaning of "knot." The stage directions instruct him to concurrently "perform the action of untying the white strip on her behalf," thereby literally translating the words of the heavenly pardon into the coded sartorial language of the stage.

The next step toward redemption occurs in scene 30, "Repenting of Love," in which Lady Yang's ghost repeatedly thinks on the past and expresses her guilt and remorse, all the while reiterating the unquenchable flame of her love for the emperor. The Earth God, overhearing her and pronouncing her repentance sincere, thereupon grants her a travel permit, that bureaucratic formality required for wandering souls in drama, releasing her from her confinement in Mawei.[26] This is the second milestone.

The opening of scene 37 finds her at last tasting a little of a ghost's freedom "to let the wind take her where it will." As she sings:

> Soundlessly, my soul rides the wind as though wandering
> in a dream.
> The road is dark and silent; I cannot tell day from night . . .
> Green will-o'-the-wisps float through blighted weeds,
> Lighting my way ahead through the murky darkness. (p. 190)

Suddenly, in the distance, she spies the corner of a palace enshrouded in mist. At first, she does not recognize where she is; then all at once she realizes she is at the gate of the Western Palace, where, as she reminisced in scene 30, she had "formerly made merry with the emperor" (p. 158).

From this point on, the stage directions for the scene décor take on a specificity virtually unprecedented in any southern drama play text. After Lady Yang acts out entering the palace, the stage directions specify the furnishings she finds: "Earlier, the former bed and curtains, along with other former implements and utensils, should have been placed on stage" (p. 191). She acts out climbing to the second story of a building, and suddenly realizes she is in the Hall of Lasting Life, where she and the emperor swore their eternal love on the lovers' festival of the Seventh Day of the Seventh Month. Again the stage directions specify the furnishings: "Earlier, the table with incense for begging favor on the Seventh Day of the Seventh Month should have been placed on stage" (p. 191).

Wu Yiyi's commentary astutely points out the extraordinary way this part of the scene is constructed, so that external landscapes and subjective states, past memory and present experience blur together: "Her wandering soul has no control over her movements. It's almost exactly like the working of a dream" (*Guben* 2. 41b). "Wherever her thoughts take her, there suddenly that place appears. These sites of the past are all illusions conjured up; they are not real scenes. The décor on stage must proceed entirely from this awareness" (*Guben* 2. 42a). In other words, as in a dream, the omnipotence of unconscious thought is paramount. We are reminded of a comment from the Three Wives' edition of *Peony Pavilion:* "A ghost is merely a dream, and a dream is nothing but a ghost,"[27] which asserts the fungibility of these two phantom states. We are also reminded that "dream" is the central trope in Chinese literature for the past, not only because of the fleeting evanescence of a dream, but because once the past has vanished, it exists only as a memory trace in the mind of the survivor.[28]

Again, what is extraordinary in Hong Sheng's conception of this scene is that these vistas in the palace are not presented as dreams. They employ none of the standard conventions for portraying dreams on stage, such as the dreamer leaning on a desk on one elbow to simulate sleeping or other mannerisms. Moreover, while in plays and stories, ghosts commonly enter the dreams of the living, ghosts themselves are virtually never portrayed as dreaming: they are the objects rather than the subjects of dreams.[29] Instead, the dream-like ambiance of this scene and the unusual insistence that the décor exactly replicate past furnishings in the palace suggest that Hong Sheng was trying to invent a mise-en-scène for memory, because no adequate stage language existed for it. A litany of phrases such as "I recall," "It comes back to me," "I painfully remember," repeatedly punctuate Lady Yang's movements through the palace, keeping the explicit focus on memory continually in the foreground.

The return of a palace lady's specter to the ruined or vanished site of an old palace, as I argued in Chapter 3, is the most persistent type of ghost story told about dynastic fall. Such tales are narrated from the viewpoint of a male visitor to the site, whose ardent longing for the past is fulfilled when a palace lady ghost appears on the spot to recite a *huaigu* poem and takes him as a lover. Such stories, steeped in the melancholy and sensuality of ruin-sentiment, constitute a standard subset of the ghost romance. But although Lady Yang's ghost repeatedly sings the expected *huaigu* verses upon her return, Hong Sheng forecloses any pleasurable outcome. As with the emperor's return to the ruined imperial gardens in his dream, Lady Yang's fantasmatic return to the abandoned Western Palace simply reinforces the other's absence and their separation.

Determined to make another attempt to rejoin the emperor in his exile, she takes flight, only to be blown backwards by a sudden gust of wind. To her horror she sees that the wind has returned her to Mawei, to the pear tree in the Buddhist chapel yard where she had hanged herself. Again, the stage directions indicate that a chapel and a pear tree should have been set up onstage earlier. The lyrics that she sings accentuate the extreme ghostliness of the scene:

> By the station wall, as the night grows colder,
> Faint light from a single lamp leaks through.
> Outside the chapel, a dank [*yin*] wind rises all around.
> See how the moon darkens the empty stable. (p. 191)

This involuntary second return as a ghost to the scene of her suicide arouses a strong feeling of the uncanny. Her experience resembles the classic examples Freud gives as sources of uncanniness in his famous essay, such as attempting to find a new path out of a maze of streets or a forest shrouded in mist but repeatedly finding oneself back in the identical spot where one began.[30] The entire scene up to this point, with its emphasis on the replication of previous sites on stage, is an attempt to convey in theatrical terms that "unintended reoccurrence of the same situation," which Freud identifies as provoking a sensation of the uncanny.[31] He further links this sensation with "the sense of helplessness experienced in some dream-states,"[32] which again seems to capture Lady Yang's experience of being blown backward against her will to the very place she has sought to escape and forget. Again, Wu Yiyi's comments underline the similarity to dream, not only because of the speed and involuntary nature of her repeated return to Mawei, but because of the indeterminacy of whether what she describes is real or imaginary: "Is this a scene in the human world? Or simply the words of a ghost?" he asks (*Guben* 2. 43a).

Dream is specifically invoked in this scene as a trope for memory in another of Lady Yang's arias:

> I look back in a vain.
> This destiny in a dream[33]
> Has vanished, like flower petals falling
>   or rivers flowing on.
> This drop of past love alone detains me,
> like a spring silkworm, which even after death,
> keeps spinning a silken thread. (p. 190)[34]

Just at this moment, when it seems that Lady Yang will be trapped forever in the spiral of her past, the Earth God reenters and announces the heavenly order restoring her to the immortal world. This is the third milestone, indicating that the curse of ghosthood has been lifted, that purgatory is over, and that she is now ready for rebirth and transcendence. Again this release is symbolically enacted through a sartorial device, by having the Earth God remove the *hun pa* (spirit kerchief), the theatrical sign of her ghostly status.[35] This action echoes his earlier untying of the strip of silk in scene 27 and brings the process of her penitence to a visible close.

In Chapter 4, I explored the multiple uses and meanings of the *hun pa* in late Ming phantom-heroine plays. As in Zang Maoxun's revision of the resurrection scene in *Peony Pavilion,* the removal of Lady Yang's *hun pa* in scene 37 is a sign that her corpse will be revived; in *West Garden* and *Man / Ghost,* the removal signifies her forthcoming rebirth as an immortal in the celestial sphere. The main difference is that in *Palace of Lasting Life,* taking off the *hun pa* precedes the phantom heroine's resurrection and transcendence, rather than signifying a completed action and the efficacy of the rituals.

Lady Yang's compulsion to revisit the past and relive her old trauma is not the only reason that she is suddenly transported back to Mawei, the site of her grave. In the context of the play, for her to achieve post-mortem immortality (as opposed to post-mortem existence as a ghost), it becomes necessary for her body to be resurrected first, so that in merging with it, her soul can obtain a permanent "release from the corpse" *(shi jie)*. This Daoist term, which can be traced back to Han times, refers to the idea of a human subject being able to achieve immortal transcendence by sloughing off the corpse after death and burial.[36] Although drawing on the stagecraft that earlier dramatists had developed to enact the merging of body and soul in phantom-heroine plays, Hong Sheng's treatment of the resurrection is much more detailed and experimental than any of his predecessors'; it also develops much more fully the theme of the double implicit in all these plays. Wu Yiyi's comment toward the end of the scene voices both the playwright's hope that the elaborate sequence will be staged exactly as he envisaged it and his suspicion that it will not: "The spirit of the preceding stage directions must be carefully conveyed; under no circumstances may performers be careless or negligent!" (*Guben* 2. 45b).

The solution to the problem of how to stage resurrection in *Palace of Lasting Life* has most in common with the basic set-up of *The Disembodied Soul.* In *Peony Pavilion,* as discussed in Chapter 4, the main female lead and the phantom heroine are never required to appear together on stage so that both roles can be played by a single performer. In the final act of *The Disembodied Soul,* the performer playing the soul (the phantom heroine) must directly confront the performer playing the body (the main female lead), who enters "in a swoon." The stage directions in all extant texts of the play instruct the phantom heroine to "act out merging with the main female lead's body and exit." Afterwards, the main female lead, who now represents the soul united with the body, pantomimes awakening, then sings in amazement: "There were two beauties exactly alike, as though I'd grown another body outside myself."[37]

This staging, which calls for two female leads to appear together on stage, both of whom sing in the act but never at the same time, contradicts the staging in Act 2 of the play, in which the main female lead is directed to play the phantom heroine. The contradiction would be resolved if, in the final act, an extra were employed to play the body, who then exited upon merging with the soul. This is precisely how Hong Sheng resolves the problem in his staging of Lady Yang's resurrection.

After removing the *hun pa,* the Earth God escorts Lady Yang's soul back to a spot that represents her grave. Then facing the stage entrance, he drags forward an extra to play her corpse. The extra is costumed exactly like the female lead, but is wrapped in a brocade coverlet, which the Earth God removes. Holding the "corpse" upright, he acts out sprinkling ritual water over it. The extra then opens its eyes, moves its limbs, and runs a few steps towards the female lead. Facing the extra in an amazed stupor, the female lead asks: "If this Lady Yang is alive, then where will I, the other Lady Yang, go?" This recognition that she is facing her own double echoes the moment in scene 27 when Lady Yang's ghost first sees her own grave marker and calls out to her unseen corpse.[38] Pointing from the female lead to the corpse and back again, the Earth God explains that the two are really one: "She is, in fact, you, and you are, in fact, her." After the extra chases the female lead once around the stage, the female lead collides with the extra and tumbles to the ground; the extra secretly exits. The Earth God's aria confirms the miracle of rebirth and reunion that has occurred: "The original spirit enters its shell / like a second quickening in the womb / or twin rings fused as one." Because Lady Yang's name "Yuhuan" means "Jade Ring," this last line is not only a metaphor but a pun. The female lead, now playing the soul unified with the body, gets to her feet and slowly starts singing: "Suddenly awaking from fogs of dream / long had I lost the 'I' that used to be. / Now spirit and body are whole again."[39] The scene ends with Lady Yang "changing into the costume of an immortal," again registering a change in status visually through the sartorial code of the stage, as she is led offstage to the immortal world in a ritual entourage of immortal maidens holding an embroidered banner.

The staging of the resurrection is set up to maximize the dramatic confrontation of the female lead with a figure who represents both her double and her reanimated corpse, the two most common manifestations of the uncanny singled out by Freud. But here any effect of terror or dread is diluted by the reassuring presence of the Earth God and by the fact that the whole event is so clearly an allegory for the process of self-realization and spiritual enlightenment. Retrospectively, we realize that one reason for Hong Sheng's extraordinary staging of the first part of the scene as a series of disorienting, hallucinatory memories was to convey with full theatrical force the sensation of resurrection as an "awaking from fogs of dream."

In staging the resurrection scene as a process of self-discovery and a triumph of the soul over the body, however, Hong Sheng again reinforces the radical divergence of *Palace of Lasting Life* from *Peony Pavilion,* and indeed from the ghost romance in general. In *Peony Pavilion,* Du Liniang's revival is in part a testament to the power of a man's sexual love to revive the body of his dead beloved. This is one of the reasons the play's imagery so heavily invokes the fecundity of the natural world, of the cosmic replay of seasonal renewal, and why *qing* (love) is equated with *sheng* (life).[40] But the emperor in *Palace of Life* is impotent and in any case unavailable to her. Lady Yang must therefore revive herself, unaided by a living male, through a purifying process of remembering and expiation. In the scene's climax, when her soul and corpse collide and fall together, Lady Yang's body is banished from the stage. What we are witnessing, therefore, is really a kind of parthenogenesis. The penitent has redeemed herself from history through her individual effort (though with divine encouragement and intervention) and thereby achieves rebirth, transcendence, and reunion with the emperor for eternity.

* * *

> During daylight, the soul adheres to the body; at night, the soul can transform itself; this is how dreams come about. After death, the body will decay, but the soul may still be potent; this is a ghost. If the soul returns to the body, then resurrection will occur; if the body is transformed by the soul, then "release from the corpse" will occur. These principles are quite commonplace, but never before have they been enacted as well as this in the theater! Accordingly,

one will be astonished by the novelty and wonder of the staging. (*Guben*, scene 37, 2. 44b–45a)

In his remarks on Lady Yang's apotheosis in *Palace of Lasting Life*, Wu Yiyi draws a continuum between the phenomenology of dreams and ghosts in that both involve the soul's freedom to act independently of the body. These remarks illuminate the logic of resurrection as enacted in this scene: the reversibility dreams are subject to also governs death. Just as we awaken from a dream, thereby undoing it, so death can be negated and a corpse live again. But such explication he dismisses as "commonplace"; what truly excites him is "the wonder and novelty of the staging." Wu Yiyi's comment reinforces a central tenet of the approach that I have adopted throughout this book: namely, that any serious attempt to grapple with the richness of the Chinese literary ghost tradition must move beyond a simple binary of belief or fiction to focus on representation. A corollary of this approach has been not only to investigate how and why ghosts are represented in a specific historical period and in specific generic contexts, but what cultural ideas ghosts reveal about representation itself.

Writing and theater constituted the two main elite media for representing specters in the seventeenth century. Woodblock illustrations of ghosts, posthumous portraits, and Land and Water Rite images also existed, but depiction of dead souls outside a ritual context was limited because pictures of this subject matter were considered inauspicious. In the case of writing, a perceived connection to ghosts was ancient, projected back onto the mythical creator of the written word, Cang Jie, whose invention reputedly caused ghosts to wail in the night.[41] Early imperial commentators struggled to explain this cryptic response by imputing to ghosts a premonition of writing's fearsome power to bind and regulate them.[42] In certain tales and anecdotes from the eighth century on, however, a stunning reversal occurs: ghosts are imagined to have mastered Cang Jie's invention so that their wailing now takes the form of writing.

As we have seen, written communication from ghosts is overwhelmingly patterned as verse, partaking of poetry's vaunted ability to make writing "go far" and the magical properties of rhyme and meter to communicate between this world and the next. Strikingly, in any number of stories, it is the materiality of the writing rather than the information conveyed by the words that most clearly registers a spectral effect. In certain cases a poem becomes imbued with the symbolic properties of the medium on which it is written. A Tang anecdote about reading a mysterious verse penned on a worn sheet of paper epitomizes this associative logic. As soon as the reader touches the paper, it crumbles to dust, proof for him that the author of the poem must have been a ghost.[43]

More often, the material traces of the characters themselves—whether as rubbed-out ink or eroded engraving—embody the instability and evanescence that are the most common physical attributes of ghost writing. In these instances the distance between signifier and signified collapses, since the writing signifies not something else but itself. In such ghost writing we detect the kind of "ontological border crossing" that Brigitte Peucker identifies in the European context as an "aim shared by trompe l'oeil in the visual arts" and those "moments in which writing aspires to invade, incorporate, or be a thing."[44]

The image of writing fading away, momentarily suspending the words between life and death, past and present, before vanishing altogether, became a conventional trope for signaling a ghostly presence in Chinese literature, first in tales and anecdotes, and later in drama. In Fan Wenruo's *An Intoxicating Dream*, the discovery that a song-lyric only recently presented to the play's male lead by his lover has inexplicably faded clinches the identity of its author as a revenant:

> OLDER WOMAN *(with an expression of surprise):* How is it that the marks of ink on the paper look as though they're not from a human hand?
> SECONDARY FEMALE LEAD: At the end there are a couple of words that you can still faintly read.
> MALE LEAD *(with an expression of surprise):*
> How could her song-lyric have been rubbed out like this?
>
> *(sings to the tune "Dahe fo"):* The characters are
> Thin like traces of a dragon in autumn;
> Leached of color, as though incised by a ghost.[45]

Pale, attenuated, worn away: the inscription is still legible in part, but only barely. Overnight the writing has become the equivalent of a ruin, a visual display of the past engulfing the present.

To write ghosts is de facto to write the relationship with the past and with history. One of the reasons for the popularity of spirit writing through the planchette among late imperial literati was the prospect it afforded of communicating directly with the ghosts of historical figures, especially famous poets.[46] Literary composition had traditionally promised a kind of immortality to the author in that his name, and his self as embodied in his words, would live on after his death; a main attraction of spirit writing was that it provided literal proof of this ideal.

The planchette was by definition a writing device, wielded either by sticking an implement in a sieve and tracing characters in sand, ashes, or powder, or by affixing a brush to a wooden crook and using paper and ink. As a consequence of these media, any imagined encounter with ghosts of the past was restricted to the domain of the written word. (Pictorial communication was also possible but was much rarer.) It was only in the realm of the theater, as Ming and Qing drama critics were fond of observing, that a writer's brush could raise the dead and bring them to life before the present's eyes. This metaphor is particularly compelling in the case of *Palace of Lasting Life*, which literally resurrects the ghost of a famous historical figure on stage.

Guided by these and other observations, this book has sought to explore the complex permutations and ramifications of a distinct pattern of imagination in seventeenth-century Chinese literature—the revival of a phantom heroine through the power of love. In this light, what is most striking about "Release from the Corpse" in *Palace of Lasting Life* is how Hong Sheng breathes new life into what was a dramatic cliché of the first order. The extravagance of the staging lends itself to an allegorical reading, suggesting the continual potential for renewal of the female-centered Chinese ghost tradition. *Palace of Lasting Life* itself may mark the endpoint of the creative phase of southern drama playwrights, but the brilliant phantom-heroine films made in Hong Kong, such as *A Chinese Ghost Story* and *Rouge*, exemplify the tradition's protean ability both to reinvent itself *and* to become part of global popular culture in our own times.

Appendix

Selected List of Major Translated Book and Film Titles

Accounts Widely Gathered in the Taiping Era (*Taiping guangji;* abbreviated *TPGJ*) comp. Li Fang

Anatomy of Love (Qingshi leilüe) comp. Feng Menglong

Anecdotes about Tang Poems (Tangshi jishi) comp. Ji Yougong

Book of Songs (Shijing)

By and about Women (Furen ji) by Chen Weisong; full title: *A Collection by and about Women*

Celestial Court Music (Juntian yue) by You Tong

A Chinese Ghost Story (Qiannü youhun) directed by Ching Siu Tung and produced by Tsui Hark

Classified Cases of Renowned Physicians (Mingyi leian) by Jiang Guan

Classified Materia Medica (Bencao gangmu) by Li Shizhen

A Collection by and about Women (Furen ji) by Chen Weisong; short title: *By and about Women*

Complete Poetry of the Tang (Quan Tangshi)

Communications from the Unseen World (Tongyou ji)

A Complete Mastery of Correct Characters (Zhengzi tong) comp. Zhang Zilie

The Complete Writings of Doctor Zhang (Jingyue quanshu) by Zhang Jiebin

Constant Words to Awaken the World (Xingshi hengyan) ed. Feng Menglong

The Disembodied Soul (Qiannü lihun) by Zheng Guangzu

Disquisitions (Lunheng) by Wang Chong

Dream of the Red Chamber (Honglou meng) by Cao Xueqin; also known as *Story of the Stone*

The Dropped Hairpin (Zhuichai ji) by Shen Jing; also known as *Yizhong qing*

Emerald Peach Flowers (Bitao hua)

Enchanted Shadow (Qiannü youhun) produced by Shaw Brothers

Flowers in the Rear Courtyard (Houting hua) by Zheng Tingyu

Fu Qingzhu's Medicine for Women (Fu Qingzhu nüke) by Fu Shan

A General Source for Remarks on Poetry (Shihua zonggui) by Ruan Yue; short title: *A General Source*

The Great Book of Marvels (Guangyi ji) by Dai Fu

The Injustice to Dou E (Dou E yuan) by Guan Hanqing

The Inner Canon (Neijing); full title: *The Yellow Emperor's Inner Canon*

An Intoxicating Dream of Flowers (Menghua han) by Fan Wenru

Jottings from the Thatched Cottage of Careful Reading (Yuewei caotang biji) by Ji Yun; short title: *Jottings from the Thatched Cottage*
Lady in the Painting (Huazhong ren) by Wu Bing
Li Huiniang (Peking opera version of *Red Flowering Plum*)
Liaozhai's Records of the Strange (Liaozhai zhiyi) by Pu Songling; short title: *Liaozhai;* abbreviated as *LZ*
The Magician's New Records (Yu Chu xinzhi) ed. Zhang Chao
The Magician (short title for the three seventeenth-century books to include Lin Yunming's version of "Lin Siniang")
Maid and Mistress (Jiao Hong ji) by Meng Chengshun
Man / Ghost, Husband / Wife (Rengui fuqi) by Fu Yichen
Mirror of the Return to Origin or The Transmission of the Lamp (Chuandeng lu Guiyuan jing) by Zhida
Missing History of the Tang and Song (Tang Song yishi)
More Tales Told by Lamplight (Jiandeng yuhua) by Li Zhen
Mulian Rescues His Mother (Mulian jiumu) by Zheng Zhizhen
A New Account of Tales of the World (Shishuo xinyu) comp. Liu Yiqing
New Tales Told by Lamplight (Jiandeng yuhua) by Qu You
Notes from Genzhai (Genzhai biji) by Li Chengzhong
Occasional Chats North of the Pond (Chibei outan) by Wang Shizhen; short title: *Occasional Chats*
Outlaws of the Marsh (Shuihi ji) by Wang Yufeng
Palace of Lasting Life (Changsheng dian) by Hong Sheng
A Patchwork of Scenes (Zhui baiqiu)
Peachblossom Fan (Taohua shan) by Kong Shangren
Peachwood Amulet (Taofu ji) by Shen Jing
Peony Pavilion (Mudan ting) by Tang Xianzu; also known as *The Soul's Return*
Pine Knoll Anthology (Songling ji) by Lu Guimeng and Pi Rixiu
Poetry from a Single Dynasty (Liechao shiji) by Qian Qianyi
The Purple Hairpin (Zichai ji) by Tang Xianzu
Qingzhou Anecdotes by An Zhiyuan
Rain on the Pawlonia Tree (Wutong yu) by Bai Renfu
Records of the Historian (Shiji) by Sima Qian
Records of the Listener (Yijian zhi) by Hong Mai
Records of Talented Ghosts (Caigui ji) by Mei Dingzuo
Red Flowering Plum (Hongmei ji) by Zhou Chaojun; Peking opera version entitled *Li Huiniang*
Ritual Canon (Liji)
Rouge (Yanzhi kou) directed Stanley Kwan
The Secret Burial Classic of the Great Han (Da Han yuanling mizang jing)
Seeking the Spirits (Soushen ji) by Gan Bao
Shandong Poetry from Our Dynasty (Guochao Shanzuo shichao) comp. Lu Jianzeng
Snow-sprinkled Hall (Saxue tang) by Feng Menglong (adapted from a play by Mei Xiaosi)

The Soul's Return (Huanhun ji) by Tang Xianzu (also known as *Peony Pavilion*); title of Zang Maoxun's revision

Spring in Nanjing (Moling chun) by Wu Weiye

The Startled Swan (Jinghong ji)

Story of the Stone (Shitou ji) by Cao Xueqin (also known as *Dream of the Red Chamber*)

Tao'an's Dream Reminiscences (Tao'an mengyi) by Zhang Dai

The Three Wives' Commentary (Wu Wushan sanfu heping Mudanting) by Wu Yiyi and Qian Yi; full title: *Wu Wushan's Three Wives' Combined Commentary to Peony Pavilion*

What Confucius Didn't Speak Of (Zi bu yu) by Yuan Mei

West Garden (Xiyuan ji) by Wu Bing

The Western Wing (Xixiang ji) by Wang Shifu

Wu Wushan's Three Wives' Combined Commentary to Peony Pavilion (Wu Wushan sanfu heping Mudan ting) by Wu Yiyi and Qian Yi; short title: *The Three Wives' Commentary*

The Yellow Emperor's Inner Canon (Huangdi neijing); short title: *The Inner Canon (Neijing)*

Zuo Tradition on the Spring and Autumn Annals (Zuozhuan); short title: *Zuo Tradition*

Notes

Introduction

1 The English title of the 1960 film is *Enchanting Shadow.* The Chinese title of both films is the same, a variation on the name of a famous thirteenth-century play, *Qiannü lihun (The disembodied soul).*

2 These are *Chinese Ghost Story II* (1990) and *Chinese Ghost Story III* (1991), all starring Joey Wang as the phantom heroine.

3 Yuan Mei's eighteenth-century tale collection *Zi bu yu (What Confucius didn't speak of)* is unusually partial to horror. The handful of horror stories in Pu Songling's *Liaozhai zhiyi* (henceforth *Liaozhai* or *LZ*) include "The Walking Corpse" ("Shi bian," 1.5–7) and "The Water Spitter" ("Pen shui," 1.8).

4 Late imperial ghost tales bear out Campany's observation that in early tales of the strange, "one's deepest impression will be a sense of sympathy, community, and fellow-feeling across the boundary between the 'light' and 'dark' realms." He links this phenomenon to Buddhist and Daoist attempts "to extend solicitude for the welfare of the dead beyond the circle of kinship" (*Strange Writing,* p. 383).

5 Laplanche and Pontalis, *The Language of Psycho-Analysis,* p. 349. (However, Freud developed this idea to explain why ghosts, as embodiments of bad conscious desires, were frightening rather than frightened; *The Language of Psycho-Analysis,* p. 352.)

6 Shen Fu, *Fusheng liuji,* 3.35. Unless otherwise indicated, all translations are my own.

7 Ibid.

8 *Erya jinzhu,* 3.116, p. 154.

9 See, for example, the list of definitions in *Zhongwen dacidian,* p. 7635; or *Hanyu dacidian* 5. 367.

10 Cited in Zhang Zilie, comp., *Zhengzi tong* under *gui, haiji,* part 1, p. 53a.

11 Cited under *gui* in *Kangxi zidian* 14. 85, p. 3309.

12 *Zuozhuan.* (Another possible reading of this passage: "If a ghost has something to rely on, it will not become a vengeful spirit.") Cited in Zhang Zilie, comp., *Zhengzi tong, haiji,* part 1, p. 53a.

13 See Poo, "The Concept of Ghost in Ancient Chinese Religion," and Myrhe, "The Appearances of Ghosts in Northern Drama," pp. 6–9, 119–135.

14 Myrhe, "The Appearances of Ghosts in Northern Drama," p. 6.

15 Xu Shen, *Shuowen jiezi,* p. 434. My translation follows Duan Yucai's commentary.

16 Brashier, "Han Thanatology and the Division of 'Souls,'" pp. 125–158.

17 Cf. Shao Yong: "A ghost is a person's shadow or reflection." Cited in *Zhengzi tong, haiji,*

part 1, p. 53a. *Oxford English Dictionary* (online ed.) defines a phantom as: (1b) "an illusion, a delusion; a deception; a figment"; (2a) "Something that appears to the sight or other sense, but has no material substance; an apparition, a spectre; a spirit, a ghost."

18 On the ghost story in late nineteenth-century newspapers, magazines, and books as mediating the modern, see Huntington, "The Weird in the Newspaper," pp. 341–396.

19 For example, according to Xu Xianglin (*Zhongguo guixi,* pp. 88–89), of the twenty-six operas banned by successive Ministry of Culture edicts between 1950–1952, more than half featured ghosts. Even in early postwar Hong Kong, ghost films were targeted in an anti-superstition campaign (Fonoroff, *Silver Light,* p. 94).

20 Titles include: Yin Feizhou et al., *Zhongguo gudai guishen wenhua daguan* (1992); Wu Kang, *Zhongguo guishen jingguai* (1992); Xu Hualong, *Zhongguo gui wenhua dacidian* (1994); Wen Yansheng, *Zhongguo guihua* (1996); *Bu pa gui de gushi* (1999), a reprint of a compilation of classical ghost tales originally published in 1961 with Chairman Mao's involvement for the express purpose of fostering disbelief in ghosts. For a survey of changing intellectual trends in Mainland discussions of ghost operas from 1949 to 2003, see Liu Chao, "Jianguo yilai guixi yanjiu huimou."

21 David Wang, "Second Haunting," pp. 262–291.

22 For example, Anthony Yu, "O, Rest, Rest, Perturbed Spirit!" pp. 397–434; or Xu Xiangling, *Zhongguo guixi.*

23 *Ducheng jisheng* (ca 1235), 13b.

24 Ji Yun, *Yuewei caotang biji,* 7. 35. On Ji Yun and the casual oral storytelling context, see Leo Chan, *Discourse on Foxes and Ghosts,* esp. chap. 2; and Huntington, *Alien Kind,* 2003.

25 Ji Yun, *Yuewei caotang biji* 7. 35.

26 There are three extant plays on this theme: a Yuan *zaju,* entitled *Hongli hua (Red Flowering Plum Blossoms),* and two Ming *chuanqi,* both entitled *Hongli ji (Red Flowering Plum).* Of these, Xu Fuxiang's *Hongli ji* (1611 preface) provides the most expansive treatment of the flower seller scene, which was subsequently elaborated into an independent extract in the performing tradition.

27 de Groot, *Religious System of China;* Doré, *Researches into Chinese Superstitions.*

28 In *Génies, Anges, et Démons* (p. 405), Schipper stated that he would ignore the Chinese literary corpus on ghosts and confine himself to fieldwork alone. Recent scholars of Chinese religion and anthropology have tended to follow his example and no longer treat *zhiguai* literature as primary source material for ethnography.

29 David Wang, *Fin-de-Siècle Splendor,* pp. 205–209; and "Second Haunting."

30 L. Chan, *Discourse on Foxes and Ghosts;* see also his "Narrative as Argument," pp. 25–62.

31 Good, *Medicine, Rationality and Experience,* pp. 14–21.

32 Watson, "Structure of Chinese Funerary Rites," pp. 9–10.

33 Schmitt, *Ghosts in the Middle Ages,* pp. 7, 221.

34 For an overview of Chinese death culture, see Zheng Xiaojiang, *Zhongguo siwang wenhua daguan;* and Watson and Rawski, eds., *Death Ritual in Late Imperial and Modern China.*

35 Watson, "Structure of Chinese Funerary Rites," p. 9.
36 Shahar and Weller, "Introduction" to *Unruly Gods,* p. 11.
37 Wolf, "Gods, Ghosts, and Ancestors"; Jordan, *Gods, Ghosts, and Ancestors.*
38 Wolf, "Gods, Ghosts, and Ancestors." Campany ("Ghosts Matter," p.18) notes that relatively few Six Dynasties stories involve deceased ancestors. The same is true for later tales. Two notable exceptions are Hong Mai, *Yijian zhi,* "Hukou miao tudi" (10. 1465) and Pu Songling's "Jiaping gongzi" (*LZ* 11. 1588–1591), which Giles translates as "His Father's Ghost" in *Strange Stories from a Chinese Studio,* pp. 349–353. In fiction, deceased parents do sometimes appear to their offspring in dreams to admonish or provide specific aid (such as revealing buried treasure), but these encounters are not the main point of the narrative.
39 Shahar and Weller, "Introduction," *Unruly Gods,* p. 11.
40 These include Guanyin (as Miaoshan), Mazu, Linshui furen, and Zigu shen.

Chapter 1: The Ghost's Body

Epigraph. From *Yifang leiju,* translated in McMahon, *Misers, Shrews, and Polygamists,* p. 39.

1 See, inter alia, Vernant, "Feminine Figures of Death in Greece"; Bronfen, *Over Her Dead Body;* and Guthke, *The Gender of Death.* The trope of personification—rendering abstract ideas as human figures—is uncommon in Chinese literature.
2 Trans. Wai-yee Li, *Enchantment and Disenchantment,* p. 50. Original in Tang Xianzu, *Mudan ting,* "Tici," p. 1. For the influence of this preface on actual love suicides in this period, see Gōyama, "Min-Shin jidai ni okeru jōshi."
3 The definition of *qing* in Xu Shen, *Shuowen jiezi* (p. 502) could pass as a definition of a ghost: "Desire in the yin vital stuff *(yin qi)* of a human being" *(qing, ren zhi yin qi you yuzhe).* For the philological and philosophical debates on *qing* in early China contexualizing this passage, see Anthony Yu, *Rereading the Stone,* chap. 2
4 Trans. Wai-yee Li, *Enchantment and Disenchantment,* p. 52, modified. Original reprinted in Pan Zhiheng, *Pan Zhiheng quhua,* p. 72.
5 Zhang Qi, "Qingchi wuyan" in *Hengqu zhutan* 4. 273.
6 Some Tang exceptions to the rule: "Zhu Qiniang" (*TPGJ* 331. 2628); "Mengshi" (*TPGJ* 345. 2735–2736); and de Groot, *Religious System of China* 5. 706–707. Poo Mu-chou ("The Completion of an Ideal World," pp. 87–103) argues that in Six Dynasties accounts, "male ghosts also figured prominently in ghost-human marriages or love stories."
7 Anthony Yu, "Rest, Rest, Perturbed Spirit!" p. 429.
8 Chao Yuanfang, *Zhubing yuanhou lun* 40. 214; Zhang Jiebin, *Jingyue quanshu* 39. 677.
9 Huntington, *Alien Kind* (p. 174), similarly argues that narratives of human women being possessed by male foxes portray their sexual relationship as illness or madness rather than as amorous fantasy. Furth, *A Flourishing Yin* (p. 90) suggests that this medicalizing strategy helped preserve a woman's reputation for chastity. An exception again is the Tang tale "Mengshi" (*TPGJ* 345. 2735–2736).
10 Wang Chong, *Lunheng* 22. 933; I follow Huang Hui's emendation that the character

jian before *de* is redundant and is most likely an error. On the changing understanding of the relationship between ghosts and disease in Chinese medical thought, see Kuriyama, "Concepts of Disease in East Asia."

11 Yi-li Wu, "Ghost Fetuses, False Pregnancies," p. 180. For a discussion of haunting in Chinese medical discourse, see Li Jianmin, "Suibing yu changsuo."

12 "Rare diseases" *(qi ji)* is a frequent heading in both medical books and in collections of the strange.

13 Some publishing houses published both medical works and fiction. See Widmer, "The Huanduzhai of Hangzhou and Suzhou."

14 Kuriyama, "Concepts of Disease in East Asia," p. 58.

15 Tang Xianzu, *Mudan ting,* scene 55, p. 286.

16 Qu You, "Mudan deng ji" in *Jiandeng xinhua,* p. 50. For an abridged translation of the story, see Bauer, *The Golden Casket,* pp. 234–240. Compare a similar formulation in the tale "Yueniang ji," in Liu Fu, *Qingsuo gaoyi, bieji* 3. 221.

17 "Chou Liu Chaisang," trans. Hightower, *The Poetry of T'ao Ch'ien,* p. 76; original in Tao Qian, *Tao Yuanming ji,* p.159.

18 Furth (*A Flourishing Yin,* pp. 27–28) distinguishes two modes of yin-yang relations: a hierarchical relationship by encompassment and bipolar complementarity. Anthony Yu (*Rereading the Stone,* p. 69) cites Dong Zhongshu's writing on the "debasement of yin and the exaltation of yang" to argue that equality between yin and yang in early philosophical writings is only really present in *The Inner Canon.*

19 On the love triangle in *Liaozhai,* see Barr, "A Comparative Study," pp. 177–193.

20 My translation. For a complete translation of the story, see Minford, *Strange Tales from a Chinese Studio,* pp. 211–228. Bray ("A Deathly Disorder," p. 236) argues that women's bodies were seen as more dominated by *yin qi,* and men's bodies by *yang qi.* From this angle too, the female ghost's body in this passage is conceptualized as "super-yin."

21 Hanan, *Chinese Vernacular Story,* p. 44.

22 Because the term *qi* (vitality, energy, psycho-physical stuff) is so fundamental and multivalent, it is impossible to fully translate the term. In this passage, the compound *shenqi* ("overall vitality") refers to the "normal vitality of the body," as Sivin explains in "State, Cosmos, and Body in China" (p. 14, n. 16), though he translates the term as "divine vitality."

The use of pulse diagnosis to deduce a supernatural encounter also occurs in "Huang Jiulang" (*LZ* 3. 318), a tale about a man who is having an affair with a fox-boy. His friend, a doctor, alerted by the darkness of his complexion, examines him and detects a "demonic pulse" *(gui mai)* in the "minor yin" *(shao yin)* position. (Here *gui* is used in a generic rather than specific sense to mean "demonic.") "Minor yin" is a medical term corresponding to a conduit connected to the Heart, but if *shao* is understood not as an adjective but as a verb, it means to disparage or to lack. In that case the phrase is also a pun: the disorder the man *is* suffering from is a "a disparagement and deficiency of yin."

23 Jiang Guan, *Mingi leian* 8. 242, first entry under "gui zhu." I follow many historians of

Chinese traditional medicine in capitalizing terms to show that they are not synonymous with their usage in modern biomedicine.

The same case is also quoted in Xu Chunfu (*Gujin yitong daquan* 49. 15b–16a), who attributes it to the thirteenth-century doctor Luo Tianyi; cf. Unschuld's translation in *Medicine in China*, p. 327. The pulse diagnosis under "*xiesui*" for a *xiemai* ("evil pulse") in Yu Tuan, *Yixue zhengchuan* 5. 271, is quite similar: "The pulse will suddenly accelerate, then slow down; grow small, then big; grow hurried, then hesitant. These are all cases of a heteropathic *(xie)* pulse." With regard to "women who dream of copulation with specters," Zhang Jiebin (*Jingyue quanshu* 39. 677) reads a wildly fluctuating pulse as a sign of externally caused demonic possession, which he distinguishes from internally provoked dreams that arise from a woman's own lustful thoughts. Similarly, in "Loushang tongnü" (Feng Menglong, *Qingshi leilüe* 10. 791) when a man falls ill from an affair with a ghost, the doctor's pulse diagnosis is that the patient is suffering not from a febrile illness, but from a yin pathogen attack.

24 Sivin, *Traditional Medicine*, p. 49.

25 Chinese physicians considered amenorrhea the sign of grave health problems for women, not just a condition impeding fertility. See Bray, "A Deathly Disorder" (p. 241), who asserts that "amenorrhoea is not a disorder in itself, but signals some fundamental dysfunction that could well develop into a fatal sickness."

26 Jiang Guan, *Mingi leian* 10. 311, "Menstruation" ("Jingshui"), entry, no. 7. For a similar diagnosis, see Fu Shan, *Fu Qingzhu nüke*, p. 4590.

27 In "Xihu nüzi," a puzzling tale in Hong Mai's *Yijian zhi* (6. 754–755), a female ghost assumes the doctor's role and prescribes medicine in advance to cure her mortal lover of the illness that he will suffer from having made love to her. He objects that he had previously read about this prescription in *Yijian zhi* (presumably an earlier installment, since the collection was published sequentially), and the medicine was too weak for the job. The ghost overrules his objections, saying that it will do to replenish his Blood and Essence.

28 Unschuld (*Medicine in China*, pp. 216–223) argues that the term *xie* (heteropath, abnormal, pathogenic, evil, malignant), which in early medical works such as *The Inner Canon* refers to physical phenomena such as excessive hot, cold, dampness, and so on, is expanded to include the popular meaning of "demonic" and so facilitates the incorporation of demonology into the province of orthodox medical discourse during the Ming and Qing. A fluctuating dialectic between the two meanings of *xie* is detectable, to varying degrees, throughout Chinese medical thought.

29 Personal communication from Sivin, email, August 17, 2006.

30 Furth, "Blood, Body, and Gender," p. 58.

31 Wu Zhiwang, *Jiyang gangmu* 69. 4a.

32 "Yueniang ji" in Liu Fu, *Qingsuo gaoyi, bieji* 3. 222.

33 Lotus-scent's preternatural gift to foresee the future course of his illness points to her fox identity, but such power was also attributed to outstanding doctors, from the earliest biographies of legendary physicians to the casebooks of Ming physicians. Kuriyama emphasizes this vaunted medical ability to see the invisible and the future

in *The Expressiveness of the Body*, pp. 154 and 178. See also my "Literary Fashioning of Medical Authority."

34 Two early textual references to the apotropaic function of spitting appear in Gan Bao, *Soushen ji*. In the first (16.199, no. 393) a ghost reveals that spitting is what ghosts fear most; in the second (16. 204, no. 397) people spit at a boy who is said to be the son of a ghost.

35 An early textual parallel from *Soushen houji, j.* 6 is translated in de Groot, *Religious System of China* 5. 679–680. In that story a doctor cures a patient's ghost-induced illness *(gui bing)* by dosing him with a purgative. The patient's "belly rumbles like thunder," heralding a copious bout of diarrhea, after which he recovers.

36 See "Jiaona" (*LZ* 1. 60) for an account of surgery performed by a female fox-doctor, which the male patient also experiences as erotic pleasure.

37 Cf. West and Idema's translation: "If only I could swallow down one drop of my missy's sweetly, sweetly delicious, aromatically, aromatically perfumed, piercingly, piercingly dripping, dropping lovable spittle then this fucking illness would be over." *The Western Wing*, Book 3, Act 4, p. 317. Original in Wang Shifu, *Xixiang ji*, p. 131.

38 An early example of the close relationship between a weird illness and illicit sex occurs in Gan Bao, *Soushen ji* 17. 209, no. 404, where a woman is suffering from a *gui bing;* her husband deduces she is having an affair; her lover turns out to be a male cicada spirit. See Gu Xuejie and Wang Xueqi, *Yuanqu shici* 1. 694, for the vernacular usage of *gui bing* as a synonym for lovesickness. Pu Songling never employs the term to mean lovesickness in *Liaozhai*, but he would certainly have been familiar with this usage.

39 My translation. Original in Wang Shifu, *Xixiang ji* Book 3, Act 4, p.132. Compare with West and Idema's translation, *The Western Wing*, p. 320. *Xieyin*, the phrase I have translated as "heteropath lust," borrows medical terminology to play on lovesickness and sexual frustration. *Xieyin* also means "the cause of a disease" but works like a pun because the cause of the disease *is* heteropathic lust.

40 Double entendres involving love, illness, and medicine are first developed in *Dong Jieyuan Xixiang ji* (5. 106), which offers the earliest usage of *gui bing* as lovesickness and in which the heroine's love letter is delivered under the guise of being a prescription.

41 In *Liaozhai*, supernatural experiences of love are routinely conjured up by the man's subjective longing or contemplation without negating their objective existence. The use of the term *ning si* suggests a causal connection between the scholar's desire and his subsequent illness. This connection is explicit in "Bai Qiulian" (*LZ* 11. 1485): After the hero is separated from his beloved, "he longed for her so intensely, he fell ill" *(ning si cheng ji)*.

42 The ghost reworks a famous line by the Tang poet Li Shangyin to give passion a posthumous existence, which can be spun out to infinity: "I'm like a spring silkworm whose threads of longing linger even after death" (*LZ* 2. 225). By contrast, in the original poem, death puts an end to those "threads" and longing is finite. This usage reinforces the pun on threads and longing offered in the story's pulse diagnosis.

43 Castle (*The Female Thermometer*, p. 123) argues that "old-fashioned" literal ghosts are displaced in much eighteenth-century British fiction and migrate inward to inhabit the

mind, creating a figural language of love as haunting. In the Chinese case, figurative and literal understandings of the ghost intermingle, especially when *qing* is involved.

44 Comment attributed to "The Historian of Love" in Feng Menglong, *Qingshi leilüe* 8. 624.

45 Sivin, "Emotional Counter-Therapy," p. 7. Shapiro ("The Puzzle of Spermatorrhea," p. 587, n. 13) notes that as early as the third century BCE, *si* "connotes a negative preoccupation," some thought which one dwells obsessively upon.

46 "Jutong lun," *Suwen* 39. 113.

47 Ibid.

48 Gan Bao, *Soushen ji* 16. 200, no. 394.

49 *Yu* is treated both as a disorder *(bing)* and as a manifestation-type *(zheng)*. In "Blood, Body, and Gender," Furth describes *yujie* as a particular type of *yu* syndrome, a melancholy one opposed to an anger-based one, but this is not borne out in the medical literature. The two characters are most often found as a verb object, describing the tendency of stasis to congest some place; when the phrase occurs as a noun compound, it may be particularly associated with the pathogenic effect of the emotions, but not one emotion in particular. For an example of *yujie* used to describe anger-related stasis in women, see Fu Shan, *Fu Qingzhu nüke* 164. 4586–4587.

50 Guo Aichun et al., eds. *Huangdi neijing cidian,* p. 438; see also relevant passages in Zhang Jiebin, *Jingyue quanshu.*

51 The definition is attributed to a Doctor Dai, probably Dai Sigong, an early Ming follower of Zhu Zhenheng. Quoted in Xu Chunfu, *Gujin yitong daquan* 26. 2177; Zhang Jiebin, *Jingyue quanshu* 19. 359; and other compendia.

52 See *Zhongyi dacidian: Neike,* p. 199, which bases its individual entries on emotionally based *yu* syndromes on Ming and Qing texts.

53 On the problem of how to translate *yu* as a medical term and how to differentiate it from related terms meaning stagnation, see Wiseman and Zmiewski, "Rectifying the Names," p. 62. Since "*yu* describes reduced and frustrated activity of physiological elements, particularly *qi,* as well as pathogens . . . and the emotions . . . ," they translate the term as "depression."

54 Sima Qian, *Shiji* 10: 130. 330.

55 Shapiro, "The Puzzle of Spermatorrhea," p. 558.

56 Xu Chunfu, *Gujin yitong daquan* 26. 24a (p. 2184).

57 Furth, "Blood, Body and Gender," pp. 60–61.

58 In *A Flourishing Yin,* Furth argues that after the Song dynasty, disorders not exclusively related to women's reproductive capacities were not categorized as part of *fuke* (medicine for women). Thus virtually all discussion of stasis or static congestion is found in sections on internal medicine, not *fuke.* Within these entries, however, specific disorders could have specific gender-based symptoms or be a gender-based syndrome.

59 Porkert (*Theoretical Foundations of Chinese Medicine,* p. 115) asserts that *qing* (emotion) and *zhi* (psychic reaction) are synonyms in Chinese medicine.

60 What is new here is that Zhang departs from the classical grouping of the "seven emotions" to select specific culprits.

61 Zhang Jiebin, *Jingyue quanshu* 19. 357–358. Zhang identifies "stasis related to the passions" as an innovation but establishes a genealogy for this new category by citing *The Inner Canon* on the nature of the emotions. Much of my discussion of *si* is based on the composite picture Zhang provides in his entry on *yu*.

62 There are three in total, all of which are also quoted in Xu Chunfu, *Gujin yitong daquan* 26.28a-b (p. 2189), along with a fourth about a man who is exposed to cold and wet immediately after a bout in the bedchamber. Of the approximately thirty-nine cases of *yu* in Wei Zhixu, *Xu Mingyi leian,* the eighteenth-century sequel to Jiang Guan's *Classified Cases of Renowned Physicians,* about half are women, but none is a maiden, and none is suffering from lovesickness; most concern anger with the *qi* congested in the Liver.

63 According to the theory of correspondences, each of the five major Organ systems is correlated with one of the Five Phases. In this system, Wood overcomes Earth. Both the Liver and anger are correlated with Wood, the Spleen and longing with Earth.

64 Zhang Jiebin (*Jingyue quanshu* 19. 3359) abridges the case; my translation is based on the version in Jiang Guan, *Mingyi leian* 2. 74–75.

65 In *The Taoist Body,* Schipper writes: "Those who die prematurely, by accident or suicide, can never become ancestors; neither their casket nor their tablet can enter the family house. These dead are not 'correct spirits' *(zhenghun),* but become wandering disinherited souls *(guhun).* The vital forces of a person who has not fulfilled his destiny leave the normal cycle and are 'left over.' The cycle has been interrupted and the souls can no longer reenter it; they neither pass on to the world of the dead nor can be reabsorbed into the family matrix. They must remain in a place where their unexpected vitality condemns them to a miserable life, as exiles in the world of the living. These orphan souls are full of resentment towards a society that they rightly or wrongly, feel has deprived them of their natural destiny." Schipper includes virgins along with victims of suicide, murder, or execution as the main types of "orphan souls."

66 See Dudbridge, *Religious Experience and Lay Society,* pp. 167–169; Ahern, *The Cult of the Dead,* pp. 127–128; and Harrell, "Men, Women and Ghosts," pp. 108–110.

67 On the insatiability attributed to female ghosts in ethnographies of Taiwan, see Wolf, "Gods, Ghosts, and Ancestors," pp. 148–152; and Jordan, *Gods, Ghosts, and Ancestors,* pp. 144–155.

68 Zhu Xi ("Guishen pian," *Zhuzi yulei* 3. 43; 3. 39) says that when someone dies a violent death (from suicide, battle, execution, or murder), since the *qi* does not have a chance to disperse fully, the person may return as a revenant. Although Zhu Xi specifically omits maidens from what is otherwise a typical roster of "lonely souls," he does include "anyone who dies with resentment or injustice" on his list of those whose *qi* does not immediately disperse upon death. The clearly pathological term *yujie* he reserves for those who die a violent death and become malignant demons *(yaonie).*

69 Freud, "The Uncanny." See Laplanche and Pontalis, *The Language of Psycho-Analysis,* pp. 398–399. For applications of this psychoanalytic concept to Chinese ghost stories, see Stephen Chan, "The Return of the Ghostwoman"; and David Wang, "Second Haunting."

70 Furth, "Blood, Body, and Gender," p. 64.

71 Sivin (personal communication, email, August 17, 2006) has found that in a wide range of medical writings, pollution and transgression are the same thing. Li's acquisition of "shame at being a ghost," accords with Cynthia Brokaw's contention (*The Ledgers of Merit and Demerit,* p. 19) that for late Ming writers, developing a sense of shame was a prerequisite for self-reform.

72 The phrase is formulaic. See, for example, Ji Yun, *Yuewei caotang biji,* 1: 1. 47, no. 47.

73 The second part of the story methodically undoes the first part to ensure that fox and ghost become indistinguishable both from each other and from ordinary women. As a prerequisite to their rebirth and co-marriage to the hero, the fox must die and her bones be buried in the same grave as the ghost's. In the end it becomes impossible even to tell whose bones are whose.

74 Van Gulik, *Sexual Life in Ancient China,* p. 189.

75 Ibid., p. 294. Van Gulik has been influenced by the romantic stereotypes of the tubercular beauty in European literature, so skillfully deconstructed in Sontag, *Illness as Metaphor.* In fact, in his memoir, Mao Xiang complains frequently of his own health and is constantly nursed by Dong Xiaowar, who maintains a stiff upper lip. It is not at all clear that she is being presented as the "sicklier" one. For a critique of the orientalism and anti-Victorianism of van Gulik's approach in *Sexual Life in Ancient China,* see Furth, "Rethinking Van Gulik."

76 See Shapiro, "The Puzzle of Spermatorrhea," pp. 553–563.

77 Wang Kentang, "Yijing," in *Zhengzhi zhunsheng* 3: 86a. See also Shapiro, "The Puzzle of Spermatorrhea," p. 560.

78 See case histories under *yijing* in Jiang Guan, *Mingyi leian* 154–155. Medical compendia such as Zhang Jiebin's *Jingyue quanshu* do not discuss the demonic possession theory of wet dreams for men, only for erotic dreams of women, though parallels are drawn between the two. A case attributed to Zhu Zhenheng involves a man suffering from recurrent oneiric emissions, who had caressed the statue of a serving girl in a temple, by implication bringing the haunting of the statue's spirit upon himself. In this case the cure is purely ritual, rather than medical; the doctor dispatches an exorcist to destroy the statue, which cures the patient. When the statue is smashed open, they discover that the clay inside the lower belly is completely wet. A similar story appears in *Guangyi ji* (*TPGJ* 368. 2930) where a man is haunted by what turns out to be the spirit of a porcelain statue; they smash it open and find blood in the statue's heart. Both stories are counterparts of the case history of the girl who developed the symptoms of phantom pregnancy after being attracted to a male statue in a temple.

79 Zhang Jiebin, *Jingyue quanshu* 29. 501. Zhang contrasts the quick-witted man to the slow-witted country bumpkin and addresses a little bromide to youths to emulate the latter rather than the former in stilling their hearts.

80 In their introduction to Mei Dingzuo, *Caigui ji,* Tian and Cha argue that in accounts prior to the Tang, ghosts with grievances tend to be forceful and inspire awe and submission but that from the Tang on, such ghosts are meek and evoke human sympathy. Though their observation is on the whole accurate, counterexamples can be found

on both sides of the equation. For instance, Dudbridge (*Religious Experience and Lay Society*, pp. 188–189) shows how in some Tang tales female ghosts are still frightening and dangerous. Conversely, Yuan Mei favored horror in his ghost tales, while even Pu Songling includes some scary specimens in his collection.

81 Tang Xianzu, *The Peony Pavilion*, trans. Birch, scene 27, pp. 151–152; original in Tang, *Mudan ting*, pp. 134–135.

82 Thompson, *Chinese Religion*, p. 7

83 On "the festivity and terror" of such nocturnal performances and their exorcistic function, see David Johnson, ed., *Ritual Opera, Operatic Ritual.*

84 Cf. Dan Minglun's comment on "Liansuo": "Where did he get this 'elegant ghost?'" (*LZ* 3. 333) and Tan Ze's comment on Du Liniang: "These lascivious words refer to the pleasures of a ghost, hence they sound elegant." Trans. Ko, *Teachers of the Inner Chambers*, p. 88; original in Wu Yiyi and Qian Yi, *Wu Wushan sanfu* 2. 84b.

85 Pacteau (*The Symptom of Beauty*, p. 12) discusses the "absence of the 'real' woman that is the necessary support of the attribution of beauty."

86 Barbara Johnson, *Critical Difference*, p. 48.

87 For my translation of the tale, see Mann and Cheng, eds., *Under Confucian Eyes*, pp. 199–205. The formula of a knight-errant rescuing the heroine on behalf of a scholar was established in Tang dynasty tales.

88 Even in *Liaozhai* tales that feature male revenants, to be a ghost is to occupy a feminine position with respect to the living. A good example is "Ye sheng" (*LZ* 1. 81–85), in which a poor scholar is so anxious to pass the examinations to requite his patron that he does not realize he is dead until he returns to his village. There he is scolded by his wife for trying to frighten the living. Throughout the story he is portrayed as tearful and pitiful rather than threatening.

89 Furth, *A Flourishing Yin*, chap. 6 (unpublished draft).

90 Ibid., p. 205.

91 For my translation of this story, see Mann and Cheng, eds., *Under Confucian Eyes*, pp. 205–214.

92 Li Shizhen, *Bencao gangmu* 52. 113, although the five categories predate Li Shizhen. On the "natural eunuch," see Furth, "Androgynous Males and Deficient Females"; and Fan Xinzhun, *Zhongguo bishi xinyi*, pp. 221–225.

93 The locus classicus of the phrase is *Shishuo xinyu* 14. 14, where it is used to convey one man's admiration for another: "Whenever [Wang Ch'i] saw Chien he would always say with a sigh, 'With such pearls and jade at my side I'm made aware of the foulness of my own body.'" Trans. Mather, *Shih-shuo hsin-yü* 14. 311, no. 14.

94 Variations on this formula are reiterated throughout the story, but assume an ironic inflection after the boy's cure.

95 There is a possible double entendre here, since the graph for bird (pronounced *diao*) was vernacular slang for penis.

96 Some wordplay with frog as the head of the penis is involved. The Chinese original employs no personal pronoun so "he" could equally be translated as "it."

97 The exception is Chinese pornography, where interest in the size and description of

the penis is common. As a tale in which a man acquires a penis, "Ingenia" reads as the inverse of "The Human Prodigy" ("Renyao"), a *Liaozhai* tale in which a man is castrated and thereby loses a penis. See my *Historian of the Strange*, pp. 99–106.

98 For women, bound feet displace genitalia as the ultimate determinant of sexual difference; for men, genitalia are always the determining factor. See my *Historian of the Strange*, p. 125.

99 Furth, *A Flourishing Yin*. In the literature on nourishing life, the focus is male immortality, whereas it is the female's whose mortality is overcome here, but the principle is similar. Furth argues (p. 199) that "internal alchemy had long appropriated the gestational female body . . . as a way of imagining the body at work fashioning its immortal transformation" and that for the "inner alchemical journey and the process of rejuvenation and rebirth . . . the most profound metaphor was gestation and the most realized body that of an infant in the womb." This metaphor also helps make sense of this story.

100 The birth of a son is overdetermined here. According to a Ming and Qing medical theory of conception, the "stronger" partner determines the sex of the fetus. In this light, by siring a son the protagonist in this tale proves that his *yang qi* is so strong it overcomes the *yin qi* of a ghost.

101 Precocious intelligence is a conventional attribute of a ghost child, presumably because the word *gui* also means clever. For additional examples, see Dudbridge, *Religious Experience*, p. 197 (*Guangyi ji*, no. 78); and Li Qing, "Guimu zhuan" in Zhang Chao, comp., *Yu Chu xinzhi* 10.190–191. In "Ingenia," the child's cleverness is also plausibly inherited from his father, who is several times described as smart and witty.

102 This may be the biggest distinction between erotic and pornographic fiction in China. Unions in pornography are sterile, just as pornographic heroines, such as Pan Jinlian in *Jin Ping Mei* or the Foolish Old Woman in *Chi pozi zhuan*, are barren.

103 Gan Bao, *Soushen ji* 16. 203, no. 397. The commentary to *Shishuo xinyu* 5. 186, no. 18, appends this story to explain the truth behind the insult "son of a ghost" as applied to a historical figure. See Mather's translation, *Shih-shuo hsin-yü*, pp. 155–161.

104 Gan Bao, *Soushen ji* 16. 202–220, no. 396.

105 Dudbridge, *Religious Experience and Lay Society*, pp. 164–169. There is one constant, however: the bride is *always* dead, never living.

106 *Da Han yuanling mizang jing*, p. 18a. Xu Pingfang, "Tang Song muzang," dates this text to the Jin-Yuan period (twelfth to fourteenth centuries) and assigns it a Shanxi provenance. The text specifies that the spirit marriage should take place years after death and that it consist of reburial of the couple's bones in a joint tomb. This resembles the spirit marriage customs that Uchida discusses in "Meikon kô," which is based on ethnographic research he conducted in Hebei and Shandong during the 1940s. One interesting difference is that *Da Han yuanling mizang jing* indicates that the bones of the deceased are to be tied together and padded to make a human form, which is then dressed in clothes to resemble a living person.

107 Dudbridge, *Religious Experience and Lay Society*, p. 166.

108 Ibid., pp. 170–172. Both types of bridegrooms are featured in *Liaozhai*, sometimes, as

in "Gongsun Jiuniang," even in the same story. See Chapter 3 for a discussion of this tale.

109 Turner, "Liminality and Performative Genres," p. 20. See also Hymes, "Personal Relations and Bureaucratic Hierarchy," p. 67; and Watson, "Structure of Chinese Funerary Rites," pp. 9–10.

110 Examples of *Liaozhai* tales preserving a discernible ritual framework for spirit marriage: "Wu Qiuyue," "Xinlang," "Gongsun Jiuniang." Examples of completely naturalized tales: "Lianxiang," "Liansuo," "Nie Xiaoqian."

111 Foxes were reputed to inhabit empty tombs. See Huntington, "Alien Kind," p. 11. Several *Liaozhai* tales feature foxes and ghosts in the same story, but they are usually rivals. (In one tale the fox seeks a human exorcist's help in getting rid of the ghost.)

112 The informant is the Shandong scholar-official Gao Heng (1612–1697), a friend of Pu Songling's and author of the first preface to *Liaozhai.*

113 Commentator He Shouqi remarks on the thematic similarity between the two stories (*LZ* 2. 264).

114 Anthony Yu, "Rest, Rest Perturbed Spirit!" p. 428.

115 Brokaw, *The Ledgers of Merit and Demerit,* p. 95.

116 Cf. Feng Zhenluan's comment: "Each of them bears a son; thus Xiaoqian actually has become human. In these sorts of places, we should only talk about the writing [*wen*] and not insist too much on the plausibility of the events [*shi*]" (*LZ* 2. 168).

117 Sawada, *Kishu dangi,* pp. 36–53. The story also furnished the plot for a scene in the chuanqi *Yinguo bao,* which was adapted into a Peking opera entitled "Buying Cakes" ("Mai gaogan") (see Xu Xianglin, *Zhongguo guixi,* p. 85). Sawada traces the source of this story's attraction to a taboo against burying a dead pregnant woman with the fetus still inside her. He cites some anecdotal evidence that there was a folk practice of cutting open the dead mother's belly to remove the dead fetus before burial.

118 Sawada, *Kishu dangi,* p. 44.

119 Li Qing, "Guimu zhuan" in Zhang Chao, comp., *Yu Chu xinzhi* 10. 190–191. This anthology contains a matching story by Song Cao entitled "The Filial Ghost," ("Gui xiaozi zhuan" 6. 111–112).

120 Bloch and Parry, "Introduction," in *Death and the Regeneration of Life,* p. 26.

121 Wai-yee Li, *Enchantment and Disenchantment,* p. 57; see also C. T. Hsia, "Time and the Human Condition."

122 Swatek, "Portrait and Plum," pp. 133–136; cf. also her *Peony Pavilion Onstage,* pp. 75–77.

123 Tang Xianzu, *The Peony Pavilion,* trans. Birch, scene 32, p. 189; Tang Xianzu, *Mudan ting,* p. 162.

124 Tang Xianzu, *Mudan ting,* scene 36, p. 175.

125 Male bodily self-sacrifice is a recurrent pattern in *Liaozhai.* In "Liancheng" (3.363) and "Abao" (2.233), men slice off flesh or fingers to prove their love. In "Xiaoxie" a scholar who initially resists the advances of two ghosts because he knows their "deathly *qi*" harms men, is so grateful to them later for saving his life that he volunteers to make love to them even though the act may prove fatal. "Today I am willing to die for you," he says. They refuse: "Loving you, how could we bear to kill you?" (*LZ* 7. 777)

The point here is that sex becomes life-threatening, a residual exaggeration of the view that all loss of semen, envisaged as a finite source of the body's vitality, is linked to death. From this perspective, a man's willingness to make love to a ghost can be extolled as an act of selfless *qing*.

126 Furth, *A Flourishing Yin:* "The Conception channel connected the generative centers around the navel in all bodies" (p. 44) and "generative vitalities [are] rooted in a Vital Gate and Cinnabar Field located somewhere beneath the navel in all human beings" (p. 29).

127 See Yi-li Wu, "Ghost Fetuses, False Pregnancies."

128 Chen Ziming, *Furen daquan liangfang* 48: 14. 742, 655–656.

129 Yu Tuan, *Yixue zhengchuan*, pp. 18–19. This passage is also discussed in Yi-li Wu, "Ghost Fetuses, False Pregnancies"; and Unschuld, *Medicine in China*, pp. 219–220.

130 Zhang Jiebin, *Jingyue quanshu* 38. 658.

131 Fu Shan, *Fu Qingzhu nüke*, p. 4589.

132 Wu Qian et al., *Yizong jinjian* 46. 1201–1202.

133 Fu Shan, *Fu Qingzhu nüke*, p. 4589. See also under *gui tai* in Wu Zhiwang, *Jiyin gangmu* 9.349–350. The verb *xia* (excrete) is occasionally replaced by *chu* (to discharge) or *xie* (have diarrhea).

134 This is a formulaic ending. See "Zhang Guo nü" (*TPGJ* 330. 2618) for a Tang example similar to the resurrection in "Liansuo." See also "Xu Xuanfang nü," (*TPGJ* 375. 2983–2984).

135 Bronfen (*Over Her Dead Body*, p. 104) cites Blanchot: "The corpse is 'neither the same as the one who was alive nor another, nor another thing.'" For Chinese representations of the relationship of ghost to corpse, see de Groot, *Religious System of China*, vol. 5, chap. 10.

136 For example, Gan Bao, *Soushen ji* 16. 206, no. 399. A hallmark of this type of story is that things done to the ghost while it is abroad (an injury inflicted on it, cosmetics or jewelry put on it) are later found registered on the corpse, "proving" that corpse and ghost are alternative forms of the same evil thing. Sometimes a small hole in the exhumed coffin is assumed to be the conduit through which the specter escaped and returned to the grave.

137 On the Victorian fascination with the female corpse, see Djikstra, *Idols of Perversity;* and Bronfen, *Over Her Dead Body.*

138 See Gan Bao, *Soushen ji* 15. 187, no. 273, for an early story of grave-robbers who violate a female corpse, but without her reviving.

139 For the sources, see Tan Zhengbi, *Sanyan liangpai ziliao*, pp. 452–457. In all but one of these tales, the heroine is rescued from premature burial by the fortuitous appearance of a grave-robber, but her revival is not sexualized and simply accompanies the opening of the grave.

140 Feng Menglong, *Xingshi hengyan*, no. 14, 724–725.

141 Ibid., p. 725.

142 Ibid., p. 734.

143 Hanan, *Chinese Short Story*, p. 60.

144 Schmitt, *Ghosts in the Middle Ages,* pp. 5–6.

145 Ibid., p. 35.

146 Freud, "Mourning and Melancholia." See also Laplanche and Pontalis, *The Language of Psycho-analysis,* pp. 485–486.

147 De Groot, *Religious System of China* 2: 546.

148 Ibid, pp. 549–553.

149 Sawada (*Kishu dangi,* p. 59) mentions this ghost tale as one of many on the subject of a woman's posthumous jealousy.

150 James Watson, "Structure of Chinese Funerary Rites," p. 8.

151 Zhang Jiebin, "Zhu you" in *Leijing* 12. 353. Translations and discussions of this case are found in Unschuld, *Medicine in China,* p. 331; and Sivin, "Emotional Counter-Therapy," II, p. 9, who translates the version in Wu Kun, *Yifang kao* under *"qingzhi men,"* 3. 86.

152 In "Xiangchun" (*LZ* 10. 1327–1328), the protagonist frequents a ghost brothel in the underworld and develops a *gui bing,* a sexually transmitted possession disorder that proves fatal.

153 The phrase *maomen aonao,* which I have translated as "trance and vertigo, anxiety and delirium," comes from "Liu yuan zhengji dalun," *Suwen,* 71B. 225, where it describes a medical condition that precedes sudden death.

154 The commentator is Feng Zhenluan. See Zeitlin, *Historian of the Strange,* p. 272, n. 22.

155 Xu Dachun, "Bing you guishen lun" in *Yixue yuanliu lun* 1. 38a-b.

156 "Mudan deng ji" in Qu You, *Jiandeng xinhua,* p. 50. "Powdered skeleton" is a derogatory Daoist term for a woman.

157 Hanan, *Chinese Vernacular Story,* p. 46; original in Feng Menglong, *Jingshi tongyan,* no. 19, p. 274.

158 On possible literary referents for this painting, see Idema, "Skulls and Skeletons in Art and on Stage."

159 For example, in "Gui ku" (*LZ* 1. 76) this ritual is performed for the ghosts of victims of a local rebellion to exorcise them from a haunted house.

160 A naked skeleton ghost is also depicted in a Land and Water mural in Pilu si temple in Hebei. Luo Pin's 1797 handscroll, *The Ghost Path (Guiqu tu),* depicts a ghost as a skeleton holding an hourglass, but his depiction clearly shows the influence of European representations of death.

161 Hertz, *Death and the Right Hand.*

162 Bloch and Parry, *Death and the Regeneration of Life,* "Introduction," p. 3. Ethnographies of southeast China—Fukien, Taiwan, and Canton—confirm the practice of second burial as a deliberate pattern in mortuary ritual for ancestors. See James Watson, "Of Flesh and Bones"; and Rubie Watson, "Remembering the Dead."

163 Naquin, "Funerals in North China."

164 Examples are provided in de Groot, *Religious System of China,* vol. 3, book 1.

165 Owen, *Remembrances,* p. 34.

166 These are de Groot's translations of the term in *Religious System of China,* vol. 3, p. 847.

167 Teiser, *Scripture on the Ten Kings,* p. 1.

168 Teiser, *Ghost Festival in Medieval China,* p. 220.

169 Zhu Xi, "Guishen pian" in *Zhuzi yulei* 3. 38.

170 Zhang Zilie, *Zhengzi tong, haiji* part 1, 4. 52a, entry for *gui.*

171 See Huntington, "Ghosts Seeking Substitutes."

172 Ji Yun, *Yuewei caotang biji* 8. 155.

173 Stewart, *Nonsense,* p. 129.

174 The locus classicus of this common phrase is "Grieving for the Departed" (*Shishuo xinyu* 17, no. 14; trans., Mather, *Shi-shuo hsin-yü,* p. 324) where it is used to defend what seems like a father's excessive grief over the death of his infant son. In late imperial times it is mainly used to refer to feelings between men and women.

175 Bronfen, *Over Her Dead Body,* p. 295.

Chapter 2: The Ghost's Voice

Epigraph. Ritual prayer in *Da Han yuanling mizang jing,* p. 18b.

1 Goodwin and Bronfen, "Introduction" in *Death and Representation,* p. 4

2 *Oxford English Dictionary* online edition.

3 Castle, *The Female Thermometer* and Gunning, "Phantom Images" have shown how ghosts were incorporated into new technologies of vision introduced in eighteenth- and nineteenth-century Europe and America—magic phantasmagoria shows in Castle's case, spirit photography in Gunning's.

4 Horace Walpole is cited as making the distinction between "apparition" and "audition" in reference to the ghost of Cock Lane in Clery, *The Rise of Supernational Fiction,* pp. 24–25. On the ghostly effect of the disembodied voice in film, see Chion, *The Voice in Cinema.*

5 Wang Chong, *Lunheng* 22. 940–941.

6 Han Yu, "Yuan gui," in *Han Yu quanji jiaozhu,* pp. 2701–2704.

7 Campany, *Strange Writing,* p. 261.

8 Kao, "Introduction" to *Classical Chinese Tales of the Supernatural,* p. 22, 26.

9 Li Jingliang, "Li Zhangwu," *TPGJ* 340. 2698.

10 *TPGJ* 332. 2635.

11 "Baxia ren," *TPGJ* 328. 2608–2609; the source given is *Jiwen.* An alternative version from *Tongyou pian,* another Tang source, involves the discovery of a giant footprint rather than a skeleton.

12 Wang Chong, *Lunheng* 20. 878. Wang Chong is not refuting the belief that the sound of moaning can be heard coming from unburied bones; he is simply arguing that the spirits of the dead do not have consciousness and therefore cannot be the force that produces the sound, which he argues is produced by a demonic *qi (yao qi)* whistling through them. For another reference to the moaning of unburied bones, see Fan Ye, *Hou Hanshu* 46. 1553.

13 Pauline Yu, *The Reading of Imagery,* p. 217.

14 Li Daoyuan, *Shuijing zhu* 34. 499.

15 Xie Guan, "Qing fu." Cited under "Baxia yuan ming" in *Zhongwen dacidian,* p. 4543.

16 Pauline Yu, *The Reading of Imagery,* p. 218.

17 Ibid., p. 217.

18 Compare another Tang anecdote, "Hemei ren" (*TPGJ* 330. 2621), in which a man who makes an offering to bones in the wilderness promptly hears a disembodied couplet chanted in thanks.

19 See, for instance, Yao Quan's comment in Wu Qiming, *Li He ziliao,* p. 219.

20 Pauline Yu, *The Reading of Imagery,* p. 121. See also Owen, *An Anthology of Chinese Literature,* p. 249.

21 For the dating, see Diény's, *Les Dix-Neuf Poèmes Anciens.*

22 For example, Sui Shusen, *Gushi shijiushou,* p. 21; and Waley, *Chinese Poems,* p. 54. "The Nineteen Old Poems" are an arbitrary grouping, the product of the anthologizing process of Xiao Tong's *Wenxuan.*

23 Translated by Owen, *Anthology of Chinese Literature,* pp. 260–261.

24 Diény, *Les Dix-Neuf Poèmes Anciens,* p. 129.

25 Wu Qi (before 1728) in Sui Shusen, *Gushi shijiushou,* p. 21.

26 Although the direct predecessors for these suites are usually considered the burial songs "Dew on the Shallot" and "Village of Weeds," Old Poem XIV, especially if read as Wu Qi suggests, is a closer progenitor because it intimates a journey and shares the same imagery.

27 See the discussion of the connection between the two in Diény, *Les Dix-Neuf Poèmes Anciens,* pp. 132–134.

28 For a full discussion of these imitations of burial songs, see A. R. Davis, *T'ao Yüan-ming* 2. 165–172.

29 Based on Hightower's trans., *The Poetry of T'ao Ch'ien,* p.249; original in Tao Qian, *Tao Yuanming ji,* 4.141.

30 The *yuefu* ballad "Zhan chengnan," which contains a dialogue with soldiers fallen in battle, employs a similar effect. The dead men complain in the first person *(wo)* at the beginning of the poem, and are addressed in the second person *(zi)* at the end when their (living) interlocutors praise their valor. In Miao Xi's (186–245 CE) burial song, the deceased also refers to himself in the first person. See Davis, *T'ao Yüan-ming* 2. 167–168.

31 There is some variation in the order of the stanzas. Only Tao Qian's final stanza is included in Xiao Tong, *Wenxuan,* while *Yuefu shiji* prints all three but in a different order. Li Shan's annotated version of *Wenxuan* reverses the order of the second and third stanzas for Lu Ji's burial songs. See Davis, *T'ao Yüan-ming* 2. 172.

32 Tao Qian, *Tao Yuanming ji,* p. 142; trans. based on Hightower, *The Poetry of T'ao Ch'ien,* p. 248.

33 See Wu Pei-yi, *The Confucian's Progress.*

34 For the deathbed argument, which is predicated on the recurrence of the ninth month as the date of death in both the burial songs and the elegy, see *Tao Yuanming shiwen huiping,* pp. 311–312. For the argument that the ninth month—the autumn season when the *qi* of Earth grows desolate—should be understood symbolically rather than

literally, see Wu Qi's reading of the final stanza. See also A. R. Davis, *T'ao Yüan-ming* 2: 172, for a refutation of the deathbed view.

35 Wu Hung, *Monumentality,* p. 257.

36 Ibid., p. 264.

37 A. R. Davis, *T'ao Yüan-ming* 2: 173.

38 *TPGJ* 337. 2672–2673.

39 Wei Huang's ghost manifests herself only as a voice, which is first heard as disembodied words, then heard coming from the mouth of a possessed servant girl. The story nonetheless strongly suggests that the poems are conceptualized as written documents: They are "fashioned" *(zhi)* and "given" *(yu)* by the ghost to her relatives and bear the subtitle *ti* ("signed").

40 *TPGJ* 337. 2673.

41 This line is a slight variation on the sixth line of Old Poem XIV.

42 There is also an echo here of Tao Qian's "Yin jiu," no. 6 ("I built my cottage in the realm of men / and yet there is no noise of horse and cart") to act as a signpost to the recluse.

43 "Chang Yi," *TPGJ* 336. 2665–2667. The learned gentleman sends someone to follow the messenger who delivered the letter and sees him disappear into an ancient tomb, but this simply confirms the deceased status of the letter writer, and the grave otherwise plays no part in the story.

44 "Li Daochang," in Ji Yougong, comp. *Tangshi jishi* 34. 529. This version of the story had to have been in circulation before 1067 because of the dating of *Tang Song yishi.*

45 Following the reading *qingsong* in Ji Yougong, *Tangshi jishi;* Lu Guimeng and Pi Rixiu, *Songling ji;* and Ruan Yue, *Shihua zonggui,* a phrase which reappears in the matching poem. The variant *gaosong* (tall pine) in *Quan Tangshi,* found also in the *Tongyou ji* version (*TPGJ* 338. 2682), makes the line more allegorical.

46 Following the reading *qing* (clear) in Lu Guimeng and Pi Rixiu's *Songling ji, Quan Tangshi,* and *TPGJ,* which works better grammatically than the variant *sheng* (sound) in Ji Yougong, *Tangshi jishi;* Ruan Yue, *Shihua zonggui;* and Mei Dingzuo, *Caigui ji.*

47 *TPGJ* gives *shengsi* (life and death), a variant noted by *Quan Tangshi.* I read *youxian* (dark and bright) as a locution for life and death.

48 Following the reading *wang le* in the Ming edition of *Caigui ji* and *Tangshi jishi,* which is superior to *san le* (three happinesses) in *Quan Tangshi* and *Songling ji,* to *sheng le* (the happiness of the living) in Ruan Yue, *Shihua zonggui,* and to *zhi le* (perfect happiness) in Tian and Cha's modern edition of Mei's *Caigui ji.* The end of the second poem is garbled in the *Tongyou ji* version in *TPGJ.*

49 They did continue to write their own epitaphs and autonecrologies, but imitations of burial songs became a gesture in imitation of Tao Qian, rather than an imitation of the original anonymous songs.

50 Foucault, "What is an Author?" pp. 107–108.

51 Trans. Owen, *Remembrances,* p. 32.

52 There is a final question in this series, but the text seems corrupt. The text of the elegy

is given only in the *Tangshi jishi* version. The modern punctuated edition of *Tangshi jishi* has wording which means "Who was the husband of your immortal self?" But since every version assumes that the anonymous author(s) are male, it would be more logical for the question to be "Where did your immortal self live?" or possibly "Where is your immortal abode now?"

"The Bones of Chuang-tzu," Zhang Heng's reworking of Zhuangzi's parable, includes questions of identity in the litany posed to the skull, but here the skull identifies himself so the poet can lay him to rest with a libation. See Owen, *Remembrances*, p. 37.

53 Li Daochang's appointment to this post in 776 is recorded in Liu Xun, *Jiu Tangshu* 11. 314. *Quan Tangwen* (458. 5916) includes Li Daochang's "Elegy to the Lord of Dark Solitude" ("Ji Youdu jun wen"), minus the last few lines.

54 Ji Yougong, *Tangshi jishi* 34. 529.

55 Ibid.

56 For the symbolism of stone in Chinese funerary architecture, see Wu Hung, *Monumentality*, pp. 121–122.

57 On this subgenre during the Tang, see Wu Chengxue, "Lun tibishi" and Luo Zongtao, "Tangren tibishi chutan." See also my "Disappearing Verses."

58 This resembles the miraculous genesis of religious images in the Liu Sahe myth described in Wu Hung, "Rethinking Liu Sahe," p. 35. The monk Liu Sahe predicted that at a certain spot the image of the Buddha would "thrust itself out" *(tingchu)* of the mountain cliff.

59 Cf. Wu Hung's discussion of the reversed Six Dynasties inscriptions in *Monumentality*, pp. 254–255.

60 Translation indebted to Owen, *Readings in Chinese Literary Thought*, p. 41.

61 Ibid.

62 Owen, *Traditional Chinese Poetry and Poetics*, pp. 25, 43.

63 In fact, Freud borrowed his definition of the "uncanny" from Schelling, who had developed a theory of the spirit world.

64 Heath, "Joan Riviere and the Masquerade," p. 45.

65 Cf. lines from *Zuozhuan*, 25th year of Duke Xiang, trans. in Owen, *Readings in Chinese Literary Thought*, p. 29.

66 *TPGJ* 338. 2682. The entry is titled "Wuqiu si," because "Hu" was a taboo character during part of the Northern Song. Li Jianguo (*Tang Wudai zhiguai*, p. 489) notes that 794 is the latest date recorded for any event in the surviving excerpts from *Tongyou ji*.

67 Here my translation follows the wording attributed to *Taiping guangji* in *Caigui ji*, rather than that in *TPGJ* 33. 2682.

68 Cf. the "signature" in the Wei Huang story, in which she is identified as "Sojourner in the Tomb."

69 Pi Rixiu wrote a preface for this book in 871. See Nienhauser, *P'i Jih-hsiu*, p. 13.

70 Ibid.

71 Ibid, p. 31, mentions the "extensive interest in local Soochow history and mythology"

that Pi Rixiu developed during his stay came from his access to the library of a prominent local scholar. It is possible that he found a copy of *Tongyou ji* there; at any rate, it seems that Pi Rixiu saw a written version, rather than simply hearing an oral version of the story. In his preface he mentions that as "a lover of antiquity, he saw the poems and enjoyed them" (*Songling ji* 2. 2a). Whatever the case, the version of the story that Lu and Pi had access to was clearly closer to the earlier *Tongyou ji* one. In *Songling ji*, the quatrain comes first, not last, and the second auto-dirge is regarded as a matching poem written in response to the first auto-dirge. The most striking similarity is the use in *Songling ji* of the sobriquet Lord of Darkness (Youjun) for one of the ghost authors. One difference is that Pi Rixiu's preface mentions that he did not know the identity or status of the matching poem's author, and the sobriquet "Dark Solitude" is assigned to the author of the first poems, not to the author of the matching poem. But these are relatively small variations.

72 "Zhuihe Youdu jun shi ciyun" in *Songling ji,* 2. 5b–7a.

73 Pi Rixiu and Lu Guimeng, "Zhuihe Huqiu si Qingyuan daoshi shi bing xu," in *Songling ji* 2. 1a-b. The two matching quatrains by Lu Guimeng and Pi Rixiu are tacked onto the end of the *Tangshi jishi* version of the Tiger Mound Hill story.

74 Sima Qian, *Shiji* 130. 3300.

75 Translated in full in Frodsham, *Poems of Li Ho,* pp. 1–2.

76 Li He, *Sanjia pingzhu,* 1. 11–13.

77 Trans. Frodsham, *Poems of Li Ho.*

78 Li Shangyin, "Li Changji xiaozhuan," in Wu Qiming, *Li He ziliao,* pp. 8–9.

79 Lu Guimeng, "Shu Li He xiaozhuan hou," in Wu Qiming, *Li He ziliao,* pp. 12–13.

80 Shang Wei, "Prisoner and Creator," p. 25.

81 The colophon is undated. Lu Guimeng's death, which occurred somewhere between 880 and 881, provides a *terminus ad quem* for it. The colophon speaks of Li Shangyin's career with a finality that suggests it must have been written after his death in 858.

82 Trans. Shang Wei, "Prisoner and Creator," p. 38.

83 Li Shangyin, "Li Changji xiaozhuan," in Li He, *Sanjia pingzhu,* p. 13.

84 Quoted in Li He, *Sanjia pingzhu,* p. 24; Wu Qiming, *Li He ziliao,* p. 35.

85 Trans. Owen, *Readings in Chinese Literary Thought,* p. 43.

86 Wang Siren, "*Li He shijie* xu," in Wu Qiming, *Li He ziliao,* p. 201

87 Li He, *Sanjia pingzhu,* p. 96. My translation has been influenced by Graham, *Poems of the Late T'ang,* p. 114. See also Frodsham's translation, *The Poems of Li Ho,* p. 116.

88 Cf. Owen, *Traditional Poetry and Poetics,* pp. 65–66.

89 Wu Qiming, *Li He ziliao,* p. 162.

90 Wang Qi suggests that the green oaks are an elegant substitution for the commonplace white poplars. The green oaks may also be reminiscent of the green maples in Du Fu's "Dreaming of Li Bai" ("Meng Li Bai"), in which the greenness of the trees signifies the outward leg of a dead soul's journey.

91 Lu Ji, in Xiao Tong, *Wenxuan* 3: 28. 1335.

92 Robertson, "Poetic Diction in the Works of Li Ho," p. 88.

93 Schafer, *The Divine Woman*, p. 134.

94 Trans. Graham, *Chuang-tzu*, p. 59, modified; original *Zhuangzi jinzhu*, "Qiwu lun," p. 85.

95 The former is from "Su Xiaoxiao mu," the latter from "Qiu lai."

96 Bronfen, *Over Her Dead Body*, p. 113.

97 In Wu Qiming, *Li He ziliao*, p. 162.

98 Li He, *Li Changji shige*, p. 242.

99 Certain compilers of later imperial collections, such as the editors of *Quan Tangshi*, even change the character *ren* to *gui* in the title for logical consistency.

100 Pi Rixiu and Lu Guimeng, *Songling ji* 2. 1b.

101 The second auto-dirge, minus any narrative frame and entitled "Ghost Poem from a Cliff at Tiger Mound Temple" is included in Zhong Xing's *Gushi gui* 32. 16b–17a. His comment implicitly supports Pi Rixiu's assumptions about dating and aesthetic judgment and also explicitly connects this Tiger Mound inscription with the Six Dynasties auto-dirges.

102 Owen, *The Poetry of Meng Chiao and Han Yü*, p. 227, argues that Li He's poetry participated in a "cult-hermetic" style, which gloried in displaying a bizarre imagination beyond the ken of ordinary poets.

103 See Kuo-ching Tu, *Li Ho*, p. 126.

104 Frodsham, *Poems of Li Ho*, p. xxv. Graham, *Poems of the Late T'ang*, p. 89. The proportion of anecdotes on this subject in Ji Yun's *Yuewei caotang biji* and other Qing sources suggests that interest in ghost poetry persisted in the eighteenth and nineteenth centuries too.

105 Wang Qiming, "Introduction," *Li He ziliao*, p. 5.

106 Shen Yazhi, "Song Li Jiao xiucai shi xu," in Wu Qiming, *Li He ziliao*, p. 6.

107 Wu Qiming, *Li He ziliao*, p. 6 and p. 46, respectively.

108 Ibid., pp. 122–123.

109 Yagi Akiyoshi, "Ho Shōrei to Ri Ga."

110 Wu Qiming, *Li He ziliao*, p. 204.

111 Ibid., p. 298. For Wang Shizhen's original remark, see Wu Qiming, *Li He ziliao*, p. 118.

112 Tang Qingmou, *Xiangzhong cao*, 2a in You Tong, *Xitang quanji*.

113 Wu Yiyi and Qian Yi, *Wu Wushan sanfu*, scene 20, 1.59a.

114 For a discussion of these features, particularly the Li He technique of "chiaroscuro"—the glimmering of light against a dark background—see Robertson, "Poetic Diction in the Works of Li Ho," pp. 89–90.

115 Ji Yun, *Yuewei caotang biji* 2. 27, no. 17.

116 Li Yi, "*Shihua zonggui* xu," in Ruan Yue, *Shihua zonggui*, pp. 1a–2b.

117 As reported in collections such as Ji Yougong's *Tangshi jishi*, p. 904.

118 See, inter alia, Su Shi, *Dongpo zhilin;* Wang Zhifang, *Wang Zhifang shihua*, p. 6; and Zhao Lingzhi, *Houqing lu* 8a–8b.

119 Xin Wenfang, *Tang caizi zhuan*, pp. 961–962.

120 Li Jianguo (*Tang Wudai zhiguai*, pp. 1195–1196) offers no firm conclusion about the dating and compilation of the earlier *Caigui ji*. There is no record of such a title exist-

ing in the Tang; in later collectanea, the title is credited variously to a Tang or Song dynasty compiler. The contents of this work vary, but only well-known Tang stories are ever included. The title predates Mei (that is, it was not a forgery by Mei), since it is included in collectanea dating before the late Ming, but it was not compiled by a Tang author, and probably not by a Song author either.

121 On elite interest in spirit poetry, see my "Spirit Writing and Performance." The chapters on spirit writing, which generally treat this pastime positively, draw upon the experiences of relatives and friends, but Mei does not mention being present at any séances himself. His literary collection, *Luqiu shi shi ji,* includes a poem entitled "Hearing Ghosts" ("Wen gui") but provides no evidence of personal involvement with spirit writing.

122 Mei Dingzuo, *Guyue yuan* 8. 52. This anthology updates *Yuefu shiji,* the main Song dynasty source on old ballads, but adds a separate ghost section.

123 Barr, "Pu Songling and *Liaozhai* zhiyi," p. 202.

124 Hu Wenkai, *Lidai funü zhuzuo kao,* p. 877.

125 Ibid., pp. 879–880.

126 Qian Qianyi was a devotee of Le'an fashi, the Suzhou intermediary spirit also worshipped by Ye Shaoyuan and his family. Qian wrote a biography of Le'an and also exchanged poems with her. See my "Spirit Writing and Performance."

127 Ye Ziqi, *Cao Muzi,* p. 79.

128 She acknowledges *Liechao shiji* as a source a number of times in this section.

129 Additional supernatural poems appear in *j.* 35, 36, and 38B.

130 Wang Duanshu listed a section entitled *bai ji* (fiction) in her table of contents as pending, in which she must have planned to include anecdotes about women writers, but as far as we know, it was never completed.

131 "Yu Yuanji," (that is, Yu Xuanji) in Wang Duanshu, *Mingyuan shiwei* 30B. 7a.

132 "Jiang ji" in ibid., 30B. 9b; "Chen ji," p. 10a.

133 "Ranzhi ji li," in Zhang Chao, comp. *Zhaodai congshu, yiji* 28. 12a-b.

134 Ibid., p. 12b.

135 Cf. Foucault, "What is an Author?" on the classificatory function of the proper name. The orthographic homogeneity of *Quan Tangshi* plus the authoritative status the compendium still enjoys today means that recent reference books include unwittingly humorous entries for ghost authors.

136 See, inter alia, Widmer, "Xiaoqing's Literary Legacy," Ko, T*eachers of the Inner Chambers,* and my "Shared Dreams."

137 Shen Yixiu, "Ji nü Qiongzhang zhuan," *Lichui ji,* inYe Shaoyuan, comp. *Wumengtang ji,* p. 128.

138 Furth, "Editor's Introduction," p. 4. (Shen Yixiu, Ye Xiaoluan's mother and a poet in her own right, would be an obvious exception to this rule, since she bore some thirteen children. She did, however, die of illness in middle age.)

139 Dan Minglun, *LZ* 3. 331.

140 Pu Songling, *Pu Songling quanji* 2. 1662. Although the poem imitates "The Grave of Little Su," it also incorporates phrases from other poems by Li He.

141 Yagi Akiyoshi, "Sho Horei to Ri Ga," p. 138. Yagi's study of Li He's influence overlooks verse included in *Liaozhai* stories.

142 Li He, *Li Changji geshi* 4. 140–141.

143 The first line is from "Tian Zicheng" (*LZ* 12. 1628); the second from "Jiaping gongzi" (*LZ* 11. 1588–1589).

144 Ji Yun, *Yuewei caotang biji* 11. 253.

145 *Liechao shiji, run ji,* 6. 8a-b. Qian Qianyi provides no source for this anecdote. For a Tang anecdote about a ghost who continues the poem of a living man, see Mei Dingzuo, *Caigui ji* 7. 129.

146 The words of the linked couplet may provide some clue as to why one line is fatal to the monk, and why the other is effective in exorcising his ghost.

147 Owen, *Traditional Chinese Poetry and Poetics,* p. 61.

148 Diény, *Dix-neuf poèmes anciens,* p. 167, trans. in Pauline Yu, *The Reading of Imagery,* p. 129.

149 "Yanzhong xian," in Zeng Zao, *Leishuo* 29. 1877.

150 Thus in "Liansuo," the action of linking couplets is reinforced by the man's finding the ghost's lost shoe ribbon, which he later refastens for her to make both shoes match.

151 See Wu Chengxue, "Jiju lun," p. 16.

152 Meng Chengshun, *Jiao Hong ji,* scene 39, p. 196.

153 "Song Meng Jiaodong xu," in *Han Yu Xuanji,* p. 202. Discussed in Robertson, "Refiguring the Feminine."

154 "Mudu xian ji xiaozhuan," *Xitang zazu, sanji,* 6. 16b, in You Tong, *Xitang quanji.*

155 Chen Zilong, *Chen Zilong shiji* 1. 27. For the story of Princess Purple Jade, whose ghost marries a living man and bears him a child, see Gan Bao, *Soushen ji* 16.294, no. 200.

Chapter 3: Ghosts and Historical Time

Epigraph. From Ricoeur, *Time and Narrative* 3: 312, n. 12.

1 Needham, "Time and Knowledge in China," pp. 92–104. The Chinese calendar consists of repeating sixty-year cycles, but it is also clearly anchored to a progressive view of time through the succession of political dynasties, rulers, and reign periods.

2 Ricoeur, *Time and Narrative* 3. 99; 113.

3 Jonathan Hay, "The Wilderness Environment." See also his "Suspension of Dynastic Time" and "Ming Palace and Tomb." The end of the dynasty may also be denoted by Chinese words closer to the English "fall," such as *fei* ("to be deposed" or "abandoned") and *dianfu* ("to be overturned").

4 Some late seventeenth-century plays are exceptions, particularly Kong Shangren's *Peach Blossom Fan (Taohua shan);* and Hong Sheng's *Palace of Lasting Life.*

5 Ricoeur, *Time and Narrative,* p. 144

6 Frankel, *The Flowering Plum,* p. 108.

7 Ibid., p. 119; Frankel, "The Contemplation of the Past," p. 361; and Owen, "Place."

8 Owen, *Remembrances,* p. 20.

9 Trans. Owen in *Remembrances,* p. 20. Original in *Mao Shi zhengyi,* no. 65, 4. 329–331.

10 Trans. Wu Hung, "But Where are the Ruins in Chinese Art?" Original in Sima Qian, *Shiji* 38. 1620–1621.

11 Ibid.

12 Wu Hung, "But Where are the Ruins in Chinese Art?"

13 Yao Silian, *Liangshu* 13.229–245. For instance, Shen Yue's ghost politely declines his host's offer of wine on the grounds that he never drinks; the *Liangshu* biography mentions that by nature Shen Yue was not fond of wine. Shen Yue's ghost mentions a dream in which he was told he would be promoted to grand councilor but would never reach the rank of prime minister; the biography mentions that there was talk of appointing Shen Yue prime minister, but that it never came about. The contrast Shen Yue's ghost draws between the carefree pleasures he enjoyed in his youth while in relative obscurity with the terrible anxiety he suffered after he rose to power parallels the sentiments expressed in the autobiographical *fu* included in his biography, and so on.

14 Here is the exact wording of Lu Qiao's objection: "I've often read the *Literary Anthology* assembled by Prince Zhaoming of the Liang and I've noticed that the poems it includes are not constrained by tonal regulations. We call this 'the style of the Qi and Liang dynasties.' Only beginning in the Tang did the poets Shen Quanqi and Song Zhiwen develop the liking for regulated verse. Now your son's poem follows the modern style. How can this be?"

15 Qian Zhongshu, *Guanzhui bian* 2. 664.

16 Ji Yun, *Yuewei caotang biji* 18.451–452, no. 13. For additional examples, see my "Spirit Writing and Performance, pp. 105–106.

17 Quotations from Owen's translation of Bao Zhao's "Weed-covered City" in *Remembrances,* p. 64.

18 Feng Menglong, *Qingshi leilüe* 20. 1773–1775.

19 Qu You, *Jiandeng xinhua,* p. 44.

20 Ibid.

21 For Du Mu's quatrain, "Bo Qinhuai," see Gao Buying, ed., *Tang Song shi juyao,* p. 830.

22 In some stories the palace-lady revenants profess ignorance about the current state of historical affairs, but they are always aware of the basic principles and contours of historical change. See, for instance, Wei Guan, "Zhou Qin xing ji," *TPGJ* 489. 4018–4023.

23 Rey Chow, "Souvenir of Love," p. 135.

24 The poem is entitled "Pillow Talk" ("Zhenshang") in Wang Duanshu's *Mingyuan shiwei* 30.3a. This story, set during the fifteenth century, involves the ghost of a palace lady from the reign of the Song Emperor Duzong (r. 1265–1675), who recites this poem to her mortal lover in bed. This story, entitled "Hua Lichun," also appears in Feng Menglong, *Qingshi leilüe* 20.1807–1811, but without the poem.

25 The Mandolin Pavilion was built to commemorate the spot in Jiangxi province where Bai Juyi met the courtesan from the capital one autumn night, as described in his "Mandolin Song." Li Zhen, the author of the story, was himself a native of Jiangxi.

26 For another example of the "tourism of ruins" during the Ming as a component fueling the ghost story, see "Chang'an yexing lu," in Li Zhen, *Jiandeng yuhua,* pp. 125–128.

27 In "Tian Zhu yu Xue Tao lianju ji" (Li Zhen, *Jiandeng yuhua,* pp. 169–178), where the

hero meets the ghost of the Tang courtesan Xue Tao, linking verses goes far beyond foreplay to become the raison d'être of the story.

28 Li Zhen, *Jiandeng yuhua*, p. 184.

29 Owen, *Remembrances*, p. 14.

30 Pu Songling's tales of obsession are prime examples. For a discussion of this theme, see my *Historian of the Strange*, chap. 3; and Wai-yee Li, *Enchantment and Disenchantment*, chap. 3.

31 Kwan's 1987 film *Rouge* is based on Li Bihua's 1984 novel of the same title. On the courtesan's ghostly return in the film to confront what Abbas terms "the déjà disparu" of Hong Kong on the eve of its return to the Mainland, see his *Hong Kong*, chap. 2. Little Su and Xue Tao are the two most ubiquitous ghosts of courtesans; for examples of the former, see Mei Dingzuo, *Caigui ji*, 8.144–145; for the latter, see "Tian Zhu yu Xue Tao lianju ji" in Li Zhen, *Jiandeng yuhua* 2.169–177. For the ghost of a chaste martyr, see "Yueye tanqin ji," in ibid., 1.138–152.

32 For ghosts of heroes slain in battle, see "Huating feng guren ji" in Qu You, *Jiandeng xinhua*, 1.20–23; for male victims of political purges, see "Xu sheng" (*TPGJ* 350.2769–2771).

33 On the practice of putting palace ladies to death so they could accompany emperors into death and be buried with them, which persisted sporadically in the Ming and Qing, see Huang Zhangyue, "Ming Qing huangshi," pp. 29–34.

34 "Xi Shi" in Feng Menglong, *Qingshi leilüe* 20. 1773.

35 A case in point is the Song dynasty romance about a man who finds a red leaf inscribed with a quatrain along a moat flowing out of the palace and falls in love with the invisible author of the verse. He inscribes a poetic reply on another red leaf and floats it back upstream to his imagined palace lady. Through a series of coincidences, the two are eventually united outside the palace ("Li Yin," *TPGJ* 354. 2807–2808). In a later version from *Beimeng suoyan*, however, she is only able to remain outside the palace by committing suicide and rejoining her lover as a ghost, and in the end she has to be exorcised by a Daoist priest. For a discussion of the different versions, see Li Jianguo, *Songdai zhiguai chuanqi shulu*, pp. 98–101.

36 A famous passage in Freud's *Beyond the Pleasure Principle* (chap. 2, pp. 13–17), describes a child's game of *fort/da*—making a favorite toy go away so that he can bring it back again. Freud reads this game of willful "disappearance and return" as the child's attempts to gain mastery over his anxiety about the mother's absence. Bronfen applies the idea of *fort/da* to explain aesthetic depictions of women's death in *Over Her Dead Body*, chap. 2.

37 The palace had been burned down by Li Zicheng upon fleeing Beijing. The process of the Qing reconstruction of the Forbidden City was a lengthy one, taking many years; see Hay, "Ming Palace and Tomb."

38 Ibid.

39 For accounts of what happened to this area of Shandong during the collapse of the Ming, see *Qingzhou fuzhi* (1859) 36. 44–49; and *Yidu xian tuzhi* 6. 11–14; Brook,

Praying for Power, pp. 228–235 for Zhucheng county; and Barr, "Pu Songling and *Liaozhai zhiyi*," pp. 11–17 for Zichuan. For an overview of Shandong's surrender and pacification, see Wakeman, *The Great Enterprise*, pp. 424–436, 491–494, 699–703. For the possible 1638 date for a temporary Qing occupation of Qingzhou, see Struve, *The Ming-Qing Conflict*, p. 206. The most detailed account of the Manchu conquest of Qingzhou appears in An Zhiyuan's biography of General Li Shiyuan, reprinted in *Yidu xian tuzhi;* abridged version in *Qingzhou fuzhi* (1859).

40 In "Gui ku" (LZ 1. 76) there is little time between the traumatic event (the mass murder of innocent victims in the Qing government's repression of the Xie Qian rebellion in 1647) and the haunting, but the ghostly weeping only begins to be heard after the owner of the house where the corpses of the victims had been piled removes them for burial and scours the place clean of bloodstains. The point is that all traces of these deaths must be eliminated before the haunting can commence.

41 Caruth, "Introduction," in *Trauma*, p. 8. On the difference between repression and disassociation, see van der Kolk and van der Hart, "The Intrusive Past," p.168.

42 Yidu city was also the site of the former palace of the Ming prince of Qi, but because this palace had burned down long before the dynasty fell, it never became a focus for Ming loyalist sentiment and sparked no notable ghost stories. On the two Ming palaces in Yidu, see Su Bai, "Qingzhou cheng kaolüe."

43 *Qingzhou shizhi*, p. 855, also includes information on the tombs of these princes and their cohorts and tables of the hereditary House of Heng. See also *Qingzhou fuzhi* (1859), 24. 10a; *Yidu xian tuzhi* 12.12a and j. 47; and Zha Jizuo, *Zuiwei lu*, p. 1287.

44 Examples include Xu Tian, "Guo gu Hengfan feigong you gan" (cited in Zhang Chongchen, "Pu Songling yu Zhucheng yimin," p. 45), which includes a line about ghosts weeping amid the ruins as farmers plow in the springtime; Wang Shizhen, "Linzi huaigu" (reprinted in Qian Zhonglian, *Qingshi jishi*, pp. 2040–2042), and Peng Ershu, "Hengfan jiudi jiunan jiangjun" (in Deng Hanyi, *Shiguan chuji* 4.11a). A *huaigu* on Qingzhou by Ding Yaokang, another famous Shandong loyalist and writer, entitled "Wangchun lou," is included in Xu Gui, *Ciyuan congtang* 9. 546, no. 30. Lu Jianzeng's *Guochao Shanzuo shichao* includes "Qingzhou huaigu," a poem by Zhu Helu, a *zhusheng* from Xincheng. Although this poem does not mention the prince of Heng's palace by name, it evokes architectural ruins and laments the absence of the prince who once resided in the town: "Since the prince left, the place is overgrown with grass / the palace eunuchs greeting one another are all white-haired."

45 For the complete text of this poem, see Gu Yanwu, *Gu Tinglin shiji* 3. 600–601. According to Hummel, (*ECCP*, p. 422), Gu Yanwu first traveled to Shandong in 1657, was imprisoned in Ji'nan, the provincial capital, in 1668, and had settled in Shanxi province by 1679. *Juan* 3 of his collected poems, where the "Hengwang fu" poem appears, includes several verses about nearby places in Shandong. For the dating of the poem, also see Zhou Kangxie, *Gong Lingting nianpu*, pp. 35–36.

46 *Qingzhou shizhi*, p. 856.

47 On the methodological distinction between early and late stories, see Barr, "A Com-

parative Study." The romantic orientation of "Lin Siniang" and its treatment of the dynastic transition suggest that it would have probably been written in the 1670s or 1680s, early in the thirty-odd years it took Pu Songling to write *Liaozhai.*

48 Wang Shizhen, *Chibei outan* 21. 512–513, no. 995.

49 Chen Weisong names Wang Shiyi as his informant for the story, which Sun Yancheng, comp., *Wang Shizhen nianpu* (p. 6) identifies as an appellation for Wang Shizhen. The text of the story is cited as "a short preface to 'The Ballad of Lin Siniang' ("Lin Siniang ge") by Wang Taishi"; *taishi* is an unofficial reference to a member of the Hanlin Academy, an office Wang Shizhen held. Neither "Lin Siniang ge" nor this preface can be found in Wang Shizhen's published collections, however. Wang Shilu, Wang Shizhen's older brother, was a close friend of Chen Weisong's and collaborated with him on *Furen ji.* It is therefore understandable that Xu Fuming ("Cong 'Lin Siniang,'" p. 205) would mistakenly identify Wang Shilu rather than Wang Shizhen as Chen Weisong's source for the Lin Siniang story. For further discussion of the Wang brothers' contribution to *Furen ji,* see my "Disappearing Verses."

50 It is possible that Lin Yuming first published "Lin Siniang" in *Yu Chu xinzhi,* rather than in a collection of his own work, if it was included in the first eight-*juan* edition of *Yu Chu xinzhi,* for which Zhang Chao wrote a 1683 preface, but which is not extant. In circulation now is the expanded version of this anthology (with a postface dated 1700). For the publication history of *Yu Chu xinzhi,* see Deng Changfeng, *Ming Qing xiqu kaolüe xubian,* pp. 156–162. Lin Yunming published three collections of his work: *Wushan kouyin* is undated but was published in Hangzhou where Lin had moved after 1677; two of the prefaces mention the year 1685, so it could not have been published before then. *Yikuilou xuangao* combines selections from *Wushan kouyin* and Lin's 1672 collection *Sunzhai fenyu.*

51 Li Chengzhong, *Genzhai biji,* reprinted in Bai Yaren, "Lüelun Li Chengzhong *Genzhai biji,*" pp. 46–55.

52 An Zhiyuan, *Qingshe yiwen,* j. 3, reprinted in Bai Yaren, "Lüetan An Zhiyuan *Qingshe yiwen,*" pp. 77–88.

53 Convenient, though abridged, sources are Zhu Yixuan, *Liaozhai zhiyi ziliao,* pp. 91–98; and Qian Zhonglian, *Qingshi jishi* 22. 16229–16236.

54 For the discovery of Li Chengzhong's version, see Barr, "The Early Qing Mystery"; and Bai Yaren, "Lüelun Li Chengzhong *Genzhai biji*"; for the discovery of An Zhiyuan's version, see Bai Yaren, "Lüetan An Zhiyuan *Qingshe yiwen.*" For additional information about these men and the Shandong loyalist circle to which they belonged, see Zhang Chongchen, "Pu Songling yu Zhucheng yimin." Barr has just discovered a seventh version by Zhejiang author Chen Yixi (1648–1709), but I have not yet seen it.

55 *Yidu xian tuzhi* 18. 46a-b. This gazetteer also notes that Zhou Lianggong assumed the office in 1662.

56 Lin Yunming (*Sunzhai fanyu,* j. 4) wrote a preface dated 1664 for Chen's literary collection entitled "Chen Lüya shi xu," but which makes clear the two had met only once or twice at this time. Barr ("Lüetan An Zhiyuan *Qingshe yiwen*") shows that Chen

Baoyao was also acquainted with Li Chengzhong and probably with An Zhiyuan as well, but neither of these men name Chen as their informant.

57 It is the first post listed in Chen Baoyao's biography in *Quanzhou fuzhi* 44. 19a. *Yidu xian tuzhi* notes that the military and maritime defense bureau was first established at the beginning of the Qing dynasty, but that it underwent a change in nomenclature in 1671.

Chen Baoyao's poetry collection was banned during the Qianlong period, apparently because it touched too much on post-Chongzhen era events, particularly relating to the Ming princes of Tang and Gui. See Wang Xuetai, "Lin Siniang gushi," p. 367.

58 See *Qingzhou fuzhi* (1709); *Qingzhou fuzhi* (1859) 11.12a-b; and *Yidu xian tuzhi* 12. 12a.

59 The problem was first raised in the late Qing by Yu Yue in his *Hudong manlu* 40. 3a-b. The question is directly posed by Nie Shiqiao and Deng Kuiying in *Gudai xiaoshuo,* p. 31.

60 Nie and Deng (*Gudai xiaoshuo,* p. 32) argue that the records show a possible relationship between the prince and local peasant rebels and that he therefore must have perished at the hands of the Manchus; Lin Siniang would therefore have died in the conquest, maybe on the same side as the local rebels. Wang Xuetai ("Lin Siniang gushi") also believes the prince fought alongside local rebels against the Qing. Mou Runsun ("Lin Siniang gushi") argues that the prince surrendered to the Manchus but that there is no evidence that he fought on the side of peasant rebels. Wang Xianming, ("*Liaozhai zhiyi* zhong de Mingdai Shandong Qinwang" 1. 96) asserts that the prince of Heng surrendered to the Manchus in 1644 and was sentenced to death three years later along with eleven other Ming princes, but he gives no sources. Qian Lianzhong (*Qingshi jishi* 24. 16233–16234) sides with *Dream of the Red Chamber;* he argues that historical records show that the prince of Heng killed several of Li Zicheng's officials and surrendered to the Qing, then was killed when rebels retook Qingzhou. In personal conversations I had in Beijing with Liu Shide during the mid 1990s, he reiterated his strong conviction that Cao Xueqin had gotten it right. The conflicting information in the primary sources suggests that even at the time no one was quite sure what had happened. This ambiguity may have contributed to the wave of ghost stories about the palace.

61 See Struve, *The Ming-Qing Conflict;* and Barr, "Pu Songling and *Liaozhai,*" pp. 120–122.

62 These tales include: "Gongsun Jiuniang" (*LZ* 4. 477–483) and "The Wild Dog" ("Yegou"; *LZ* 1. 70–71) about the Manchu suppression of the Yu Qi uprising in 1662; "The Weeping Ghosts" ("Gui ku" *LZ* 1.76–77) about the Qing reprisals against the Xie Qian rebellion of 1647; and "The Ghost Runners" ("Gui li" *LZ* 11. 1558) about the Ji'nan massacre of 1639. See Barr, "Pu Songling and *Liaozhai,*" pp. 116–119.

63 Schmitt, *Ghosts in the Middle Ages,* p. 100.

64 For a discussion of women's chaste martyrdom as an emblem of resistance to foreign invasions, see Carlitz, "Desire, Danger, and the Body."

65 Both Chen Weisong and Lin Yunming provide an explicit conversational frame for the provenance of the story. The claim that a story was heard at a social gathering is admi-

rably portrayed in "The Winsome Colonel" episode in *Dream of the Red Chamber.* On its own, the internal claim that a tale was heard by its author is not sufficient evidence to establish an "oral" provenance or circulation for the tale, because as with all literary conventions, such a claim can be easily used to subvert what it substantiates. However, the presence of a number of different versions of a story in roughly contemporaneous versions does provide convincing external evidence for oral circulation. On this phenomenon in the early Kangxi, see Barr, "The Early Qing Mystery," pp. 385–386. The seventeenth-century Lin Siniang narratives involve a rather small circle, since virtually all the major recorders of the story were personally acquainted with Wang Shizhen.

66 Ivy, *Discourses on the Vanishing,* pp. 163–164.

67 Nora, "Between Memory and History," pp. 8–9.

68 Xu Fuming, "Cong 'Lin Siniang,'" and Wai-yee Li, "Women as Emblems of Dynastic Fall," discuss the contrasts between these two deaths in further detail.

69 Trans. Hawkes, *Story of the Stone* 3. 567, chap. 78; original in Cao Xueqin, *Honglou meng* 2. 1124.

70 Clothes betraying no trace of a seam are a common sign of otherworldly status in Chinese tales of the strange.

71 Dudbridge, *Religious Experience and Lay Society,* p. 132.

72 Huntington, *Alien Kind,* pp. 99, 135–136.

73 Dudbridge, *Religious Experience and Lay Society,* p. 127.

74 Dudbridge hints at, but does not make explicit, the idea that the city of Ye's displacement by the city of Anyang may be one of the other causes for resentment attributed to the general's ghost, along with his suicide, his posthumous decapitation, and the slaying of his sons.

75 Dudbridge, *Religious Experience and Lay Society,* p. 117.

76 Based on Dudbridge's translation in ibid., 129.

77 His account of Lin Siniang is too lacking in details to draw any conclusions about the significance of the father's prison sentence. Still, the implication may be that both father and daughter suffered injustices under the former dynasty.

78 This change is the opposite of demon stories such as "The Painted Skin," ("Hua pi" *LZ* 1. 119–123) or "The White Snake" ("Baishe zhuan," in Feng Menglong, *Jingshi tongyan,* no. 28) in which a beautiful woman's true form is revealed to be that of a monster.

79 On the Xie Qian rebellion and its relationship to *Liaozhai,* see Barr, "Pu Songling and *Liaozhai zhiyi,*" pp. 112–115 and Xie Guozhen, *Mingmo Qingchu,* pp. 264–268. Zichuan, Pu Songling's home town, was a rebel stronghold. When the Manchu army stormed the city, many innocent people were put to death along with the rebels.

80 Chen Baoyao's biography (*Quanzhou fuzhi* 45. 19a) includes an account of how he rid Qingzhou of a scourge of bandits and purchased coffins for the victims. It is possible that the local reputation he acquired for pacifying the district contributed to his association with the Lin Siniang story.

81 Xu Fuming, "Cong 'Lin Siniang,'" pp. 205–209.

82 However, Lin Yunming says that he heard the story from Chen Baoyao when Chen was serving in the Jiangnan postal service circuit, rather than in Fujian. In Lin Yunming's own comments to the story, which are usually omitted from modern reprints, he defends the veracity of the story by appealing to Chen Baoyao as an upright gentleman and fellow *Landsmann* who would be incapable of making up something like this (Zhang Chao, *Yu Chu xinzhi* 5. 76).

83 Wang Shilu's heavy involvement with *By and about Women* strengthens this book's links to Shandong, even though Chen Weisong himself was from the south. In both this collection and *Occasional Chats*, Lin Siniang is said to be originally from Nanjing. The *Occasional Chats* version adds another Shandong link: a Li Wuxian from Changshan in Shandong is said to have a manuscript of Lin Siniang's poems. Li is mentioned as an informant for several tales in *Liaozhai*. See Zhou Shaoliang, "Lin Siniang gushi," p. 159.

84 See Zhang Chongchen, "Pu Songling yu Zhucheng yimin" and Barr, "The Early Qing Mystery."

85 An Zhiyuan participated in compiling the local gazetteer for Qingzhou prefecture and wrote several important works on the area's local history. See Bai Yaren, "Lüetan An Zhiyuan *Qingshe yiwen*." An's version of "Lin Siniang" underscores the local audience for the tale by adding the possessive *wu* (my, our) when he first mentions Qingzhou, and by specifying that Lin Siniang's volume of poems circulated among the Qingzhou elite. Lin Siniang herself is from Fujian in this story. As in Lin Yunming's story, she tells Chen Baoyao that she is from his hometown.

86 Lu Jianzeng, *Guochao shanzuo shichao* 60. 6b. Lu's source for both Lin Siniang's poem and the framing narrative is Wang Shizhen, *Chibei outan*.

87 The typology also obscures the relationship between the accounts in *The Magician* and those in *Notes from Genzhai* and *Qingzhou Anecdotes* by authors with Shandong loyalist credentials. All three versions give related names for a ghost maid who accompanies Lin Siniang ("Dong'er" or "Dong gu"), and there are also some plot resemblances. For these reasons alone, we should not accept the premise of two entirely separate regional branches for the story.

88 "Shang Wang Ruanting neihan" in *Yikuilou xuangao*, *j.* 9.

89 See my "Disappearing Verses," pp. 98–108.

90 "Gufan zhi" in Wang Shizhen, *Chibei outan* 22. 533, no. 1039. This extract is also reprinted in the *Yidu xian tuzhi* entry on the prince of Heng's palace.

91 Official documents dated 1661–1662 pertaining to the disposal of the estates of the former Ming palaces in Shandong, including those of the princes of Heng and De, are reprinted in *Qingdai dang'an shiliao*, pp. 205–220, 226–227.

92 Cf. Zhang Chao's comment in *Yu Chu xinzhi* 5. 92: "How could Lin Siniang have changed shape like that? Is it true, then, that a wronged soul can become a vengeful ghost?"

93 The only difference in wording is that Pu Songling gives "*li ruo*" whereas Wang Shizhen gives "*li bo*."

94 A common allusion to a king of Shu, who, legend has it, turned into a whippoorwill after his death. This bird, whose cry sounds mournful, was said to weep until it spit blood. Here the allusion simply means the prince is dead.

95 Qian Zhonglian, *Qingshi jishi* 22. 16, 234, suggests that *"haiguo"* refers to Taiwan, but this seems farfetched. In my view it is much more likely to refer to the coastal region of Shandong, since Qingzhou abutted the sea. I take lines 3–5 as a flashback with Lin Siniang's ghost remembering the death of her prince and the Manchu conquest in 1644, rather than as a description of the state of the empire in 1662, when she is supposed to have written the poem.

96 Literally, "loudly sing songs from the Pear Garden." The Pear Garden is the site where court entertainers trained during the reign of the Tang Emperor Xuanzong, but became a common allusion for court entertainers and for entertainers in general.

97 The corresponding line in *Occasional Chats* is "The palace has been locked tight; but I remember the past." Li Zhen's *Jiandeng yuhu* has a similar couplet attributed to a female revenant: "Ruined ramparts gleam amid yellow reeds in the evening sun / Emerald grass and chilly mist lock in the former palace." Another similar couplet appears in a verse credited to a palace-lady revenant in Wang Duanshu, *Mingyuan shiwei:* "How many autumns have passed deep within the sealed palace? / My dusty cosmetic case is locked and cannot bear my sorrow."

98 Her musical performances are overheard by other members of the household, who are similarly affected and shed tears.

99 An exception is "An Autumn Night's Visit" in Li Zhen, *Jiandeng yuhua.*

100 Translated and discussed by Yim Chi-hung, "The Poetics of Historical Memory," p. 119 (modified); original in Yuan Zhen, *Yuan Zhen ji,* p. 169. Another example is the Tang tale "Dugu Mu" (*TPGJ* 342. 2709–2716) about a man, the eighth-generation grandson of a Sui general, who is taken to the tomb of a Sui dynasty princess who had perished during the fall of the dynasty. Here she does say that she died in an attempted rape when pillaging soldiers stormed the palace, but when the man queries her on events and people of the last reign period of the Sui, the text skips her account, contenting itself with the observation that what she said was "mostly the same as the *Sui History.*" The princess is more forthcoming about her past a bit later in the tale.

101 For example, one entry involves a nun who had formerly served in the Ming imperial palace and who always "talked about past events in the palace." She recounts a few poignant details about the flight of the palace ladies after the Chongzhen Emperor's suicide. See Chen Weisong, *Furen ji,* 1b.

102 In *Remembrances,* Owen describes composing a *huaigu* as a ritual act and emphasizes the "rememberer remembered" as a major theme in Chinese literature. I see the interest in remembering as an active verb predominating over any idea of memory as a reified noun in Chinese writings on the past.

103 Qu You, *Jiandeng xinhua,* p. 45. This is the kind of virtuoso tale that aims to show off the poetic abilities of the author. From the author's point of view, then, the reason it would be inappropriate to sing an old tune is that it would deprive him of an opportunity to versify.

104 Wei Guan, "Zhou Qin xing ji," *TPGJ* 489. 4018–4023.

105 Wai-yee Li, "Women as Emblems of Dynastic Fall," p. 134. Ghosts do shed blood in other *Liaozhai* tales. The weirdest is "Xiangchun" (*LZ* 10. 1325), in which an underworld ghost punctures her vein to make the blood flow as proof that she is ready to accompany the mortal protagonist back to the world of the living. See also my discussion of "Gongsun Jiuniang" below.

106 Jonathan Hay, "The Wilderness Environment."

107 Kong Shangren, *Taohua shan,* supplementary scene 20, p. 135. In this scene, the terrifying mutilated apparitions of those slain in battle usher in the consoling vision of the emperor and empress's apotheosis.

108 In Zhang Chao, *Yu Chu xinzhi* 5. 91.

109 The retiring hall was a space where a prince's ladies could accompany him; the choice of this particular building also hints that the spectral writer of the verse is female.

110 Li Chengzhong, *Genzhai biji,* reprinted in Bai Yaren, "Lüelun Li Chengzhong *Genzhai biji.*"

111 The major discrepancy is that the *Notes from Genzhai* poem reads "eighteen years"; *Liaozhai* gives "seventeen years."

112 *By and about Women* includes several poignant anecdotes about finding poems on ruined walls said to be by Ming palace ladies.

113 There may be an implied connection here with the unlocking of the palace and the disintegration of the clothes on the racks.

114 Li Chengzhong, *Genzhai biji,* reprinted in Bai Yaren, "Lüelun Li Chengzhong *Genzhai biji.*"

115 Chen Baoyao's biography in *Quanzhou fuzhi,* j. 45 mentions that he did indeed resign his position in Qingzhou on account of his mother's death.

116 One puzzling anecdote in the entry has no counterpart in any of the other Lin Siniang versions and seems misplaced. Following Lin Siniang's visit to the brother, on the Lantern Festival, a girl emerges from the inner quarters of Chen Baoyao's official residence and lectures his clerk(s) on their moral duty. Her identity is not revealed but her hand looks like the bark of a tree, which seems to suggest she is a tree spirit rather than a palace-lady ghost. If so, there might some connection to the ancient pine tree at the site mentioned by Wang Shizhen in his description of the ruins of the prince of Heng's palace in *Occasional Chats.* It is possible, however, that two entirely different girls/spirits are intended.

117 This distinguishes the *Notes from Genzhai* account from the other seventeenth-century ones. Even in *The Magician*'s treatment, the spirit is propitiated and a close friendship between ghost and official ensues.

118 For examples of this motif in *Liaozhai,* see "Liansuo" and "Wu Qiuyue."

119 See, inter alia, "Liu Fangxuan" (*TPGJ* 345. 2731), "Taiyuan Yiniang" (Hong Mai, *Yijian zhi (dingzhi)* 9. 608–609). For other classical versions of this tale, see Tan Zhengbi, *Sanyan liangpai ziliao.* This story is the basis for Feng Menglong's vernacular retelling, "Yang Siwen Yanshan feng guren," *Gujin xiaoshuo,* no. 24. For a discussion of these and other instances of ghost writing on walls, see my "Disappearing Verses."

120 "Dujuan xing" in Chen Zilong, *Chen Zilong shiji* 1. 299–300. I have been influenced by Kang-i Sun Chang's translation in *The Late Ming Poet*, pp. 106–107.

121 Based on Wang Yi's commentary to "Tian wen" in *Chu ci*. For a discussion of this commentary and the fictitiousness of the story, see Hawkes, *Songs of the South*, p. 123.

122 "Questions to Heaven" ("Wen cangtian") is also the name of the song that the Master of Ceremonies composes in the last scene of Kong Shangren's *Taohua shan*, scene 40, pp. 263–264. In Wu Weiye's loyalist play *Reaching Heaven Terrace (Tongtian tai)*, scene 1, p. 1390, the protagonist passes by the ruins of Emperor Han Wudi and jointly mourns his own Liang dynasty together with the previous Han dynasty. He says: "Here I am at Reaching Heaven Terrace, but where is Heaven? Let me question him a moment."

123 Chang, *The Late Ming Poet*, p. 107.

124 Cf. Ricoeur (*Time and Narrative*, 3. 188): "Horror attaches to events that must never be forgotten. It constitutes the ultimate ethical motivation for the history of victims. . . . Every other form of individuation is the counterpart to a work of explanation that connects things together. But horror isolates events by making them incomparable, incomparably unique, uniquely unique."

125 Schmitt, *Ghosts in the Middle Ages*, pp. 5–6.

126 In "Chimerical Early Modernity," Struve draws upon Mannheim's theory of "cohorts" to distinguish a "conquest generation." Pu Songling was born too late to belong to this cohort. In identifying with a traumatic historical event, young adulthood is apparently the most decisive time in an individual's life-cycle, exactly Pu Songling's age during the Yu Qi rebellion.

127 On the historical background of the Yu Qi rebellion and its impact on Pu Songling, see Xie Guozhen, *Mingmo Qingchu*, pp. 268–272; Nie Shiqiao and Deng Kuiying, *Gudai xiaoshuo*, pp. 36–41; and Barr, "Pu Songling and *Liaozhai zhiyi*," pp. 115–119. Nie and Deng (p. 37) mention that Pu Songling's examiner Shi Runzhang was forced to resign from office because of the incident and that another friend of his was imprisoned for two years. Supposedly anyone who had so much as exchanged name cards with Yu Qi was arrested and executed.

128 A common allusion to Chang Hong, a loyal statesman of antiquity who was unjustly murdered. His blood was said to have crystallized into jasper upon spilling to the ground as a sign of his martyrdom.

129 The niece is his sister's daughter, for whom, in the patrilineal structure of Chinese kin relations, he would have been considered less responsible than for his brother's daughter. Complicating the relationship between uncle and niece is that she had been brought up in his household after the early death of her mother and had only returned to her father's house after she came of age. So the scholar from Laiyang has already previously served generously in loco parentis for this niece.

130 He objects that she has her own father, so why must he be involved? He also objects that the living cannot serve as matchmakers to the dead.

131 Earlier in the story, a living cousin of hers moved her father's coffin away.

132 The arrangement is that he spends nights with her in the village of ghosts and days at home in the ordinary world.

133 Another unusual example is "Yueniang ji" (Liu Fu, *Qingsuo gaoyi, bieji* 3. 218), where the poverty-stricken interior of the ghost's dwelling is meant to show the inadequacy of her burial.

134 Freud, "The Uncanny." When Jiuniang first walks into the niece's cottage and perceives the scholar from Laiyang, the niece prevents her from fleeing by saying: "You don't have to avoid him. He's my uncle, not a stranger."

135 Based on Arthur Waley's "The Graveyard" in his *Translations from the Chinese,* p. 33; original reprinted in Shen Deqian, comp., *Gushi yuan qianzhu,* p. 95.

136 Here I distinguish Buddhist-influenced narratives in which someone visits the hells of the underworld from ghost stories, which imagine the living quarters of the dead inside a grave or graveyard.

137 Quoted in Nie and Deng, *Gudai xiaoshuo,* p. 39; original in *Laiyang xianzhi,* volume on military affairs, 5b-6a.

138 The legendary liaison of a king and a goddess took place at "Sunlit Terrace"; along with the clouds and rain, it signals lovemaking. For a similar line in a ghost poem, see "Dugu Mu" (*TPGJ* 342. 2711).

139 My second stanza is influenced by Barr's translation in "Pu Songling and *Liaozhai zhiyi,*" p. 118.

140 For further examples, see "Dugu Mu" (*TPGJ* 342. 2711), "Zhang Yunrong" (*TPGJ* 69. 430), and "Yueniang ji" (Liu Fu, *Qingsuo gaoyi, bieji* 3. 220).

141 Qu You, *Jiandeng xinhua,* p. 45. Tang Xianzu also uses this metaphor in *Peony Pavilion* when Liu Mengmei agrees to resurrect Du Liniang and she retorts: "Then my hopes in you are fulfilled. In cold secluded vale / you urge a flower to bloom through the night." On the sexual nature of this recurrent imagery in the play, see Swatek, "Plum and Portrait," p. 137.

142 The loss of Jiuniang's virginity —through the shedding of blood and the violence to her person, through the general association of weddings and death—replicates in some way the original traumatic situation (her mother's death and her suicide). It therefore acts as a triggering mechanism for "traumatic memory," according to van der Kolk and van der Hart's theory ("The Intrusive Past," p. 163) that when one element of a traumatic experience is evoked, all other elements follow automatically. Recounting the story of her death to the scholar does not provide Jiuniang any relief but instead seems to drive her to chant the poems, through which she reproduces again the moment of her own death. The abruptness of her opening the casket in the final lines also suggests the automatic behavior van der Kolk and van der Hart refer to. Caruth (*Trauma,* p. 5) stresses the "surprising literality and non-symbolic nature of traumatic dreams and flashbacks" but in "Jiuniang," symbolic displacement is a basic feature of lyric poetry, the heightened linguistic space in which she can act out the symptoms of trauma.

143 This stock speech is again filled with formulaic phrases, as in "Dugu Mu" (*TPGJ* 342.2711).

144 For a Tang example of a ghost raising a sleeve before disappearing, see "Tang Xuan qi" (*TPGJ* 332. 2635–2638); for early Ming examples, see "Qiuxi fang Pipa ting ji" in Li Zhen, *Jiandeng yuhua,* p. 189; and Ye Ziqi, *Cao Muzi* 4. 80.

145 The story, set in 841, is "Xu sheng" (*TPGJ* 350. 2768–2771). On this purge, the Sweet Dew Incident of 835–836, see Twitchett, *The Cambridge History of China* 3.1, pp. 654–659, especially p. 657. The incident, which involved the failure of an imperially supported assassination attempt against eunuchs usurping power at court, not only resulted in the executions of the chief conspirators (loyal subjects in Confucian historiography), but led to the mass murder of a large number of innocent people.

146 Kong Shangren, "*Taohua shan* benmo," *Taohua shan*, p. 6.

147 Garber, *Shakespeare's Ghost Writers*, p. 130.

148 The set phrase in Classical Chinese for posthumous handwriting is "the hand's moisture" *(shouze)*, which underscores the intimate connection of writing with the body that produced it. The locus classicus is from *Liji* ("Yuzao," in Ruan Yuan et al., eds., *Shisanjing* 2. 1484): "A son may not read his late father's writings because they still bear 'the moisture of his hand'; a man may not drink from his late mother's cup and bowl because they still bear the 'breath of her mouth.'"

149 Owen, *Remembrances*, p. 23.

150 Nie and Deng, *Gudai xiaoshuo*, p. 38.

151 Ibid., pp. 39–40.

152 Barr, "Pu Songling and *Liaozhai zhiyi*," p. 119.

153 For another example of how shared imagery helps bridge comment and main story in *Liaozhai*, see my *Historian of the Strange*, p. 106.

154 Ricoeur, *Time and Narrative*, vol. 3, p. 100.

Chapter 4: Ghosts and Theatricality

Epigraph. From Michael Goldman, *The Actor's Freedom*, p. 9.

1 Yuan Yuling, "*Fenxiang ji* xu." In Chen and Ye, *Zhongguo lidai julun*, p. 229. On Yuan Yuling, see Deng Changfeng, *Ming Qing xiqu kaolüe xubian*, pp. 99–104. For statistics on the increase of new plays in the Wanli era, see Song Junhua, *Zhongguo gudai xiju fushi*, p. 105.

2 Li Yu, "Xuan ju," in *Xianqing ouji* 2.61.

3 Some plays have survived only in later manuscript copies; others survive in multiple printed and manuscript versions; but a huge number of plays mentioned by title in various records have been lost altogether.

4 Xu Xianglin, *Zhongguo guixi*, p. 47.

5 Guo Yingde, *Ming Qing chuanqi shi*, p. 239.

6 Zhang Dai, "Da Yuan Tuoan," in *Zhang Dai shiwen ji*, p. 230. On Zhang Dai's friendship with Yuan Yuling, see Hu Yimin, *Zhang Dai yanjiu*, p. 191.

7 Zhang Dai, "Da Yuan Tuoan," in *Zhang Dai shiwen ji*, p. 230.

8 See Tanaka Issei, "The Social and Historical Context of Ming-Ch'ing Local Drama," pp. 143–160; and his *Zhongguo xiju shi*.

9 Zhang Dai, "Mulian xi" in *Tao'an mengyi* 6. 52–53. Zhang Dai doesn't mention when the performance took place, but says that his uncle had a large stage built, selected the cast himself, and that the audience was terrified. On the Mulian operas and their

terrifying aspects, see David Johnson, ed. *Ritual Opera, Operatic Ritual,* especially his "Actions Speak Louder than Words."

10 His memoirs mention one literati friend whose obsessions included a passion for ghost operas, loud percussion music, and football, all of which presumably fall into the category of "noisy excitement." "Qi Zhixiang" in Zhang Dai, *Tao'an mengyi* 4. 39.

11 Li Yu, "Xuan ju," in *Xianqing ouji* 2.60.

12 Li Yu, "Jie huangtang," in *Xianqing ouji* 1.12.

13 Davis and Postlewait, "Theatricality," in *idem,* ed. *Theatricality,* p. 2.

14 See Yung, *A Critical Study of Han-tan chi,* Part 2, Chapter 1, on the adaptability of various scenes in plays to different performance contexts. Liao Ben (*Zhongguo gudai juchang shi,* p. 63) argues that with the decline of public theaters, from the mid to late Ming, banquets in private settings were the main performance venue for secular theater. Private performances were mainly held in the halls or gardens of people's houses, but also included boats and other open air settings. See Guangren Shen, "Theatre Performance During the Ming Dynasty"; and *Elite Theatre in Ming China,* pp. 129–143. For the effect of shifting performance venues on the conception of the theater in this period, see Volpp, *Worldly Stage,* chap. 2.

15 In one of those uncanny coincidences, the entry for *fantôme* ("ghost") that appears in Pavis, *Dictionnaire du Théâtre* (pp. 165–166), which notes the theater's affinity for ghosts and illusions, has mysteriously vanished from the English translation, *Dictionary of the Theatre,* although it is still cross-referenced in several entries.

16 Liu Chuhua, "Ming Qing chuanqi zhong de *hun dan,*" p. 73.

17 In a coma: Zheng Guangzu, *The Disembodied Soul;* as the spirit of a portrait, Wu Bing, *Lady in the Painting;* as a reflection in water: Fan Wenruo, *An Intoxicating Dream;* as a reflection in the metal surface of a cup: Wu Weiye, *Spring in Nanjing (Moling chun).* Although ghosts frequently enter and exit during the dream of a mortal protagonist onstage, living souls who leave their bodies during a dream do not assume the *hun dan* role. For example, in *Peony Pavilion,* the *hun dan* designation is used only during Du Liniang's ghost scenes, and not during the famous dream sequence in the garden. On the differences between "living" dream souls and "dead" souls in Chinese theater, see Liao Tengye, *Zhongguo mengxi yanjiu,* chap. 5.

18 Wu Yiyi and Qian Yi, *Wu Wushan sanfu,* scene 26, 1. 83a-b; on ghosts as "copies," see Garber, *Shakespeare's Ghost Writers,* pp. 15–16; my *Shared Dreams,* pp. 162–163; and Tina Lu, *Persons, Roles, and Minds,* p. 118.

19 The *hun dan* is not listed as a separate entry in modern encyclopedias or dictionaries on drama; *Zhongguo dabaike quanshu: Xiqu quyi* (p. 57) mentions the *hun dan* (or *gui hu dan*) as a regional specialty of Sichuan opera.

20 When the heroine's ghost makes her entrance in Guan Hanqing's, *Injustice to Dou E,* the stage directions in the *Guming jia* and *Gujin mingju hexuan* editions read: *dan hun shang* and then refer to her simply as *dan* for the remainder of the scene. Zang Maoxun's edition (*Yuanqu xuan* 4. 1512) reverses the order of the words so the directions read: *hun dan shang,* but the usage is not uniform even in this anthology. In

scene 3 of Zheng Tingyu's *Flowers in the Rear Courtyard (Houting hua)*, the stage directions in Zang's edition read "the dan's soul enters" *(dan hunzi shang)* (*Yuanqu xuan*, 4: 42); the anonymous *Emerald Peach Flower (Bitao hua)* uses the appellation *zheng dan* for both the living woman and her ghost. In fact, late Ming and early Qing southern drama play texts are similarly flexible, though *hun dan* is the term used with the most regularity.

21 For the phantom's first entrance, the *Gu mingjia* edition (scene 2, 8b) reads: "The principal heroine enters costumed differently as a disembodied soul"; thereafter the stage directions refer to her as *hun dan*. The same wording is followed in the other two late Ming editions of the play, *Gu zaju* and *Yuanqu xuan*.

22 The term *hunzi* is only used in a theatrical context.

23 Liu Chuhua ("Ming Qing chuanqi zhong de *hun dan*," p. 73), argues that based on a rough estimate of all Song and Yuan play *titles* (rather than extant plays), female ghosts outnumbered male ghosts even in the Song and Yuan theater, but she still concedes that the disparity grows even larger in the Ming.

24 Myrhe ("Appearances of Ghosts in Northern Drama," p. 248, n.1) suggests that "in earlier dramas martial heroism and loyalty were ascendant, while in later productions and collections ghosts were more often female and tended to have romantic as opposed to political concerns. If this is primarily the result of a shift of tastes over time then the proliferation of female ghosts in later productions is coherent with an increasing interest in romantic themes in the Ming and Qing." Sieber argues that the late Ming interest in romance is evident in the selection of which Yuan plays to anthologize for publication and that late Ming editors of Yuan plays "select [ed] romantic plots at significantly higher rates" than previous editors had (*Theaters of Desire*, p. 116).

Tanaka Issei (*Zhongguo xiju shi*, pp. 187, 193) sees a change in late Ming Jiangnan from hero-centered plays to wronged female ghost plays, which he argues formed the core of the earliest southern drama *(nanxi)*. However, since Tanaka is not interested in literati plays, his history touches only briefly on *Peony Pavilion* (pp. 219–220, 235), which he classifies under "romance," and whose ghost content he does not remark on. He ignores the phantom-heroine plays composed in *Peony Pavilion*'s wake that I focus on in this chapter.

25 For the observation that the *dan* and *sheng* did not engage in the kind of doubling of parts that other role types routinely did, see Lu Eting, *Kunju yanchu shigao*, p. 66. As Kong Shangren explains (*Xiao hulei*, "Se mu" 1. 15a-b): "The *sheng* and *dan* are the main roles. As a rule, they can't be assigned indiscriminately to other characters. All other roles can be 'borrowed' so that one role can be used for dozens of characters."

26 The underworld scene is 23 ("Ming pan"); the revenant scenes are scene 27 ("Hun you"), scene 28 ("You gou"), scene 30 ("Huan nao"), and scene 32 ("Ming shi").

27 See Swatek, *Peony Pavilion Onstage* for this process.

28 In "My Year of Peonies," I discuss the staging of ghosts and resurrection in three productions of the play in 1999–2000.

29 Dorothy Ko, *Teachers of the Inner Chambers,* chap. 2; Widmer, "Xiaoqing's Literary Legacy;" Hua Wei, *Ming Qing funü zhi xiqu;* and my "Shared Dreams."

30 Shen Jing's revision was never published and has been lost. The extant late Ming revisions are Feng Menglong, *Fengliu meng;* Zang Maoxun, *Huanhun ji;* and Xu Rixi, *Shuoyuan shanding Mudan ting.*

31 Swatek, *Peony Pavilion Onstage,* chaps. 2 and 3. On Zang's revision, see also Idema, "Zang Maoxun as a Publisher."

32 Meng Chengshun, *Jiao Hong ji,* scenes 39 and 40.

33 Many examples are reprinted in Xu Fuming, *Mudan ting yanjiu,* section 4.

34 Wu Bing, *Huazhong ren,* scene 29, 2. 33a.

35 Sieber, *Theaters of Desire,* p. 75. She also argues (p. 79) that Tang Xianzu had access to "the same stash of manuscripts" that Zang Maoxun used to compile *Yuanqu xuan.*

36 Zhuang Yifu, *Gudian xiqu cunmu,* p. 54, lists two lost chuanqi versions of *The Disembodied Soul* as well as adaptations into other dramatic and prosimetric genres, none of which survive.

37 Fan Wenruo, *"Menghua han xu"* under his sobriquet Wunong xunya. For an annotated version see, Chen and Ye, eds. *Zhongguo lidai julun,* pp. 224–225.

38 Wu Bing, *Huazhong ren,* scene 14, 1. 45b.

39 Ibid., scene 16 ("She hun"), 1. 53b.

40 Such a technique is used in an early twentieth-century Peking opera play text of *Flowering Red Plum (Hongmei ge)* in *Xikao,* no. 242. Stage directions read: *"dai guilian."*

41 Wu Bing, *Huazhong ren,* scene 15, 1. 49a-b. Shen Jing, *Boxiao ji,* scenes 24–25, also features an exorcist charlatan who dons multiple "false" ghost masks *(jia gui mian).*

42 Xu Zichang, *Shuihu ji,* scene 31, 2. 54a. In the scene, Sanlang protests that he didn't kill her, so why has she come to find him and not her murderer? And what, he asks, has made her decide to copy *Peony Pavilion* and become a revenant, manifesting herself to him? Two other vengeful female ghosts in contemporaneous plays are Guiying in Wang Yufeng, *Fenxiang ji* and Li Huiniang in Zhou Chaojun, *Hongmei ji.* All three stayed in the repertory, indicating the appeal of this theme.

43 Wu Bing, *Xiyuan ji,* scene 26, 2. 22a.

44 Cited in Ye Changhai, *Zhongguo xijuxue shi,* p. 302. *Rou shi* is a play on *rou shen*— "fleshly body," a term of Buddhist origin.

45 See especially John Hay's pioneering essay, "The Human Body as a Microcosmic Source."

46 From *Shishuo xinyu* 7, no. 16, pp. 220–221. On this locution, see my "Notes of Flesh."

47 For example, Cheng Yuwen's preface to *Shengming zaju* (*Xiqu xuba* 1. 462) mentions "traces of the dead being made to live on stage"; Xu Shijun's preface to his play about Xiaoqing *(Chunbo ying)* asserts he is transmitting her story so that she will not truly die; Zhuo Renyue's poem on this play imagines the "fragrant soul" of Xiaoqing descending from Heaven and lending her blood and tears as ink to the playwright so that he might "give voice to her sobs" (discussed in Shi Kaiti, "Tiaodeng xiankan Feng Xiaoqing" and translated in Swatek, "Two Feng Xiaoqing Dramas"); Wang Siren's

preface to *Xixiang ji* (*Xiqu xuba* 2. 654) notes that each line of the playwright's seems to raise the dead and make them come to life before our eyes.

48 Barthes, "Baudelaire's Theatre," p. 26.

49 On changes in the staging of *kunqu*, see, inter alia, Swatek, *Peony Pavilion Onstage;* and Lu Eting, *Kunju yanchu shigao.* Few of the seventeenth-century revenant scenes stayed in the later performing repertory; most do not appear in the eighteenth- and nineteenth-century anthologies of scene excerpts, such as *Zhui baiqiu* or *Shenyin jiangu lu,* which theater historians think register changes introduced through performance and reflect the preferences and repertory of the theatergoing audiences and amateur performers.

50 Cf. the definition in Pavis, *Dictionary of the Theatre:* "Stage directions include any text (usually written by the playwright but sometimes added by editors. . . .) which is not spoken by the actors and is meant to clarify the understanding and mode of presentation for the reader." Scene titles, tune titles, musical modes, and indications of the type of poem to be recited should also be considered "stage directions" in Chinese drama but will not be discussed in this chapter as part of the staging apparatus. In modern Chinese, much of this is subsumed under the term *paichang.* The term itself is an old one and appears in premodern sources, but its elaboration and theorization is a modern phenomenon. See Xu Zihan, "Ming chuanqi paichang sanyaosu," p. 16.

51 West, "Text and Ideology," p. 351. McLaren (*Chinese Popular Culture,* p. 50) makes a similar argument for an early Ming commercial imprint of Yuan drama, the famous 1498 Bejing edition of *The Western Wing.* "With complete dialogue, stage directions, arias and illustrations on each folio it is thus possible to 'read' the play as one would a narrative, with full understanding of the continuity of the plot."

52 Pavis (*Dictionary of the Theater,* p. 356) attributes this change to the rise of bourgeois drama with "the character becom[ing] more than just a role, taking on individual and naturalistic traits" as well as with the playwright's "awareness of the need for mise-en-scène. . . . The stage directions then have to do not only with coordinates of space and time, but mainly with the character's interiority and the mood of the stage. This information is so precise and subtle that it requires a narrative voice. Here the theatre approaches the novel."

53 Stage directions in medieval English drama were in Latin; for the process through which the Elizabethans developed the beginnings of a modern language of stage directions, see McJannet, *The Voice of Elizabethan Stage Directions.*

54 Goldman, *The Actor's Freedom,* p. 35.

55 Although modern gaslight or electric lighting was not introduced until the late nineteenth century, Shen ("Theater Performance during the Ming," pp.188–189) notes that artificial illumination by lantern or torch was common in late Ming productions since plays were often staged at night or in dark interior spaces, and lighting was perceived to contribute to the theatrical effect. Even curtains, both for concealing and revealing (as with a scrim), and the alternation of darkness and light to create sudden appearance and disappearance and to convey a magical atmosphere, seem to have been used

on special occasions. See Zhang Dai's description (*Tao'an mengyi* 5. 49) of a spectacular production of "Emperor Minghuang's Trip to the Moon" ("Liu Huiji nüxi"); translated in Fei, *Chinese Theories of Theater,* pp. 71–72.

56 Zhou Yibai, "Zhongguo xiqu de shangxia chang," pp. 184–186. Zhou was undoubtedly influenced by Qi Rushan's essay "Shangxia chang," which listed the multiple types of entrances and exits current in Peking opera.

57 Qi Rushan defines a "stealthy exit" in Peking opera as an informal one.

58 See Act 4 of Guan Hanqing, *Dou E yuan,* for the use of the empty exit to convey the phantom heroine's appearance and disappearance. In Peking opera, an actor moves upstage and turns his back on the audience during an empty exit. Upstage is referred to as the inner stage *(neichang)* and is demarcated from downstage (the outer stage or *waichang*) by a set of table and chairs. See Hsü, *Chinese Conception of the Theater;* and Zhou Yibai, "Zhongguo xiqu de shangxia chang," p. 186.

59 Gu and Wang, *Yuanqu shici* (3. 283–284) define a *shan* exit as a rushed one. In *West Garden,* the two are used in tandem, as the phantom heroine "gives a ghostly wail and makes a rushed lightning exit" (Wu Bing, *Xiyuan,* scene 29, 2. 34b).

60 Fan Wenruo, *Menghua han,* scene 15, 1.44a; scene 17, 1.53a.

61 Inter alia: Wang Anqi, *Mingdai chuanqi zhi juchang;* Liao Ben, *Zhongguo gudai juchang shi,* p. 64; Zhou Yibai, "Zhongguo juchang shi."

62 For Ming usages of *xifang,* see Liao Ben, *Zhongguo gudai xiju shi,* p. 64; *Pipa ji* uses *houfang* (cited in Zhou Yibai, "Zhongguo juchang shi," pp. 185–186). For *neichang* as offstage, see Fan Wenruo, *Menghua han,* scene 34, 2. 59a, which includes these stage directions: *wai ru neichang jie,* having previously announced *"laofu ru nei chulai."*

63 Zhu Quan, *Taihe zhengyin pu,* 3. 54–55.

64 Liao Ben, *Zhongguo gudai juchang shi,* pp. 49–50.

65 Che Wenming, *Ershi shiji xiqu wenwu,* p. 35.

66 On the use of the left doorway for entering and the right for exiting, see Zhou Yibai, "Zhongguo juchang shi," pp. 482–485. Zhou is extrapolating from Peking opera practice but cites a reference to "entering the ghost doorway" *(shang gui men)* from Li Dou's eighteenth-century *Yangzhou huafang lu.* Idema and West *(Chinese Theater 1100–1450)* assume that the "ghost doorways" the prince describes, which they translate as "paths to ghost doors," were "double doorways."

67 Liao Ben, *Zhongguo gudai juchang shi,* p. 64; Wang Anqi, *Mingdai chuanqi zhi juchang,* p. 161. In *The Chinese Conception of the Theater* (p. 486), Hsü emphasizes that the openings that provided stage entrance and exit never represented actual doors and that, at least in Peking opera, actors mime crossing the threshold and going through a door into a room after making their entrance. Crossing through the ghost doorway does not on its own signify entering or exiting a room.

68 As far as I know, although entrances and exits are marked in some plays in our only Yuan imprint, stage doors are not mentioned. The *Mowangguan* manuscripts are considered more reliable as an index for Yuan practices than Ming imprints such as Zang's *Yuanqu xuan.*

69 Tanaka Issei, *Zhongguo xiju shi,* p. 121.

70 Wang Guowei was in turn influenced by early twentieth-century scholarship on the ritual origins of Greek drama.

71 Tanaka Issei has dedicated himself to this area of study, combining ethnography with history. New research in the 1990s on *nuoxi* and the history of the material remains of theatrical culture, such as manuscripts, steles, and tomb décor have also reconfirmed the strong interconnection between ritual and social functions for Chinese theater.

72 Riley, *Chinese Theatre and the Actor in Performance,* p. 143: "The most striking aspect of Chinese performance is the analogy of theatre play to the afterworld, or world of the dead as world of 'other.'"

73 Zhang Dai, "Guo jianmen," in *Tao'an mengyi* 7. 69–70.Wang Anqi (*Mingdai chuanqi zhi juchang,* p. 153) argues that courtesan establishments during the Ming were not equipped with permanent stages, and that the stage space there would have resembled that of banquet performances in private households.

74 Carlson, *Places of Performance,* p. 131.

75 Wu Bing, *Xiyuan ji,* scene 23, 2. 15a-b.

76 Tang Xianzu, *Mudan ting,* p. 187. In scene 23 (p. 122), the stage directions instruct the underworld judge to "make a low whistle toward the ghost door" to summon Du Liniang's ghost, who is immediately led onstage by a clown playing one of the judge's ghost assistants. Here the ghost door is quite literally that—the entry way through which ghosts enter the underworld courtroom.

77 Marginal comment to the original scene 17 ("Gui bian") in *Guben xiqu* I 1. 46.

78 The rewrite is entitled "Jianxiaoge *xin'gai Hongmei ji* di shiqi zhe" and therefore attributed to Yuan Yuling (Jianxiaoge is Yuan's studio name). It is possible that Yuan had done a revision of the whole play, but only this scene survives. It is also possible that this is a false attribution. The Wanli edition (*Guben xiqu* I) prints both the original and rewrite of scene 17. Both the "general comments" appended to the scene and the "general comments" in the prolegomena to this edition strenuously argue that the rewrite, rather than the original of this scene, should be performed. The rewrite replaces the original altogether in a revised and abridged late Ming edition of the play, which was published anonymously under the title *Dangui ji.*

79 Zhou Chaojun, *Hongmei ji,* scene 17, p. 88. (Unless otherwise indicated all page references to this play are keyed to the 1985 edition.)

80 Ibid., scene 13 ("You hui"), p. 60.

81 Song Junhua, *Zhongguo gudai xiju fushi,* p. 187. Song emphasizes the symbolic properties of color and material in Chinese costume and is careful to distinguish between different contexts and historical periods, but unfortunately he does not fully explore the meanings assigned to individual colors.

82 Riley, *Chinese Theatre and the Actor in Performance,* p. 64. According to *Zhongguo dabaike quanshu: Xiqu quyi,* p. 44, condemned prisoners being led to execution and their judges wore red on the stage to keep such ill-fortune at bay.

83 The title of this painting, *Gui qu,* is usually mistranslated into English as *Ghost*

Amusement because of its witty portrayal of ghosts. Although one meaning of *qu* is "amusement" and a play on words may be involved here, the phrase *gui qu* is a set Buddhist term denoting one of five paths of existence.

84 *Chunfang pu,* p. 75. The lover's knot alludes to the final couplet of the Six Dynasties *yuefu* "The Song of Little Su": "Where shall we tie our lover's knot? Beneath cypress and pine at West Mound."

85 In private conversation in 2000, Xu Shuofang suggested that the color red here expressed pity for Li Huiniang, but Lu Eting suggested that it was intended to ward off malign influences *(bi xie).* Lu Xun ("Nü diao," p. 617) also mentions that the hanged female ghost in Mulian performances of his youth was costumed in red.

86 Zhou Chaojun, *Hongmei ji,* p. 88.

87 The most common phrase is *gui sheng*—ghost sound. I follow Birch, (Tang Xianzu, *The Peony Pavilion,* p.151) in translating it as "wailing," but we do not know exactly what a ghost sound would have sounded like on the Ming stage.

88 For example, in Tang Xianzu, *Mudan ting* (scene 28, p. 153), right before Du Liniang's ghost enters, the wind blows out Liu Mengmei's lamp; in *Houting hua* (Act 3, p. 939), the *hun dan* knocks on the male lead's door to borrow a light and twice blows it out; the same device is borrowed in Shen Jing's southern drama adaptation, *Taofu ji,* scene 18, pp. 559–560. In both cases, the phantom is trying to get the male lead to open the door and let her in, but the stage business still underscores the ghostly connection between wind and flickering lamps.

89 The best example is Guan Hanqing, *Dou E yuan,* Act 4 (*Yuanqu xuan* 4: 1512–1513), where there is lots of stage business for the ghost to manipulate the light, making it now grow dim, now grow bright, until finally her father realizes there must be a ghost involved. In Wu Bing, *Huazhong ren* (scene 21, 11a), when the phantom heroine runs into the male lead carrying a lamp, she immediately extinguishes it. In Wu Bing, *Xiyuan ji* (scene 29, 2. 34b), a sound cue is given for a whirlwind that extinguishes the lamp while the ghost is onstage.

90 Meng Chengshun, *Jiao Hong ji,* scene 41, p. 205.

91 Han Yu's essay "Yuan gui" *(Han Yu quanji jiaoshu)* gives wind as an example of a phenomenon that has sound but no form. His point is to distinguish a ghost from wind, but the essay nonetheless reinforces the ubiquitous association of the two. On ghosts and wind on stage, see also Liao Tengye, *Zhongguo mengxi yanjiu,* pp. 227–228.

92 Hong Sheng, *Changsheng dian,* scene 27, p. 143. In Fan Wenruo, *Menghua han* (scene 20, 2.10a), before "Auntie Wind" enters and runs around the stage holding a wind flag, the stage directions cue the gongs to sound within *(nei mingluo).* Lu Eting (*Kunqu yanchu shigao,* p. 71) asserts that for southern drama, *nei* refers both to the greenroom *(xifang)* and to musicians backstage *(houchang siyue).*

93 Hsü, *Chinese Conception of the Theater* (p. 41, n. 4) notes that in Peking opera, "wind flags carried in front of an actor sometimes mean that the actor is a ghost riding the wind," but I have found no traces of such a technique in southern drama play texts.

94 See also *Zhongguo kunqu dacidian* under "Huo zhuo," p. 832, which describes "gui

bu" as requiring the actor to walk in a straight line or arc; making a turn requires performing a whirlwind first. However the entry for "gui bu" (p. 584) notes that ghost walks differ depending on the play. In films or videos of contemporary *kunqu* or Peking opera, the eerie ghost walk effect is often enhanced with dry ice. In *A Chinese Ghost Story* (photo in Ho and Ho, eds. *The Swordsman*, p. 130), to achieve a gliding ghost walk, the actors were pushed on dollies.

95 Wu Bing, *Huazhong ren*, scene 21, 2. 9b.

96 Zang Maoxun, ed., *Huanhun ji*, scene 15, 1. 56a.

97 Shen Jing, *Taofu ji*, scene 22, p. 574.

98 Hsiao ("The Eternal Present"), argues that some drama illustrations reflect the influence of staging both in the deployment of space and in use of gesture.

99 Weng Minhua ("Lun Yuandai zaju liang 'hun dan,'" p. 35), suggests that the opening arias sung by the *hun dan* in *The Disembodied Soul* and *Injustice to Dou E* are related to ghost movement and dance on stage.

100 On the iconography of this painting, see Laing, "Erotic Themes and Romantic Heroines," pp. 78–88.

101 Yang Youhe, *Chuanju danjiao biaoyan yishu*, p. 15.

102 Entry for "gui bu" in *Zhongguo kunqu dacidian*, p. 584. A more detailed description of the ghost walk for this role is given in *Zhongguo xiqu zhi: Jiangsu juan*, p. 547; see also Liao Tengye, *Zhongguo mengxi yanjiu*, p. 230.

103 An exception is Wu Bing, *Huazhong ren*, scene 21, 1. 11a, where the phantom heroine "acts out stirring up a whirlwind" before she exits to signal her presence.

104 Zheng Tingyu, *Houting hua*, *Gu mingjia* ed., 10b.

105 Guan Hanqing, *Injustice to Tou O*, trans. Chung-wen Shih, p. 239. (Her translation is based on the *Yuanqu xuan* edition, but the text of this passage in the other two late Ming editions is the same.)

106 Lu Eting (*Kunju yanchu shilüe*, p. 76) argues that there were fewer and less elaborate dances in sixteenth- and seventeenth-century *kunqu* performance than later on, because the performance of full plays rather than excerpts meant that the action had to proceed at a faster clip. The exception, he says, were ghost roles, which always involved dance routines.

107 Zhou Chaojun, *Hongmei ji*, scene 17, p. 91.

108 Qu You, "Jinfeng chai ji," *Jiandeng xinhua*, pp. 24–28. For the Yuan writer Liu Guan's authorship of this tale, see Tan Zhenbi, *Sanyan liangpai ziliao*, p. 692. The vernacular version was published as story no. 23 in both of Ling Mengchu's collections *Paian jingqi* and *Erke Paian jingqi*. *Man / Ghost* was published as play no. 9 in Fu Yichen's *Sumen xiao* collection of twelve *zaju*, all of which are based on stories from Ling Mengchu's collections. The unusual format of *Sumen xiao*—a collection of multiple short plays by a single author—imitates a story anthology in dramatic form.

109 For the dating of *Zhuichai ji*, see Xu Shuofang, *Wanming qujia nianpu*, 1. 315. As far as I know, the play, which circulated under the alternative title *Yizhong qing*, was not published until modern times.

110 Stevenson, "Text, Image, and Transformation," pp. 32–33.

111 Fu Yichen, *Rengui fuqi,* Act 7, 25b.

112 On this tomb, see Zhengzhou shi wenwu kaogu yanjiu suo, "Henan Xinmishi," pp. 26–32; and Stuer, "Double Passage to Heaven."

113 Stevenson, "Text, Image, and Transformation," p. 56

114 Zhida, *Guiyuan jing,* scene 39, 2. 37b.

115 Fu Yichen, *Rengui fuqi,* Act 7, p. 26a.

116 Zheng Guangzu, *Qiannü lihun, Gu mingjia* ed., Act 2, p. 8b.

117 See tables in Song Junhua, *Zhongguo gudai xiju fushi,* p. 330. Ghost masks are also listed, but these would have been for the ghosts who staffed the underworld courts.

118 Ibid, pp. 157, 193.

119 Costuming ghosts in winding cloths or sheets was one option in English Renaissance drama; see Jones and Stallybrass, *Renaissance Clothing,* pp. 249, 252. Chinese mortuary ritual is complex, and involved textiles in various ways. Sima Guang (*Sima shi shuyi* 5. 54) lists the conjoined ritual use of a *pa* and a *hun bo* (made of knotted white silk): "Set up a clothes rack to the south of the corpse and cover it with a *pa;* place a table and chair in front of it, and place the *hun bo* on the chair; set an incense burner, a cup with wine, and food on the table—this is the 'spirit seat' [*lingzuo*]." The *hun bo* would be buried at the funeral.

120 *Zhongguo dabaike quanshu: Xiqu quyi,* p. 44. For the underworld scene from *Peony Pavilion, Kunju chuandai,* a costume list transcribed in the early 1960s, describes Du Liniang's dead soul as wearing a silver *pa* on her head, with black gauze draped over her *(pi hei sha);* all the dead souls in this scene wear black gauze.

121 Although the term *pa* is not used in the *Hongmei ji* stage directions, the ghost's headdress is clearly a version of the same thing. The verb *meng* is used in scene 13, p. 60; the verb *dou* in the rewrite of scene 17, p. 88. *Pi* (to drape) is never used.

122 Xu Shuofang, private conversation, spring 2000. He also suggested that a *gui pa* was a "square white handkerchief."

123 Ouyang Xiu and Song Qi, *Xin Tangshu,* "Liyue zhi" 10. 451. With cloth, *mo/pa* as a verb is mainly used in a funerary context.

124 Garber, *Shakespeare's Ghost Writers,* p. 130.

125 Zang Maoxun, ed., *Huanhun ji,* scene 15, 1. 56

126 Fu Yichen, *Rengui fuqi,* Act 3, p. 8b.

127 Sofer, *The Stage Life of Props,* pp. 11–12.

128 Zang Maoxun, ed., *Huanhun ji,* scene 15, 1.57a.

129 Shen Jing, *Zhuichai ji,* scene 9, p. 625; facsimile of 1689 ms. in *Guben xiqu* I: 1. 15. Fu Xihua (*Mingdai chuanqi quanmu,* p. 75) lists a 1650 manuscript that I have not seen, but if the 1689 manuscript reflects what Shen Jing actually wrote when he composed the play some seventy years earlier, it would be the earliest usage of *hun pa* I have found.

130 Shen Jing, *Zhuichai ji,* scene 9, p. 627; *Guben xiqu* I: 1. 17a.

131 *Zhui baiqiu* (first series) in *Shanben xiqu* 52: 172.

132 Zang Maoxun, ed. *Huanhun ji,* scene 20, 2.9b. Zang still draws upon the otherworldly

significance of offstage space by having the company first burn paper money, a standard offering to the dead, in the direction of the stage door (though here called *gu men* rather than *gui men*).

133 Ibid., scene 19, 2. 5a-b.

134 Ibid., scene 20, 2. 10b.

135 Wu Bing, *Xiyuan ji,* scene 32, 2. 47a.

136 Ibid., 2. 47b.

137 A direct case of textual borrowing is likely here. Another possibility is that this bit of stage business with the *hun pa* was already common in performances of *Peony Pavilion.*

138 Called a "sutra hall" *(jingtang)* in the scene. The buildings in the West Garden, which form part of the family's residence, have been converted into a ritual space for the Land and Water Rite.

139 Wu Bing, *Xiyuan ji,* scene 33, 2. 51a.

140 Ibid.

141 Fu Yichen, *Rengui fuqi,* scene 6, p. 18b.

142 Ibid., p. 19a. *Jiu ren* is a double entendre here that also means "old friend" or "former person"—the deceased.

143 Schechner, *Performance Theory,* p. 197.

144 Cole, *The Theatrical Event,* p. 33.

145 Shen Jing, *Zhuichai ji,* scene 26, p. 677.

146 Cole, *The Theatrical Event,* pp. 42–43, citing Stanislavski and Salvino. See also Bauman, "Performance," pp. 46–48.

147 Shen Jing, *Zhuichai ji,* scene 11, p. 631.

148 Ibid., scene 7, p. 621.

149 Wu Bing, *Huazhong ren,* scene 8, 1. 26a.

150 Shen Jing, *Zhuichai ji,* scene 26, p. 679. The character *cui,* misprinted in Xu Shuofang's edition, should read *tui* as it does in the manuscript in *Guben xiqu* I.

151 Rewritten version of scene 17, attributed to Yuan Yuling. In Zhou Chaojun, *Hongmei ji,* p. 91.

152 Bronfen (*Over Her Dead Body,* p. 325) argues that a perfect resemblance between two women is often fatal for the second woman.

153 Shen Jing, *Zhuichai ji,* scene 26, p. 679.

154 Ibid. scene 9, p. 627.

155 Li Zhen, "Jia Yunhua huanhun ji," in *Jiandeng yuhua,* pp. 269–302.

156 Feng reprinted Mei Xiaosi's 1628 preface to the play in his own edition. See Xu Shuofang, *Feng Menglong nianpu,* 1. 433–434, year 1635.

157 Feng Menglong, *Saxue tang,* scene 36, 2. 40b.

158 Ibid., 2. 41a.

159 Ling Mengchu's version of "The Golden Hairpin" adds a little epilogue in which both sisters and the husband are eventually buried as a trio in the same grave (*Erke paian jingqi,* no. 23, 2. 276).

160 In addition to *Peony Pavilion, An Intoxicating Dream* heavily borrows from the Xiaoqing plays and Wu Bing's *Lady in the Painting* and *West Garden.*

161 The *cha dan,* a variant of the term *cha*[a] *dan,* did not designate an "extra" female lead in Yuan drama, but was a broad term for a range of young or middle-aged women, including lively courtesans. See *Zhongguo quxue dacidian,* p. 822.

162 The sole upper marginal note in the play text not concerned with musical issues of pronunciation reiterates that the *cha dan* now replaces the *dan* on stage and that everything must be done to make the spectators grasp this. Fan Wenruo, *Menghua han,* 2. 37b.

163 Stewart (*Nonsense,* p. 121) notes that "infinity and repetition implicate each other" and that repetition and reversal are frequently conjoined in the play with infinity.

164 Tina Lu, *Persons, Roles, and Minds* (p. 100), discusses the word play involving *gui hua* in *Peony Pavilion,* where, as in *Menghua han,* it works as pun to mean both nonsense and matters discussed by a ghost.

165 Usages of *gui hua:* scene 18, 2. 3a; scene 28, 2. 34a; scene 33, 2. 54a; as well as scene 32. Usage of *dao gui:* scene 18, 2.3a; and scene 32.

166 Four plays (two Yuan *zaju* and two Ming *chuanqi*) involve tricking the male lead into believing his lover is a ghost so that he will leave her to take the exams. The *zaju* are *Hongli hua* and *Zhuwu tingqin;* both *chuanqi* are entitled *Hongli ji.*

167 In 2000 I saw a *kunqu* performance of this play in Suzhou that excised the "real" ghost part of the plot and kept only the misidentification of the "false" ghost. This has become the standard modern adaptation of the play.

168 Fan Wenruo, *Menghua han,* scene 32, 2. 48b.

169 Ibid., scene 32, 2. 49b.

170 Garber, *Shakespeare's Ghost Writers,* p. 15.

171 Fan Wenruo, *Menghua han,* scene 31, 2.45a.

172 Goldman, *The Actor's Freedom,* p. 37.

173 Fen Wenruo, *Menghua han,* scene 34, 2. 60a.

174 Stewart, *Nonsense,* pp. 133–134.

175 Fan Wenruo, *Menghua han,* scene 34, 2. 61a-b.

Coda

1 The other is Kong Shangren's *Taohua shan.* Full-length southern dramas did continue to be written after 1700 (Lu Eting, "Qingdai quanbenxi yanchu shulun"), but after this point, theater reverts from a playwright's to an actor's theater.

2 On the influence of Wu Weiye's plays on *Palace of Lasting Life,* see Tschantz, "Early Qing Drama," pp. 275–276.

3 Hong Sheng, "Liyan," *Changsheng dian,* p. 1. All page numbers in the text are keyed to Hong Sheng, *Changsheng dian,* ed. Xu Shuofang, except for those preceded by *Guben,* which refer to Wu Yiyi's commentary in the facsimile of Hong Sheng's authorized edition.

4. Before the play was banned, it was staged in at least two different venues in Beijing, a

public theater and a private household, but it cannot be ascertained where the performance that got Hong Sheng into trouble took place. See Zhou Huabin, *Jingdu guxilou*, pp. 102–104. The phrase "gala performance" is Ay-ling Wang's ("The Artistry of Hong Sheng's *Changshengdian*," p. 2). Wang's is the fullest account of the scandal in English, but she probably overstates the Kangxi emperor's objections to the Han-nationalist Ming-loyalist implications of the play's content as the underlying reason for his reaction. Wang's account is based on those in Zhang Peiheng, *Hong Sheng nianpu;* and Chen Wannai, *Hong Sheng yanjiu.*

5. Hong Sheng, *Changsheng dian*, "Liyan," p. 1.
6. Zhang Peiheng, *Hong Sheng nianpu*, pp. 365–366. Hong Sheng was the honored guest and sat together with his host watching the entire performance with script in hand. There could have been other complete performances of the play at the time, but none of the brief accounts of other performances specify how much was performed. My feeling is that this anecdote mentions that the complete play was performed and specifies the amount of time it took *because* it was unusual.
7. Hong Sheng was well versed in the vast array of texts on the court of Emperor Minghuang and his relationship with Lady Yang and An Lushan. Because Hong Sheng's treatment of this material does not privilege "official" works of history, such as *Zizhi tongjian* or the *Old* and *New Tang Histories,* over unofficial or private works, such as *biji (Yang Taizhen waizhuan),* poems (by Bai Juyi and other Tang poets), tales ("Changhen ge zhuan" and "Mei fei zhuan"), or plays *(Wutong yu),* there is arguably no real distinction in *Palace of Lasting Life* between the historical and the legendary. In effect, all past treatments of the story occupy the same position in the textual universe as potential source material for Hong Sheng.
8. Scenes 31, 34, and 35. An exception is scene 28, in which one of the former musicians from the emperor's court denounces An Lushan to his face and is executed.
9. Liu Yanjun, *Lan'gan paibian*, p. 209.
10. Wei Guan, "Zhou Qin xing ji," *TPGJ* 489. 4018–4023.
11. *Jinghong ji* (*Guben* II, no. 29) scene 39, 2. 40a.
12. Wang Jilie, *Yinlu qutan* 2. 30.
13. That is to say, none of these scenes are included in *Zhui baiqiu* or *Shenyin jiangu lu.* A 1750 manuscript of the play, which reduces the play from fifty acts to forty-five, shows much more evidence of use, such as cross-outs and comments, for Part I than for Part II. Stage directions and costume indications are significantly abridged, and some scenes are rearranged to make them better conform to standard performing conventions and to clarify the action for the audience. These signs suggest that this manuscript may have been a text more geared to performance; if so, it also suggests that Part II was less frequently performed than Part I.
14. One exception is the court. *Chuandai gangmu* (Vol. II), a nineteenth-century Qing manuscript from the court drama bureau, which provides cast and costume lists for play excerpts staged in the palace, includes "Ming zhui" (scene 27). Apart from stage performances, evidence from song formularies suggests that the arias from the ghost scenes remained part of the amateur singing tradition up through the begin-

ning decades of the twentieth century. Ye Tan's *Nashuying qupu* scores all three ghost scenes: scene 27 (*xuji*, 2: 1. 89–95), scene 30 (*zhengji*, 1: 4. 577–580), and the first half of scene 37 (*zhengji*, 1: 4. 593–596). So-called full-length *(quanben)* stagings of the play in recent years, which are usually excerpts from the traditional repertory cobbled together, omit the ghost interlude. An exception is the twenty-seven-scene Suzhou Kunju troupe production, which premiered February 17–22, 2004, in Taipei's Novel Theater (Xin wutai), and which "resurrected" all three of the play's major ghost scenes (available on DVD as *The Palace of Eternal Youth*).

15 On Wu's involvement with the publication of *Changsheng dian*, see Liu Hui's introduction to *Hong Sheng ji*, pp. 4–5, and his "Lun Wu Shufu." The publication of Volume II was postponed for four years because of the death of Wu's mother. Hong Sheng lacked the financial resources to publish his work, and it is likely that Wu, who had experience in publishing drama and medical works, helped raise the capital to publish *Changsheng dian*.

16 On the story of this edition, see my "Shared Dreams"; Ko, *Teachers of the Inner Chambers*, pp. 68–89; and Hua Wei, *Ming Qing funü zhi xiqu*, pp. 337–360. For the text of the colophon, see Mao Xiaotong, *Tang Xianzu yanjiu ziliao* 2: 905.

17 Hong Sheng's foreword ("Liyan," p. 1) explicitly distances himself from Tang on musical and prosodic grounds. In a comment to scene 39 (*Guben* 2.56a), Wu Yiyi noted: "[The arias here] employ the same tune as the sacrifice to Du Liniang in *Peony Pavilion*, but the offering of fading plum blossoms has been changed to an offering of peonies. *Thus, although this scene duplicates that scene, not one word or meaning is exactly alike*" (italics mine).

18 Although Lady Yang appears in a dream after her death to the grieving emperor in Bai Renfu, *Wutong yu* (Act 4), the play does not specify that she is a phantom or employ any of the normal stage business for the phantom-heroine role.

19 Wu Yiyi's commentary glosses the monster as An Lushan, but he interprets the dream mainly as a projection of the emperor's psychological state (*Guben* 2. 76a).

20 Zheng Zhizhen, *Mulian jiumu*, "Guo wangxiang tai" (*Guben xiqu* I), j. 2.

21 Teiser, *Scripture on the Ten Kings*, pp. 1–2.

22 Zeng Yongyi, *Zhongguo gudian xiju*, p. 697. Zeng feels that northern tunes are meant to be perceived as sad and therefore that the sadness of Lady Yang's perspective permeates the scene. But it is doubtful that northern tunes can be assigned such a blanket emotional affect.

23 Scene 27 ("Ming zhui") partially occupies the position of scene 23 ("Ming pan") in *Peony Pavilion*. The 1750 forty-five-scene manuscript of the play rewrites this scene so that it better conforms to the "Ming pan" performing tradition by setting it in the underworld and adding a colorful underworld judge.

24 In the final act of *West Garden*, the phantom heroine returns to the garden and discovers the spirit tablet with her name on it as part of the Land and Water Rite, but here too the garden has pleasant associations because she had her dream tryst there.

25 In scene 26 of Wang Yufeng, *Fenxiang ji*, a late Ming phantom-heroine play in which the courtesan Guying is abandoned by the scholar Wang Kui, Guying sings a lengthy

aria apostrophizing her gauze kerchief *(luo pa)* before she hangs herself with it. This scene, renamed "Yang gao" became a famous excerpt.

26 Beginning with *Peony Pavilion,* the underworld judge typically provides the phantom heroine with a travel permit to provide at least a bureaucratic fig leaf of control over the revenant's return to the human world.

27 Qian Yi, marginal comment to scene 54 in Wu Yiyi and Qian Yi, *Wu Wushan sanfu* 2:84b.

28 The use of dream as a metaphor for the vanished past surfaces specifically in early Qing reminiscences of life before the fall of the Ming. Zhang Dai's two memoirs, *Tao'an's Dream Reminiscences (Tao'an mengyi)* and *Seeking West Lake in a Dream (Xihu mengxun)* exemplify this tendency.

29 An exception that proves the rule is Pu Songling's "Zhang Aduan," discussed in Chapter 1, in which the ghost who falls ill with a "ghost-induced illness" dreams of the vengeful "ghost of a ghost" of her former husband.

30 Freud, "The Uncanny," p. 138.

31 Ibid.

32 Ibid. p. 139.

33 My translation of these lines is indebted to Owen's translation in his *Anthology of Chinese Literature,* p. 1071.

34 "Silken thread" *(si*[a]*)* is punned with *(si)* "longing" to mean: even death cannot put an end to my longing. This aria alters the famous line by Li Shangyin in which death cuts off the silkworm's thread and therefore longing. For a similar emendation of this line by a female ghost to express the infinity of longing, see "Lianxiang" (*LZ* 2. 225), discussed in Chapter 1, n. 42.

35 *Chuandai gangmu* (Vol. II), lists a *hun pa* and dancing clothes *(wuyi)* for Lady Yang's costume in this scene; Lady Guo also wears a *hun pa.*

36 Seidel, "Post-mortem Immortality"; Wu Hung, "Handai daojiao meishu shitan."

37 Zheng Guangzu, *Qiannü lihun, Guzaju, ce* 3, p. 23a; *Gujin zaju, ce* 13, p. 12a.

38 Wu Yiyi's comment in scene 27 points out how this action anticipates facing her own corpse in scene 37 (*Guben* 2. 8a).

39 Passages in this paragraph translated by Owen, *Anthology,* p. 1074.

40 See C. T. Hsia, "Time and the Human Condition," pp. 249–250; Wai-yee Li, *Enchantment and Disenchantment,* pp. 56–57; Swatek, "Portrait and Plum," pp. 131–133.

41 *Huai nan zi,* "Ben jing," 8. 4a

42 Boltz, *The Origin and Early Development,* pp. 131–134; and Connery, *Empire of the Text,* pp. 34–35.

43 "Jiewei gui" in *Quan Tangshi* 865. 9778.

44 Peucker, *Incorporating Images,* p. 104.

45 Fan Wenruo, *Menghua han,* scene 18, 2. 4a-b.

46 See my "Spirit Writing and Performance" for a fuller exposition of these ideas.

Glossary

"Abao" 阿寶
"Ainu" 愛奴
an 暗
An Zhiyuan 安致遠
Anyang 安陽
bai ji 稗集
Bai Juyi 白居易
Bao Zhao 鮑照
"Baxia gui" 巴峽鬼
"Baxia ren" 巴峽人
"Baxia yuan ming" 巴峽猿鳴
Beimang 北邙
Beimeng suoyan 北夢瑣言
"benmo" 本末
bi 斃
bi xie 避邪
bian 變
bieji 別集
bing 病
"Bing you guishen lun" 病有鬼神論
bingbei haifang dao 兵備海防道
"Bo Qinhuai" 泊秦淮
bu zhi gui[a] 不知歸
Caishen ji 才神記
Caixian ji 才仙記
Cang Jie 倉頡
Cao Yin 曹寅
cha dan 搽旦
cha[a] dan 茶旦
"Chang Yi" 常夷
"Chang'an yexing lu" 長安夜行錄
"Changhen ge zhuan" 長恨歌傳
Changji ti 長吉體
Chen Baoyao 陳寶鑰
Chen ji 陳姬
"*Chen Lüya shi* xu" 陳綠崖詩序
Chen Yixi 陳奕禧
Chen Youliang 陳有諒
Cheng Yuwen 程羽文
chi 癡
Chi pozi zhuan 癡婆子傳
chou zhuang lei gui 醜狀類鬼
chu 出
chuanqi 傳奇
chui shou shang 垂手上
Chunbo ying 春波影
cui 摧
"Cui yanei baiyao zhao yao" 崔衙內白鷂招妖
cuoren 錯認
"Da Yuan Tuoan" 答袁籜庵
dai guilian 戴鬼臉
dai/luo gui mian 戴落鬼面
dan hun shang xuanfeng ke 旦魂上旋風科
dan hun shang 旦魂上
dan hunzi shang 旦魂子上
Danyang 丹陽
dao gui 搗鬼
dianfu 顛覆
Ding Yaokang 丁燿康
"Dinggui pian" 訂鬼篇
Dong gu 東姑
Dong Xiaowan 董小宛
Dong'er 東兒
dou 兜
Du Liniang 杜麗娘

Du Mu 杜牧
Duan Yucai 段玉裁
"Dujuan xing" 杜鵑行
Erya 爾雅
Fan Yun 范雲
fei 廢
fei qi[a] bu chuan 非奇不傳
Feng Cuiliu 馮翠柳
"Feng mujiang" 馮木匠
Feng Zhenluan 馮鎮巒
"*Fenxiang ji* xu" 焚香記序
fuji 扶乩
fuke 婦科
gai 蓋
"Ganfeng" 感風
ganjiu 感舊
gaosong 高松
"Gechuang gui" 隔窗鬼
"Gongsun Jiuniang" 公孫九娘
gu 古
gu men 古門
gu men dao[a] 古門道
gu men dao[b] 鼓門道
guai 怪
guaihuan 怪幻
Guan Yu 關羽
"Gufan zhi" 故藩址
guhun 孤魂
gui 鬼 ("ghost")
gui[a] 歸 ("to return")
"Gui bian" 鬼辯
gui bing 鬼病
gui bu 鬼步
gui cai 鬼才
gui, gui ye 鬼, 歸也
gui hu dan 鬼狐旦
gui hua 鬼話
gui ji 鬼擊
gui jing 鬼境
"Gui ku" 鬼哭
"Gui li" 鬼隸
gui mai 鬼脈
gui men 鬼門
gui men dao 鬼門道
gui qi 鬼氣
"Gui qi" 鬼妻
gui sheng 鬼聲
gui shi 鬼詩
gui tai 鬼胎
gui wu 鬼物
gui xi 鬼戲
"Gui xiaozi zhuan" 鬼孝子傳
gui zhe, ren suo [jian] de bing zhi qi ye 鬼者人所[見]得病之氣也
gui zhu 鬼注
"Guihua ci" 媿嫿詞
guihun bu 鬼魂步
"Guimu zhuan" 鬼母傳
Guiqu tu 鬼趣圖
"Guishen pian" 鬼神篇
Guiying 桂英
guizhong zhi gui 鬼中之鬼
guo 果 ("indeed")
guo 裹 ("to wind")
"Guo gu Hengfan feigong you gan" 過故衡藩廢宮有感
"Guo jianmen" 過劍門
"Guo Wangxiang tai" 過望鄉臺
Gushi gui[a] 古詩歸
"Gushi shijiu shou" 古詩十九首
haiji 亥集
haiguo 海國
"Hao li" 蒿里
He Shouqi 何守奇
"Hengfan jiudi nan jiangjun" 衡藩舊邸南將軍
Hongli hua 紅梨花
Hongli ji 紅梨記
Hongmei ge 紅梅閣
hou yin 後陰
houchang siyue 後場司樂
houfang 後房
"hu bian gui lian" 忽變鬼臉
"hu bian zuo gui xing" 忽變作鬼形
"Hu hun" 呼魂
Hu Yinglin 胡應麟

"Hua Lichun" 花麗春
"Hua pi" 畫皮
huaigu 懷古
"Huan nao" 歡撓
huanhun 還魂
huan ji 幻集
"Huating feng guren ji" 華亭逢故人記
"Hukou miao tudi" 湖口廟土地
hun 魂
hun bo 魂帛
hun bu 魂步
hun dan 魂旦
hun dan shang 魂旦上
"Hun hua" 魂話
hun pa 魂帕
hun po 魂魄
"Hun you" 魂遊
hunzi 魂子
hunzi yi 魂子衣
"Huo zhuo" 活捉
ji 祭 ("sacrifical elegy")
ji[a] 急 ("rushed")
"Ji nü Qiongzhang zhuan" 季女瓊章傳
ji si mu 寄思慕
"Ji Youdu jun wen" 祭幽獨君文
jia gui mian 假鬼面
Jia Sidao 賈似道
"Jia Yunhua huanhun ji" 賈雲華還魂記
jian 蹔
jian wang gongde 薦亡功德
Jiang ji 江姬
"Jianxiaoge xin'gai *Hongmei ji*" 劍嘯閣新改紅梅記
"Jiaona" 嬌娜
"Jiaping gongzi" 嘉平公子
jie 結
jie[a] 解 ("to untie")
"Jie huangtang" 戒荒唐
jieshi huanhun 借屍還魂
"Jinfeng chai ji" 金鳳釵記
jing 景 ("scene")
jing 淨 ("painted face role")
jingshen 精神
"jingshui" 經水
jingtang 經堂
Jiong Yuchi 迥尉遲
Jishan 稷山
jiu ren 舊人
Jiu Tangshu 舊唐書
Jiwen 紀聞
Kong Shangren 孔尚任
Kulou huanxi tu 骷髏幻戲圖
Laixia 萊霞
Laiyang 萊陽
laofu ru nei chang jie 老夫入內場介
Le'an fashi 泐庵法師
lei ze nisha 淚澤泥沙
li bo 力薄
"Li Changji xiaozhuan" 李長吉小傳
Li Daochang 李道昌
"*Li He shijie* xu" 李賀詩解序
Li Hu 酈琥
Li Huiniang 李慧娘
Li Jingliang 李景亮
Li Qing 李清
li ruo 力弱
Li Shangyin 李商隱
Li Shiyuan 李士元
Li Song 李嵩
Li Yi 李易
"Li Yin" 李茵
"Li Zhangwu" 李章武
Li Zicheng 李自成
"Lianchang gongci" 連昌宮詞
"Liancheng" 連城
"Lianxiang" 蓮香
Liangzhou[a] 梁州
Liangzhou[b] 涼州
"Liansuo" 連瑣
"lianwai yanshuang jie dao fei" 簾外嚴霜皆倒飛
Lichui ji 酈吹集
lie hun 烈魂
Lin Siniang 林四娘
"Lin Siniang ge" 林四娘歌
lingguai 靈怪

lingzuo 靈座
Linshui furen 臨水夫人
"Linzi huaigu" 臨淄懷古
"Liu Fangxuan" 劉方玄
"Liu Huiji nüxi" 劉暉吉女戲
Liu Sahe 劉薩訶
Liu Shide 劉世德
Liu Yong 柳永
"Liu yuan zhengji dalun" 六元正紀大論
"liuying re cao fu zhan wei" 流螢惹草復沾幃
"Liyan" 例言
"Liyue zhi" 禮樂志
"Loushang tongnü" 樓上童女
Lu Guimeng 陸龜蒙
Lu Ji 陸機
Lu Qiao 陸喬
"Lü Wubing" 呂無病
luan si 亂思 ("thoughts of longing")
luan si[a] 亂絲 ("tangled threads")
luo pa 羅帕
Luo Pin 羅聘
"Mai gaogan" 賣糕乾
Mao Xiang 冒襄
maomen aonao 瞀悶懊憹
Mawei 馬嵬
Mawei po 馬嵬坡
Mazu 媽祖
"Mei Fei zhuan" 梅妃傳
Mei Xiaosi 梅孝巳
meng 蒙
Meng Jiao 孟郊
"Meng Li Bai" 夢李白
meng yu gui jiaotong 夢與鬼交通
"*Menghua han* xu" 夢花酣序
"Mengshi" 孟氏
mengyi 夢遺
Miaoshan 妙善
mie 滅
"Ming pan" 冥判
"Ming shi" 冥誓
"Ming you" 冥佑
"Ming zhui" 冥追
"Minghun yili pian" 冥婚儀禮篇
minghun 冥婚
mo 帕 ("to wrap")
mo 末 ("older male role")
Moling chun 秣陵春
Mowangguan 脈望館
"Mudan deng ji" 牡丹燈記
"Mudu xianji xiaozhuan" 木瀆仙姬小傳
Mulian 目連
"Mulian xi" 目連戲
"Nanshan tianzhong xing" 南山田中行
nanxi 南戲
"Nao Panlou duoqing Zhou Shengxian" 鬧潘樓多情周勝仙
naore 鬧熱
nei 内
nei mingluo 内鳴鑼
nei mingluo zuo feng qi ke 内鳴鑼作風起科
neichang 内場
neidan 内丹
"Nie Xiaoqian" 聶小倩
ning gui 獰鬼
ning si 凝思
ning si cheng ji 凝思成疾
nuoxi 儺戲
pa 帕
paichang 排場
Pan Jinlian 潘金蓮
"Pen shui" 噴水
Peng Ershu 彭二述
pi 披
pi hei sha 披黑紗
Pi Rixiu 皮日休
Pilu si 毗盧寺
Pingmo 平陌
"Pipa xing" 琵琶行
po 魄
pohuai 破壞
"Puji youhun" 普濟幽魂
qi[a] 奇 ("extraordinary")
qi 氣 ("vital stuff")
qi ji 奇疾

"Qi Zhixiang" 祁止祥
qian yin 前陰
Qiannü youhun 倩女幽魂
Qiaoniang 巧娘
qifeng 淒風
Qilai li 棲萊里
qing 情
qing 清 ("clear")
"Qing fu" 清賦
qing gui 情鬼
"Qing hui" 情悔
qing, ren zhi yin qi you yu zhe 情，人之陰氣有欲者
"Qingchi wuyan" 情癡寤言
Qingniang 慶娘
Qingshe yiwen 青社遺聞
qingsong 青松
Qingxiang 青箱
qingzhi yu 情志鬱
Qingzhou 青州
"Qingzhou huaigu" 青州懷古
"Qiu lai" 秋來
"Qiuxi fang Pipa ting ji" 秋夕訪琵琶亭記
"Qiwu lun" 齊物論
Qixia 棲霞
quanben 全本
"*Ranzhi ji* li" 燃脂集例
re 惹
ren 人
rendao 人道
"Renyao" 人妖
rou 肉
rou shen 肉身
rou shi 肉尸
"Ruiyun" 瑞雲
run ji 閏集
Sadula 薩都剌
san 散
san le 三樂
Sanlang 三郎
Saxue tang 灑雪堂
"Se mu" 色目
shan 閃
"Shang Wang Ruanting neihan" 上王阮亭內涵
shao 少
shao yin 少陰
Shao Yong 邵雍
"She hun" 攝魂
Shen Deqian 沈德潛
Shen Quanqi 沈佺期
Shen Yazhi 沈亞之
Shen Yixiu 沈宜修
Shen Yue 沈約
shendao 神道
sheng 聲
sheng le 生樂
shengsi 生死
shenqi 神氣
Shensheng 申生
shi 事
"Shi bian" 尸變
"Shi jie" 尸解
Shi nüshi 詩女史
"shi you guiqi" 詩有鬼氣
Shi Zhenlin 史震林
shifang 石坊
shihua 詩話
"shiying zhan ancao" 濕螢沾暗草
shouze 手澤
"Shu Li He xiaozhuan hou" 述李賀小傳後
"Shu qiong" 術窮
Shuilu daochang 水陸道場
Shuilu hua 水陸畫
Shuilu zhai 水陸齋
"Shuli" 黍離
si 思 ("longing")
si 死 ("to die")
si[a] 絲 ("silken thread")
simie 死滅
Song Cao 宋曹
"Song Li Jiao xiucai shi xu" 送李膠秀才詩序
"Song Meng Jiaodong xu" 送孟郊東序
Song Zhiwen 宋之問
Songling ji 松陵集

Su Xiaoxiao 蘇小小
"Su Xiaoxiao mu" 蘇小小墓
Suwen 素問
Taishi 太史
"Taiyuan Yiniang" 太原意娘
Tang Qingmou 唐卿謀
Tang Song yishi 唐宋遺史
"Tang Xuan" 唐晅
Tangshi sanbai shou 唐詩三百首
Taohua shan 桃花扇
"*Taohua shan* benmo" 桃花扇本末
"Teng Mu zuiyou Jujingyuan ji" 騰穆醉游聚景園記
ti 題
"Tian wen" 天問
Tian Yiheng 田藝蘅
"Tian Zhu yu Xue Tao lianju ji" 田洙逾薛濤聯句記
tianyan 天閹
tibishi 題壁詩
"Tici" 題詞
tie 貼
tingchu 挺出
Tongguan yibian 彤管遺編
Tongtian tai 通天臺
Tongyou ji 通幽記
tuanyuan 團圓
tui 推
waichang 外場
wai ru neichang jie 外入內場介
wang 亡
Wang Kui 王魁
wang le 王樂
Wang Shilu 王士錄
Wang Shiyi 王十一
Wang Shizhen 王世貞 (Ming)
Wang Shizhen 王士禎 (Qing)
Wang Siren 王思任
Wang Taishi 王太史
Wang Yuying 王玉英
Wang Zhaojun 王昭君
Wangchun lou 望春樓
wei 僞
Wei Guan 韋瓘
Wei Huang 韋璜
Wei Huiqi 衛輝戚
wen 文
"Wen cangtian" 問蒼天
wo 我
wu 吾
Wu Qi 吴淇
"Wu Qiuyue" 伍秋月
Wu Yiyi 吳儀一
"Wucheng fu" 蕪城賦
Wunong xunya 吳儂荀鴨
"Wuqiu si" 武丘寺
Xi Shi 西施
xia ewu 下惡物
xian qiao 仙橋
"Xiangchun" 湘春
"Xiangyu" 香玉
Xiangzhong cao 湘中草
Xiangzhou 相州
xiao dan 小旦
xiao sheng 小生
Xiaoqing 小青
"Xiaoxie" 小謝
xie 瀉
xie 邪
Xie Guan 謝觀
"Xie lu ge" 薤露歌
xie qi 邪氣
Xie Qian 謝遷
Xie Qiantao 謝蒨桃
xiemai 邪脈
xiesui 邪祟
xieyin 邪因 (cause of heteropathy)
xieyin 邪淫 (heteropathic lust)
xifang 戲房
Xihu nüzi 西湖女子
xin gui 新鬼
xin ren 新人
Xin Tang shu 新唐書
Xin wutai 新舞臺
Xincheng 新城
Xing Jushi 邢居實

"Xinggong" 行宮
xinghui 形穢
Xingniang 興娘
"Xinlang" 新郎
Xiqing sanji 西青散記
Xitang zazu 西堂雜俎
xu 虛
"Xu guishi" 續鬼詩
"Xu sheng" 許生
Xu Shijun 徐士俊
Xu Tian 徐田
"Xu Xuanfang nü" 徐玄方女
"Xuan ju" 選劇
xuanfeng xia 旋風下
"xuanye qifeng que dao chui" 玄夜淒風卻倒吹
xue man xiongyi 血滿胸臆
Xue Tao 薛濤
Xueguan ting 血灌亭
xueye yinjing 血液陰精
xun 殉
ya gui 雅鬼
Yan Poxi 閻婆惜
Yan Yu 嚴羽
"Yang gao" 陽告
Yang Guifei 楊貴妃
Yang Guozhong 楊國忠
Yang Jian 楊堅
yang qi 陽氣
"Yang Siwen Yanshan feng guren" 楊思溫燕山逢故人
Yang Taizhen waizhuan 楊太真外傳
Yang Yuhuan 楊玉環
"Yangzhou shiri ji" 揚州十日記
"Yanzhong xian" 烟中仙
yao qi 妖氣
Yao Quan 姚佺
yaonie 妖孽
Ye 鄴
Ye Shaoyuan 葉紹袁
"Ye sheng" 葉生
Ye Xiaoluan 葉小鸞
"Ye zuo yin" 夜坐吟
"Yegou" 野狗
yeshi 野史
yi si 遺思
Yidu 益都
Yifang leiju 醫方類聚
yijing 遺精
yin 隱
yin chu 隱出
yin du 陰毒
"Yin jiu" 飲酒
yin qi 陰氣
Yinguo bao 因果報
yinyou 陰幽
Yizhong qing 一種情
"You gou" 幽媾
you gui wuhai lun 有鬼無害論
you guiqi 有鬼氣
"You hui" 幽會
youhun 幽婚 ("spirit marriage")
you[a]hun 幽魂
you[b]hun 遊魂
Youjun 幽君
"Youming dahui" 幽明大會
yu 與 ("given")
Yu Qi 于七
Yu Xuanji 魚玄機
Yu Yuanji 魚元機
"Yuan gui" 原鬼
Yuan Hongdao 袁宏道
yuan jie 冤結
yuan qi 怨氣
Yuan Yuling 袁于令
Yuan Zhen 元稹
yuanhun 冤魂
yuanman 圓滿
yuefu 樂府
Yuefu shiji 樂府詩集
"Yueniang ji" 越娘記
"Yueye tanqin ji" 月夜彈琴記
yujie 鬱結
Yunqi Zhuhong 雲棲袾宏
"Yuzao" 玉藻
yu 鬱 ("stasis")

Zeng Yi 曾益
"Zhan chengnan" 戰城南
zhan 沾
"Zhang Aduan" 章阿端
"Zhang Guo nü" 張果女
zhaohun zang 招魂葬
zhen hun 真魂
zheng 症
zheng dan 正旦
zheng qi 正氣
zhenghun 正魂
"Zhenshang" 枕上
zhi 志
zhi 制 ("fashioned")
zhi le 至樂
zhiguai 志怪
Zhong Kui 鍾馗
zhong yin 中陰
Zhou Bida 周必大
"Zhou Qin xingji" 周秦行記
Zhou Youde 周有德
zhu 屬
zhugongdiao 諸宮調
Zhu Helu 朱和陸
"Zhu you" 祝由
Zhu Yuanzhang 朱元璋
Zhucheng 諸城
"Zhuihe Huqiu si Qingyuan daoshi shi bing xu" 追和虎丘寺清遠道士詩並序
"Zhuihe Youdu jun shi ciyun" 追和幽獨君詩次韻
Zhuo Renyue 卓人月
Zhuwu tingqin 竹塢聽琴
zi 自
"Zi ji wen" 自祭文
Zichai ji 紫釵記
Zichuan 淄川
Zigu shen 紫姑神
"Ziyu ge" 紫玉歌
Zizhi tongjian 資治通鑑
zuo ying xia/ying xia 作影下/影下

Works Cited

Abbas, Ackbar. *Hong Kong: Culture and the Politics of Disappearance.* Minneapolis: University of Minnesota Press, 1997.

Ahern, Emily M. *The Cult of the Dead in a Chinese Village.* Stanford: Stanford University Press, 1973.

Bai Renfu 白仁甫. *Wutong yu* 梧桐雨. *Gu mingjia* 古名家 ed. In *Mowangguan chaojiaoben Gujin zaju* 脈望館鈔校本古今雜劇, no. 27. Facsimile reprint, *Guben xiqu* IV.

———. *Wutong yu* 梧桐雨. In *Yuanqu xuan* 元曲選, ed. Zang Maoxun 臧懋循, 1: 348–364. Beijing: Zhonghua shuju, 1958.

Bai Yaren 白亞仁 (Allan Barr). "Lüelun Li Chengzhong *Genzhai biji* ji qi yu *Liaozhai zhiyi* de gongtong ticai." 略論李澄中艮齋筆記及其與聊齋誌異的共同題材. *Pu Songling yanjiu* 蒲松齡研究 (2000.1): 46–55.

———. "Lüetan An Zhiyuan *Qingshe yiwen* ji qi yu *Liaozhai zhiyi* de guanxi." 略談安致遠青社遺聞及其與聊齋誌異的關係. *Pu Songling yanjiu* 蒲松齡研究 (2002.1): 77–88.

Barr, Allan. "A Comparative Study of Early and Late Tales in *Liaozhai zhiyi.*" *HJAS* 45.1 (1985): 157–202.

———. "The Early Qing Mystery of the Governor's Stolen Silver." *HJAS* 60.2 (Dec. 2000): 385–412.

———. "Pu Songling and *Liaozhai zhiyi*: A Study of Textual Transmission, Biographical Background, and Literary Antecedents." PhD diss., Oxford University, 1983.

Barthes, Roland. "Baudelaire's Theatre." In *Critical Essays*, trans. Richard Howard, pp. 25–32. Evanston, IL: Northwestern University Press, 1972.

Bauer, Wolfang, and Herbert Franke, trans. *The Golden Casket: Chinese Novellas of Two Millennia.* London: Allen and Unwin, 1965.

Bauman, Richard. "Performance." In *Folklore, Cultural Performances, and Popular Entertainments*, ed. Richard Bauman, pp. 46–48. New York: Oxford University Press, 1992.

Bitao hua 碧桃花. [Anonymous]. In *Zaju xuan* 雜劇選. Facimile reprint of Xijizi 息機子's edition (1598 author's preface), *Guben xiqu* IV.

———. In *Yuanqu xuan* 元曲選 (1615/16), ed. Zang Maoxun 臧懋循, 4: 1684–1702. Beijing: Zhonghua shuju, 1958.

Birch, Cyril, trans. *Mistress and Maid: Jiaohongji*, by Meng Chengshun. New York: Columbia University Press, 2001.

———, trans. *The Peony Pavilion*, by Tang Xianzu. Bloomington: Indiana University Press, 1980.

Bloch, Maurice, and Jonathan Parry, eds. *Death and the Regeneration of Life*. Cambridge: Cambridge University Press, 1982.

Boltz, William G. *The Origin and Early Development of the Chinese Writing System*. New Haven, CT: American Oriental Society, 1994.

Brashier, Kenneth. "Han Thanatology and the Division of Souls." *Early China* 21 (1996): 125–158.

Bray, Francesca. "A Deathly Disorder: Understanding Women's Health in Late Imperial China." In *Knowledge and the Scholarly Medical Traditions*, ed. Donald Bates, pp. 235–250. Cambridge: Cambridge University Press, 1995.

Brokaw, Cynthia J. *The Ledgers of Merit and Demerit: Social Change and Moral Order in Late Imperial China*. Princeton, NJ: Princeton University Press, 1991.

Bronfen, Elisabeth. *Over Her Dead Body: Death, Femininity and the Aesthetic*. New York: Routledge, 1992.

Brook, Timothy. *Praying for Power: Buddhism and the Formation of Gentry Society in Late-Ming China*. Cambridge, MA: Council on East Asian Studies, 1993.

Bu pa gui de gushi 不怕鬼的故事. Comp. Zhongguo shehui kexue yuan 中國社會科學院. Revision of 1961 edition. Beijing: Renmin chubanshe, 1999.

Cai Jiudi 蔡九迪 [Judith T. Zeitlin]. "Chongshen yu fenshen—Mingmo xiqu zhong de *hun dan*" 重身與分身—明末戲曲中的「魂旦」. In *Tang Xianzu yu Mudan ting yanjiu* 湯顯祖與《牡丹亭》研究, ed. Hua Wei, pp. 512–536. Taibei: Zhongyang yanjiuyuan Zhongguo wenzhe yanjiusuo, 2006.

Cai Yi 蔡毅, ed. *Zhongguo gudian xiqu xuba huibian* 中國古典戲曲序跋彙編. Ji'nan: Qi-Lu shushe, 1989.

Campany, Robert F. "Ghosts Matter: The Culture of Ghosts in Six Dynasties *zhiguai*." *CLEAR* 13 (Dec. 1991): 15–34.

———. *Strange Writing: Anomaly Accounts in Early Medieval China*. Albany: State University of New York Press, 1996.

Cao Xueqin 曹雪芹. *Honglou meng* 紅樓夢. 3 vols. Beijing: Renmin wenxue chubanshe, 1982.

Carlson, Marvin A. *Places of Performance: The Semiotics of Theatre Architecture*. Ithaca, NY: Cornell University Press, 1989.

Caruth, Cathy. "Introduction." In *Trauma: Explorations in Memory*, ed. Cathy Caruth, pp. 3–12. Baltimore, MD: Johns Hopkins University Press, 1995.

Carlitz, Katherine. "Desire, Danger, and the Body: Stories of Women's Virtue in Late Ming China." In *Engendering China: Women, Culture, and the State*, eds. Christina K. Gilmartin et al., pp. 101–124. Cambridge, MA: Harvard University Press, 1994.

Castle, Terry. *The Female Thermometer: Eighteenth-century Culture and the Invention of the Uncanny*. New York: Oxford University Press, 1995.

Chan, Leo Tak-hung. *The Discourse on Foxes and Ghosts: Ji Yun and Eighteenth-century Literati Storytelling*. Honolulu: University of Hawai'i Press, 1998.

———. "Narrative as Argument: The *Yuewei caotang biji* and the Late Eighteenth-century Elite Discourse on the Supernatural." *HJAS* 53.1 (Jun. 1993): 25–62.
Chan, Stephen Chingkiu. "The Return of the Ghostwoman: A Critical Reading of Three Sung Hua-pen stories." *Asian Culture Quarterly* 15.3 (1987): 47–72.
Chang, Kang-i Sun. *The Late Ming Poet Ch'en Tzu-lung: Crises of Love and Loyalism.* New Haven, CT: Yale University Press, 1991.
Chao Yuanfang 巢元方. *Zhubing yuanhou lun* 諸病源候論. Facsimile of 1891 ed. Beijing: Renmin weisheng chubanshe, 1955.
Che Wenming 車文明. *Ershi shiji xiqu wenwu de faxian yu quxue yanjiu* 二十世紀戲曲文物的發現與曲學研究. Beijing: Wenhua yishu chubanshe, 2001.
Chen Duo 陳多, and Ye Changhai 葉長海, eds. *Zhongguo lidai julun xuanzhu* 中國歷代劇論選注. Changsha: Hunan wenyi chubanshe, 1987.
Chen Wannai 陳萬鼐. *Hong Sheng yanjiu* 洪昇研究. Taibei: Taiwan xuesheng shuju, 1970.
Chen Weisong 陳維崧. *Furen ji* 婦人集. In *Zhaodai congshu guangbian, yiji* 昭代叢書廣編, 已集, eds. Yang Fuji 楊復吉 and Shen Maozhi 沈楙直. Shikaitang 世楷堂 edition, 1833. Academy of Sciences Library, Beijing.
Chen Zilong 陳子龍. *Chen Zilong shiji* 陳子龍詩集, eds. Shi Zhecun 施蟄存 and Ma Zuxi 馬祖熙. Shanghai: Shanghai guji chubanshe, 1983.
Chen Ziming 陳自明. *Furen daquan liangfang* 婦人大全良方. Taibei: Shangwu yinshuguan, n.d. (facsimile of Wenyuange siku quanshu ed., vol. 14).
Chion, Michel. *The Voice in Cinema*, ed. and trans. Claudia Gorbman. New York: Columbia University Press, 1999.
Chow, Rey. "A Souvenir of Love." In *Ethics After Idealism: Theory, Culture, Ethnicity, Reading*, ed. Rey Chow, pp. 133–148. Bloomington: Indiana University Press, 1998.
Chuandai gangmu 穿戴綱目. Photocopy of 1820–1845 Shengping shu 昇平署 ms. Palace Museum Library, Beijing. (n.p.)
Chunfang pu: Nüxing de xingxiang yu caiyi 春芳譜：女性的形象與才藝, eds. Liu Fangru 劉芳如 and Zhang Huazhi 張華芝. Taibei: National Palace Museum, 2003.
Clery, E. J. *The Rise of Supernatural Fiction, 1762–1800.* Cambridge: Cambridge University Press, 1995.
Cole, David. *The Theatrical Event.* Middletown, CT: Wesleyan University Press, 1975.
Connery, Christopher Leigh. *The Empire of the Text: Writing and Authority in Early Imperial China.* Lanham, MD: Rowman and Littlefield, 1998.
Da Han yuanling mizang jing 大漢原陵秘葬經. Attributed to Dili yinyang ren Zhang Jingwen 地理陰陽人張景文. Facsimile reprint of *Yongle dadian* 永樂大典. Beijing: Zhonghua shuju, 1959, *ce* 冊 no. 91.
Dai Fu 戴孚. *Guangyi ji* 廣異記. In *Mingbao ji/Guangyi ji* 冥報記/廣異記, ed. Fang Shiming 方詩銘. Beijing: Zhonghua shuju, 1992.
Dangui ji 丹桂記. Facsimile reprint of Wanli ed. *Guben xiqu* I, no. 99.
Davis, A. R. *T'ao Yüan-ming, A.D. 365–427: His Works and Their Meaning.* Hong Kong: Hong Kong University Press, 1983.
Davis, Tracy C., and Thomas Postlewait. "Theatricality: An Introduction." In *Theatricality*,

eds. Tracy C. Davis and Thomas Postlewait, pp. 1–39. Cambridge: Cambridge University Press, 2003.

Deng Changfeng 鄧長風. *Ming Qing xiqu kaolüe xubian* 明清戲曲考略續編. Shanghai: Shanghai guji chubanshe, 1997.

Deng Hanyi 鄧漢儀, comp. *Shiguan chuji* 詩觀初集. Preface dated 1672. Photocopy of Kangxi Shenmotang 慎墨堂 edition in the Library of Congress.

Diény, Jean-Pierre, ed. and trans. *Les Dix-neuf Poèmes Anciens.* Paris: Université Paris VII, Centre de publication Asie orientale, 1974.

Djikstra, Bram. *Idols of Perversity: Fantasies of Feminine Evil in Fin-de-siècle.* New York: Oxford University Press, 1986.

Dong Jieyuan Xixiang ji 董解元西廂記, ed. Ling Jingyan 凌景埏. Beijing: Renmin wenxue chubanshe, reprint of 1962 ed., 1986.

Doré, Henri. *Researches into Chinese Superstitions.* Trans. M. Kennelly. Taibei: Cheng-Wen Publishing Company, 1966.

Ducheng jisheng 都城紀勝. Comp. Naide weng 耐得翁 (pseud.). *Siku quanshu zhenben* 四庫全書珍本, ninth series, no. 162. Taibei: Taiwan Commercial Press, 1979.

Dudbridge, Glen. *Religious Experience and Lay Society in T'ang China: A Reading of Tai Fu's Kuang-i chi.* Cambridge: Cambridge University Press, 1995.

Erya jinzhu 爾雅今注. Annotated by Xu Chaohua 徐朝華. Tianjin: Nankai daxue chubanshe, 1987.

Fan Xingzhun 范行准. *Zhongguo bingshi xinyi* 中國病史新義, ed. Yi Guangqian 伊廣謙. Beijing: Zhongyi guji chubanshe, 1989.

Fan Wenruo 范文若. *Menghua han* 夢花酣. Preface dated 1632. Fascimile reprint of Ming Boshan tang 博山堂 ed. *Guben xiqu congkan* II, no. 84.

Fan Ye 范曄. *Hou Hanshu* 後漢書. Beijing: Zhonghua shuju, 1965.

Fei, Faye Chunfang, ed. and trans. *Chinese Theories of Theater and Performance from Confucius to the Present.* Ann Arbor: University of Michigan Press, 1999.

Feng Menglong 馮夢龍, ed. *Fengliu meng* 風流夢. Revised and abridged version of Tang Xianzu, *Mudan ting.* In *Mohanzhai dingben chuanqi* 墨憨齋定本傳奇, vol. 3. Beijing: Zhongguo xiju chubanshe, 1960.

———, ed. *Gujin xiaoshuo* 古今小說. Beijing: Renmin daxue chubanshe, 1981.

———, ed. *Jingshi tongyan* 驚世通言. Beijing: Beijing renmin daxue chubanshe, 1986.

———, ed. *Qingshi leilüe* 情史類略. In *Feng Menglong quanji* 馮夢龍全集, ed. Wei Tongxian 魏同賢. Vols. 37–38. Shanghai: Shanghai guji chubanshe, 1993.

———, ed. *Saxue tang* 灑雪堂. In *Mohanzhai dingben chuanqi* 墨憨齋定本傳奇, vol. 2. Beijing: Zhongguo xiju chubanshe, 1960.

———, ed. *Xingshi hengyan* 醒世恒言. In *Feng Menglong quanji* 馮夢龍全集, ed. Wei Tongxian 魏同賢, vol. 24. Shanghai: Shanghai guji chubanshe, 1993.

Fonoroff, Paul. *Silver Light: A Pictorial History of Hong Kong Cinema 1920–1970.* Hong Kong: Joint Publishing, 1997.

Foucault, Michel. "What is an Author?" In *The Foucault Reader*, ed. Paul Rabinow, pp. 101–120. New York: Pantheon Books, 1984.

Frankel, Hans. "The Contemplation of the Past in Tang Poetry." In *Perspectives on the*

Tang, eds. Arthur Wright and Denis Twitchett, pp. 345–366. New Haven, CT: Yale University Press, 1973.

———. *The Flowering Plum and the Palace Lady*. New Haven, CT: Yale University Press, 1976.

Freud, Sigmund. *Beyond the Pleasure Principle*. Trans. and ed. James Strachey. New York: Norton, 1961.

———. "Mourning and Melancholia." In *The Standard Edition of the Complete Psychological Works of Sigmund Freud*, ed. James Strachey, vol. 14, pp. 239–258. London: The Hogarth Press, 1953–1974.

———. "The Uncanny." Trans. Alix Strachey. In Sigmund Freud, *Psychological Writings and Letters*, ed. Sandor Gilman, pp. 120–153. New York: Continuum Publishing Company, 1995.

Frodsham, J. D. *The Poems of Li Ho (791–817)*. Oxford: Clarendon Press, 1970.

Fu Shan 傅山. *Fu Qingzhu nüke nanke erke* 傅青主女科男科兒科. Taiyuan: Shanxi renmin chubanshe, 1992.

Fu Xihua 傅惜華. *Mingdai chuanqi quanmu* 明代傳奇全目. Beijing: Renmin wenxue chubanshe, 1959.

Fu Yichen 傅一臣. *Rengui fuqi* 人鬼夫妻 in *Sumen xiao* 蘇門嘯. Preface dated 1642. Facsimile of Qiaoyuezhai 敲月齋 edition, play no. 9, pp. 1–28.

Furth, Charlotte. "Androgynous Males and Deficient Females: Biology and Gender Boundaries in Sixteenth- and Seventeenth-Century China." *Late Imperial China* 9.2 (1988): 1–31.

———. "Blood, Body, and Gender: Medical Images of the Female Condition in China, 1600–1845." *Chinese Science* 7 (1986): 43–66.

———. "Editor's Introduction." *Late Imperial China* 13, no. 1 (Jun 1992): 1–8.

———. *A Flourishing Yin: Gender in China's Medical History, 960–1665*. Berkeley: University of California Press, 1999.

———. "Rethinking Van Gulik: Sexuality and Reproduction in Traditional Chinese Medicine." In *Engendering China: Women, Culture and the State*, ed. Christina K. Gilmartin et al., pp. 125–146. Cambridge, MA: Harvard University Press, 1994.

Gan Bao 干寶. *Soushen ji* 搜神記, ed. Wang Shaoying 汪紹楹. Beijing: Zhonghua shuju, 1979.

Gao Buying 高步瀛, ed. *Tang Song shi juyao* 唐宋詩舉要. Beijing: Zhonghua shuju, 1978.

Garber, Marjorie B. *Shakespeare's Ghost Writers: Literature as Uncanny Causality*. New York: Methuen, 1987.

Goldman, Michael. *The Actor's Freedom: Toward a Theory of Drama*. New York: Viking Press, 1975.

Gong Zizhen 龔自珍. *Gong Zizhen quanji* 龔自珍全集. Shanghai: Zhonghua shuju, 1959.

Good, Byron. *Medicine, Rationality and Experience: An Anthropological Perspective*. Cambridge: Cambridge University Press, 1994.

Goodwin, Sarah Webster, and Elisabeth Bronfen, eds. *Death and Representation*. Baltimore: Johns Hopkins University Press, 1993.

Gōyama Kiwamu 合山究. *Min-Shin jidai ni okeru jōshi to sono bungaku* 明清時代における

情死とその文學. In *Itō Sōhei Kyōju taikan kinen Chūgokugaku ronshū* 伊藤漱平教授退官中國學論集, pp. 417–448. Tokyo: Kyūko shoin, 1986.
Graham, A. C., trans. *Poems of the Late T'ang.* Harmondsworth: Penguin Books, 1965.
———, trans. *Chuang-tzu: The Seven Inner Chapters and Other Writings from the Book Chuang-tzu.* London: Allen & Unwin, 1981.
Groot, J. J. M. de. *The Religious System of China: Its Ancient Forms, Evolution, History and Present Aspect, Manners, Customs and Social Institutions Connected Therewith.* 6 vols. Reprint of 1892–1910 Brill ed. Taibei: Ch'eng-wen Publishing Company, 1969.
Gu Xuejie 顧學頡, and Wang Xueqi 王學奇. *Yuanqu shici* 元曲釋詞. 4 vols. Beijing: Zhongguo shehui kexue chubanshe, 1983–1990.
Gu Yanwu 顧炎武. *Gu Tinglin shiji huizhu* 顧亭林詩集彙注, eds. Wang Quchang 王蘧常 and Wu Piji 吳丕績. Shanghai: Shanghai guji chubanshe, 1983.
Guan Hanqing 關漢卿. *Dou E yuan* 竇娥冤. *Gu mingjia* 古名家 ed. In *Mowangguan chaojiao ben Gujin zaju* 脈望館鈔校本古今雜劇, no. 23. Facsimile reprint, *Guben xiqu* IV.
———. *Dou E yuan* 竇娥冤. In *Gujin mingju hexuan* 古今名劇合選. Ed. Meng Chengshun 孟稱舜. Facsimile reprint of 1633 edition, *Guben xiqu* IV.
———. *Dou E yuan* 竇娥冤. In *Yuanqu xuan* 元曲選. Ed. Zang Maoxun 臧懋循, 4: 1499–1517. Beijing: Zhonghua shuju, 1958.
Guben xiqu congkan chuji 古本戲曲叢刊初集. Shanghai: Shangwu yinshuguan, 1955. Abbreviated as *Guben xiqu* I.
Guben xiqu congkan erji 古本戲曲叢刊二集. Shanghai: Shangwu yinshuguan, 1955. Abbreviated as *Guben xiqu* II.
Guben xiqu congkan siji 古本戲曲叢刊四集. Shanghai: Shangwu yinshuguan, 1958. Abbreviated as *Guben xiqu* IV.
Guben xiqu congkan wuji 古本戲曲叢刊五集. Shanghai: Shanghai guji chubanshe, 1984. Abbreviated as *Guben xiqu* V.
Gunning, Tom. "Phantom Images and Modern Manifestations: Spirit Photography, Magic Theater, Trick Films, and Photography's Uncanny." In *Fugitive Images: From Photography to Video*, ed. Patrice Petro, pp. 42–71. Bloomington: Indiana University Press, 1995.
Guo Aichun 郭靄春 et al., eds. *Huangdi neijing cidian* 黄帝内經詞典. Tianjin: Tianjin kexue jishu chubanshe, 1991.
Guo Yingde 郭英德. *Ming Qing chuanqi shi* 明清傳奇史. Nanjing: Jiangsu guji chubanshe, 1999.
Guthke, Karl Siegfried. *The Gender of Death: A Cultural History in Art and Literature.* London: Cambridge University Press, 1999.
Han Yu 韓愈. *Han Yu quanji jiaozhu* 韓愈全集校注, eds. Qu Shouyuan 屈守原 and Chang Sichun 常思春. Chengdu: Sichuan daxue chubanshe, 1996.
———. *Han Yu xuanji* 韓愈選集, Ed. Sun Changwu 孫昌武. Shanghai: Shanghai guji chubanshe, 1996.
Hanyu dacidian 漢語大詞典, ed. Luo Zhufeng 羅竹風. 12 vols. Shanghai: Hanyu dacidian chubanshe, 1994.

Hanan, Patrick. *The Chinese Short Story: Studies in Dating, Authorship and Composition.* Cambridge, MA: Harvard University Press, 1973.

———. *The Chinese Vernacular Story.* Cambridge, MA: Harvard University Press, 1981.

Harrell, Stevan. "Men, Women, and Ghosts in Taiwanese Folk Religion." In *Gender and Religion: On the Complexity of Symbols*, eds. Carolyn Walker Bynum et al., pp. 97–116. Boston: Beacon Press, 1986.

Hawkes, David, trans. *The Songs of the South: An Ancient Chinese Anthology of Poems by Qu Yuan and Other Poets.* Harmondsworth: Penguin Books, 1985.

———, trans. *The Story of the* Stone (*Dream of the Red Chamber*). By Cao Xueqin. 5 vols. Harmondsworth: Penguin Books, 1973–1986.

Hay, John. "The Human Body as a Microcosmic Source of Macrocosmic Values in Calligraphy." In *Theories of the Arts in China*, eds. Susan Bush and Christian Murck, pp. 74–102. Princeton: Princeton University Press, 1983.

Hay, Jonathan. "Ming Palace and Tomb in Early Qing Jiangnan: Dynastic Memory and the Openness of History." *Late Imperial China* 20.1 (Jun 1999): 1–48.

———. "The Suspension of Dynastic Time." In *Boundaries in China*, ed. John Hay, pp. 171–197. London: Reaktion, 1994.

———. "The Wilderness Environment of the Remnant Subject." Unpublished paper.

Heath, Stephen. "Joan Riviere and the Masquerade." In *Formations of Fantasy*, eds. Victor Burgin, James Donald, and Cora Kaplan, pp. 45–61. New York: Methuen, 1986.

Hertz, Robert. *Death and the Right Hand.* Trans. Rodney and Claudia Needham. Glencoe, IL: Free Press, 1960.

Hightower, James Robert, trans. *The Poetry of T'ao Ch'ien.* Oxford: Clarendon Press, 1970.

Ho, Sam 何思穎, and Ho Wai-leng 何慧玲, eds. *The Swordsman and his Jiang Hu: Tsui Hark and Hong Kong Film/Jianxiao jianghu: Xu Ke yu Xianggang dianying* 劍嘯江湖：徐克與香港電影. Bilingual ed. Hong Kong: Hong Kong Film Archives, 2002.

Hong Mai 洪邁. *Yijian zhi* 夷堅志. 4 vols. Beijing: Zhonghua shuju, 1981.

———. *Wanshou Tangren jueju* 萬首唐人絕句. Facsimile of Ming ed. Beijing: Wenxue guji kanxingshe, 1955.

Hong Sheng 洪昇. *Changsheng dian* 長生殿, ed. Xu Shuofang 徐朔方. Beijing: Renmin wenxue chubanshe, 1986.

———. *Changsheng dian* with commentaries (1700–1704). Facsimile reprint of author's Baiqicao tang 稗畦草堂 edition in *Guben xiqu* V.

———. *Changsheng dian.* 1750 manuscript copied by Shen Wencai 沈文彩. 45 scenes, 2 vols. Zhongguo yishu yanjiuyuan 中國藝術研究院, Xiqu yanjiusuo ziliao shi 戲曲研究所資料室, Beijing.

———. *Changsheng dian* (31 acts). In *Nashuying qupu* 納書楹曲譜, scored by Ye Tang 葉堂. 3 vols. Facsimile reprint of 1792 ed. Taibei: Shengzhai chubanshe, 1969.

———. *Changsheng dian* in *Zhongguo gudian xiju xuanzhu* 中國古典戲劇選注, annotated by Zeng Yongyi 曾永義, pp. 501–822. Taibei: Guojia chubanshe, 1985.

———. *Palace of Eternal Youth* (*Quanben liantai Changsheng dian* 全本連台長生殿), performed by the Suzhou Kunju *Changsheng dian* yishu tuan 江蘇蘇州昆劇長生殿藝術團. Taibei: Shitou chubanshe, 2004.

Hongmeige 紅梅閣. In *Xikao daquan* 戲考大全, no. 242. Ed. Wang Dacuo 王大錯. Zhonghua tushuguan edition, 1915–1925. Reprint. Shanghai: Shanghai shudian, 1990.

Hsia, C. T. "Time and the Human Condition in the Plays of T'ang Hsien-tsu." In *Self and Society in Ming Thought*, ed. Theodore de Bary, pp. 250–290. New York: Columbia University Press, 1990.

Hsiao, Li-ling. "The Eternal Present of the Past: Performance, Illustration, and Reading in the Drama Culture of the Wanli Period (1573–1619)." PhD diss., Oxford University, 2002.

Hsü, Tao-Ching. *The Chinese Conception of the Theatre.* Seattle: University of Washington Press, 1985.

Hu Wenkai 胡文楷. *Lidai funü zhuzuo kao* 歷代婦女著作攷. Shanghai: Shanghai guji chubanshe, 1985.

Hu Yimin 胡益民. *Zhang Dai yanjiu* 張岱研究. Hefei: Anhui jiaoyu chubanshe, 2002.

Hu Zi 胡仔. *Tiaoxi yuyin conghua* 苕溪漁隱叢話. Taibei: Shijie shuju, 1961.

Hua Wei 華瑋. *Ming Qing funü zhi xiqu chuangzuo yu piping* 明清婦女之戲曲創作與批評. Taibei: Zhongyang yanjiu yuan Zhongguo wenzhe yanjiusuo, 2003.

———, ed. *Tang Xianzu yu Mudan ting yanjiu* 湯顯祖與《牡丹亭》研究. 2 vols. Taibei: Zhongyang yanjiu yuan Zhongguo wenzhe yanjiusuo, 2006.

Hua Wei, and Wang Ay-ling 王愛玲, eds. *Ming Qing xiqu guoji yantaohui lunwen ji* 明清戲曲國際研討會論文集. 2 vols. Taibei: Zhongyang yanjiu yuan Zhongguo wenzhe yanjiusuo, 1998.

Huai nan zi. 淮南子. Comp. Liu An 劉安. *Sibu congkan* 四部叢刊, first series, no. 70. Shanghai: Shangwu yinshuguan, 1929.

Huang Zhanyue 黃展岳. "Ming Qing huangshi de gongfei xunzang zhi." 明清皇室的宮妃殉葬制. *Gugong bowuyuan yuankan* 故宮博物院院刊 (1988. 1): 29–34.

Hummel, Arthur. *Eminent Chinese of the Ch'ing Period.* Taibei: Ch'eng-wen, 1967. Abbreviated as *ECCP.*

Huntington, Rania. *Alien Kind: Foxes in Ming-Qing Narrative.* Cambridge, MA: Harvard Asia Center Publications, 2003.

———. "Ghosts Seeking Substitutes: Female Suicide and Repetition." *Late Imperial China* 26.1 (June 2005): 1–40.

———. "The Weird in the Newspaper." In *Writing and Materiality in China: Essays in Honor of Patrick Hanan*, eds. Judith T. Zeitlin and Lydia H. Liu, pp. 341–396. Cambridge, MA: Harvard Asia Center Publications, 2003.

Hymes, Robert P. "Personal Relations and Bureaucratic Hierarchy: Evidence from the Song Dynasty." In *Unruly Gods: Divinity and Society in China*, eds. Meir Shahar and Robert P. Weller, pp. 37–60. Honolulu: University of Hawai'i Press, 1996.

Idema, Wilt L. "Skulls and Skeletons in Art and on Stage." In *Conflict and Accommodation in Early Modern East Asia: Essays in Honor of Erik Zürcher*, eds. Leonard Blussé and Harriet Zurndorfer, pp. 191–216. Leiden: E. J. Brill, 1993.

———. "Zang Maoxun as a Publisher." In *Higashi Ajia shuppan bunka kenkyū ni wa tazumi* 東アジア出版文化研究にわたずみ, ed. Isobe Akira 磯部彰, pp. 19–29. Tokyo: Nigensha, 2004.

Idema, Wilt L., and Stephen H. West. *Chinese Theater 1100–1450: A Sourcebook.* Wiesbaden: Steiner, 1982.

Ivy, Marilyn. *Discourses of the Vanishing: Modernity, Phantasm, Japan.* Chicago: University of Chicago Press, 1995.

Ji Yougong 計有功, comp. *Tangshi jishi* 唐詩紀事. Beijing: Zhonghua shuju, 1965.

Ji Yun 紀昀. *Yuewei caotang biji* 閱微草堂筆記. 2 vols. Shanghai: Shanghai guji chubanshe, 1980.

Jiang Guan 江瓘. *Mingyi leian* 名醫類案. Facsimile reprint of Qianlong ed. Taibei: Hongye shuju, 1971.

Jin Weinuo 金維諾. *Shanxi Jishan Qinglong si bihua* 山西稷山青龍寺壁畫. Shijiazhuang: Hebei meishu chubanshe, 2001.

Jinghong ji 驚鴻記. Facsimile reprint of Wanli ed. (1590 preface). *Guben xiqu* II, no. 29.

Jinghong ji/Yanmei ji 驚鴻記/鹽梅記. Ed. Kang Baocheng 康保成. Beijing: Zhonghua shuju, 2004.

[Jiaozheng] Kangxi zidian [校正]康熙字典. 1716. 2 vols. Taibei: Yiwen yinshuguan, 1973.

Johnson, Barbara. *The Critical Difference: Essays in the Contemporary Rhetoric of Reading.* Baltimore: Johns Hopkins University Press, 1980.

Johnson, David, ed. *Ritual Opera, Operatic Ritual: "Mu-Lien Rescues His Mother" in Chinese Popular Culture.* Berkeley: University of California Press, 1989.

Jones, Ann Rosalind, and Peter Stallybrass. *Renaissance Clothing and the Materials of Memory.* Cambridge: Cambridge University Press, 2000.

Jordan, David K. *Gods, Ghosts, and Ancestors: The Folk Religion of a Taiwanese Village.* Berkeley: University of California Press, 1972.

Kangxi zidian. See *[Jiaozheng] Kangxi zidian.*

Kao, Karl, ed. *Classical Chinese Tales of the Supernatural and the Fantastic: Selections from the Third to the Tenth Century.* Bloomington: Indiana University Press, 1985.

Ko, Dorothy. *Teachers of the Inner Chambers: Women and Culture in Seventeenth-century China.* Stanford: Stanford University Press, 1994.

Kong Shangren 孔尚任. *Xiao Hulei chuanqi* 小忽雷傳奇. Shanghai: Nuanhongshi ed., 1919.

———. *Taohua shan* 桃花扇, eds. Wang Jisi 王季思 et al. Beijing: Renmin chubanshe, 1997. Reprint of 1959 edition.

Kunju chuandai 昆劇穿戴. Comp. Suzhou shi xiqu yanjiu shi. Based on oral interviews with Zeng Changsheng 曾長生. 1963.

Kuriyama, Shigehisa. *The Expressiveness of the Body and the Divergence of Greek and Chinese Medicine.* New York: Zone Books, 1999.

———. "Concepts of Disease in East Asia." *The Cambridge World History of Human Disease,* eds. Kenneth F. Kiple et al., pp. 52–59. Cambridge: Cambridge University Press, 1993.

Laing, Ellen Johnston. "Erotic Themes and Romantic Heroines Depicted by Ch'iu Ying." *Archives of Asian Art* 49 (1996): 68–91.

Laiyang xianzhi 萊陽縣志. Comp. Wang Pixu 王丕煦 et al. China, 1935.

Laplanche, J., and J.-B. Pontalis. *The Language of Psycho-Analysis.* Trans. Donald Nicholson-Smith. New York: W. W. Norton, 1973.

Li Chengzhong 李澄中. *Genzhai biji* 艮齋筆記. Photocopy of unpaginated ms. in National Central Library, Taiwan.

Li Daoyuan 酈道元. *Shuijing zhu* 水經注. Eds. Tan Shuchun 譚屬春 and Chen Aiping 陳愛平. Changsha: Yuelu shushe, 1995.

Li Fang 李昉 et al., comp. *Taiping guangji* 太平廣記. 10 vols. Bejing: Zhonghua shuju, 1981. Abbreviated as *TPGJ*.

Li He 李賀. *Sanjia pingzhu Li Changji geshi* 三家評注李長吉歌詩, annotated by Wang Qi 王琦 et al. Beijing: Zhonghua shuju, 1959.

Liji 禮記. In *Shisanjing zhushu* 十三經注疏, ed. Ruan Yuan 阮元. Beijing: Zhonghua shuju, 1980.

Li Jianguo 李劍國. *Songdai zhiguai chuanqi xulu* 宋代志怪傳奇敍錄. Tianjin: Nankai daxue chubanshe, 1997.

———. *Tang Wudai zhiguai chuanqi xulu* 唐五代志怪傳奇敍錄. Tianjin: Nankai daxue chubanshe, 1993.

Li Jianmin 李建民. "Suibing yu changsuo: Chuantong yixue dui suibing de yizhong jieshi." 祟病與場所：傳統醫學對祟病的一種解釋. *Hanxue yanjiu* 12.1 (Jun 1994): 101–148.

Li Shizhen 李時珍. *Bencao gangmu* 本草綱目. 5 vols. Reprint of 1930 edition. Beijing: Zhongguo shudian, 1988.

Li, Wai-yee. *Enchantment and Disenchantment: Love and Illusion in Chinese Literature.* Princeton: Princeton University Press, 1993.

———. "Women as Emblems of Dynastic Fall in Qing Literature." In *Dynastic Crisis and Cultural Innovation: From the Late Ming to the Late Qing and Beyond*, eds. David Wang and Shang Wei, pp. 95–150. Cambridge, MA: Harvard Asia Center Publications, 2005.

———. "Heroic Transformation: Woman and National Trauma in Early Qing Literature." *HJAS* 59.2 (Dec. 1999): 363–443.

Li Yu 李漁. *Xianqing ouji* 閒情偶記, ed. Bei Jinheng 卑錦珩. Hangzhou: Zhejiang guji chubanshe, 1999.

Li Zhen 李禎. *Jiandeng yuhua* 剪燈餘話. Author's preface dated 1420. In *Jiandeng xinhua wai erzhong* 剪燈新話外二種, ed. Zhou Yi 周夷. Shanghai: Gudian wenxue chubanshe, 1957.

Liao Ben 廖奔. *Zhongguo gudai juchang shi* 中國古代劇場史. Zhengzhou: Zhongzhou guji chubanshe, 1997.

Liao Tengye 廖藤葉. *Zhongguo mengxi yanjiu* 中國夢戲研究. Taibei: Xuexi chubanshe, 2000.

Lin Yunming 林雲銘. *Sunzhai fenyu* 損齋焚餘. Kangxi edition. National Library of China.

———. *Wushan kouyin* 吳山鷇音. Kangxi edition. National Library of China.

———. *Yiguilou xuanji.* 挹奎樓選集. Kangxi edition. National Library of China.

Ling Mengchu 凌濛初. *Erke Paian jingqi* 二刻拍案驚奇. Facsimile reprint of 1628 Shangyou tang 尚友堂 ed. 2 vols. Shanghai: Shanghai guji chubanshe, 1985.

———. *Paian jingqi chuke* 拍案驚奇初刻. Facsimile reprint of 1628 Shangyou tang 尚友堂 ed. 2 vols. Shanghai: Shanghai guji chubanshe, 1985.

Liu Chao 劉超. "Jianguo yilai guixi yanjiu huimou" 建國以來鬼戲研究回眸 in *Wuhan daxue yishuxi jikan luojia yilin* (2004.2): 41–49.
Liu Chuhua 劉楚華. "Ming Qing chuanqi zhong de *hun dan*." 明清傳奇中的魂旦. In *Ming Qing wenxue yu xingbie yanjiu* 明清文學與性別研究, ed. Zhang Hongsheng 張宏生, pp. 71–91. Nanjing: Jiangsu guji chubanshe, 2002.
Liu Fu 劉斧. *Qingsuo gaoyi* 青瑣高議. Shanghai: Shanghai guji chubanshe, 1983.
Liu Hui 劉輝, ed. *Hong Sheng ji* 洪昇集. Hangzhou: Zhejiang guji chubanshe, 1992.
———. "Lun Wu Shufu." 論吳舒鳧. *Xiju yanjiu* 戲劇研究 37.1 (1987): 108–117.
Liu Xun 劉昫, comp. *Jiu Tangshu* 舊唐書. Beijing: Zhonghua shuju, 1977.
Liu Yanjun 劉彥君. *Lan'gan paibian: Gudai juzuojia xinlu* 欄杆拍遍：古代劇作家心路. Beijing: Wenhua yishu chubanshe, 1995.
Lu Eting 陸萼庭. *Kunju yanchu shigao* 昆劇演出史稿. Shanghai: Shanghai wenyi chubanshe, 1980.
———. "Qingdai quanbenxi yanchu shulun." 清代全本戲演出述論. In *Ming Qing xiqu guoji yantao hui lunwen ji*, eds. Hua Wei and Wang Ay-ling, pp. 327–363. Taibei: Zhongyang yanjiu yuan Zhongguo wenzhe yanjiusuo, 1998.
Lu Guimeng 陸龜蒙 and Pi Rixiu 皮日休. *Songling ji* 松陵集. In *Hubei xianzheng yishu* 湖北先正遺書, comps. Lu Jing 盧靖 and Lu Shen 盧慎. Shenshiji zhai, 1923.
Lu Jianzeng 盧見曽. *Guochao Shanzuo shichao* 國朝山左詩鈔. Author's preface dated in 1758. Qing edition in Regenstein Library, University of Chicago.
Lu, Tina. *Persons, Roles, and Minds: Identity in Peony Pavilion and Peach Blossom Fan.* Stanford: Stanford University Press, 2001.
Lu Xun 魯迅. "Nü diao" 女吊. In *Lu Xun quanji* 魯迅全集, 6: 614–621. Beijing: Renmin wenxue chubanshe, 1981.
Luo Zongtao 羅宗濤. "Tangren tibishi chutan" 唐人題壁詩初探. *Zhonghua wenshi luncong* 中華文史論叢 47 (1991): 153–186.
Mann, Susan, and Yu-yin Cheng, eds. *Under Confucian Eyes: Writings on Gender in Chinese History.* Berkeley: University of California Press, 2001.
Mao Shi zhengyi 毛詩正義. In *Shisanjing zhushu* 十三經注疏. Ed. Ruan Yuan 阮元 et al. Beijing: Zhonghua shuju, 1979.
Mao Xiaotong 毛效同, ed. *Tang Xianzu yanjiu ziliao huibian* 湯顯祖研究資料彙編. 2 vols. Shanghai: Shanghai guji chubanshe, 1986.
Mather, Richard B., trans. *Shih-shuo hsin-yü: A New Account of Tales of the World.* Comp. Liu Yiqing. Minneapolis: University of Minnesota Press, 1976.
McJannet, Linda. *The Voice of Elizabethan Stage Directions: The Evolution of a Theatrical Code.* Newark: University of Delaware Press, 1999.
McLaren, Anne. *Chinese Popular Culture and Ming Chantefables.* Leiden: Brill, 1998.
McMahon, Keith. *Misers, Shrews, and Polygamists: Sexuality and Male-Female Relations in Eighteenth-century Chinese Fiction.* Durham: Duke University Press, 1995.
Mei Dingzuo 梅鼎祚. *Caigui ji* 才鬼記, eds. Tian Pu 田璞 and Cha Hongde 查洪德. Zhengzhou: Zhongzhou guji chubanshe, 1989.
———, comp. *Guyue yuan* 古樂苑. *Yingyin wenyuange Siku quanshu* 影印文淵閣四庫全書, vol. 1394. Taibei: Taiwan Shangwu yinshuguan, 1983–1986.

———. *Luqiu shi shi ji* 鹿裘石室集. 1633 preface. Hishi photocopy of Ming ed. in Naikaku Bunko. Gest Library, Princeton.

"Mei fei zhuan" 梅妃傳. In *Gudai wenyan duanpian xiaoshuo xuanzhu* 古代文言短篇小說選注, ed. Cheng Boquan 成柏泉, 2: 40–47. Shanghai: Shanghai guji chubanshe, 1984.

Meng Chengshun 孟稱舜. *Jiao Hong ji* 嬌紅記. Ed. Ouyang Guang 歐陽光. Shanghai: Shanghai guji chubanshe, 1988.

Mowangguan chaojiaoben Gujin zaju 脈望館鈔校本古今雜劇. Facsimile reprint of Zhao Qimei's 趙琦美 (1563–1624) collection, *Guben xiqu* IV.

Mou Runsun 牟潤孫. "Lin Siniang gushi zhengshi" 林四娘故事徵實. *Lianhe shuyuan xuebao* 聯合書院學報 12 (1974): 1–9.

Myrhe, Karin. "The Appearances of Ghosts in Northern Drama." PhD diss., University of California, Berkeley, 1998.

Needham, Joseph. "Time and Knowledge in China." In *The Voices of Time: A Cooperative Survey of Man's Views of Time as Expressed by the Sciences and by the Humanities*, ed. J. T. Fraser, pp. 92–135. New York: George Braziller, 1966.

Nie Shiqiao 聶石樵, and Deng Kuiying 鄧魁英. *Gudai xiaoshuo xiqu luncong* 古代小說戲曲論叢. Beijing: Zhonghua shuju, 1985.

Nienhauser, William H. *P'i Ji-hsiu*. Boston: Twayne Publishers, 1979.

Nora, Pierre. "Between Memory and History: Les Lieux de Mémoire." *Representations* 20 (Spring 1989): 7–25.

Ouyang Xiu 歐陽修, and Song Qi 宋祁. *Xin Tangshu* 新唐書. Beijing: Zhonghua shuju, 1986.

Owen, Stephen, trans. *An Anthology of Chinese Literature: Beginnings to 1911*. New York: W. W. Norton, 1996.

———. "Place: Meditations on the Past at Chin-ling." *HJAS* 50.2 (Dec. 1990): 417–457.

———. *The Poetry of Meng Chiao and Han Yü*. New Haven, CT: Yale University Press, 1975.

———, ed. *Readings in Chinese Literary Thought*. Cambridge, MA: Council on East Asian Studies, Harvard University, 1992.

———. *Remembrances: The Experience of the Past in Classical Chinese Literature*. Cambridge, MA: Harvard University Press, 1986.

———. *Traditional Chinese Poetry and Poetics: Omen of the World*. Madison: University of Wisconsin Press, 1985.

Oxford English Dictionary, The. Online at http://dictionary.oed.com/.

Pacteau, Francette. *The Symptom of Beauty*. Cambridge, MA: Harvard University Press, 1994.

Pan Zhiheng 潘之恆. *Pan Zhiheng quhua* 潘之恆曲話, ed. Wang Xiaoyi 汪效倚. Beijing: Zhongguo xiju chubanshe, 1988.

Pavis, Patrice. *Dictionary of the Theatre: Terms, Concepts, and Analysis*. Trans. Christine Shantz. Toronto: University of Toronto Press, 1998.

———. *Dictionnaire du Théâtre*. Paris: Messidor/Éditions sociales, 1987.

Peucker, Brigitte. *Incorporating Images: Films and the Rival Arts*. Princeton, NJ: Princeton University Press, 1995.

Poo, Mu-chou. "The Completion of an Ideal World: The Human Ghost in Early-medieval China." *Asia Major* 10.1–2 (1997): 69–94.

———. "The Concept of Ghost in Ancient Chinese Religion." In *Religion and Chinese Society*, ed. John Lagerwey, pp. 173–191. Hong Kong: The Chinese University Press/ Paris: École française d'Extrême-Orient, 2004.

Porkert, Manfred. *Theoretical Foundations of Chinese Medicine: Systems of Correspondence.* Cambridge, MA: MIT Press, 1974.

Pu Songling 蒲松齡. *Liaozhai zhiyi huijiao [huizhu huiping ben]* 聊齋誌異[會校會註會評本], ed. Zhang Youhe 張友鶴. 4 vols. Shanghai: Shanghai guji chubanshe, 1983. Abbreviated to *Liaozhai* in text and *LZ* in citations.

———. *Liaozhai zhiyi [quanjiao huizhu jiping ben]* 聊齋誌異[全校會註集評本], ed. Ren Duxing 任篤行. 3 vols. Ji'nan: Qilu shushe, 2000.

———. *Pu Songling quanji* 蒲松齡全集, ed. Sheng Wei 盛偉. 3 vols. Shanghai: Xuelin chubanshe, 1998.

———. *Strange Stories from a Chinese Studio.* Trans. Herbert Allen Giles. London: T. De la Rue & Co., 1880.

———. *Strange Tales from a Chinese Studio.* Trans. John Minford. London: Penguin Books, 2006.

Qi Rushan 齊如山. "Shangxia chang" 上下場. Preface dated 1932. Reprinted in *Qi Rushan quanji* 齊如山全集, 1: 1–51. Taibei: Chongguang wenyi chubanshe, n.d.

Qian Qianyi 錢謙益. *Liechao shiji* 列朝詩集. Early Qing edition, Peking University Library.

Qian Zhonglian 錢仲聯. *Qingshi jishi* 清詩紀事. Vol. 22. Nanjing: Jiangsu guji chubanshe, 1987.

Qian Zhongshu 錢鍾書. *Guanzhui bian* 管錐編. 4 vols. Beijing: Zhonghua shuju, 1979.

Qingdai dang'an shiliao congbian 清代檔案史料叢編. Fourth collection. Beijing: Zhonghua shuju, 1979.

Qingzhou fuzhi 青州府志. 1709. Harvard-Yenching Library.

Qingzhou fuzhi 青州府志. 1859. Regenstein Library, University of Chicago.

Qingzhou shizhi 青州市志. Tianjin: Nankai daxue chubanshe, 1989.

Qu You 瞿佑. *Jiandeng xinhua* 剪燈新話. Author's preface dated 1379. In *Jiandeng xinhua wai erzhong* 剪燈新話外二種, ed. Zhou Yi 周夷. Shanghai: Shanghai guji chubanshe, 1981.

Quan Tangshi 全唐詩. Comps. Peng Dingqiu 彭定求 et al. Beijing: Zhonghua shuju, 1979.

Quan Tangwen. 全唐文. Comps. Dong Gao 董誥 et al. Wuyingdian kanben 武英殿刋本, 1818. Regenstein Library, University of Chicago.

Quanzhou fuzhi 泉州府志. Comp. Huang Ren 黃任. Facsimile reprint 1870 edition.

Ren Yingqiu 任應秋 et al., eds. *Huangdi neijing zhangju suoyin* 黃帝內經章句索引. Beijing: Renmin weisheng chubanshe, 1986.

Ricoeur, Paul. *Time and Narrative.* Trans. Kathleen Blarney and David Pellauer. 3 vols. Chicago: University of Chicago Press, 1988.

Riley, Jo. *Chinese Theatre and the Actor in Performance.* Cambridge: Cambridge University Press, 1997.

Robertson, Maureen. "Poetic Diction in the Works of Li He." PhD diss., University of Washington, 1970.

———. "Refiguring the Feminine." Unpublished paper.

Ruan Yuan 阮元 et al., eds., *Shisanjing zhushu* 十三經注疏. Beijing: Zhonghua shuju, 1980.

Ruan Yue 阮閱, comp. *[Zengxiu] Shihua zonggui* [增修]詩話總龜. Facsimile reprint of 1545 *Yuechuang daoren jiaokanben* 月窗道人校刊本 ed. Shanghai: Hanfenlou, 1929.

Sawada Mizuho 澤田瑞穗. *Kishu dangi* 鬼趣談議. Tokyo: Kokusho kankōkai, 1976.

Schafer, Edward. *The Divine Woman: Dragon Ladies and Rain Maidens in T'ang Literature.* Berkeley: University of California Press, 1973.

Schechner, Richard. *Performance Theory.* New York: Routledge, 2003.

Schipper, Kristofer. *Génies, Anges, et Démons.* Paris: Éditions du Seuil, 1971.

———. *The Taoist Body.* Trans. Karen C. Duval. Berkeley: University of California Press, 1993.

Schmitt, Jean-Claude. *Ghosts in the Middle Ages: The Living and the Dead in Medieval Society.* Trans. Teresa Lavender Fagan. Chicago: University of Chicago Press, 1998.

Seidel, Anna. "Post-mortem Immortality, or the Taoist Resurrection of the Body." In *Gilgul: Essays on Transformation, Revolution and Permanence in the History of Religions,* ed. S. Shaked et al., pp. 223–237. Leiden: E. J. Brill, 1987.

Shahar, Meir, and Robert P. Weller. "Introduction." In *Unruly Gods: Divinity and Society in China,* eds. Meir Shahar and Robert P. Weller, pp. 1–36. Honolulu: University of Hawai'i Press, 1996.

Shanben xiqu congkan 善本戲曲叢刊. Comp. Wang Qiugui 王秋桂. Taibei: Xuesheng shuju, 1984–1987.

Shang, Wei. "Prisoner and Creator: The Self-image of the Poet in Han Yu and Meng Jiao." *CLEAR* 16 (1994): 19–40.

Shapiro, Hugh. "The Puzzle of Spermatorrhea in Republican China." *positions* 6.3 (Winter 1998): 551–581.

Shen Deqian 沈德潛, comp. *Gushi yuan qianzhu* 古詩源箋注. Annotated by Wang Chunfu 王蒓父. Taibei: Huazheng shuju, 1983.

Shen Fu 沈復. *Fusheng liuji* 浮生六記. Beijing: Renmin wenxue chubanshe, 1999.

Shen, Guangren Grant. *Elite Theatre in Ming China, 1368–1644.* London and New York: Routledge, 2005.

———. "Theatre Performance during the Ming Dynasty." PhD diss., University of Hawai'i, 1994.

Shen Jing 沈璟. *Boxiao ji* 博笑記 in *Shen Jing ji* 沈璟集, 2: 696–782. Shanghai: Shanghai guji chubanshe, 1991.

———. *Shen Jing ji* 沈璟集, ed. Xu Shuofang 徐朔方. 2 vols. Shanghai: Shanghai guji chubanshe, 1991.

———. *Taofu ji* 桃符記 in *Shen Jing ji,* 2: 508–595. Shanghai: Shanghai guji chubanshe, 1991.

———. *Zhuichai ji* 墜釵記 in *Shen Jing ji,* 2: 598–693. Shanghai: Shanghai guji chubanshe, 1991.

———. *Zhuichai ji.* [under the alternate title *Yizhong qing*]. Facsimile reprint of the manuscript dated 1689 in *Guben xiqu* I, no. 85.

Shenyin jiangu lu 審音鑒古錄. Comp. Qinyinweng 琴隱翁. 1834 ed. Facsimile reprint in *Shanben xiqu*, vols. 73–74.

Shih, Chung-wen, trans. *Injustice to Tou O*, by Guan Hanqing. Cambridge: Cambridge University Press, 1972.

Shi Kaiti 史愷悌 (Catherine Swatek). "Tiaodeng xiankan Feng Xiaoqing: Lun liangbu Feng Xiaoqing xiqu dui 'Mudan ting' de 'nianjie.'" 挑燈閑看馮小青—論兩部馮小青戲曲對牡丹亭的拈借. In *Tang Xianzu yu Mudan ting* 汤显祖与牡丹亭, ed. Hua Wei 華瑋, pp. 537–590. Taibei: Zhongyang yanjiu yuan Zhongguo wenzhe yanjiusuo, 2006.

Shishuo xinyu jiaojian 世說新語校箋. Comp. Liu Yiqing 劉義慶, ed. Xu Zhen'e 徐震堮. Beijing: Zhonghua shuju, 1984.

Sieber, Patricia. *Theaters of Desire: Authors, Readers, and the Reproduction of Early Chinese Song-drama, 1300–2000.* New York: Palgrave Macmillan, 2003.

Sima Guang 司馬光. *Sima shi shuyi* 司馬氏書儀. In *Congshu jicheng chubian* 叢書集成初編. Vol. 182. Shanghai: Shangwu yinshu guan, 1936.

Sima Qian 司馬遷. *Shiji* 史記. 10 vols. [1959]. Reprint. Beijing: Zhonghua shuju, 1985.

Sivin, Nathan. "Emotional Counter-therapy." In idem., *Medicine, Philosophy and Religion in Ancient China: Researches and Reflections*, vol. 2, pp. 1–19. Aldershot: Variorum, 1995.

———. "State, Cosmos, and Body in China in the Last Three Centuries B.C." *HJAS* 55.1 (Jun. 1995): 5–37.

———. *Traditional Medicine in Contemporary China: A Partial Translation of Revised Outline of Chinese Medicine (1972), with an Introductory Study on Change in Present Day and Early Medicine.* Ann Arbor: Center for Chinese Studies, University of Michigan, 1987.

Sofer, Andrew. *The Stage Life of Props.* Ann Arbor: University of Michigan Press, 2003.

Song Junhua 宋俊華. *Zhongguo gudai xiju fushi yanjiu* 中國古代戲劇服飾研究. Guangzhou: Guandong gaodeng jiaoyu chubanshe, 2003.

Songren huace 宋人畫冊. Eds. Zhen Zhenduo 鄭振鐸 et al. Beijing: Zhongguo gudian yishu chubanshe, 1959.

Sontag, Susan. *Illness as Metaphor.* New York: Farrar, Straus and Giroux, 1978.

Stevenson, Daniel. "Text, Image, and Transformation in the History of the *Shuilu fahui*, the Buddhist Rite for Deliverance of Creatures of Water and Land." In *Cultural Intersections in Later Chinese Buddhism*, ed. Marsha Weidner, pp. 30–70. Honolulu: University of Hawai'i Press, 2001.

Stewart, Susan. *Nonsense: Aspects of Intertextuality in Folklore and Literature.* Baltimore: Johns Hopkins University Press, 1979.

Struve, Lynn. "Chimerical Early Modernity: The Case of 'Conquest Generation' Memoirs." In *The Qing Formation in World-historical Time*, ed. Lynn Struve, pp. 335–372. Cambridge, MA: Harvard University Asia Center, 2004.

———. *The Ming-Qing Conflict, 1619–1683: A Historiography and Source Guide.* Ann Arbor: Association for Asian Studies, Monograph and Occasional Paper Series, Number 56, 1998.

Stuer, Catherine. "Double Passage to Heaven in Pingmo, Henan, 1108 CE: Buddhist Rebirth in Sepulchral Context." Unpublished paper.

Su Bai 宿白. "Qingzhou cheng kaolüe" 青州城考略. *Wenwu* 8 (1999): 47–56 and *Wenwu* 9 (1999): 37–42.

Su Shi 蘇軾, comp. *Dongpo zhilin* 東坡志林. Annotated by Wang Songling 王松齡. Beijing: Zhonghua shuju, 1981.

Sui Shusen 隋樹森. *Gushi shijiushou jishi* 古詩十九首集釋. Beijing: Zhonghua shuju, 1955.

Sun Yancheng 孫言誠, comp. *Wang Shizhen nianpu* 王士禎年譜. Beijing: Zhonghua shuju, 1992.

Suwen 素问. In Ren Yingqiu 任應秋 et al., eds. *Huangdi neijing zhangju suoyin* 黃帝內經章句索引. Beijing: Renmin weisheng chubanshe, 1986.

Swatek, Catherine C. *Peony Pavilion Onstage: Four Centuries in the Career of a Chinese Drama.* Ann Arbor: Center for Chinese Studies, 2002.

———. "Plum and Portrait: Feng Meng-lung's revision of *The Peony Pavilion.*" *Asia Major* 3.6 (1992): 127–160.

———. "Two Feng Xiaoqing Dramas: 'Dark Alternatives' to *Mudan ting.*" Unpublished paper.

Tan Zhengbi 譚正璧, ed. *Sanyan liangpai ziliao* 三言兩拍資料. Shanghai: Shanghai guji chubanshe, 1980.

Tanaka Issei. "The Social and Historical Context of Ming-Ch'ing Local Drama." In *Popular Culture in Late Imperial China*, ed. David Johnson, Andrew Nathan, and Evelyn Rawski, pp. 143–160. Berkeley: University of California Press, 1985.

———. *Zhongguo xiju shi* 中國戲劇史, trans. Yun Guishan 云貴杉 and Yu Yun 于允. Beijing: Beijing guangbo xueyuan chubanshe, 2002.

Tang Xianzu 唐顯祖. *Fengliu meng* 風流夢. Revised and abridged ed. of *Mudan ting* by Feng Menglong 馮夢龍. In *Mohanzhai dingben chuanqi* 墨憨齋定本傳奇, vol. 3. Beijing: Zhongguo xiju chubanshe, 1960.

———. *Huanhun ji* 還魂記. (1618). Revised and abridged ed. of *Mudan ting* by Zang Maoxun 臧懋循. In *Yuming xinci sizhong* 玉茗新詞四種. Jinling: Wenlinge, Wanli edition. In the National Central Library, Taiwan.

———. *Mudan ting* 牡丹亭. Eds. Xu Shuofang 徐朔方 and Yang Xiaomei 楊笑梅. Beijing: Renmin wenxue chubanshe, 1978.

———. *Shuoyuan shanding Mudan ting* 碩園刪定牡丹亭. Abridged and revised ed by Xu Rixi 徐日曦. In *Liushizhong qu* 六十種曲, comp. Mao Jin 毛晉. Beijing: Xinhua shudian, 1982.

Tao Qian 陶潛. *Tao Yuanming ji* 陶淵明集, ed. Lu Qinli 逯欽立. Beijing: Zhonghua shuju, 1979.

Tao Yuanming shiwen huiping 陶淵明詩文彙評. Comp. Beijing daxue Zhongwenxi wenxueshi jiaoyanshi jiaoshi wuliu ji si ban tongxue 北京大學中文系文學史教研室教師五六級四班同學. Beijing: Zhonghua shuju, 1961.

Tschantz, Dietrich. "Early Qing Drama and the Dramatic Works of Wu Weiye (1609–1672)." PhD diss., Princeton University, 2002.

Teiser, Stephen F. *The Ghost Festival in Medieval China.* Princeton, NJ: Princeton University Press, 1988.

———. *The Scripture on the Ten Kings and the Making of Purgatory in Medieval Chinese Buddhism.* Honolulu: University of Hawai'i Press, 1994.

Thompson, Lawrence. *Chinese Religion: An Introduction.* Encino, CA: Dickenson Pub. Co., 1975.

Tian Yiheng 田藝蘅. *Shinü shi* 詩女史. Facsimile reprint of Jiajing ed. In *Siku quanshu cunmu congshu* 四庫全書存目叢書, jibu 集部, 321. Tainan, Taiwan: Zhuangyan wenhua shiye youxian gongsi, 1997.

Tu, Kuo-ching. *Li Ho.* Boston: Twayne Publishers, 1979.

Turner, Victor. "Liminality and Performative Genres." In *Rite, Drama, Festival, Spectacle: Rehearsals Toward a Theory of Cultural Performance*, ed. John J. MacAloon, pp. 19–41. Philadelphia: ISHI, 1984.

Twitchett, Denis, ed. *The Cambridge History of China: Sui and T'ang China, Part 1.* Cambridge: Cambridge University Press, 1979.

Uchida Tomoo 內田智雄. "Meikon kō" 冥婚攷. *Shinagaku* 11.3 (1944): 311–373.

Unschuld, Paul U. *Medicine in China: A History of Ideas.* Berkeley: University of California Press, 1985.

Van der Kolk, Bessel A., and Van der Hart, Onno. "The Intrusive Past: The Flexibility of Memory and the Engraving of Trauma." In *Trauma: Explorations in Memory*, ed. Cathy Caruth, pp. 158–182. Baltimore: Johns Hopkins University Press, 1995.

Van Gulik, Robert Hans. *Sexual Life in Ancient China: A Preliminary Survey of Chinese Sex and Society from ca. 1500 B.C. till 1644 A.D.* Leiden: E. J. Brill, 1974.

Vernant, Jean-Pierre. "Feminine Figures of Death in Greece." In *Mortals and Immortals: Collected Essays*, ed. Froma I. Zeitlin, pp. 95–110. Princeton: Princeton University Press, 1991.

Volpp, Sophie. *Worldly Stage: The Figure of the Theater in Seventeenth-century China.* Cambridge, MA: Harvard Asia Center Publications, forthcoming.

Wakeman, Frederic, Jr. *The Great Enterprise: The Manchu Reconstruction of Imperial Order in Seventeenth-century China.* Berkeley: University of California Press, 1985.

Waley, Arthur, trans. *Chinese Poems.* London: Allen and Unwin, 1976.

———. *Translations from the Chinese.* New York: A. A. Knopf, 1941.

Wang Anqi 王安祈. *Mingdai chuanqi zhi juchang ji qi yishu* 明代傳奇之劇場及其藝術. Taibei: Xuesheng shuju, 1985.

———. *Mingdai xiqu wulun* 明代戲曲五論. Taibei: Da'an chubanshe, 1990.

Wang, Ay-ling. "The Artistry of Hong Sheng's *Changshengdian.*" PhD diss., Yale University, 1992.

Wang Chong 王充. *Lunheng jiaoshi* 論衡校釋, ed. Huang Hui 黃暉. 4 vols. Beijing: Zhonghua shuju, 1990.

Wang, David Der-wei. *Fin-de-siècle Splendor: Repressed Modernitites of Late Qing Fiction, 1848–1911.* Stanford: Stanford University Press, 1997.

———. "Second Haunting." In *The Monster That is History: History, Violence, and Fictional Writing in Twentieth-century China*, ed. David Wang, pp. 262–291. Berkeley: University of California Press, 2004.

Wang, David Der-wei, and Shang Wei, eds. *Dynastic Crisis and Cultural Innovation: From the Late Ming to the Late Qing and Beyond.* Cambridge, MA: Harvard Asia Center Publications, 2005.

Wang Duanshu 王端淑. *Mingyuan shiwei* 名媛詩緯. Qing edition in Beijing University Rare Book Library.

Wang Jilie 王季烈. *Yinlu qutan* 螾廬曲談. Taibei: Taiwan shangwu yinshuguan, 1971.

Wang Kentang 王肯堂. *Zhengzhi zhunsheng* 證治準繩. In *Liuke zhunsheng* 六科準繩. Taibei: Xinwenfeng chuban gongsi, 1974.

Wang Qishu 王啟淑. *Xiefang ji* 擷芳集. Photocopy of 1773 ed. in the Fudan University Library. Regenstein Library, University of Chicago.

Wang Shifu 王實甫. *[Jiping jiaozhu] Xixiang ji* [集評校注]西廂記, ed. Wang Jisi 王季思 and Zhang Renhe 張人和. Shanghai: Shanghai guji chubanshe, 1987.

———. "*Ranzhi ji* li." 燃脂集例. In *Zhaodai congshu* 昭代叢書, comp. Zhang Chao 張潮, *yiji* 乙集 28.1–15b. In *Zhaodai congshu guangbian* 昭代叢書廣編, ed. Yang Fuji 楊復吉 and Shen Maozhi 沈楙直. Shikaitang 世楷堂 ed., 1833. Academy of Sciences Library, Beijing.

———. "*Ranzhi ji* li." Reprinted in Hu Wenkai 胡文楷, *Lidai funü zhuzuo kao* 歷代婦女著作攷, pp. 61–69. Shanghai: Shangwu yinshuguan, 1957.

Wang Shizhen 王士禎. *Chibei outan* 池北偶談. Beijing: Zhonghua shuju, 1982.

Wang Xianming 王憲明. "*Liaozhai zhiyi* zhong de Mingdai Shandong Qinwang" 聊齋誌異中的明代山東親王. *Pu Songling yanjiu* 1 (1999): 93–97.

Wang Xuetai 王學太. "Lin Siniang gushi de yanbian ji qi lishi zhenxiang" 林四娘故事的演變及其歷史真象. *Pu Songling yanjiu jikan* 蒲松齡研究集刊 1 (1980): 366–373.

Wang Yufeng 王玉峰. *Fenxiang ji* 焚香記. Facsimile of late Ming ed. *Guben xiqu* I, no. 55.

Wang Zhifang 王直方. *Wang Zhifang shihua* 王直方詩話. In *Song shihua jiyi* 宋詩話輯佚, comp. Guo Shaoyu 郭紹虞, pp. 1–110. Beijing: Zhonghua shuju, 1980.

Watson, James L. "Of Flesh and Bones." In *Death and the Regeneration of Life*, eds. Maurice Bloch and Jonathan Parry, pp. 155–186. Cambridge: Cambridge University Press, 1982.

———. "The Structure of Chinese Funerary Rites: Elementary Forms, Ritual Sequence, and the Primacy of Performance." In *Death Ritual in Late Imperial and Modern China*, eds. James L. Watson and Evelyn Rawski, pp. 3–19. Berkeley: University of California Press, 1988.

———, and Evelyn S. Rawski, eds. *Death Ritual in Late Imperial and Modern China.* Berkeley: University of California Press, 1988.

Watson, Rubie S. "Remembering the Dead: Graves and Politics in Southeastern China." In *Death Ritual in Late Imperial and Modern China*, eds. James L. Watson and Evelyn Rawski, pp. 203–227. Berkeley: University of California Press, 1988.

Wei Zhixiu 魏之琇. *Xu Mingyi leian* 續名醫類案, annoted by Huang Hanru 黃漢儒. Beijing: Renmin weisheng chubanshe, 1997.

Wen Yansheng 文彥生. *Zhongguo guihua* 中國鬼話. Shanghai: Shanghai wenyi chubanshe, 1996.

Weng Minhua 翁敏華. "Lun Yuandai zaju liang 'hun dan' jian ji qita." 論元代雜劇兩魂旦兼及其他. *Shanghai shifan daxue xuebao* 上海師範大學學報 1 (1998): 33–36.

West, Stephen H. "Text and Ideology: Ming Editors and Northern Drama." In *Ming Qing xiqu guoji yantaohui lunwen ji*, eds. Hua Wei and Wang Ay-ling, pp. 235–284. Taibei: Zhongyang yanjiu yuan Zhongguo wenzhe yanjiusuo, 1998.

West, Stephen H., and Wilt L. Idema, trans. *The Moon and the Zither: The Story of the Western Wing*. Berkeley: University of California Press, 1995.

Widmer, Ellen. "The Huanduzhai of Hangzhou and Suzhou: A Study in Seventeenth-century Publishing." *HJAS* 56.1 (Jun. 1996): 77–122.

———. "Xiaoqing's Literary Legacy and the Place of the Woman Writer in Late Imperial China." *Late Imperial China* 13.1 (1992): 111–155.

Wiseman, N., and P. Zmiewski. "Rectifying the Names: Suggestions for Standardizing Chinese Medical Terminology." In *Approaches to Traditional Chinese Medical Literature: Proceedings of an International Symposium on Translation Methodologies and Terminologies*, ed. Paul U. Unschuld, pp. 55–66. Boston: Kluwer Academic Publishers, 1989.

Wolf, Arthur. "Gods, Ghosts, and Ancestors." In *Religion and Ritual in Chinese Society*, ed. Arthur Wolf, pp. 141–176. Stanford: Stanford University Press, 1974.

Wu Bing 吳炳. *Canhuazhai wuzhong* 粲花齋五種. Facsimile reprint of Nuanhong shi ed. Yangzhou: Jiangsu Guangling guji keyinshe, 1982.

———. *Huazhong ren* 畫中人. In *Canhuazhai wuzhong*.

———. *Xiyuan ji* 西園記. In *Canhuazhai wuzhong*.

———. *Xiyuan ji* 西園記. Late Ming ed. in Nanjing Library.

Wu Chengxue 吳承學. "Jiju lun" 集句論. *Wenxue yichan* 文學遺產 4 (1993): 12–20.

———. "Lun Tibishi jian ji xiangguan de shige zhizuo yu chuanbo xingshi" 論題壁詩兼及相關的詩歌製作與傳播形式. *Wenxue yichan* (1994.4): 4–13.

Wu Hung [巫鴻]. "But Where are the Ruins in Chinese Art?" Unpublished paper.

———. "Handai daojiao meishu shitan" 漢代道教美术试探. In *Liyi zhong de meishu: Wu Hung Zhongguo gudai meishushi wenbian* 禮儀中的美術：巫鴻中國古代美術史文編, eds. Zheng Yan 鄭岩 and Wang Rui 王睿. Vol. 2, pp. 455–484. Beijing: Sanlian shudian, 2005.

———. *Monumentality in Early Chinese Art and Architecture*. Stanford: Stanford University Press, 1995.

———. "Rethinking Liu Sahe: The Creation of a Buddhist Saint and the Invention of a 'Miraculous Image.'" *Orientations* 27.10 (November 1996): 32–43.

Wu Hung, and Katherine R. Tsiang, eds. *Body and Face in Chinese Visual Culture*. Cambridge, MA: Harvard Asia Center Publications, 2005.

Wu Kang 吳康. *Zhongguo guishen jingguai* 中國鬼神精怪. Changsha: Hunan wenyi chubanshe, 1992.

Wu Kun 吳崑. *Yifang kao* 醫方攷. In *Wu Kun yixue quanshu* 吳崑醫學全書, ed. Guo Junshuang 郭君雙. Beijing: Zhongguo zhongyiyao chubanshe, 1999.

Wu Pei-yi. *The Confucian's Progress: Autobiographical Writings in Traditional China.* Princeton, NJ: Princeton University Press, 1990.

Wu Qian 吳謙 et al., comps. *Yizong jinjian* 醫宗金鑑. 1742 ed. Beijing: Renmin weisheng chubanshe, 1977.

Wu Qiming 吳企明, ed. *Li He ziliao huibian* 李賀資料彙編. Beijing: Zhonghua shuju, 1994.

Wu Weiye 吳偉業. *Moling chun* 秣陵春. In *Wu Meicun quanji* 吳梅村全集, ed. Li Xueying 李學穎. Vol. 3. Shanghai: Shanghai guji chubanshe, 1990.

———. *Tongtian tai* 通天臺. In *Wu Meicun quanji* 吳梅村全集, Vol. 3. Shanghai: Shanghai guji chubanshe, 1990.

Wu, Yi-li. "Ghost Fetuses, False Pregnancies, and the Parameters of Medical Uncertainty in Classical Chinese Gynecology." *Nannü* 4.2 (2002): 170–206.

Wu Yiyi 吳儀一, and Qian Yi 錢宜, eds. *Wu Wushan sanfu heping Mudan ting* 吳吳山三婦合評牡丹亭. Photocopy of the edition based on 1694 woodblocks in the Tōyō bunka kenkyūjō, Tokyo.

Wu Zhiwang 武之望. *Jiyang gangmu* 濟陽綱目. Facsimile reprint of Xianfeng ed. Yangzhou: Jiangsu guangling guji keyinshe, 1982.

———. *Jiyin gangmu* 濟陰綱目, ed. Wang Qi 汪淇. Shanghai: Keji weisheng chubanshe, 1958.

Xikao daquan 戲考大全. 5 vols. Ed. Wang Dacuo 王大錯. Zhonghua tushuguan edition, 1915–1925. Reprint, Shanghai: Shanghai shudian, 1990.

Xiao Tong. *Wenxuan, or, Selections of Refined Literature.* Trans. David R. Knechtges. Princeton, NJ: Princeton University Press, 1982–1996.

Xie Guozhen 謝國楨. *Mingmo Qingchu de xuefeng* 明末清初的學風. Beijing: Renmin chubanshe, 1982.

Xin Wenfang 辛文房. *Tang caizi zhuan jiaozhu* 唐才子傳校注, annotated by Sun Yingkui 孫映逵. Beijing: Zhongguo shehui kexue chubanshe, 1991.

Xu Chunfu 徐春甫. *Gujin yitong daquan* 古今醫統大全. First published 1556. Facsimile reprint. Taibei: Xin wenfeng chuban gongsi, 1978.

Xu Dachun 徐大椿. *Yixue yuanliu lun* 醫學源流論. In *Xu Lingtai yixue quanshu* 徐靈胎醫學全書. Ed. Lin Yang 劉洋 et al. Beijing: Zhongguo zhongyiyao chubanshe, 1999.

Xu Fuming 徐扶明. "Cong 'Lin Siniang,' 'Guihua ci,' dao 'Guihua feng.'" 從《林四娘》《姽嫿詞》到《姽嫿封》. *Honglou meng yuanjiu jikan* 8 (March 1982): 205–219.

———, ed. *Mudan ting yanjiu ziliao* 牡丹亭研究資料. Shanghai: Shanghai guji chubanshe, 1987.

Xu Fuxiang 徐復祥. *Hongli ji* 紅梨记. Preface dated 1611. *Guben xiqu* I, no. 97.

Xu Gui 徐軌. *Ciyuan congtan jiaojian* 詞苑叢談校箋. Ed. Wang Baili 王百里. Beijing: Renmin wenxue chubanshe, 1988. First printed 1689.

Xu Hualong 徐華龍. *Zhongguo gui wenhua dacidian* 中國鬼文化大辭典. Shanghai: Guangxi minzu chubanshe, 1994.

Xu Pingfang 徐苹芳. "Tang Song muzang zhong de 'mingqi shensha' yu 'muyi' zhidu: du *Da Han yuanling mizang jing* zhaji." 唐宋墓葬中的《明器神煞》與《墓儀》制度：讀《大漢原陵秘葬經》札記. *Kaogu* 2 (1963): 87–106.

Xu Rixi 徐日曦, ed. *Shuoyuan shanding Mudan ting* 碩園刪定牡丹亭. Abridged and revised ed. of Tang Xianzu, *Mudanting.* In *Liushizhong qu* 六十種曲, comp. Mao Jin 毛晉. Beijing: Xinhua shudian, 1982.
Xu Shen 許慎. *Shuowen jiezi* 說文解字. Shanghai: Shanghai guji chubanshe, 1988.
Xu Shuofang 徐朔方. *Feng Menglong nianpu* 馮夢龍年譜. In idem, *Wanming qujia nianpu* 晚明曲家年譜. Vol. 1. Hangzhou: Zhejiang guji chubanshe, 1993.
Xu Xianglin 許祥麟. *Zhongguo guixi* 中國鬼戲. Tianjin: Tianjin jiaoyu chubanshe, 1997.
Xu Zichang 許自昌. *Shuihu ji* 水滸記. Facsimile ed of late Ming Jiguge 汲古閣 ed. *Guben xiqu* I, no. 93.
Xu Zihan 許子漢. "Ming chuanqi paichang sanyaosu fazhan licheng zhi yanjiu." 明傳奇排場三要素發展歷程之研究. PhD diss., Guoli Taiwan daxue, 1999.
Yagi Akiyoshi 八木章好. "Ho Shorei to Ri Ga" 蒲松齢と李賀. *Geibun kenkyū* 藝文研究 54 (1989): 134–151.
Yang Youhe 陽友鶴. *Chuanju danjiao biaoyan yishu* 川劇旦角表演藝術. Beijing: Zhongguo xiju chubanshe, 1959.
Yao Silian 姚思廉. *Liangshu* 梁書. Beijing: Zhonghua shuju, 1992.
Ye Changhai 葉長海. *Zhongguo xijuxue shi* 中國戲劇學史. Taibei: Luotuo chubanshe, 1993.
Ye Shaoyuan 葉紹袁, comp. *Wumengtang ji* 午夢堂集, ed. Ji Qin 冀勤. Beijing: Zhonghua shuju, 1998.
Ye Tang 葉堂. *Nashuying qupu* 納書楹曲譜. 3 vols. Facsimile reprint of 1792 ed. Taibei: Shengzhai chubanshe, 1969.
Ye Ziqi 葉子奇. *Cao Muzi* 草木子. 1957 ed. Reprint. Beijing: Zhonghua shuju, 1997.
Yidu xian tuzhi 益都縣圖志. Ed. Fa Weitang 法偉堂 et al. China, 1907.
Yim, Chi-hung. "The Poetics of Historical Memory in the Ming-Qing Transition: A Study of Qian Qianyi's (1582–1664) Later Poetry." PhD diss., Yale University, 1998.
Yin Feizhou 尹飛舟 et al., *Zhongguo gudai guishen wenhua daguan* 中國古代鬼神文化大觀. Nanchang: Baihuazhou wenyi chubanshe, 1992.
You Tong 尤侗. *Juntian yue* 鈞天樂. In *Xitang quanji.* Qing edition. Regenstein Library, University of Chicago.
———. *Xitang quanji* 西堂全集. Qing edition. Regenstein Library, University of Chicago.
———. *Xitang zazu* 西堂雜俎. In *Xitang quanji.* Qing edition. Regenstein Library, University of Chicago.
Yu, Anthony C. *Rereading the Stone: Desire and the Making of Fiction in the Dream of the Red Chamber.* Princeton, NJ: Princeton University Press, 1997.
———. "'Rest, Rest, Perturbed Spirit!' Ghosts in Traditional Chinese Fiction." *HJAS* 47.2 (Dec. 1987): 397–434.
Yu, Pauline. *The Reading of Imagery in the Chinese Literary Tradition.* Princeton, NJ: Princeton University Press, 1987.
Yu Tuan 虞摶. *Yixue zhengchuan* 醫學正傳. Beijing: Renmin weisheng chubanshe, 1965.
Yu Yue 俞樾. *Hudong manlu* 壺東漫錄. In *Chunzaitang congshu* 春在堂叢書. 1902.
Yuan Mei 袁枚. *Zi bu yu* 子不语. In *Yuan Mei quanji* 袁枚全集. Annotated by Zhou Xin 周欣. Vol. 4. Nanjing: Jiangsu guji chubanshe, 1997.
Yuan Zhen 元稹. *Yuan Zhen ji* 元稹集, ed. Ji Qin 冀勤. Beijing: Zhonghua shuju, 1982.

Yung, Sai-shing. "A Critical Study of Han-tan chi." PhD diss., Princeton University, 1992.

Zang Maoxun 臧懋循, ed. *Huanhun ji* 還魂記 (1618). Revised and abridged version of Tang Xianzu, *Mudan ting*. In *Yuming xinci sizhong* 玉茗新詞四種, ed. Zang Maoxun. Wanli edition in the National Central Library, Taiwan.

———, comp. *Yuanqu xuan* 元曲選 (1616). 4 vols. Beijing: Zhonghua shuju, 1958.

———, comp. *Yuanqu xuan tu* 元曲選圖. Facsimile of illustrations from the 1616 edition. In *Zhongguo gudai banhua congkan erbian* 中國古代版畫叢刊二編. Shanghai: Shanghai guji chubanshe, 1994.

Zeitlin, Judith T. "Disappearing Verses: Writing on Walls and Anxieties of Loss in Late Imperial China." In *Writing and Materiality in China: Essays in Honor of Patrick Hanan*, eds. Judith T. Zeitlin and Lydia H. Liu, pp. 73–132. Cambridge, MA: Harvard Asia Center Publications, 2003.

———. *Historian of the Strange: Pu Songling and the Chinese Classical Tale*. Stanford: Stanford University Press, 1993.

———, trans. "Ingenia." In *Under Confucian Eyes: Writings on Gender in Chinese History*, eds. Susan Mann and Yu-yin Cheng, pp. 205–213. Berkeley: University of California Press, 2001.

———, trans. "Liansuo." In *Under Confucian Eyes: Writings on Gender in Chinese History*, eds. Susan Mann and Yu-yin Cheng, pp. 199–205. Berkeley: University of California Press, 2001.

———. "The Life and Death of the Image: Ghosts and Female Portraits in Sixteenth- and Seventeenth-century Literature." In *Body and Face in Chinese Visual Culture*, eds. Wu Hung, and Katherine R. Tsiang, pp. 229–257. Cambridge, MA: Harvard Asia Center Publications, 2005.

———. "The Literary Fashioning of Medical Authority: A Study of Sun Yikui's Case Histories." In *Thinking with Cases: Specialist Knowledge in Chinese Cultural History*, eds. Charlotte Furth, Judith T. Zeitlin, and Ping-chen Hsiung. Honolulu: University of Hawai'i Press, 2007.

———. "My Year of Peonies." *Asian Theatre Journal* 19.1 (Spring 2002): 124–133.

———. "Notes of Flesh: The Courtesan's Song in Seventeenth-century China." In *The Courtesan's Arts: Cross-cultural Perspectives*, eds. Martha Feldman and Bonnie Gordon, pp. 75–99. London: Oxford University Press, 2006.

———. "Shared Dreams: The Story of the Three Wives' Commentary on *The Peony Pavilion*." *HJAS* 54.1 (July 1994): 127–179.

———. "Spirit Writing and Performance in the Work of You Tong." *T'oung Pao* 84 (1998): 102–135.

———, and Lydia H. Liu, eds. *Writing and Materiality in China: Essays in Honor of Patrick Hanan*. Cambridge, MA: Harvard Asia Center Publications, 2003.

Zeng Yongyi 曾永義, ed. *Zhongguo gudian xiju xuanzhu* 中國古典戲劇選注. Taibei: Guojia chubanshe, 1985.

Zeng Zao 曾慥, ed. *Leishuo* 類說. Facsimile reprint of Ming edition. Beijing: Wenxue guji kanxingshe, 1955.

Zha Jizuo 查繼佐. *Zuiwei lu* 罪惟錄. Hangzhou: Jiangsu guji chubanshe, 1986.

Zhang Chao 張潮, comp. *Yu Chu xinzhi* 虞初新志. Shijiazhuang: Hebei renmin chubanshe, 1985.

———, comp. *Zhaodai congshu, yiji* 昭代叢書, 乙集. In *Zhaodai congshu guangbian* 昭代叢書廣編, ed. Yang Fuji 楊復吉 and Shen Maozhi 沈楙直. Shikaitang 世楷堂, 1833. Academy of Sciences Library, Beijing.

Zhang Chongchen 張崇琛. "Pu Songling yu Zhucheng yimin jituan" 蒲松齡與諸城遺民集團. *Pu Songling yanjiu* 蒲松齡研究 3 (1989): 24–51.

Zhang Dai 張岱. *Tao'an mengyi/Xihu mengxun* 陶菴夢憶/西湖夢尋. Shanghai: Shanghai guji chubanshe, 1982.

———. *Zhang Dai shiwen ji* 張岱詩文集. Shanghai: Shanghai guji chubanshe, 1991.

Zhang Jiebin 張介賓. *Jingyue quanshu* 景岳全書. 1959 ed. Reprint. Shanghai: Shanghai kexue jishu chubanshe, 1984.

———. *Leijing* 類經. Beijing: Renmin weisheng chubanshe, 1965.

Zhang Qi 張琦. *Hengqu zhutan* 衡曲麈談. *Gudian xiqu*. Vol. 4. Beijing: Zhongguo xiju chubanshe, 1959.

Zhang Peiheng 章培恆. *Hong Sheng nianpu* 洪昇年譜. Shanghai: Shanghai guji chubanshe, 1979.

Zhang Zilie 張自烈, comp. *Zhengzi tong* 正字通. 1685; preface dated 1670. Collated by Liao Wenying 廖文英. Xiushui qingwei tang ed. 秀水清畏堂. In Regenstein Library, Univerity of Chicago.

Zhao Lingzhi 趙令畤. *Houqing lu* 侯鯖錄. Beijing: Zhonghua shuju, 2002.

Zheng Guangzu 鄭光祖. *Qiannü lihun* 倩女離魂. *Gu mingjia* 古名家 ed. In *Mowangguan chaojiaoben Gujin zaju* 脈望館鈔校本古今雜劇, no. 37. Facsimile reprint, *Guben xiqu* IV.

———. *Qiannü lihun* 倩女離魂. *Gu zaju* 古雜劇. Facsimile reprint of 1615–1621 edition, *Guben xiqu* IV.

———. *Qiannü lihun* 倩女離魂. In *Yuanqu xuan* 元曲選, ed. Zang Maoxun 臧懋循, 2: 705–719. Beijing: Zhonghua shuju, 1958.

Zheng Tingyu 鄭廷玉. *Houting hua* 後庭花. *Gu mingjia* 古名家 ed. In *Mowangguan chaojiaoben Gujin zaju* 脈望館鈔校本古今雜劇, no. 52. Facsimile reprint in *Guben xiqu* IV.

———. *Yuanqu xuan* 元曲選, ed. Zang Maoxun 臧懋循. Beijing: Zhonghua shuju, 1958, 3: 929–949.

Zheng Xiaojiang 鄭小江. *Zhongguo siwang wenhua daguan* 中國死亡文化大觀. Nanchang: Baihuazhou wenyi chubanshe, 1995.

Zheng Zhizhen 鄭之珍. *Mulian jiumu* 目連救母. Facsimile reprint of Wanli Gaoshi shanfang 高石山房 ed. *Guben xiqu* I, no. 67.

Zhengzhou shi wenwu kaogu yanjiusuo 鄭州市文物考古研究所 et al. "Henan Xinmishi pingmo Songdai bihua mu." 河南新密市平陌宋代壁畫墓. *Wenwu* 12 (1998): 26–32.

Zhengzhou Song Jin bihua mu 鄭州宋金壁畫墓. Ed. Zhengzhou Municipal Institute of Cultural Relics and Archaeology. Shenzhen: Kexue chubanshe, 2005.

Zhida 智達. *[Yifang bian jingtu] Chuandeng lu Guiyuan jing* [異方便淨土]傳燈錄歸元鏡. Facsimile reprint of 1770 ed. In *Guben xiqu* V, no. 68.

Zhong Xing 鍾惺. *Gushi gui* 古詩歸. Late Ming ed. Harvard-Yenching Rare Book Library.

Zhongguo dabaike quanshu: Xiqu quyi 中國大百科全書: 戲曲曲藝. Beijing: Zhongguo dabaike quanshu chubanshe, 1983.

Zhongguo kunju dacidian 中國昆劇大辭典, ed. Wu Xinlei 吳新雷 et al. Nanjing: Nanjing daxue chubanshe, 2002.

Zhongguo quxue dacidian 中國曲學大辭典, ed. Qi Senhua 齊森華 et al. Hangzhou: Zhejiang jiaoyu chubanshe, 1997.

Zhongguo xiqu zhi: Jiangsu juan 中國戲曲志: 江蘇卷. Beijing: Zhongguo ISBN zhongxin chuban, 1992.

Zhongwen dacidian 中文大辭典, ed. Zhang Qiyun 張其昀 et al. Taibei: Zhonghua xueshu yuan, 1976.

Zhongyi dacidian 中醫大辭典, ed. Zhongyi dacidian bianji weiyuanhui 中醫大辭典编輯委員會. Beijing: Renmin weisheng chubanshe, 1981.

Zhou Chaojun 周朝俊. *Hongmei ji* 紅梅記, ed. Wang Xingqi 王星琦. Shanghai: Shanghai guji chubanshe, 1985.

———. Facsimile reprint of Wanli ed. *Guben xiqu* I, no. 89.

Zhou Huabin 周華斌. *Jingdu guxilou* 京都古戲樓. Beijing: Haiyang chubanshe, 1998.

Zhou Kangxie 周康燮. *Gu Tinglin xiansheng nianpu huibian* 顧亭林先生年譜彙編. Hong Kong: Chongwen shudian, 1975.

Zhou Shaoliang 周紹良. "Lin Siniang gushi zhi zhuihe gen bikan." 林四娘故事之綴合跟比勘. In *Guoji Liaozhai lunwenji* 國際聊齋論文集, eds. Gu Meigao 辜美高 and Wang Zhizhong 王枝忠, pp. 155–160. Beijing: Beijing shifan xueyuan chubanshe, 1992.

Zhou Yibai 周貽白. "Zhongguo xiqu de shangxia chang" 中國戲曲的上下場. In *Xiju lunwen xuan* 戲劇論文選, pp. 182–193. Changsha: Hunan renmin chubanshe, 1982.

———. "Zhongguo juchang shi." 中國劇場史. In *Zhou Yibai xiaoshuo xiqu lunji* 周貽白小說戲劇論集, ed. Shen Xieyuan 沈燮元, pp. 465–543. Ji'nan: Qilu shushe, 1986.

Zhu Quan 朱權. *Taihe zhengyin pu* 太和正音譜. *Gudian xiqu.* Vol. 3. Beijing: Zhongguo xiju chubanshe, 1959.

Zhu Xi 朱熹. *Zhuzi yulei* 朱子語類, ed. Li Jingde 黎靜德. Beijing: Zhonghua shuju, 1986.

Zhu Yixuan 朱一玄, comp. *Liaozhai zhiyi ziliao huibian* 聊齋誌異資料匯編. Zhengzhou: Zhongzhou guji chubanshe, 1985.

Zhuang Yifu 莊一拂. *Gudian xiqu cunmu huikao* 古典戲曲存目彙考. Shanghai: Shanghai guji chubanshe, 1982.

Zhuangzi jinzhu jinyi 莊子今注今譯. Annoted by Chen Guying 陳鼓應. Beijing: Zhonghua shuju, 1983.

Zhui baiqiu 綴白裘. Comp. Wanhua zhuren 玩花主人, ed. Qian Decang 錢德蒼 et al. Facsimile reprint of 1777 Hongwen tang 鴻文堂 ed. In *Shanben xiqu*, vols. 58–72.

Index

Bold page numbers refer to figures.

accounts of the strange *(zhiguai)*, 5, 15, 54, 120

actors: association with ghosts, 145; possession of, 172. *See also* role types

"Ainu," 40

An Lushan rebellion, 93, 95, 115, 182

An Zhiyuan, 110; *Qingzhou Anecdotes (Qingshe yiwen)*, 100, 101, 104, 110, 111–112, 118

Anatomy of Love (Qingshi leilüe), 21, 93–94

ancestors, boundaries with ghosts, 11

ancestral worship, 10, 47, 122

Anecdotes about Tang Poems (Tangshi jishi), 62–65, 67, 80

authorship: anonymity, 63–64, 67; ghostly authors, 68–69; immortality, 67, 196; of poetry, 63, 70. *See also* ghost authors

auto-dirges, 60–65, 66, 67

autonecrology, 60

"Autumn Moon" ("Wu Qiuyue"), 25–27, 28

"Autumn Night's Visit to the Mandolin Pavilion, An" ("Qiuxi fang Pipa ting ji"), 95–96, 104

Bai Juyi, 95

Bao Zhao, 93

Barr, Allan, 78, 100, 129–130

Barthes, Roland, 141

beauty: changes in visual representations, 25; of ghosts, 24–25, 27–28, 40, 107; ideal, 25, 82; of phantom heroines, 138; of revenants, 82

Beijing, 97

belief, 9–10

Biographies of Tang Poets (Tang caizi zhuan), 77

Bloch, Maurice, 37, 47

blood, 38, 120, 125–126, 233n105

bodies: emotional influences, 21–23; hybrid, 33–34; imagery, 140; male self-sacrifice, 38, 214n125; separation of soul from, 5, 135, 173, 193–194. *See also* corpses; skeletons

bones: reburials, 48. *See also* skeletons

Book of Liezi (Liezi), 4

Book of Songs (Shijing), 65, 70, 76, 89

bound feet, 27, 213n98

Brashier, Kenneth, 5

"Bridegroom, The" ("Xinlang"), 123

bridge of immortality *(xian qiao)*, 160–163, **161, 162**

Bronfen, Elisabeth, 27, 52, 53, 74

Buddhism: Ghost Festival, 9, 27, 133; hagiographies, 161–163; purgatory, 50, 116–117, 188. *See also* Land and Water rite; Mulian legend

burial songs, 59–61, 62, 63, 72, 124. *See also* auto-dirges

burials: of clothing and personal articles, 50; double, 47; second, 47–48, 51. *See also* graves; tombs

By and about Women. See *Collection by and about Women*

"Camelia" ("Xiangyu"), 26, 37

Campany, Robert F., 54

candles and lamps, 3, 149

Cang Jie, 195

Cao Xueqin, 181; *Dream of the Red Chamber*

(Honglou meng), 25, 101–103, 105–106, 113
Cao Yin, 181
Carlson, Marvin, 146
"Carpenter Feng" ("Feng mujiang"), 113
Caruth, Cathy, 99
Celestial Court Music (Juntian yue), 135, 142
cemeteries. *See* graveyard poems; tombs
Chang, Kang-i Sun, 120
Chao Yuanfang, *Etiology and Symptomology of All Diseases (Zhubing yuanhou lun)*, 15
Characters Explained (Shuowen jiezi), 4
Che Wenming, 144
Chen Baoyao, 100–101, 229n57, 230n80, 233n115. *See also* "Lin Siniang"
Chen Weisong, *Collection by and about Women, A (Furen ji)*, 100, 103, 110–111, 112, 113–114, 115, 118
Chen Zilong, 86, 120
Chen Ziming, *Complete Good Prescriptions for Women (Furen daquan liangfang)*, 39
childbirth: to ghosts, 32–34, 35–36; male fantasy, 38; posthumous, 36–37. *See also* pregnancy
Chinese Ghost Story, A (Qiannü youhun), 1–2, **2,** 11, 35, 197
Chow, Rey, 95
chuanqi. *See* southern drama; tales of the marvelous
Classic Poetry by Renowned Women (Mingyuan shiwei), 79–80
clothing: burial of, 50; of ghosts, 127, 148, **148;** mourning, 72; shoes, 38; sleeves, 126–127, 152–153, **154,** 165; stockings, 38, 126, 127. *See also* costumes
clowns, 137, 176
Cole, David, 172
Collection by and about Women, A (Furen ji), "Lin Siniang" tale, 100, 103, 110–111, 112, 113–114, 115, 118
collective memory, 183
colors: red, 148; white, 72, 189
Communications from the Unseen World (Tongyou ji), 66, 67
Complete Mastery of Correct Characters, A (Zhengzi tong), 50
Complete Poetry of the Tang (Quan Tangshi), 80–81
Complete System of Medicine Past and Present, A (Gujin yitong daquan), 22
Confucianism: filial piety, 37; poetics, 67, 70
Confucius, 66
Constant Words to Awaken the World (Xingshi hengyan), 40
"Continuing a Ghost's Poem" ("Xu guishi"), 85
corpses: decay, 37, 126; ghosts' relationship to, 39–40; of phantom heroines, 193–194; reanimation, 39–40; release from, 193; violation of, 40–41. *See also* bodies; burials
costumes: of ghosts, 163–165, 168–171; instructions, 141; of Lady Yang, 189, 191, 194; in northern drama, 164; of phantom heroines, 148, 152–153, **154,** 163–165, 168–171

Dai Fu, *Great Book of Marvels (Guangyi ji)*, 34, 61–62
dan (female lead), 134–135, 136, 156; splitting, 171–174, 193–194; surplus of, 172, 175–180. See also *hun dan;* phantom heroines
dances: of ghosts, 2; of phantom heroines, 152, 156–158
Davis, A. R., 61
Davis, Tracy C., 133
death: analogy to dynastic fall, 87–88; analogy to marriage, 73, 74; anticipation of, 60; in Chinese culture, 10; of ghosts, 50, 51, 52, 117; relationship to exile, 59, 73, 87; subjective experience of, 53, 57, 58, 59; written markers, 127–129. *See also* mourning; suicides
death rituals: cloths to cover or represent dead, 164, 245n119; gaps in memorialization, 104; headgear of mourners, 165;

Land and Water rite, 47, 109, 158–163, 169–171, 188; obligations of living, 10, 122, 124, 130, 188. *See also* burials
demon tales, 17–18, 19, 46
demonology, 18
Deng Kuiying, 127–129
depression, 21, 22–23, 82
desire. See *qing*
Disembodied Soul, The (Qiannü lihun): hun dan role, 135, 136, 237n17; illustrations, 152, **153;** as source for *Peony Pavilion*, 137; stage directions, 164, 193
Dong Xiaowan, 25
doubling: of actors, 134, 171, 173; of body by ghost, 135; of ghosts, 51–52, 193–194; by phantom heroines, 136, 193–194; role types, 177–178; of roles, 175; splitting female lead, 171–174, 193–194
drama. *See* northern drama; ritual drama; southern drama; theater
drama criticism, 140–141, 196
Dream of the Red Chamber (Honglou meng), 25, 101–103, 105–106, 113
dreams: of emperor in *Palace of Lasting Life*, 186–187; of intercourse with ghosts, 15, 26; of intercourse with gods, 18, 39; of intercourse with statues, 39, 211n78; memory and, 191, 192; relationship to ghosts, 195
Dropped Hairpin, The (Zhuichai ji), 159, 168, 171, 172–174
Du Liniang: costumes, 245n120; death, 132; as embodiment of *qing*, 14; illustrations, 165, **166–167;** resurrection, 14, 37–38, 132, 146–147, 169, 178, 194; scenes as phantom heroine, 136–137, 168–169, 170, 188; stage directions for, 127, 151, 165, 168–169. See also *Peony Pavilion*
Du Mu, 68–69, 94, 95
Dudbridge, Glen, 34, 107, 108
"Dugu Mu," 232n100
dynastic transitions, 87–88, 108–109, 121, 191. *See also* Ming dynasty, fall of; palace ladies
Emerald Peach Flower (Bi taohua), 137, 175, 177, 237n20
emotions: of dying, 23; links to bodily health, 21–23; in poetry, 83, 86; of women, 22
entrances and exits, 141, 142–149. *See also* ghost doorways
eroticism: in ghost poetry, 83; of ghosts, 3–4, 30; in veneration of past, 96
Erya, 4
eunuchs, natural, 29–33
exile, relationship to death, 59, 73, 87
exorcisms, 27, 145, 160
exorcists, 18, 43

Fan Wenruo, *Intoxicating Dream of Flowers (Menghua han)*, 137, 143, 177–180, 196, 237n17
femininity: of ghosts, 17, 82, 136; of past, 96
Feng Menglong: *Anatomy of Love (Qingshi leilüe)*, 21, 23, 93–94; *Constant Words to Awaken the World (Xingshi hengyan)*, 40; *Jingshi tongyan*, 46; revision of *Peony Pavilion*, 136; *Snow-Sprinkled Hall (Saxue tang)*, 175–177
Feng Zhenluan, 51, 83, 84
fertility, 29, 33. *See also* pregnancy
filial piety, 37
films: *A Chinese Ghost Story (Qiannü youhun)*, 1–2, **2,** 11, 35, 197; *Rouge (Yanzhi kou)*, 96, 197, 226n31
fireflies, 83, 84, 186
Flowers in the Rear Courtyard (Houting hua), 151, 156, 237n20
Foucault, Michel, 63
foxes, 24
fox-spirits, 17–20, 25, 35, 107
fox-woman, 29–33
Frankel, Hans, 89
Freud, Sigmund, 27; interest in spiritualism, 65–66; "Mourning and Melancholia," 42; on repressed memory, 99; on uncanny, 74, 124, 191–192
Frodsham, J. D., 75

Fu Qingzhu's Medicine for Women (Fu Qingzhu nüke), 39
Fu Yichen. See *Man / Ghost Husband / Wife*
funerary rituals. *See* death rituals
Furth, Charlotte, 19, 22, 24, 29, 82

Gan Bao, *Seeking the Spirits (Soushen ji)*, 33–35
Garber, Marjorie B., 127, 179
Garden of Old Ballads, A (Guyue yuan), 77
gender: in afterlife, 10; of ghost story writers, 14; of ghosts, 3–4, 14, 16–17; roles, 29. *See also* femininity; men; women
General Source for Remarks on Poetry (Shihua zonggui), 76
ghost authors, 57, 62, 63, 67, 77, 80–81. *See also* ghostly authors
ghost doorways *(gui men)*, 144–145, 146–149
Ghost Festival, 9, 27, 133
"Ghost Mother, The" ("Guimu zhuan"), 36–37
ghost opera *(gui xi)*, 9
ghost poetry: chanted in ghost stories, 54, 64, 82–83, 84–85; codification, 76–77; collections, 67, 76–81; communication through, 57, 195–196; distinction from ghostly poetry, 57; feminization, 81; formulaic nature, 84; graveyard poems, 61–65; images, 75–76; in "Lin Siniang," 101, 112, 113–114, 117–118, 120, 127; manifestations, 64–65, 120, 195; popularity, 76–77; in Tang anecdotal literature, 77; by women, 78–80, 82–83, 86; written on walls, 65, 120. *See also* ghostly poetry
ghost rooms *(gui fang)*, 145
ghost tales: accounts of the strange, 5; anti-superstition campaigns, 6; classical, 5, 8; compilations, 6; genres, 5–6, 8–9; literary, 3, 6–7, 14; oral traditions, 7–8, 27–28; political allegories, 9; publication, 6; satiric, 9; scholar-ghost romances, 23–24, 28–29, 123, 130; tales of haunted posts, 107–109, 110–113, 119. *See also* historical ghost tales
"Ghost Wife, The" ("Gui qi"), 43
ghostly authors, 68–69
ghostly poetry, 55–57, 81
ghosts: association with disease, 15, 18, 20, 174; auditory perception of, 54–56, 84–85, 149; beauty, 24–25, 27–28, 40, 107; boundaries with gods and ancestors, 11; communities, 123–124; compulsive repetition, 84–85; of dead wives, 45–46; deaths of, 50, 51, 52, 117; definitions, 4, 50, 73, 85; English terms, 53–54; femininity, 17, 82, 136; fragility and vulnerability, 24, 25, 27, 38; gender, 3–4, 14, 16–17; gesture of covering face with sleeve, 126–127, **128,** 165; hanged, 189; humorous side, 178; illnesses of, 45–46, 52; as manifestation of emotions, 23; meanings of *gui* character, 4–5; medical view of, 14–16; painted images, 47, 127, **128,** 195; rebirths, 50–51, 116–117, 125; relationships to corpses, 39–40; returns of, 4, 73; sexual desire, 3, 30; symbols of, 2; ugly, 27–28; virgins, 23, 25, 27, 37, 116, 124; writing of, 195–196. *See also* palace ladies; phantom heroines; revenants
ghosts, interaction with human males: analogy to human male-female relations, 16–17, 23–24; children, 32–34, 35–36; defloration of virgins, 116, 125–126; effects of rebirth, 116–117; living in tomb, 30, 32, 123–124; love affairs, 14, 17, 116, 125; marriages, 2–3, 34–36; resurrection by male agency, 14, 26–27, 32–34, 37–38, 39, 194; scholar-ghost romances, 23–24, 28–29, 123, 130
gods, 11, 18, 39
"Golden Hairpin, The" ("Jinfeng chai ji"), plays based on, 159, 174–175. See also *Dropped Hairpin; Man / Ghost Husband / Wife*
Golden Mirror of Medicine (Yizong jinjian), 39

Goldman, Michael, 143, 179
"Gongsun Jiuniang," 121–126, 127–130; geographic setting, **98;** memories of trauma, 235n42; postscript, 129–130
Good, Byron, 9–10
Goodwin, Sarah, 53
Gorges of Ba, 55–56
Graham, A. C., 75
grave-robbers, 40–41
graves, exhumation of, 40, 129, 146, 158, 177, 183. *See also* burials; tombs
graveyard poems: "Criticism ("Ganfeng"), no. 3," 71–74; development, 63; "Nineteen Old Poems," 57–59, 61, 62, 63, 186; in Tang anecdotal literature, 61–65
Great Book of Marvels (Guangyi ji), 34, 61–62
Green Dragon Temple (Qinglong si), murals, 47, **49,** 164
grief. *See* mourning
Gu Yanwu, 99
gui. See ghosts
Guo Yingde, 132

Han Yu, "On the Origin of Ghosts" ("Yuan gui"), 54, 86, 243n91
Hanan, Patrick, 18, 40–41, 42
haunted posts, tales of, 107–109, 110–113, 119
"Haunting of Pan's Wineshop, The" ("Nao Panlou duoqing Zhou Shengxian"), 40–42
Hay, Jonathan, 87
hell. *See* Mulian legend; underworld
Heng, prince of, 99–100, 101–103, 110, 112–113, 118–120
historical events: An Lushan rebellion, 93, 95, 115, 182; cycles, 87, 121; traumatic, 88, 99, 117, 121; veneration of past, 96; Yu Qi rebellion, 101, 121, 122–123, 124–125, 126. *See also* dynastic transitions; Ming dynasty, fall of
historical ghost tales: awareness of loss, 88; about dynastic falls, 88, 93–97, 191; traumatic events, 88, 99, 121. *See also* "Gongsun Jiuniang"; *huaigu;* "Lin Siniang"; palace ladies
History of the Liang Dynasty (Liangshu), 91, 92
History of Women Poets, A (Shinü shi), 78
Hong Mai, 77, 80
Hong Sheng. See *Palace of Lasting Life*
Hong Zhize, 185
Hu Yinglin, 75
Hu Zi, 76
huaigu: description, 88–89; early instances, 89–90; elements in tales of palace ladies, 93, 94–96, 111, 114, 116, 118; exchanged poems, 96; "Lu Qiao," 90–93; on palace of prince of Heng, 99; ruins as sites, 90, 93, 96; set in Nanjing, 98; in tales of the marvelous, 90
hun. See soul
hun dan (soul of female lead), 135, 237n17. *See also* phantom heroines
hun pa. See spirit kerchief
Huntington, Rania, 107

illnesses: association with ghosts, 15, 18, 20, 174; of ghosts, 45–46, 52, 174; lovesickness, 20, 82, 86, 139; mourning, 43–44. *See also* medical writings
"Ingenia" ("Qiaoniang"), 29–33, 35
"Inhabitant of the Gorges of Ba, The" ("Baxia ren"), 54–56, 64, 74
Injustice to Dou E (Dou E yuan), 156, 237n20
inner alchemy, 29
Intoxicating Dream of Flowers (Menghua han), 137, 143, 177–180, 196, 237n17
Ivy, Marilyn, 104

Ji Yun, *Jottings from the Thatched Cottage of Careful Reading (Yuewei caotang biji),* 8, 50–51, 76, 84
Jiang Guan, *Classified Cases of Renowned Physicians (Mingyi leian),* 18, 22–23, 39
Ji'nan, 113, 121, 122, 124, 125, 126
jing (painted face roles), 137, 176
Jiong Yuchi, 108

Johnson, Barbara, 27
Jottings from the Thatched Cottage of Careful Reading (Yuewei caotang biji), 8, 50–51, 76, 84
"Journey to Zhou and Qin, A," 116, 183

Kangxi emperor, 80, 101
Kao, Karl, 54
kerchief. *See* spirit kerchief
kinship, patrilineal and patrilocal, 10–11, 73
Kong Shangren, *Peach Blossom Fan (Taohua shan)*, 93, 98, 117, 127
kunqu (*kun*-style opera), 136, 150, 156, 164
Kuriyama, Shigehisa, 16
Kwan, Stanley, 96

Lady in the Painting (Huazhong ren), 137, 138, 150, **151**, 173, 237n17
Lady Yang (Yang Guifei or Yang Yuhuan): costumes, 189, 191, 194; historical figure, 182; in purgatory, 188–192; *Rain on the Pawlonia Tree*, 186; resurrection of body, 192–195, 197; reunion with emperor, 182, 183; as revenant, 183–184, 185–186, 187; *The Startled Swan*, 189, **189;** suicide, 182, 185, 188–189, 191–192. See also *Palace of Lasting Life*
Lamp Oil Collection, The (Ranzhi ji), 80
Land and Water paintings (Shuilu hua), 47, 127, **128**, 164, 216n160
Land and Water rite (Shuilu zhai), 47, 109, 158–163, 169–171, 188
latency, 65, 99
Li Chengzhong, 110; *Notes from Genzhai (Genzhai biji)*, 100, 103–104, 110, 118–120
Li Daoyuan, *Commentary on the Classic of Waterways (Shuijing zhu)*, 55
Li Fang. See *Wide Gleanings from the Taiping Era*
Li He: "At Night, Sitting and Chanting" ("Ye zuo yin"), 84; biography of, 69, 70; "Criticism ("Ganfeng"), no. 3," 71–74; "Ghostly Genius" reputation, 68–69, 70–71, 75, 81; "The Grave of Little Su" ("Su Xiaoxiao mu"), 84; imitations of poetry, 75, 84; influence, 84; poetry, 68, 70–71, 74–75; popularity, 75
Li Hu, 78–79
Li Huiniang, 6
Li Shangyin, 59, 69, 70
Li Shizhen, *Classified Materia Medica (Bencao gangmu)*, 29–30
Li Song, *Skeleton Puppet Master*, **48**
Li, Wai-yee, 37, 103, 116
Li Yu, 131, 133
"Li Zhangwu," 54
Li Zhen, 95–96
Li Zicheng, 99
Liang Guyin, 156, **157**
"Liansuo," 28–29, 38, 39, 82–85, 86
Liao Ben, 144
Liaozhai's Records of the Strange (Liaozhai zhi-yi): "Ainu," 40; "Autumn Moon" ("Wu Qiuyue"), 25–27, 28; "The Bridegroom" ("Xinlang"), 123; "Camelia" ("Xiangyu"), 26, 37; "Carpenter Feng" ("Feng mujiang"), 113; ghost poetry, 84; ghost stories, 7, 25; "The Ghost Wife" ("Gui qi"), 43; "Ingenia" ("Qiaoniang"), 29–33, 35; "Liansuo," 28–29, 38, 39, 82–85, 86; "Lin Siniang," 100, 103, 104, 113–115, 117–118, 120; "Lotus-scent" ("Lianxiang"), 17–21, 24–25; "Lü the Flawless" ("Lü Wubing"), 48–50, 51; "Nie Xiaoqian," 1, 2–3, 35–36, 37; "The Painted Skin" ("Hua pi"), 28; "Ruiyun," 27–28; "Weeping Ghosts" ("Gui ku"), 109; "Xiangchun," 16, 233n105; "Zhang Aduan," 44–46, 47, 48, 51–52
"Lin Siniang": *Collection by and about Women* version, 100, 103, 110–111, 112, 113–114, 115, 118; differences among versions, 106, 109–110; *Dream of the Red Chamber* version, 101–103, 105–106; geographic setting, 97–100, **98,** 101, **102,** 110; ghost poetry, 101, 112, 113–114, 117–118, 120, 127; historical records, 103–104; *Liaozhai* version, 100, 103, 104, 113–115,

117–118, 120; *Magician's New Records* version, 100–101, 106–107, 108–110, 118; nineteenth-century dramas, 103; *Notes from Genzhai* version, 100, 103–104, 110, 118–120; *Occasional Chats* version, 100, 103, 112, 113, 114, 115, 118; oral circulation of tale, 104; *Qingzhou Anecdotes* version, 100, 101, 104, 110, 111–112, 118; references to fall of Ming, 114–115; temporal frame, 100–101; versions, 100, 106
Lin Yuan, *Sima Caizhong's Dream of the Courtesan Su Xiaoxiao*, **128**
Lin Yunming, 110; "Lin Siniang" tale, 100–101, 106–107, 108–110, 118
Ling Menchu, 159
Little Su. *See* Su Xiaoxiao
Liu Yanjun, 182–183
Liu Yong, 116
"Lost Frontiers" ("Liangzhou"), 94–95
"Lotus-scent" ("Lianxiang"), 17–21, 24–25
lovesickness, 20, 82, 86, 139
Lu Guimeng, 66–67, 69, 74
Lu Ji, 59, 60–61, 63, 72
Lu Jianzeng, 81, 110
"Lu Qiao," 90–93
"Lü the Flawless" ("Lü Wubing"), 48–50, 51
Luo Pin, *The Ghost Path (Guiqu tu)*, 148, **148**, 216n160

Magician's New Records, The (Yu Chu xinzhi): "The Ghost Mother" ("Guimu zhuan"), 36–37; "Lin Siniang" tale, 100–101, 106–107, 108–110, 118; publication, 36
male potency. *See* men
Manchu conquest, 7, 87, 97, 98, 99. *See also* Ming dynasty, fall of
Man / Ghost Husband / Wife (Rengui fuqi): death ritual scene, 159, 160, 163–164, 169, 170–171; female leads, 171, 172, 174; spirit kerchief, 164, 169; stage directions, 163, 165, 168
Mao Xiang, 25
marriage: analogy to death, 73, 74; ghosts of dead wives, 45–46; of men and ghosts, 2–3, 34–36; patrilocal, 73; posthumous, 34, 122–123, 124; spirit, 34–35, 123; uxorilocal, 123
marvelous *(qi[a])*, 131. *See also* tales of the marvelous
masculinity, 28–29, 96
masks, 138
matching poetry. *See* poetry
medical writings: on emotions and bodily health, 21–23; on fertility, 29; on ghostly possession, 15, 18, 46; on ghosts, 14–16; on illnesses related to mourning, 43–44; images of women, 23–24; on natural eunuchs, 29–30; on nocturnal emissions, 26; on phantom pregnancy, 38–39; publication, 15; on sexual health, 19
Mei Dingzuo: *A Garden of Old Ballads (Guyue yuan)*, 77; *Records of Talented Ghosts (Caigui ji)*, 6, 7, 77–78, 93
Mei Xiaosi, *Snow-Sprinkled Hall (Saxue tang)*, 176
melancholy. *See* depression
memorialization, 104–105
memory: collective, 183; cultural act, 115; of dead, 42; dreams and, 191, 192; in *Palace of Lasting Life*, 182–183, 191; repressed, 99; of traumatic events, 99, 130, 235n142
men: bodily self-sacrifice, 38, 214n125; creativity, 29; martial, 28–29; masculinity, 28–29, 96; nocturnal emissions, 26; phantom pregnancies, 38–39, 82; potency, 29–34, 37–38, 116; semen (Essence), 19, 26, 29. *See also* gender; ghosts, interaction with human males
Meng Chengshun: anthologies, 137; *Mistress and Maid (Jiao Hong ji)*, 86, 137, 150
metatheatricality, 134
Min Qiji, 152, **154**
Ming dynasty: founding, 95; loyalists, 87, 99, 110, 120; nostalgia for, 7, 101; palaces, 97; prince of Heng, 99–100, 101, 110, 112–113, 118–120; rebellions against, 103
Ming dynasty, fall of: cultural responses,

103, 104–105, 114–115; dramas on theme, 98, 181; responses of loyalists, 87; trauma of, 7, 101. *See also* "Lin Siniang"
Minghuang emperor, 115, 182. See also *Palace of Lasting Life*
Mirror of the Return to Origin (Guiyuan jing), 161–163
Missing History of the Tang and Song, The (Tang Song yishi), 62, 67
Mistress and Maid (Jiao Hong ji), 86, 137, 150
More Tales Told by Lamplight (Jiandeng yuhua), 175–176; "An Autumn Night's Visit to the Mandolin Pavilion" ("Qiuxi fang Pipa ting ji"), 95–96, 104
mourning: ambivalence toward dead, 44; end of, 52; for fallen dynasties, 7, 104–105, 114; headgear, 165; illnesses, 43–44; purpose, 52; rituals, 42–43; for wife, 42–43, 45; work of, 42
Mulian legend: illustrations, 127, **128,** 165; plays, 9, 27, 133, 187–188

Nanjing, 97–98, 145
natural eunuchs. *See* eunuchs, natural
necrophilia, 40–41
New Tales Told By Lamplight (Jiandeng xinhua), 16; "Teng Mu's Drunken Excursion to the Jujing Gardens" ("Teng Mu zuiyou Jujingyuan ji"), 94–95, 104, 115–116, 125
New Tang History (Xin Tangshu), 165
Nie Shiqiao, 127–129
"Nie Xiaoqian," 1, 2–3, 35–36, 37
"Nineteen Old Poems" ("Gushi shijiu shou"), 57–59, 61, 62, 63, 186
nocturnal emissions, 26
northern drama *(zaju)*: adaptations in southern drama, 6–7, 137; conventions, 136; costumes, 164; *The Disembodied Soul (Qiannü lihun)*, 135, 137, 152, **153,** 164, 193; *Emerald Peach Flower (Bi taohua)*, 137, 175, 177, 237n20; false ghosts, 178–179; ghost stories, 5–7, 137; male revenants, 135; phantom heroines, 135, 136; publication, 6, 137, 141, 152; singing roles, 136, 175; stages, 144; themes, 238n24
Nosegay of Verses, A (Xiefang ji), 81
nostalgia: association with palace ladies, 93, 95; as loop, 95; for Ming, 7, 101
Notes from Genzhai (Genzhai biji), "Lin Siniang" tale, 100, 103–104, 110, 118–120
Nymph of the Luo River (Woman in Spring Longing), 153, **155**

Occasional Chats North of the Pond (Chibei outan), 81; "Lin Siniang" tale, 100, 103, 112, 113, 114, 115, 118
officials, tales of haunted posts, 107–109, 110–113, 119
Old Official History of the Tang (Jiu Tangshu), 64
opera: ghost, 9; *kunqu* (*kun*-style), 136, 150, 156, 164; Peking, 6, 144, 164; Sichuan, 135, 150, 156. *See also* theater
Outlaws of the Marsh (Shuihu ji), 138, 150
Owen, Stephen, 48, 65, 89, 96, 127

painted face roles, 137, 176
paintings: of ghosts, 47, 127, **128,** 195; Land and Water, 47, 127, **128,** 164, 216n160; of skeletons, 47, **48, 49;** tomb murals, 160, **161**
palace ladies: burial sites, 96–97; deaths, 97, 104, 226n35; returns of, 93–97, 115, 183, 191; symbolism, 97, 114; "Teng Mu's Drunken Excursion to the Jujing Gardens," 94–95, 104, 115–116, 125. *See also* "Gongsun Jiuniang"; Lady Yang; "Lin Siniang"
Palace of Lasting Life (Changsheng dian): comparison to *Peony Pavilion*, 185, 194; historical basis, 182; music, 188; performances, 181, 184, 247n4, 248n6; phantom heroine scenes, 7, 183–192; plot, 182; publication, 181, 185; reflections on fall of Ming, 181; resurrection scene, 192–195, 197; stagecraft, 150, 184, 187, 190, 193;

structure, 182–183; success, 181; Wu Yiyi's commentary, 185, 190, 192, 195
palaces: of Ming prince of Heng, 99–100, 101, 110, 112–113, 118–120; ruins, 93, 94, 110, 118–120
Pan Zhiheng, 13
Parry, Jonathan, 37, 47
past. *See* historical events; *huaigu;* memory
Patchwork of Scenes, A (Zhui baiqiu), 168
Pavis, Patrice, 142
Peach Blossom Fan (Taohua shan), 93, 98, 117, 127
Peachwood Amulet (Taofu ji), 151–152
Peking opera, 6, 144, 164
"Peony Lantern, The" ("Mudan deng ji"), 46
Peony Pavilion (Mudan ting): comic scenes, 178; comparison to *Palace of Lasting Life,* 185, 194; expressions of *qing,* 138, 140; finale, 16; influence, 136, 137–138, 147, 185; parodies, 41; phantom heroine, 7, 132, 136, 165, 188, 193; popular reception, 13, 81; preface, 14; revised editions, 136–137, 151, 165, 168–169, 192; sources, 137; stage directions, 27, 127, 142, 151, 165, 170; Three Wives' commentary, 76, 185, 191; underworld scene, 137–138, 150, 165, **166–167,** 168–169. *See also* Du Liniang
People's Republic of China (PRC), anti-superstition campaigns, 6
Peucker, Brigitte, 196
phantom heroines: arias, 138–139; beauty, 138; costumes, 148, 152–153, **154,** 163–165, 168–171, 194; dance movements, 152, 156–158; differences from other stage ghosts, 137; distinctiveness of sub-role, 135; as doubles of living heroines, 136, 193–194; expressions of *qing,* 138–140; jealousy, 174; Land and Water rites for, 158–163; in northern drama, 135, 136; postures, 156, **157;** relation with second female lead, 171–174, 193; resurrections, 196–197; role types, 134–135; use of another body, 175–180; walk routines, 150–152, **151,** 156, 187; in *West Garden,* 138–139, 146, 149, 152–153, **154.** *See also* Du Liniang; Lady Yang
phantom pregnancy, 38–39, 82
phantoms, 5
Pi Rixiu, 66–67, 74
Pine Knoll Anthology (Songling ji), 66–67, 74
planchette *(fuji),* 77, 79, 196
play rooms *(xifang),* 144, 145
plays. *See* theater
poetics: fusion of scene and emotion, 83; imagery, 56; inner/outer movement, 65, 66; intent, 67; omissions, 85; political implications, 70
poetry: authorship, 63, 96; auto-dirges, 60–65, 66, 67; burial songs, 59–61, 62, 63, 72, 124; emotions expressed in, 86; exchanges by lovers, 82, 83–84, 85–86, 94, 96; ghostly qualities, 75–76; imitations of dead masters, 96; laments on past, 91–92; Ming loyalist, 120; "old style," 74–75, 78; as relic of dead, 64; Tang regulated verse, 74, 92; by women, 78–80, 81; writing as negative, transgressive act, 69–70, 81; writing surfaces, 65. *See also* ghost poetry; graveyard poems; *huaigu*
Poetry from an Individual Dynasty (Liechao shiji), 79
poets: early deaths, 81; social status, 79, 81; women, 78, 81–82, 85–86. *See also* authorship
pollution, 24
popular culture, ghosts, 3, 6, 197. *See also* films
popular religion: ancestral worship, 10, 47, 122; ghosts, 27; gods, 11, 18, 39
possession: of actors by roles, 172; medical writings on, 15, 18, 46
Postlewait, Thomas, 133
pregnancy: of ghosts, 32–34, 36; phantom, 38–39, 82. *See also* childbirth
print culture: medical publications, 15;

Ming publishing boom, 78, 131; poetry anthologies, 78; published plays, 141–142
procreation, 29–33, 35–36
props, 141, 168, 189–190
Pu Songling: "Gongsun Jiuniang," 121–126, 127–130; hometown, 109, 110; "Mawei Slope" ("Mawei po"), 84. See also *Liaozhai's Records of the Strange*
pulse diagnosis, 18, 206nn22, 23
purgatory, 50, 116–117, 188–192
Purple Hairpin, The (Zichai ji), 140, 142

qi: building up, 20; congestion, 21; medical writings on, 18; nocturnal emissions, 26
qi[a] (amazing, novel, marvelous), 131–132
Qian Qianyi, 79
Qian Zhongshu, 92
qing (sentiment): association with female revenants, 7; culture of, 7, 13–14, 21, 81; in drama, 13, 138–140, 185; as life-force, 37; manifestation between life and death, 13–14
Qing dynasty: acceptance of, 101; founding, 7; rebellions against, 99, 101, 109, 121, 122–123, 124–125. *See also* Manchu conquest
Qingzhou Anecdotes (Qingshe yiwen), "Lin Siniang" tale, 100, 101, 104, 110, 111–112, 118
Qingzhou prefecture, 97, 99–100. *See also* "Lin Siniang"; Shandong province
Qiu Ying, *Woman in Spring Longing*, 153, 155
Qu Yuan, "Questions to Heaven" ("Tian wen"), 120

Rain on the Pawlonia Tree (Wutong yu), 186
rebirth: cycle of, 37, 50–51, 87; of ghosts, 50–51, 116–117, 125; by male sexual agency, 7, 14, 32–34, 37–38, 194; metaphors, 125; staging in plays, 169, 177, 193–194, 196–197
"Record of Ten Days in Yangzhou, A" ("Yangzhou shiri ji"), 99
Records of Talented Ghosts (Caigui ji), 6, 7, 77–78, 93
Records of the Historian (Shiji), 89–90
Records of the Listener (Yijian zhi), 77
red, symbolism of, 148
Red Flowering Plum (Hongmei ji), 147–149, 156–158, 164, 174
Remarks Collected by the Fisherman Hermit of the Tiao River (Tiaoxi yuyin conghua), 76
Remnants from Ladies' Writing Brushes (Tongguan yibian), 78–79
resurrection. *See* rebirth
revenants: beauty, 82; literary tales of, 5; male, 135–136; power, 11; in southern drama plots, 132, 135–136. *See also* Lady Yang; palace ladies; phantom heroines
Ricoeur, Paul, 87, 130
Riley, Jo, 148
Ritual Canon (Liji), 4
ritual drama, 27
rituals. *See* death rituals
Robertson, Maureen, 72
role types: *cha dan* (third female lead), 177–178; clowns, 176; conventions, 135; *dan* (female lead), 134–135, 136, 156, 171–174, 175–180; *hun dan* (soul of female lead), 135, 237n17; painted face roles, 137, 176; splitting female lead, 171–174, 193; stage directions, 142; *tie* (supporting female role), 135, 147–148, 176, 183. *See also* phantom heroines
Rouge (Yanzhi kou), 96, 197, 226n31
Ruan Yue, 76
ruins *(xu)*: of palaces, 93, 94, 110, 118–120; poetic imagery, 93, 96; sites, 90

sarcophagi, images on, 60
Sawada Mizuho, 36
Schafer, Edward, 72
Schmitt, Jean-Claude, 10, 42, 104, 121
scholar-ghost romances, 23–24, 28–29, 123, 130
Secret Burial Classic of the Great Han, The

(Da Han yuanling mizang jing), 34, 53 (epigraph)
Seeking the Spirits (Soushen ji), 33–35
Selected Yuan Plays (Yuanqu xuan), 152, **153**
semen (Essence), 19, 26, 29
sentiment. See *qing*
sexual desire. See *qing*
sexual intercourse: dreams of, 18, 26, 39, 211n78; with ghosts, 2–3, 14, 17, 34–36, 116, 125–126; medical writings, 18, 19; poetic euphemisms, 125
shadow puppets, 28, **28**
Shahar, Meir, 10, 11
shamans, 18, 43, 46, 172
Shandong Poetry from Our Dynasty (Guochao Shanzuo shichao), 81, 110
Shandong province: map, **98;** palace of Ming prince of Heng, 99–100, 101, 110, 112–113, 118–120; Qingzhou prefecture, 97, 99–100; rebellions against Qing, 101, 109, 121, 124–125; violence during Ming-Qing transition, 99, 101, 122–123; Yu Qi rebellion, 101, 121, 122–123, 124–125, 126. *See also* "Lin Siniang"
Shang dynasty, 89–90
Shang Wei, 69
Shen Deqian, 75
Shen Fu, *Six Chapters of a Floating Life (Fusheng liuji)*, 3
Shen Jing, 137; *Dropped Hairpin, The (Zhuichai ji)*, 159, 168, 171, 172–174; *Peachwood Amulet (Taofu ji)*, 151–152; revision of *Peony Pavilion*, 136
Shen Yazhi, 75
Shen Yixiu, 81
Shen Yue, 90–92, 93
Shi Zhenlin, 81
si (longing), 21, 22–23, 52
Sichuan opera, 135, 150, 156
Sieber, Patricia, 137
Sima Caizhong's Dream of the Courtesan Su Xiaoxiao, **128**
Sima Qian, 21, 67, 89–90
Sivin, Nathan, 18–19, 21
Six Dynasties, fall of, 92
Skeleton Puppet Master, The (Kulou huanxi tu), **48**
skeletons: animated, 46–47; images of, 47, **48, 49,** 216n160. *See also* bodies
sleeves, 126–127, 152–153, **154,** 165
Snow-Sprinkled Hall (Saxue tang), 175–177
Sofer, Andrew, 168
Song dynasty: fall of, 94; paintings, 47
Song Junhua, 164
soul (spirit): dwellings, 5; *hun dan* (soul of female lead), 135, 237n17; martyred, 109; meaning of concept, 5; release from body, 193; separation from body, 5, 135, 173, 193–194; yin and yang, 5. *See also* phantom heroines; revenants
sound effects, 141, 149–150
sounds: chanting of poetry, 54, 64, 82–83; disembodied, 54, 64, 149; of ghosts, 54–56, 149; wails or cries, 149, 169
southern drama *(chuanqi)*: conventional plots, 132; ghost themes, 6, 131, 132–133, 136–137, 238n24; male revenants, 135–136; proliferation of plays, 131; published versions, 131; use of northern drama plots, 6–7, 137. *See also* role types; stage directions
spirit. *See* soul
spirit kerchief *(hun pa)*, 163–165, 168–171, 192
spirit marriage *(youhun/minghun)*, 34–35, 123
spirit verse. *See* ghost poetry
spiritualism, 65–66
spring, 125
stage directions: entrances and exits, 141, 142–149; expansion of, 141–142; gestures, 127, 141, 152; ghost walk, 150–152, 156, 187; language of, 142; lighting, 143, 240n55; props, 141, 168, 189–190; sound effects, 141, 149–150; in southern drama, 140–142, 240n50; whirlwinds, 156–158, 187. *See also* costumes; role types

Startled Swan, The (Jinghong ji), 183, **184**, 189, **189**
stasis *(yu)*, 21–22, 85, 209n49
Stevenson, Daniel, 159
Stewart, Susan, 51, 178
Su Shi, 76–77, 86, 144
Su Xiaoxiao (Little Su), 84, **128**, 226n31, 243n84
suicides: ghosts' deaths, 11, 23, 50; of Lady Yang, 182, 185, 188–189, 191–192; linked to defloration, 126
Swatek, Catherine, 37, 136–137

Taizu emperor, 108
tales of haunted posts, 107–109, 110–113, 119
tales of the marvelous *(chuanqi)*, 5, 15, 90
Tanaka Issei, 145
Tang regulated verse, 74, 92
Tang Xianzu, 137, 147; *The Purple Hairpin (Zichai ji)*, 140, 142. See also *Peony Pavilion*
"Tang Xuan," 54
Tao Qian, 16–17, 59–60, 62, 63, 72
Teiser, Stephen, 50
Ten Thousand Tang Quatrains (Wanshou Tangren jueju), 77
"Teng Mu's Drunken Excursion to the Jujing Gardens" ("Teng Mu zuiyou Jujingyuan ji"), 94–95, 104, 115–116, 125
theater: amazing or marvelous qualities, 131–132; differences from other literary genres, 133; offstage areas, 144, 145, 146, 149; performance venues, 9, 133, 143–146, 237n14; *qing* in, 13, 138–140, 185; reading plays as narrative literature, 141, 142; romantic themes, 238n24; shadow puppet, 28. *See also* northern drama; opera; role types; southern drama
theater, representation of ghosts: characters mistaken for ghosts, 178–179; clowns, 137; costumes, 163–165, 168–171; entrances and exits, 141, 142–149; gestures, 127, 141, 152; illustrations in printed plays, **151**, 152, **153**, **154**, **155**, **158**; increase in, 238n24; painted face roles, 137; semiotic code, 134; sound effects, 141, 149–150; timidity, 27; visibility and invisibility, 142, 149, 158, 165, 168, 171; wails or cries, 149, 169. *See also* phantom heroines; stage directions
theatricality, 127, 133–134, 141
Thompson, Laurence, 27
300 Tang Poems (Tangshi sanbai shou), 75
Tian Yiheng, 78
tibishi (poems on walls), 65
tie (supporting female role), 135, 147–148, 176, 183
tombs: as healing locus, 32; links to historic sites, 96–97; living with ghost in, 30, 32, 123–124; murals, 160, **161**; of palace ladies, 96–97; as residences of souls, 5. *See also* burials; graves
traumatic events: historical, 88, 99, 117, 121; in historical ghost tales, 88, 99, 121; memory of, 99, 130, 235n142. *See also* Ming dynasty, fall of

uncanny: in actor's relationship to role, 172; behavior of candle or lamp, 3; Freud on, 74, 124, 191–192; in ghost stories, 69, 124; hybrid bodies, 33–34; opposites as, 74; plurality of ghosts, 179
underworld: *Peony Pavilion* scene, 137–138, 150, 165, **166–167**, 168–169; poetic descriptions, 72; tales of, 50–51; theatrical representation, 146, 174. *See also* purgatory
unheimlich. See uncanny
Unschuld, Paul, 18

van Gulik, Robert Hans, 25
vernacular tales, 5, 40–41, 46, 159
visibility and invisibility, 142, 149, 158, 165, 168, 171

Wang Chong, 15, 54, 55
Wang, David, 6
Wang Duanshu, 79–80

Wang Guowei, 145
Wang Jilie, 184
Wang Kentang, 26
Wang Qishu, 81
Wang Shilu, 80, 110
Wang Shizhen, 75, 110; *Occasional Chats North of the Pond (Chibei outan),* 81, 100, 103, 112, 113, 114, 115, 118
Wang Siren, 71
Wang Yufeng, *Fenxiang ji,* 249n25
Watson, James L., 10
"Weeping Ghosts" ("Gui ku"), 109, 229n62
Weller, Robert, 10, 11
Weng Minhua, 152
West, Stephen H., 141
West Garden (Xiyuan ji): arias, 138–139; death ritual, 160, 169–170; ending, 171; female leads, 171; illustrations, 152–153, **154;** phantom heroine, 138–139, 146, 149, 152–153, **154;** sources, 159; stage directions, 146, 149
Western Wing, The (Xixiang ji), 20, 152, **154**
whirlwinds, 156–158, **158,** 187
white, symbolism of, 72, 189
"White Falcon, The" ("Cui yanei baiyao zhao yao"), 46
Wide Gleanings from the Taiping Era (Taiping guangji), 66, 78, 80; "Dugu Mu," 232n100; "Inhabitant of the Gorges of Ba, The" ("Baxia ren"), 54–56, 64, 74; "Lu Qiao," 90–93
will-o'-the-wisps, 73–74, 83, 93, 186, 190
wind: association with ghosts, 2, 83, 149–150, 153, 187–188; poetic images, 58, 72, 84, 85; sound effects in theatrical performances, 149–150, 187–188; whirlwinds, 156–158, **158,** 187
"Winsome Colonel, The" ("Guihua ci"), 101–103, 113
Wolf, Arthur, 11
women: anthologists, 79–80; deaths as virgins, 23; emotionality, 22; ghost poetry by, 78–80, 82–83, 86; as Other, 14, 17; poetry anthologies, 78, 79–80, 81; poets, 78, 81–82, 85–86; pollution associated with, 24; repressed sexual desire, 22. *See also* gender; palace ladies; phantom heroines; pregnancy
writing: of ghosts, 127, 195–196; traces of writer, 127, 236n148. *See also* authorship; poetry
Wu Bing, 137; *Lady in the Painting (Huazhong ren),* 137, 138, 150, **151,** 173, 237n17. See also *West Garden*
Wu Hung, 60, 90
Wu Qi, 58, 59
Wu Qiming, 75
Wu Weiye, *Spring in Nanjing (Moling chun),* 237n17
Wu Wushan's Three Wives' Combined Commentary on Peony Pavilion (Wu Wushan sanfu heping Mudan ting), 76, 185, 191
Wu, Yi-li, 15
Wu Yiyi, 185, 190, 192, 195
Wu Zhiwang, *A Flourishing Yang (Jiyang gangmu),* 19

Xi Shi, 81, 93–94, 97
"Xiangchun," 16, 233n105
Xie Guan, 55
Xie Qian rebellion, 109
Xin Wenfang, 77
Xu Dachun, 46
Xu Fuming, 103, 109–110
Xu Xianglin, 131
Xu Zichang, *Outlaws of the Marsh (Shuihu ji),* 138, 150

Yagi Akiyoshi, 75, 84
Yan Yu, 75
Yang Guifei. *See* Lady Yang
Yang Youhe, 156
Ye Xiaoluan, 81
Yellow Emperor's Inner Canon, The (Huangdi neijing), 21
Yidu city, 99, 101, **102**
yin-yang, 2, 5, 16, 17, 20

You Tong, 75, 86, 135; *Celestial Court Music (Juntian yue)*, 135, 142
Yu, Anthony C., 14
Yu, Pauline, 56
Yu Qi rebellion, 101, 121, 122–123, 124–125, 126
Yu Tuan, *Correct Transmission of Medicine (Yixue zhengchuan)*, 39
Yuan drama. *See* northern drama
Yuan Hongdao, 147
Yuan Yuling, 131, 132
Yuan Zhen, 115
Yunqi Zhuhong, 161–163

zaju. See northern drama
Zang Maoxun: revision of *Peony Pavilion*, 136, 151, 165, 168–169, 192; *Selected Yuan Plays (Yuanqu xuan)*, 152, **153**
Zeng Yi, 71, 72, 74
Zeng Yongyi, 188
"Zhang Aduan," 44–46, 47, 48, 51–52
Zhang Chao, 36. See also *Magician's New Records*
Zhang Dai, 132–133, 145
Zhang Jiebin, 22, 26, 39, 44
"Zhang Yunrong," 125
Zheng Guangzu, *The Disembodied Soul (Qiannü lihun)*, 135, 136, 137, 152, 164, 193, 237n17
Zheng Tingyu, *Flowers in the Rear Courtyard (Houting hua)*, 151, 156, 237n20
Zheng Zhizhen, *Mulian Rescues his Mother*, **128**
Zhida, *Mirror of the Return to Origin (Guiyuan jing)*, 161–163, **162**
Zhou Bida, 70
Zhou Chaojun, *Red Flowering Plum (Hongmei ji)*, 147–149, 156–158, 164, 174
Zhou Yibai, 143, 144
Zhu Quan, 144
Zhu Xi, 23, 50
Zhu Zhenheng, 18, 22–23, 26, 44
Zhuangzi, 64, 73
Zuo Tradition on the Spring and Autumn Annals (Zuozhuan), 4

About the Author

Judith T. Zeitlin is the William R. Kenan, Jr., Professor in the Department of East Asian Languages and Civilizations and the Committee on Theater and Performance Studies at the University of Chicago. She is the author of *Historian of the Strange: Pu Songling and the Chinese Classical Tale* (1993) and coeditor of *Writing and Materiality in China* (2003); *Thinking with Cases: Specialist Knowledge in Chinese Cultural History* (2007); *Chinese Opera Film,* a special double issue of *The Opera Quarterly* (2010); and *Performing Images: Opera in Chinese Visual Culture* (2014).